The Italian Tragedy
in the Renaissance

The Italian Tragedy in the Renaissance

Cultural Realities and Theatrical Innovations

Salvatore Di Maria

Lewisburg
Bucknell University Press
London: Associated University Presses

©2002 by Rosemont Publishing & Printing Corp.

All rights reserved. Authorization to photocopy items for internal or personal use, or the internal or personal use of specific clients, is granted by the copyright owner, provided that a base fee of $10.00, plus eight cents per page, per copy is paid directly to the Copyright Clearance Center, 222 Rosewood Drive, Danvers, Massachusetts 01923, [0-8387-5490-2/02, $10.00 + 8¢ pp, pc.]

Associated University Presses
440 Forsgate Drive
Cranbury, NJ 08512

Associated University Presses
16 Barter Street
London WC1A 2AH, England

Associated University Presses
P.O. Box 338, Port Credit
Mississauga, Ontario
Canada L5G 4L8

The paper used in this publication meets the requirements
of the American National Standard for Permanence
of Paper for Printed Library Materials Z39.48-1984.

Library of Congress Cataloging-in-Publication Data

Di Maria, Salvatore.
   The Italian tragedy in the Renaissance : cultural realities and theatrical innovations / Salvatore Di Maria.
   p. cm.
   Includes bibliographical references and index.
   ISBN 0-8387-5490-2 (alk. paper)
   1. Italian drama (Tragedy)—History and criticism. 2. Italian drama—To 1700—History and criticism. 3. Theater—Italy—History—16th century. 4. Theater—Italy—History—Medieval, 500–1500. I. Title.
PQ 4147 .D5 2002
852'.05120903—dc21   2001035662

PRINTED IN THE UNITED STATES OF AMERICA

To all my loved ones both living and dead.

Contents

Preface   9

Part I: Renaissance Cultural Realities

1. The Making of Italian Renaissance Tragedy   17
   Revitalization Process   20
   Realism and Living Realities on the Stage   29
   Dramaturgical Novelties: Sounds and Dramatic Space   32
2. Renaissance Living Traditions and the Revival of
   Ancient Tragedy   35
   Length of the Dramatic Text: Political Imperatives and
   Verbal Rhetoric   37
   Contemporary Spatial Setting and Courtly Ambiance   46
   Brigands and Pirates   54
3. Their Gods, Our God: Christian Religion in the Tragic
   World of Myth   58
   Religion in Christian and Mythological Settings   61
   The Deus ex Machina Expedient: Martelli's *Tullia* and
   Aretino's *Orazia*   71
4. The Nature of Kingship: The Debate on Machiavellism   79
   The Machiavellian Notion of Kingship and the Tragic Stage   81
   Giraldi's *Orbecche*   85
   Theater as Rhetoric of Power   97
5. Tragic Heroines: The Debate on the Emerging Question
   of Women   101
   The Traditional Notion of Womanhood   103
   The Stage View of Women   105
   Theater's Ambivalent Endorsement of Women   121

Part II: Theatrical Innovations

6. The Evolving Concept of Stage and Dramatic Space   129
   The Notion of Scenic and Dramatic Space   136
   Aretino's *Orazia*: A Case in Point   144

7. Representing the Unrepresentable: The *Hic et Nunc* of
   Tragedy ... 155
   Dramatic Limitations of Stage Narrative: The Role of the
   Messenger ... 158
   The Immediacy of the Tragic Here and Now: Giraldi's
   Orbecche and Aretino's *Orazia* ... 162
8. The Theatrical Language of Sounds and Movements ... 177
   Dramaturgical Elements in Rucellai's *Oreste*: Sounds,
   Retardation Technique, and Movements ... 181
   Three Dramatizations of Dido's Death: Pazzi, Giraldi, and
   Dolce ... 193

Conclusion ... 203

Notes ... 209
Bibliography ... 257
Index ... 268

Preface

MY PRIMARY AIM FOR WRITING THIS BOOK IS TO ANSWER, AT LEAST IN part, Marco Ariani's call for the reevaluation of Italian Renaissance tragedy, which, he notes, has been left in one of the several "*zone morte*" [dead areas] of Italian literature. I take up this challenge by focusing the discussion on the Renaissance revival of ancient tragedy. As Lodovico Dolce claims in the epilogue to his *Ifigenia*, tragedy came from Athens to cinquecento Florence, after a reluctant sojourn in classical Rome. It was through the efforts of Italian Renaissance playwrights wishing to revive ancient theater that tragedy, or the noble genre, as it was called, reached the theaters of Europe, thus making its way into modern Western culture. The Italian experience paved the way for great tragedians like Racine and Shakespeare, the standards of comparison for all scholarly discourse on Renaissance drama. This influence notwithstanding, theater scholarship, interested mostly in the great accomplishments of English and French tragedy, has practically neglected Italian tragedy other than to acknowledge the usefulness of its experiments. The limited critical attention it does receive has focused largely on the playwrights' attempts to imitate ancient texts and on the extent to which they observed Aristotelian precepts.[1]

Though important studies on the poetics of the Italian dramatic stage, few as they are, have contributed to a better understanding of its strengths and limitations, we still lack a clear perspective on the literary and theatrical innovations that truly characterize Italian Renaissance tragedy. More specifically, we lack a broad perspective on the function of cinquecento theater as a reflection of the times and as a forum for debating cultural issues, such as the political nature of kingship and the question of women. We know little about its dramatic and dramaturgical innovations, especially the evolving concept of dramatic space and its use. This vacuum is in part due to the monumental challenge to define a theater that, having slowly emerged from centuries of darkness, had to be assimilated and adapted to the changing aesthetic and cultural exigencies of modern audiences. Adding to the difficulty is the wide range and diversity of cultural elements informing most tragedies, as playwrights of diverse sociopolitical background brought their individual preferences to bear on their work.

A comprehensive account of the innovations informing a theater that evolved from the newly discovered ancient tragedy into a distinctive Renaissance art form is a huge task requiring significant research on specific aspects of the genre and on the cultural dynamics that prompted them. Recent studies, such as Michael Lettieri's critical edition of Aretino's *Orazia* (1991); Ronnie Terpening's excellent monograph on Dolce (1997); Mary Morrison's critical presentation of Giraldi's tragedies (1997); the modern editions of several of Giraldi's tragedies, the latest being *Gli Antivalomeni* edited by Philip Horne (1999); and Maria Passaro's commendable English translation of Tasso's *Torrismondo* (1997) point to a growing scholarly interest in the critical fortunes of Renaissance tragedy. Building on these contributions, I propose to discuss major cultural realities (part 1) and dramaturgical innovations (part 2) that contributed in a meaningful way to the revival of tragedy in the Italian Renaissance.

In keeping with my primary aim, I intend to show how Italian playwrights "clothed" the genre with their own living realities in order to make it relevant to their spectators. They set classical myths in contemporary spatial settings, dressed ancient kings in Renaissance princely attires, had mythological characters speak a language reminiscent of Dante and Petrarch, and had them voice religious beliefs similar to those of cinquecento audiences. They also proposed the stage as a forum for debating issues of major social and political concern, such as the question of womankind and the nature of princeship. They brought the genre from the page onto the stage, where a highly creative stagecraft introduced legions of theatrical innovations that amused and amazed audiences. The social themes, the cultural traditions, and the technical aspects of the tragic stage of the Renaissance are too diverse and often too complex to be treated without an appropriate contextualization. Thus, I begin the book with an overview of the evolution of the genre, briefly calling attention to the cultural and theatrical elements that made it modern and typical of Renaissance Italy.

In the second chapter, I focus on the customs, the language, the æsthetic preferences, and other living traditions that made tragedy relevant to contemporary audiences. I place particular emphasis on the formal aspects of the written text and on the function of theater as a cultural event. The following three chapters deal with the three basic elements of classical tragedy: religion, the king or tyrant, and the heroic victim. I view their respective roles as expressions of ideological issues of major concern to Renaissance society. Part 2 of the book deals with innovations both textual and theatrical that helped to establish Renaissance tragedy as a poetic composition meant to be performed on stage. Proceeding from didascalic directions, which in most texts are embedded in the discourse of the characters, I explore the concepts of dramatic space, gestures, movements, sounds, and other sensory percepts that facilitate a virtual performance of the written text, or what theater semioticians call the spectacle text.

The ensuing discussion also aims to enhance our understanding of an æsthetic taste that, though grounded in verbal rhetoric, came to value nonlinguistic signs as an effective means of communication in dramatic representation. Taken out of the reading "closet" where it was first thought to belong,[2] tragedy was brought on stage where it evolved into a representation in many aspects more spectacular than its classical counterpart. The growing emphasis on stage techniques, together with the moral underpinning of the plot, points to a developing notion of a genre meant to entertain without relinquishing its didactic function. Dramatic performances became cultural events that, among other functions, reflected the taste and the realities of the times. It is my intention to argue that, contrary to traditional notions perpetuated uncritically in the histories and surveys of literary criticism, Italian Renaissance tragedy evolved into a dramatized poetic expression of social and political issues relevant to cinquecento audiences. However, it would be a misconception to view Renaissance tragic theater as a simple reflection of culture, for it often intervened in the making of social history. By forcing attention on specific issues, such as the nature of kingship discussed in chapter 2, or the *querelle des femmes* in chapter 3, tragedy helped to plant the seed of change in a society that saw the arts as a mirror image of itself and as a means for defining and redefining changing cultural trends.

I trust that the views and arguments proposed here emerge from the book itself and that they help to foster a dialogue on the merits of cinquecento drama. My final aim is to encourage a serious assessment of the Italian Renaissance tragedy and, thus, vindicate its literary and theatrical relevance, which for centuries has been obscured by the inevitable comparison with its French and English counterparts. Sound critical analysis will undoubtedly dispel many negative perceptions that have prevailed in the past and assign to it a more deserving place in the history of theater. In the end, relevant scholarship will show that if the Italian tragedy of the Renaissance never achieved the reputation enjoyed by both the French and the English dramatic stage, it was not because it lacked distinguishing qualities, as has been suggested, but because Italy never had its Shakespeare, just as England never had its Dante. Benedetto Croce dismisses speculations about the comparison by paraphrasing Carlo Cattaneo, who attributed the difference to the mere chance that Shakespeare was born in England and not in Italy.[3]

My interest on the subject dates back to 1992, when I presented a paper on Aretino's *Orazia* at the International Conference on Aretino held in Toronto. I noticed then how little critical attention the tragic theater of the Renaissance had received both from scholars and editors. In this century the scholarly effort had been mostly limited to Neri's *Tragedia del Cinquecento* (1904), Herrick's *Italian Tragedy in the Renaissance* (1965), and Musumarra's *Poetica* (1972). Though insightful and informative, these works do not deal in depth or in a systematic way with the major cultural issues informing the genre nor do they insist on its theatrical aspect. Editorial activity has also been rather feeble, being limited to republishing collections of the usual half-dozen or so tragedies edited thus far. Hardly a major effort considering the scores of plays still in manuscript form.

The idea for this project grew out of my essay on Rucellai's *Oreste* (*Modern Language Notes*, 1996), in which I touched on several aspects of the tragic theater, especially its cultural and theatrical elements. The article became the actual blueprint for the book, and several ideas from the article as well as from the earlier essay on *Orazia* are expressed throughout the book. Although no parts of this volume have appeared in print in their present form, an abridged version of chapter 1 appeared in the *Encyclopedia of the Italian Renaissance* (1999), and chapter 6 is a revised and expanded version of my "Hic et nunc," published in *Italica* in 1995.

I benefited immensely from the sound advice of many dear friends and colleagues who gave generously of their time. Chris Craig, Denise Di Puccio, Les Essif, Michael Handelsman, Albert Mancini, John Romeiser, and the punctilious Carl Cobb all suffered through readings of various parts of this study. To them I give my thanks, and to myself I attribute the errors and oversights that in these endeavors tend to elude one's best efforts.

* * *

Unless otherwise indicated, all translations are my own. I cite both in translation and in the original texts that receive extensive analysis or have a linguistic bearing on the discussion. Also, citations from Renaissance plays are by act, scene, and line (e.g., *Orbecche*, 5.3.2906); act and line numbers if the edition is not divided into scenes (e.g., *Marianna*, 5.2870); only the line number if there are no other divisions (e.g., *Rosmunda*, 520); and, where the lines are not numbered, the page number is given (e.g., *Didone*, 5. p. 125).

The Italian Tragedy
in the Renaissance

Part I

Renaissance Cultural Realities

1
The Making of Italian Renaissance Tragedy

ALL DISCOURSE ON TRAGEDY SOONER OR LATER GOES BACK TO ARIStotle, whose dramatic precepts continue to be a point of reference for all theater scholarship. Debates on the aesthetic and technical aspects of tragedy, such as the notion and function of tragedy, the meaning of catharsis, or the use of deus ex machina, proceed from the *Poetics* or from the various interpretations and commentaries that arose from its often vague principles of poetics. In fact, the treatise came to Western culture through the Italian Renaissance, which discovered, translated, and interpreted it in ways that reflected its own cultural taste and realities.[1] The formulation of the so-called Aristotelian unities, for instance, was developed by Renaissance critics reacting to incidental comments that Aristotle casually makes about the time span of dramatic action.[2] Their interest in the treatise was not purely academic; it was especially practical, since cinquecento playwrights needed formal guidance in their endeavors to revive the newly discovered ancient tragedy. As it was, they knew little about the genre and much less about its theatrical representation, since no relevant testimony on the subject survived the Middle Ages. Lamenting the lack of information about games, spectacles, pageantry, and other forms of public amusement that the people of Italy might have enjoyed between the fall of the Roman Empire and the year 1000, Lodovico Muratori commented with resignation that "alios frustra in Chartis quaerimus" [in vain do we search the documents].[3]

To be sure, the concept of tragedy was much discussed throughout the Middle Ages. Since few ancient dramatic texts were known and those mainly in excerpts or in anecdotal form, scholars believed that tragedy was about ghastly crimes, often precipitated by women. Donatus thought of it as a literary composition dealing with noble characters, great horrors, and a sorrowful conclusion.[4] Isidore of Seville considered it a mournful poem dealing with the bloody crimes of wicked rulers. Dante, expanding this view to include Lucan's understanding of the genre as involving "mastery of grand style,"[5] concluded that tragedy consists of a serious subject treated in sublime style and having a horrible conclusion. He expressed this conception of tragedy in the *De vulgari eloquentia,* in the letter to Cangrande della Scala, and in the *Divine Comedy,* where Virgil refers to his *Aeneid* as the "high tragedy [written] in lofty verses."[6] Significantly, in this evolving notion of the genre there was no mention of tragedy as a theatrical representation other than incidental references to its being recited or mimed in public. "It was thought," suggests Jonas Barish, "that plays were recited aloud by the writer from some sort of lectern or pulpit, while below him stood an actor who gesticulated, miming the actions indicated or implied by the text."[7]

The idea of tragedy as a poem intended mostly for a reading audience was further substantiated by the discovery of Seneca's plays in the early fourteenth century, first printed in 1478–84. The Senecan emphasis on speech rather than action met with great favor in a culture that placed high value on the art of verbal rhetoric. The Latin model inspired several humanist authors, who followed the Roman predilection for dramatic reading even when they adapted contemporary source material for their plots. The humanist legacy, then, consisted of a number of Latin tragedies that, adhering to Medieval and Senecan poetics, emphasized the literary aspect of drama while neglecting its stage properties. It did not propose to revive the ancient art with living realities, although, in some instances, it dramatized recent historical events. Albertino Mussato's *Ecerinis* (c.1315), one of the better-known humanist tragedies, features relatively few modern elements and has virtually no theatrical qualities. The only modern aspect of the drama is the plot, which is based on the brutal deeds of the contemporary Ezzelino III da Romano. While the play rivals Seneca for its atrocities and moral maxims, much in the text suggests that Mussato is more interested in imitating the classical art form than in reviving it. It is also clear that he, like other humanist playwrights, was never fully aware of the genre's theatrical dimension.[8]

This view of tragedy as a literary form essentially "absolved of all stage possibilities," to quote Henry Buckley Charleton,[9] continued to prevail well into the sixteenth century as the genre was beginning to take hold in Western culture. Gian Giorgio Trissino's *Sofonisba* (1515), for instance, though reprinted six times and already translated into French (1554), was performed for the first time in 1562.[10] Giovanni Rucellai's *Rosmunda* (c.1515)[11] was reprinted at least five times in the course of the century, but we have no knowledge of its ever being performed before the eighteenth century. In 1524, Alessandro Pazzi de' Medici was still referring to his tragedies as poems to be either "lecte et recitate" (read or recited), and hoped that his *Cyclope*, a loose translation of Euripides' *The Cyclops*, was worthy of publication either as a book to be read or recited in public.[12] And yet, while no tragedy had yet appeared on stage, there was a growing awareness of its theatrical dimension. Playwrights and commentators were beginning to identify the spectator rather than the reader as the intended audience of the genre. Trissino, in his letter presenting *Sofonisba* to Pope Leo X, defended his writing it in Italian, arguing, much like Pazzi, that if it were written in another language, say French, it would not be understood by the "listeners." In addition, it would preclude its stage representation, which he considered the most delightful aspect of tragedy.[13] Echoing this belief, he later wrote in his *Poetica* that the representation is the first thing that comes before the eyes of the spectators, as well as the principal source of pleasure.[14]

The occasional discovery of ancient Greek texts contributed considerably to the growing interest in the tragic genre. The belief that many tragedies by Æschylus, Euripides, and Sophocles were still missing inspired fruitful searches in private as well as in public and in religious libraries.[15] Discoveries led to a flurry of Latin translations, responding to scholarly interest and curiosity. But, as Agostino Pertusi has pointed out, it soon became apparent that these translations and most humanist Latin plays were but expressions of an academic world out of step with the times.[16] The eagerness to divulge to a wider audience the content of newly found ancient texts led to translations into the vernacular and reworkings appropriately called "volgarizzamenti." These scholarly activities were a significant first step in the recovery of the long-lost art, for they made classical tragedy more accessible to audiences outside the world of the literati and, at the same time, provided firsthand knowledge of the genre's most basic features. Lodovico Dolce (1510?–1568), an indefatigable translator of tragedies and other ancient texts, stands out for his commitment to make the ancients available to a new class of readers.[17] The common effort revealed a literature whose æsthetic principles and cultural realities had long since vanished and could only be appreciated as one appreciates archaeological findings, that is, as testimony of a glorious but distant past. Though fascinated by ancient culture, playwrights with a keen sense of theater were not content merely to translate or imitate an art form that was not particularly relevant to their lives. Thus, with all due reverence to the genius of the past, they set out to give dramatic expression to their own culture and individual aspirations, inaugurating a revitalization process that brought the classical genre to life.

Revitalization Process

The process was facilitated by the diffusion of Aristotle's *Poetics*, which, together with Horace's *Ars poetica*, provided guidance and formal authority to authors willing to try their dramaturgical skills. A basic guideline, deduced from Aristotle's comments, was, as already noted, the notion of the three unities. Unity of action, time, and place, although later maligned by the Romantics, who saw these rules as stifling poetic creativity, played an important role in the assimilation of the genre. As Luigi Russo suggested, the rules imposed coherence on the various elements of tragedy, preventing theater from dissipating into endless and formless representations.[18] Though of fundamental importance, classical precepts such as these were open to a wide range of interpretations and did not constitute, therefore, undisputed canons of dramatic theory. Neither Trissino nor Rucellai, for example, adhered to the rule of unity of place. In *Sofonisba*, though the scene is set before the royal palace, at least one episode is represented in the Roman camp outside the city. And in *Rosmunda* the scene shifts back and forth from Rosmunda's hideout to Alboino's camp. Differences of opinion about various elements of theater poetics led to lively debates ranging from whether it was better to imitate the Greeks or the Romans, to whether plots should be based on historical or fictional events. There were also questions about the form: what type of verse was befitting to tragedy, how long should a representation last, how many characters might there be in a scene. Playwrights, thus left with plenty of freedom in the composition of their works, appealed to the authority of Horace whenever their innovations departed from Aristotelian precepts, and vice versa. At times, they simply bent ancient precepts to fit their own theatrical preferences.

If the debates failed to reach general consensus on several important issues, they succeeded in generating wide interest in the genre, as questions of poetics, usually discussed in letters to friends or influential patrons, reached an ever-widening audience. The rising popularity of the genre caught the interest of members of the nobility, who proffered financial support to authors eager to experiment with a literary form so new and so revered as ancient drama. The patrons' and the artists' involvement proceeded mainly from an infatuation with classical learning and, for the artists in particular, from the instinctual desire to vie with the ancients as well as with each other. It was not unusual, in fact, for playwrights to boast about their poetic feats and to solicit expressions of approval from the audience. In Giraldi's *Altile*, for instance, Prologue, having called attention to the author's creativity and theatrical expertise, asks the audience to show "grata udienza" [grateful appreciation]. Of course, the invitation, normally expressed in the prologue, was meant for an audience sophisticated enough to pass judgment on the creative achievements exhibited both in the text and on the stage. The spectators of dramatic representations were typically educated individuals openly appreciative of artistic experimentation and, thus, most anxious to experience the newly discovered art form.[19]

Their appreciation went beyond pure literary gratification as tragedy began to regain its rightful place on the stage. The honor of restoring tragedy to the stage went to Giambattista Giraldi Cinthio (1504–1573), one of the most prolific dramatists of the century.[20] Writing of the success of *Orbecche* performed in Parma by the Accademia, Giraldi boasts that "doppo tanti secoli ho rinovato l'uso dello spettacolo delle tragedie, il quale era poco meno che andato in oblivione" [after so many centuries I reintroduced the use of the spectacle of tragedies, which had been almost forgotten].[21] In fact, the 1541 performance of his *Orbecche*, the first Italian tragedy ever to be performed in Renaissance Italy, revived a long-lost theatrical tradition that was promptly received with much enthusiasm. That same year *Orbecche* was performed two more times at the request of illustrious prelates and signors.[22] Stage performances thus became more and more frequent as artists and patrons sought to quench an ever-growing thirst for dramatic representations. Patrons commissioned plays and sponsored performances that, in the absence of public theaters, were given either at the court of the local lord or in private residences before large but select groups of spectators. In one reported instance, the 1565 representation of Dolce's *Marianna* in Ferrara, the size of the audience grew so big in number that it actually hindered the performance.[23]

This popularity notwithstanding, the representation of tragedies never reached the level of frequency enjoyed by comedy. Lodovico Dolce, who wrote comedies as well as tragedies, complained through the prologue of his *Medea* that comedy was so popular that tragedy appeared to be neglected. The difference was partly due to the fact that the high style of tragedy and the gravity of its subject matter appealed only to the educated few. A more pragmatic reason was undoubtedly the prohibitive cost associated with the stage production. Unlike comedy, tragedy required the construction of majestic sets and the use of elaborate costumes for its royal characters and their large retinues. As such expense could only be sustained, in the words of Angelo Ingegneri, by a deep "borsa reale" [royal purse], performances were usually sponsored by the reigning prince or other members of the ruling class.[24] Undoubtedly, high costs made stage productions rare. However, the pageantry they engendered made them an ideal setting for the celebration of important events, such as state weddings or official state visits. The representation was a cultural event in itself and, as we shall see in the next chapter, was normally characterized by carefully staged protocol and pageantry that projected the sponsors' wealth and political influence. Members of the nobility, in ostentatious display of family colors and prestige, would participate in the festivities and sanction with their presence the sociopolitical system that legitimized their privileged status. It was a rhetorical show of power in which both the ruler and individual nobles reaffirmed their place in the hierarchy of the social order and displayed their ability, albeit virtual, to defend it. They were all mindful that attempts against one's power, whether a prince's sovereignty or a noble's privilege, came both from other nobles with expansionist aims as well as from ambitious members of their own family and entourage.[25]

It is important to keep in mind that this overtly heavyhanded political instrumentation of the genre did not extend to the dramatic text, but only to the pageantry occasioned by the performance. And, though the rhetoric of power spilled into the auditorium, where seating arrangements projected status and influence, the stage representation itself remained largely an artistic presentation of a fictional world. The failure to distinguish between textual import and extratextual concerns has led critics to reduce Renaissance tragedy to the role of state propaganda and to view playwrights as servile courtiers. The strength of their argument lies in the assumption that playwrights were members of the ruling nobility and tended, therefore, to promote the preservation of the sociopolitical system in which they had vested interests.[26] The seeming plausibility of this view, arising from the common belief that the educated were implicitly nobles, has contributed to its being accepted uncritically, that is, without taking into account that some dramatists were actually poor and of humble origins. Aretino, for instance, was the son of a shoemaker and made his living by threatening the rich and powerful with disparaging publicity. His pernicious and unscrupulous pen was so feared that it earned him a very comfortable living and the epithet "scourge of princes." Lodovico Dolce fought poverty by teaching children and working at a printing press. And the self-taught Luigi Groto, the blind man of Adria, found sporadic employment as a tutor and as a spokesman for various causes.[27] Though sponsorship was crucial to their success as artists, these playwrights had such a marginal stake in the socioeconomic order that it is difficult to see what interest they could have had in promoting a system that essentially excluded them.

Equally debatable is the argument that the ideology informing a play tended to support the (political) expectations of the nobles who subsidized it. This observation, consistent with the business notion that service must always satisfy the customer, not only reduces the value of art to a mere instrument of politics, but, more seriously, fails to take into account the irrepressible urge that normally inspires poetic creativity. True art does not capitulate to the demands and restrictions of sponsors or patrons, it only responds to the inner need to express emotions and ideas not readily perceptible by the common individual. Speaking of the artists' independence from socioeconomic forces and of the agonistic spirit that drives them, Harold Bloom has observed most perceptively that "throughout Western history the creative imagination has conceived of itself as the most competitive of modes, akin to the solitary runner, who races for his own glory."[28] Sponsors could, and often did, request a specific literary piece, such as a tragedy, a comedy, or a religious play, but it was the poet who determined the type of plot and how to dramatize it. With regard to other forms of artistic expression such as painting, patrons often provided the artist with specific historical or mythological details to be included in the work, since, as Burke points out, artists "generally lacked a classical education."[29] But, again, the rich and powerful could commission the labor, not the genius, which alone determines a work's artistic value.

In dedicating a play to a benefactor, it was common for playwrights to take pride in their creative genius. They also hoped, with all the modesty demanded by the rhetoric of the time, that the play would bring them recognition and do great honor to the generous patron. What sponsors bought, then, was not a political propaganda machine, but the prestige that their magnanimous patronage of the arts conferred upon their family name. Aretino's dedication of his *Orazia* to Pope Paul III exemplifies this relationship, as he humbly proposes to glorify, honor, and praise the pontiff with the creative qualities that are born out of the genius with which nature endowed him. In return, he asks for the pope's generosity, without which, he complains in a letter to Luigi Farnese's secretary, he is forced to live modestly. However, he is quick to add that only fame, honor, and praise are the true "food, sustenance, and fare of [creative] virtue."[30]

As the patron's prestige and generosity was proportionate to the artist's reputation, it was important for playwrights to excel in their work and, thus, further their fame. To this end they often called attention, usually in the prologue, to their poetic feats, lest they go unnoticed. Though the wish for patronage was undoubtedly a driving force behind the artists' work, it was the inner urge to rise above their rivals that ultimately inspired their poetic genius to greater achievements. They aimed to go beyond the mere imitation of the classics and to bring on stage a world that, while retaining its ancient allure, drew meaningful parallels to their own. Building on the knowledge and experience acquired through the translations of Greek and Roman tragedies, playwrights began to compose their own plays, drawing plot material from historical legends of the near and distant past, from classical mythology, or simply adapting story lines already dramatized in antiquity. This last alternative was perhaps the most popular, as it provided a rich source of tested material and a basic model of the genre's formal aims and limitations.

The excessive reliance on ancient dramas for plot material caused modern scholars to dismiss the Italians as slavish imitators lacking originality. Marvin Herrick, to name one of the most recent and authoritative critics, suggests that "the Italians did not succeed in modernizing their neoclassical tragedies," and that ultimately "they remained imitators of Seneca, Euripides, Sophocles, Virgil, and Ovid in the sense of copyists."[31] This view is rather narrow on two counts. First, there is no significant evidence to support the assertion that Italian dramatists were not innovators. It is a mere but persisting assumption that unfortunately continues to perpetuate the traditional, uncritical view of Italian Renaissance tragedy as ordinary theater. Second, the label "copyists" is barely appropriate, since there were considerable advantages in the recasting of old plots. The most obvious advantage was that well-known plots allowed the spectators to concentrate less on the story line and more on the playwright's innovations. In a letter describing the 1568 performance of Gabriele Bombace's *Alidoro* in Reggio Emilia, the anonymous author justifies the notion of representing "cose note" [known things] on the grounds that the spectators, "intendendo subito l'invenzione, non avessero da gir vagando con l'intelletto per interpretarle" [being familiar with the plot, did not have to wander about its meaning].[32]

Herrick's view also postulates the rather questionable assumption that good theater must perforce be original. What then, of Euripides, Sophocles, and Æschylus, whose tendency to rewrite popular stories moved the comic playwright Antiphanes to exclaim with envy:

> Comedy? Now Tragedy's a lucky sort of art.
> First the house knows the plot before you start;
> You 've only to remind it. "Oedipus"
> You say, and all's out—father Laïus,
> Mother Jocasta, daughters these, sons those,

> His sin, his coming punishment. Or suppose
> You say "Alcmaeon"; in saying that, you've said
> All his sons too, how he's gone off his head
> And killed his mother, and how . . .
> . . . .
> We Comic writers have more clamant needs;
> There's all to invent, new names, new words, new deeds,
> Prologue, presuppositions, action, ending.[33]

Lodovico Dolce justified the innovations that distinguished his *Didone* from the original source by reminding the audience that both Sophocles and Euripides took similar liberties in adapting familiar plots.[34] Thus, following in the footsteps of the ancients, the Italians found guidance in the poetics of imitation, best exemplified by the classical simile of the bees and their honey producing activity. Recalling Horace and Seneca, Petrarch suggested that in writing one should imitate the bees, that is, not by picking flowers, but by turning them into honeycombs, thereby creating something different from and even better than the original.[35] Imitation, as Castelvetro argued, consists in the creative use of basic source elements (story, characters, themes) and in the novelty of the work that these elements help to produce. Not an act of thievery or duplication, reiterates Castelvetro, but a dynamic process that leads to the creation of a thing clearly distinguishable from the source.[36] In adapting classical myths or dramas, playwrights actually challenged themselves to produce a work that would be at least as meaningful and as entertaining to their spectators as the original had been to its ancient audiences.

But whether proposing original plots or imitating classical texts, playwrights were primarily driven by an agonistic spirit to outdo their counterparts, both ancient and contemporary, and even to surpass the aesthetic standards of the times. Their achievements were measured not in terms of the story line, which was often based on well-known historical or mythological events, but in terms of the innovations that distinguished their work. Thus, the adaptation of an old plot was not construed as lack of originality, but as a significant dramaturgical expedient meant to orient the spectators' response vis-à-vis the type of performance they were about to see (tragedy, as opposed to comedy or pastoral). It would also allow for comparison between the new and the old and for a critical appraisal of their differences. Advance knowledge tends to form what Pfister calls "a contrasting inter textual background which emphasizes the elements that deviate from the older version."[37] Prior knowledge facilitated the audience's assessment of the playwright's creativity to transform a classical source into a modern drama, that is, to make it significant both ideologically and theatrically in the context of existing cultural realities. Ultimately, what the audience came to appreciate was the playwright's innovations and dramaturgical skills, which helped to narrow the gap between the fiction of the stage and the reality of the auditorium.

This bridging certainly made it easier for theater to fulfill its basic function of *docere et diligere* (to teach and to delight), which was expected of all poetry. Prologue usually voiced the didactic scope of a play, and often called attention to the forces of good and evil informing the dramatic action. He also exhorted the audience to learn from the tragic events that they were about to see represented. Commenting on the moral role of theater, Prologue in Giraldi's *Selene* asserts that theaters were conceived for the purpose of teaching the way to a virtuous life to thousands of people, all in one day. Through the dramatized events, audiences would quickly learn to follow virtue and eschew evil:

> Per insegnare adunque in un sol giorno
> A migliaia di gente il vero modo
> Di compir con onor la vita frale,
> *In uso posti for teatri e scene*
> Perché, veggendo indi gli spettatori
> Varie sembianze d'uomini e di donne,
> Di varii uffici e qualità diverse
> E di varii costumi e varie leggi,
> Sortir diversi fini e varie sorti,
> Fatti acuti, sapesser da sé in tanta
> Varietà di genti e di costumi
> Seguir la loda et ischivare il biasmo
> E veder che chiunque virtù segue
> Giunge a buon fine e chi 'l mal segue a reo.
> (*Selene*, 24–37)[38]

[To teach, then, in one day / to thousands of people the true way / of fulfilling with honor his fragile life / *stages and scenes were instituted.* / In this way, spectators can see there / various types of men and women, / of various status and different qualities, / and of various customs and various laws / come to diverse ends and various fates. / Thus aware, they (spectators) might learn, through so wide / a variety of peoples and customs, / to follow praise and eschew blame, / and see that those who follow virtue / reach a blessed end, and those who follow evil, an evil one.]

The notion of right and wrong, of good and evil is often shaped by changing cultural trends and is, therefore, peculiar to a given moment in the cultural history of a society. In the Middle Ages, for instance, reaping profits from commercial transactions was considered wrong and sinful because, as Dante points out in the *Inferno*, "usury offends divine goodness" (11.95). However, in the following century, as banking and commerce became a common means of interaction among individuals, public institutions, and even among nations, profit-making came to symbolize business acumen. And so, whereas at the end of the thirteenth century Dante disdained "the newcomers and quick gains" (*Inferno*, 16.73), a mere half century later Boccaccio sang their *gesta* and praised them as the paladins of commerce.[39] And in the quattrocento, the humanists considered honor, glory, and magnanimity intrinsic princely virtues. However, a generation later, with the proliferation of armed conflicts, fraud and violence became the basic qualities of an ideal prince. Hardly a century went by that reason-of-state writers found these Machiavellian qualities objectionable and sought to redefine them according to Counter-Reformation ideology.

The didactic function of theater, then, was not merely to teach the difference between right and wrong or show the effects of good and evil in absolute terms. Rather, it was to encourage the audience to reflect upon, define, or redefine the evolving values and ideological notions (moral, political, religious, social) underpinning their social institutions. This is indeed one of the most basic functions of theater, for in discussing a play, opines William McCollum, "we actually ask 'How does the action of the play apply to the society which produced it?'"[40] In this sense, the stage served as a forum for dramatizing issues of major concern to the society. A topic of great relevance to the times and dominant in many a tragedy, was the notion of kingship, which Machiavellian theory had brought to the forefront of political discourse.[41] The ideology informing the role of most stage rulers mirrors the ongoing debate on royal prerogatives and princely virtues. The king's usual dismissal of his counselor's advice to forsake deception and violence and to govern instead with justice, prudence, and other princely qualities dramatizes Machiavelli's rejection of humanist notions of princeship as too idealistic and incompatible with factual reality. However, in the violent death of bloodthirsty stage tyrants, audiences recognized the rejection of Machiavellian amoralism and the emergence of a political philosophy more in keeping with the prevailing moral and religious values of Counter-Reformation Italy.

Another topic of profound cultural implications that found a forum on the dramatic stage was the growing challenge to the traditional view of womankind, which denied women the intellectual potential to be men's equal. As women became more vocal about their rights and more demonstrative of their intellectual ability, their cause began to gain momentum, putting the traditional, misogynist view on the defensive. The stage dramatization of the debate, which would become better known in France as the *querelle des femmes,* proceeds from the conflicting perspectives articulating the role of the female heroine. On the one hand, she is characterized as subservient, of limited intellect, and given to quick display of emotions and other frailties. On the other hand, she is portrayed as the victim of cultural prejudice who demands the recognition of her intellectual ability and, inherently, of her right to live with the human dignity that derives from one's freedom of action and expression. In most dramas, the debate normally ends with the heroine's tragic demise; however, the composed resolve with which she faces death earns her the *admiratio* of men and elevates her to the status of man's equal.

Tragedy, then, was no longer seen as a poem merely dealing with the bloody crimes of wicked rulers. Nor was it considered just an opportunity for playwrights to show their creative talents and ingratiate themselves with their audiences and with powerful lords. It was also widely conceived as a vehicle for expressing society's views of its changing world, which, as it evolved, prompted the constant reassessment of existing beliefs and values. Admittedly, Renaissance tragedy remained largely within the parameters of the classical Sophoclean conflict between the interests of the state and the rights of the individual. What distinguished playwrights and their individual plays was the attention they called to specific aspects of the conflict. As the state was most often represented by the king, questions arose about the extent to which the king's personal interests and ambitions coincided with the welfare of his subjects. They also dealt with the ways (force or tolerance, punishment, or forgiveness) in which a prince might best defend and preserve the state. On the other side of the conflict stood the individual, whose claims or deeds were perceived by the ruling tyrant as threatening the integrity of the state. The motives behind such deeds vary from personal pride, as is the case of Horace in *Orazia,* to claims of human dignity, as voiced by Orbecche, to ideals of liberty, claimed by Sofonisba, or the right to pursue love as one chooses, professed by several tragic heroines such as Aretino's Celia and Groto's Adriana. The specific nature of the conflict, then, makes each tragedy unique and, at the same time, accounts for the ideological diversity that distinguishes both the genre and the individual dramatist.

It must be noted that whatever the issues informing the tragic conflict, the debate inevitably involved the audience, who was not simply invited to watch, but was also encouraged to favor one view or the other. Undoubtedly, vivid dramatizations drew the attention of even the most indifferent spectators, forcing a social dialogue that could lead, depending on the issue dramatized, to the questioning and perhaps the redefinition of existing values and beliefs. Italian Renaissance tragedy, then, was more than just the product and the mirror of profound ethicopolitical or religious crises, as Luigi Russo observed.[42] It was also the expression of a society eager to take a serious look at its most pressing issues. In this sense, tragedy was a vehicle that helped to determine the course of evolving cultural trends. By calling attention to critical social problems and prompting discussions about alternatives and solutions, it intervened meaningfully in the making of social history.

Realism and Living Realities on the Stage

The extent to which theater succeeded as a significant forum for cultural debates hinged largely upon its power to involve the audience in the dramatic action. To this end, playwrights would often boast that they presented events with virtual reality or "con sembianza del ver," as Prologue claims in Giraldi's *Antivalomeni*. Their guiding principle was the much debated notion of verisimilitude, which proposed that theatrical representations bear a strong resemblance to actual reality. Accordingly, the fictional world of the stage was to be represented in ways so realistic as to easily suspend the audience's instinctive reluctance to be drawn from their real world into the illusion of theater. Some authors called attention to the creative endeavors through which they brought realism on stage. Others, such as Dolce, went so far as to exhort spectators to imagine themselves as living, if not physically, at least in spirit, in the fictional world of the stage. In the prologue to his *Giocasta*, he tells the spectators

> Ora pensate di trovarvi in Tebe. . . .
> E, se non sete in lei con la persona,
> Siatevi con la mente e col pensiero.

[Picture yourselves in ancient Thebes . . . / And if you cannot be there in person, / you can at least be there with your imagination.][43]

Of course, it was not enough simply to ask for the spectators' involvement. In order to obtain their full intellectual and emotional participation, the representation had to be enlivened with current traditions that would not only speak to the audience about themselves and their problems, but would do so in ways that were both intelligible and captivating to them.

Whether writing comedies or tragedies, playwrights insisted on the novelty of the genre and argued against slavish imitation of long dead traditions. Taking heart from the Romans' practice of adapting Greek works to their own culture, they insisted that stage representation should be articulated in the vernacular and in other contemporary, living customs. Among those who argued for the modernity of theater, including well-known playwrights such as Anton Francesco Grazzini, Angelo Beolco o Ruzzante, and Giraldi, it was Dolce who gave the most vivid account of this principle of poetics. In the speech appended to his *Ifigenia*, the character Tragedia tells the audience that the author adapted the best from the Greek source and is now presenting it "con altra lingua, & altra forma" [in another tongue and in another form]. And in his *Medea*, Prologue informs the spectators that they are about to see

> Una Tragedia nova,
> Nova dico, per esser novamente
> Con nuovi panni da colui vestita.

[A new tragedy, / I say new, for it has been / dressed with new clothes by him (the author).]

A basic article of the new "clothes" was the language itself. Playwrights, drawing heavily on literary tradition, took pride in their stylistic virtuosity. They took pride in giving detailed descriptions of actions and scenes that they thought could not and should not be represented, such as crowds, fights, and bloody killings. In these narratives, writers often flaunted their familiarity with the Italian classics by employing commonplaces found in works of well-known authors. The spectators were undoubtedly gratified by their own ability to recognize in these descriptions resonances of Dante, Petrarch, Ariosto, and other famous poets. The emphasis on language, due in part to humanist influence and in part to the restrictions that decorum imposed against staging violent deeds, contributed to a mostly verbal representation of the dramatic world. The end result was a tragedy articulated by words rather than lively action, robbing the stage of its intrinsic theatrical function. Those with a keen appreciation for the stage, such as Angelo Ingegneri, himself a stage theorist and sometime director, were openly critical of the excessive reliance on verbal rhetoric. Reflecting his contemporaries' annoyance with wordy plays, Ingegneri complained that one could actually sleep through long monologues without missing much of the action.⁴⁴ Notwithstanding the call for shorter soliloquies and narratives, the practice persisted long enough to earn Renaissance tragedy the reputation of talky and static theater meant to be read rather than performed.

As with all generalizations, here too one finds exceptions, for many tragedies were actually better suited for the stage than for the "closet." The movements, the cries, the sounds, the blocking, and other auditory and visual percepts articulating the theatricality of many a tragedy make it difficult to sustain Cesare Molinari's contention that playwrights only rarely considered the relationship between the stage and the poetic text.⁴⁵ The sounds of trumpets, the shouting of crowds, the heartrending screams that animate Aretino's *Orazia*, for example, acquire full signification only when experienced on stage before a live audience. Only a viewing public, as against a reading public, could appreciate the petrifying screams of a murder victim or the shocking sight of hacked human body parts as in *Orbecche*. Underscoring the impact of representation on the spectators, Giraldi tells of a lady spectator who, during the 1541 performance of the play, fainted upon seeing Oronte's and the children's severed heads and hands placed on a silver platter for Orbecche to behold.⁴⁶

Dramatists sensitive to the theatrical function of the stage sought in earnest to enliven tragic representations by introducing a variety of changes. For instance, they reduced lengthy narratives that tended to put spectators to sleep. Also, departing from ancient tradition, which normally allowed no more than three speaking characters on stage at one time, they animated the stage with five or more characters in the same scene. Aretino and Rucellai each enlivened with five characters the closing scenes of *Orazia* and *Rosmunda* respectively. Giraldi, too, cast five characters with speaking parts in *Orbecche* 3.4. And Groto, in *Adriana* 4.4, filled the stage with seven characters all with active roles. This is indeed a novelty, especially when one considers that in all of Seneca's plays and in many Greek tragedies seldom are there more than three characters with speaking roles in one scene. Playwrights also dramatized the *antefactum*, traditionally a monological exposition *ad spectatores* who were implicitly considered active participants in the theatrical event. Facts leading to the dramatic action were told in dialogue form with one character telling the story and the other interrupting with comments, questions, and exclamations that often reflected the audience's concerns and reactions. The innovation gave rise to the concept of the invisible fourth wall between the stage and the auditorium. Giraldi formally addressed this notion of the fourth wall by arguing that the actor must not take into account the presence of spectators because they do not figure in the performance.[47] Leone de' Sommi, too, believed that the actor should not address the spectators because, he explained, they are not always in the same city or location where the actor pretends to be.[48]

Playwrights also opted, when possible, for a more visual representation either by actual showing or by spatial techniques. One such technique, to be discussed in chapter 7, was what I call the *hic et nunc* expedient, whereby a violent scene was described as it was developing, there and then, out of sight but within earshot of the audience. Such is Orbecche's murder of her father Sulmone just inside the palace doors. Although the spectators cannot see the killing, they experience it in all its immediacy and brutality through other sensory perceptions as they hear Sulmone's agonizing cries for help and see his blood running out from within the palace. The scene is rendered more vivid as the horrified chorus, beholding Orbecche furiously swinging the ax at the dying king, describes and comments upon the gruesome killing. The technique thus reduced the need for the traditional messenger and the lengthy narratives normally associated with his or her role. It also had a great emotional impact on the spectators, who could not remain indifferent to the commotion of the action taking place beyond the scenic space or ignore the anxiety of the character(s) witnessing and describing it.

Dramaturgical Novelties: Sounds and Dramatic Space

Inherent in this technique was the notion that dramatic space expanded beyond the physical limits of the stage to include areas visibly inaccessible to the audience. In several instances, the expansion led to the representation of events easily signified by sensorial signs, such as sounds and lighting. In Aretino's *Orazia*, both the stage and the theater public are startled by the sounds of trumpets and cries of joy coming from afar. In an instinctive attempt to see what is happening, they all turn toward the direction of the incoming noise, reinforcing the illusion that the stage extends beyond the physical limits of the theater. And, though neither the characters on the stage nor the spectators can see what is going on, they can all hear and appreciate the euphoria of the Roman people celebrating Horace's victory over the Curiace brothers. Thus, one of the most obvious and immediate effects of the noise is to expand the mimetic space of the dramatic action to the streets of Rome, the stage, as it were, of the events signified by the sensorial signs. Rome, then, visible only in scenic perspective, comes to life as the staging ground of events that through sensorial signs converge on the actual stage, where they acquire relevance to the main action.

The significance of these sounds is chiefly obtained when they are brought on the scenic space where all signs are interpreted and assigned a proper place in the development of the plot. The noises and cries of celebration heard coming from afar indicate that Horace has defeated the Curiaces and that the plot has now moved along into the next sequence. The stage is, however, more than a mere decoding center, for the mimetic spaces defining the set, such as royal palaces, temples, private residences, and public streets tend to confer specific semantic import to events that take place within their spatial domain. Horace's victory, then, seen in the context of the scenic layout projecting the city of Rome, becomes a Roman victory. The city featured on the backdrop emerges as a living space vibrating with life, hence promoting the theatrical illusion that the general euphoria is actually spilling out of the streets, of the houses and rooftops crowding, albeit in perspective, the skyline of the city. A dramatic space that expands in this way beyond the visibly perceptible allows for the representation, if only virtually, of otherwise unrepresentable deeds and, in so doing, reduces the need for messengers with lengthy narratives. As a result, the spectators enjoy a fuller theatrical experience, since they come to learn about dramatic events not as having taken place somewhere, but as unfolding there and then within earshot of both stage and theater audiences.

Admittedly, speech remained the most basic form of theatrical communication and practically indispensable for the full appreciation of theater, for often only verbal decoding can assign specific meaning to some signs and events happening on or beyond the visible scene. However, the increasing tendency to signify space and events through sensorial signs points to a growing awareness of the true nature of theater as a mimetic vehicle of reality. In a significant departure from the Aristotelian emphasis on the written text, Giraldi in particular recognized the effect of the spectacle, insisting that a mediocre, but well-performed, poetic text was better than a good play that was poorly staged.[49] And, Angelo Ingegneri, stressing the importance of the spectacle, inveighed against those playwrights who, lacking a sense of the genre's theatrical dimension, did not care whether their work was suitable for the stage, for which, he laments, they have no regard.[50] This emphasis on the dramaturgical aspect of drama undoubtedly encouraged the introduction and use of mechanical devices meant to show, rather than tell, the occurrence of specific sensorial phenomena. Thus, a luminous contraption representing the sun or the moon moving slowly across the fictional skies of the stage would suggest the time of day and its passing.[51] Prismatic devices, called "periatti," facilitated the change of scenes by simply rotating their painted surfaces to form new perspectives. And the rolling of a large stone on the floor above the stage produced the sound of thunder, while flashes of burning powder created the illusion of lightning. Serlio even suggested ways for simulating thunderbolts.[52]

The effect of these technical innovations was both entertaining and engaging, as spectators, always eager for entertainment, undoubtedly marveled at the ingenuity of the inventions.[53] Serlio called for the use of mechanical devices precisely because he believed that sensory percepts delight the spectators and excite their fancy. He thought that the spectators would enjoy hearing familiar noises, such as the sounds of trumpets, of human voices and footsteps, and the hoofbeats of horses.[54] Most amusing was perhaps the realistic reproduction of certain natural phenomena, which in the past were usually suggested through verbal constructs. But, whereas words could only evoke the idea of, say, thunder, the noise simulating the sound of thunder appealed to the spectators' senses, causing them to focus on its signifier. In this sense, the stage engaged the spectators both intellectually and sensorially, predisposing them to ignore the barrier between fictional and real and to accept more readily the illusion of theater. So totally involved in the representation, the public was primed to reflect upon the contrasts and similarities that the fiction of the stage bore to the reality of their own world.

2
Renaissance Living Traditions and the Revival of Ancient Tragedy

LUDOVICO DOLCE, IN THE EPILOGUE THAT FOLLOWS HIS *IFIGENIA*, sketches a brief history of tragedy, noting that Lady Tragedy after its glorious days in Greece refused to live in Rome and has now come to Florence where she has been honored by well known playwrights such as Trissino, Alamanni, Rucellai, Aretino, Giraldi, Speroni and, of course, himself.[1] Indeed, once Italian Renaissance authors discovered classical drama and felt its appeal, they proceeded to make it appealing to their contemporaries by imbuing it with their own living traditions. They expressly sought to present Tragedy "dressed in new clothes," namely, a new form, language, and situations reflecting their own realities. Trissino, in particular, spoke of the need to *Italianize* theater in order to make it intelligible and relevant to spectators. Anton Francesco Grazzini, among others, called for theatrical representations to reflect existing customs and institutions, noting that theater should mirror the culture in which it is produced. He reminded diehard imitators of the ancients that modern times, notably customs, religion, and way of life, were different from those of Aristotle and Horace.[2] And Giraldi, in the prologue to his *Altile*, insisted that classical rules were not so rigid that a poet could not depart from them in order to reflect the times and the taste of modern audiences. After all, he noted, the Romans departed form Greek dramatic traditions in order to represent their own living reality. D'Alembert saw this tendency as a symptom of the general intellectual awakening or rebirth that he characterized as one of those "révolutions qui font prendre à la terre une face nouvelle" [revolutions that change the face of the earth].[3] It was in part this urge to look beyond the ancients that led to the revitalization and modernization of classical tragedy.[4]

Playwrights knew that a dramatic work had to be culturally relevant in order to delight and instruct the public. A tragedy had to draw the spectators both emotionally and intellectually into the events of the stage before they could appreciate its spectacle and ponder the ideological import of its poetic message. To facilitate this experience, the representation had to be so realistic as to engage the concerns (human, political, religious) of contemporary audiences, appeal to their taste, and stir their emotions.[5] More specifically, it had to suggest that what was happening on stage could happen in real life. True theatrical experience happens as the gap between the world of theater and the auditorium narrows to the point that the fiction of the stage evokes in the minds of the spectators their own reality. Lest the parallel be lost on the spectators, the chorus in *Marianna* underscores how a seemingly distant danger can actually be very close, as he warns that when a neighbor's house is burning it is possible that the fire may spread to our own houses (4.2773–75). And in the prologue to his *Giocasta*, Dolce, having informed the spectators that the atrocities that they are about to witness take place in Thebes, exhorts them to praise the Lord for living in a city "ove mai crudeltà non ebbe albergo" [where cruelty was never the norm] (p 9). In *Orbecche*, Prologue draws a comparison between stage and auditorium by reminding the audience that the city on the backdrop is not the peaceful Ferrara, but a far away city, once happy and now plunged into bloodshed and despair (53).

The extent of verisimilitude in which to cast dramatic representations vexed playwrights and theorists alike throughout the sixteenth century. The dilemma was particularly evident when dealing with the representation of mythological characters, specifically how to make them come to life and behave in a way so realistic as to engage the spectator both emotionally and intellectually. Left in their ancient setting, they would appear as fossilized remains of a distant civilization and, thus, hardly relevant to contemporary audiences. Inevitably, the cultural and temporal distance separating the stage from the auditorium would hinder the spectators' involvement, leaving them unconcerned about a character's plight or a dramatic situation that bore no relation to their own reality. If, on the other hand, mythological characters were removed from their original milieu, they risked losing credibility and, again, failure to win acceptance by an audience deeply rooted in their own world. Although the issue was never settled satisfactorily, an unusual notion of realism seems to have prevailed: one that, while respecting the historical and cultural identity of characters, made them appear and behave in a manner somewhat consistent, if blatantly anachronistic, with contemporary decorum. Thus, Oedipus would be identified by his name and deeds as the mythological king of Thebes, but his appearance and behavior would be informed by living realities befitting a modern king. To Renaissance audiences, a character resembling a contemporary prince in both customs and manner was certainly more real than a character wearing, say, a mask symbolizing a king. This compromised notion of realism allowed playwrights to enliven ancient theater with current traditions, thus bringing the past closer to the present. Audiences could easily identify with, and take interest in, a world that, though remote, resembled their own. The effort to acculturate classical tragedy by informing it with cinquecento realities led to a series of innovations that gave dramatic theater a distinct Renaissance quality, and, at the same time, offered modern readers a precious insight into the aesthetic taste and the cultural climate of the times. Though a catalogue of these innovations would provide data that would help identify and quantify preferences and peculiarities of individual playwrights, it would ultimately prove too dispersive and void of meaningful analysis. For a productive discussion, we must focus our attention on those changes that may offer a reasonable measure of the extent to which ancient theater was Italianized, and, at the same time, lead to the appreciation of the cultural forces that brought it about. Innovations to consider should include the length of the written texts, costumes, spatial and courtly setting, and the mythical characters' fears of unsafe travel, which evoke the dangerous environment in which cinquecento audiences lived.

Length of the Dramatic Text:
Political Imperatives and Verbal Rhetoric

Of all the characteristics peculiar to the Italian Renaissance tragedy, the most obvious is perhaps the excessive length of the written texts, which in many cases count more than 3,300 lines. On the average, cinquecento tragedies, be they original compositions or adaptations, are nearly twice as long as a typical Greek or Roman tragedy. Anguillara's *Edippo*, for instance, is 3,180 lines long, double the number of lines of its source Sophocles' *Oedipus the King*, which has 1,530 lines. Dolce's *Medea* has approximately 2,350 lines, more than double the 1,000 lines of Seneca's *Medea*.[6] Charleton's suggestion that this difference resulted from the "tendency in closet-dramas to increase the narrative of events"[7] is inadequate because plays meant to be read are often shorter or as long as those expressly written for the stage. Mussato's *Ecerinis*, for example, though a closet tragedy, has only 629 lines; and Niccolò da Correggio's *Fabula di Cefalo* (1487) is only 638 lines long. Conversely, Groto's *Adriana*, which according to Prologue was meant for the stage, is about 4,420 lines long (perhaps the longest of all Italian Renaissance tragedies). Also, Giraldi's tragedies of horror, which, he concedes, are better suited for reading, are as long as those with a happy ending, which he proposes for the stage.[8] As the length of the dramatic text does not appear to depend on whether a play was meant to be read or represented, more plausible explanations may be found in the cultural forces that produced it. In this context, one may consider the sociopolitical significance that theatrical representations of tragedy acquired in the Renaissance and the impact that this new function had on the length of the text.

In antiquity dramatic performances were often one of several events taking place in public during major cultural festivities such as the annual Greek festivals or the Roman games honoring the gods, celebrating victories, and commemorating great men. Perforce, the stage had to compete with several other forms of entertainment for a share of the public's attention. In the Renaissance, the stage performance of a tragedy became a unique cultural event that often lasted an entire day and was attended by a large and select audience. It typically marked festive, stately occasions, such as princely weddings, state visits, peace treaties, and similar public celebrations. The magnificence and the pageantry characterizing the theatrical event bespoke the prestige of the guests of honor and of the sponsor's munificence. Performances were so costly that only princes or other members of the ruling class could afford to finance them. Giraldi, having made the point that a comic scene should be "popolaresca" [common] and the tragic regal, recalls that his *Orbecche* was staged "non perdonando né a spesa né a fatica" [without regard for cost or labor].[9] Comic representations, too, could be expensive, especially if sponsored by a prince intent upon projecting his power and wealth. Jano Pencaro reported to Isabella Gonzaga that people listened in disbelief when told that the duke of Ferrara spent the exorbitant amount of nearly two thousand ducats for the 1499 representation of Terence's *The Eunuch*.[10]

It was not unusual in Renaissance performances to see large casts of more than eighty characters and supernumeraries all sumptuously dressed with fine cloth draped in gold and other precious metals. Spectators came from miles around, taking up residence in public inns, those who could not stay with friends or relatives. For the 1568 performance of Gabriele Bombace's *Alidoro* in honor of Queen Barbara of Austria, so many nobles traveled to Reggio Emilia that, according to an anonymous account, local gentry were not allowed to attend opening night in order to accommodate the visitors.[11] Filippo Pigafetta, who attended the 1585 representation of Orsato Giustiniano's *Edippo il tiranno* (a free translation of Sophocles' *Oedipus the King*) at the Teatro Olimpico in Vicenza, reported that of the three thousand spectators in attendance more than two thousand were from out of town. We can only imagine the festive atmosphere reigning in merry ballrooms and in noisy streets bustling with people and carriages. Pigafetta notes that one did not see in the streets anything but noblemen, noblewomen, carriages, horses, and visitors who had come for the representation. It was a propitious occasion for the nobility to gather in ostentatious display of family colors and influence. Armed honor guards in their colorful uniforms contributed to the cheerful mood of pomp and pageantry. Their ubiquitous presence underscored the importance of the event and subtly reminded both subjects and foreign dignitaries of the prince's power and majesty.[12] The ruling prince attended the performance with full regalia and ceremony. Sitting on a raised platform in the center of the auditorium, and surrounded by other nobles and dignitaries according to rank and influence, he vied with the stage for the public's attention and approval.[13]

Considering the high cost of production and the political importance of the occasion, it was not unusual for patrons to demand that the play be long enough to allow for a lengthy performance. Giraldi tells that Ercole d'Este requested that *Didone*, which he commissioned from Giraldi, be at least six hours long because a work such as this, the Duke thought, should not be represented in less time.[14] The length of the representation included intermezzi, types of self-contained spectacles meant to provide a light distraction from the seriousness of the staged events or, as an anonymous observer put it, a break from the somber tone and the slow pace of the play.[15] With time allowed for honored guests to arrive and be seated according to protocol, the whole event could conceivably last the whole day or night. Pigafetta noted that *Edippo* lasted over twelve hours: spectators began arriving at four in the afternoon, the play started at one-thirty and was over at little after five o'clock in the morning.[16] Another eyewitness, Giacomo Dolfin, reported that spectators had to wait from seven o'clock until half past one in the morning for the performance to begin. However, he adds, the play, which began with the sound of trumpets, the roll of drums, and the rumbling of artillery rounds, was so gratifying that it was worth the wait. The spectators, he writes, considered well spent the six hours that elapsed from the moment they entered the theater to the fall of the curtain.[17]

The time required for so much pageantry surely contributed to the development of formal literary standards that eventually established the "appropriate" length of dramatic plays. Playwrights and theorists such as Giraldi and Angelo Ingegneri, recognizing the cultural function of theater, recommended that stage representations last between three and a half and four hours.[18] Although the duration of a performance included intermezzi, featuring nymphs, muses, satyrs, music, dances, and similar forms of entertainment, writers still had to produce texts considerably longer then the classical models in order to meet the new time demands. Whether adapting ancient plots or dramatizing myths or novellas, playwrights tended to stretch the length of their texts by elaborating selected scenes, spinning subplots, adding characters with speaking parts, and other dramatic features, such as appending a long, argumentative epilogue. The task was facilitated by the prevailing predilection for verbal rhetoric inherited from the humanist emphasis on *bene dicere*. This partiality for language favored the sublimation of emotions and events through elaborate description rather than action. Preference for telling over showing, which would have been least effective with a popular audience such as that of Renaissance England, found a most receptive public in the well-educated guests that normally attended the performance or, in some cases, the reading. Dramatists were encouraged to rely on verbal representation by several factors, including 1) the traditional definition of tragedy as a poem of sublime style and language, 2) the example of Seneca's "wordy" plays, and, not least, 3) the authority of Aristotle's recommendation that speech be given priority over performance.[19]

The strong emphasis on verbal language accounts, in part, for the eagerness of several authors to revisit and improve upon classical theater, placing themselves in agonistic rapport with the ancients and with each other.[20] They freely translated ancient tragedy, offering expanded Italian versions that often betrayed the wish to rival the original. Luigi Alamanni's *Antigone* (1533), for example, though a faithful translation of Sophocles' play, is about 300 lines longer than the original and features innovations that call attention to the translator's culture and to his intent to exhibit his own art. This is especially evident in his treatment of the chorus, which often sounds more modern than ancient. In the Greek version, soon after Teiresias has prophesied ruin upon the Thebes, the chorus sings the praise of Dionysus and begs him to "come with healing step from Parnassus' slope" to deliver them from the threat of the "grim disease" (1118–51). In the Italian translation, this piety gives way to a secular protestation against the capriciousness of powerful and "fallacious" Fortune, which the chorus characterizes in typically Renaissance terms:

> fragil, senza fede,
> Instabil, varia, e leve,
> Lubrica et inconstante.
>
> (p. 197)

[fragile, untrustworthy, / Unstable, shifting, and volatile, / Slippery and inconstant.]

In addition, the chorus sings the protestation in a lyrical Petrarchan Canzone, reflecting both the taste of the times and the author's intent to exhibit his poetic talent.[21] Ludovico Dolce, too, boasts great heights of rhetorical elegance in the prologue to his *Giocasta*. Although conceding that his style may not reach the high level of perfection worthy of tragic poems, he is confident that no other playwright has reached it yet. Also, in the prologue to his *Marianna*, he declares the play not so arrogant as to disdain comparison with well-known contemporary tragedies such as *Sofonisba, Orbecche*, and others. And Pietro Aretino, in the prologue to *Orazia*, promises the spectators a story told "in note or di mèle ora d'assenzio" [in notes here of honey there of absinthe], and asks to be judged a better dramatist than his learned counterparts (74–83). Others, such as Giraldi, pledged to entertain audiences with plots and "things" never heard or seen before in drama.[22]

The dramatists' pursuit of acclaim coupled with the sponsors' pragmatic demands for long-lasting performances led playwrights to produce works with intricate plots and elaborate narratives. Ludovico Martelli's *Tullia* (1533) is a good example of this tendency, as it features long-winded scenes and complicated subplots. Drawing from the myth of Merope, the Oresteia, Roman history and legends, Martelli weaves an intricate plot of murder and revenge reminiscent of Senecan tragedies. Events leading to the stage action tell of how young Tullia, driven by unbridled political ambition, had her peace-loving husband and her own sister killed so that she could marry her widower brother-in-law Lucius Tarquinius. The action starts as young Lucius, presumed dead, returns to Rome incognito, seeking to avenge his father's death and ascend to the throne. He first reveals himself to his wife, Tullia, and with her approval kills King Servius, Tullia's father, who had assassinated the previous king, Lucius's father. After the murder of both Servius and his queen, Tullia, in a brutal burst of capricious rage, rolls her chariot over her father's dead body before having it thrown in the gutter. The savage coup sparks a popular revolt against the murderers, but it is quickly checked by a divine voice ex machina telling the Roman people to return home and let there be peace. Though the plot is richly woven with interesting events, the pace of the action is often slow, being stalled by frequent and long narratives. The 212-line monologue in which Lucius reveals his identity to Tullia (pp. 89–96) is among the longest in Renaissance tragedy.[23]

Renaissance preference for lengthy and embellished descriptions can be observed especially in adaptations, where elaborate scenes contrast sharply with the relative brevity and simplicity of the original version. The description of the capture scene in Rucellai's *Oreste* (1520–25),[24] for example, is much longer and more elaborate than its source, Euripides' *Iphigenia in Tauris*. In the Greek original, a messenger recounts in about eighty lines (260–339) how Taurian herdsmen captured Orestes and his boyhood friend Pylades; in the Italian version the same episode is 129 lines long (1.429–558).[25] The expansion details the epic resistance put up by the young protagonists, whose *gesta* are reminiscent of Ariosto's heroes. The messenger reports that they retreated like lions facing their hunters and fought with the ferocity of tigers fearful for the life of their cubs. He also likens them to two stinging hornets fighting against a cloud of bees or an army of ground ants. The narrative abounds in rhetorical devices, especially hyperbole, a figure of speech most peculiar to the then-popular chivalric poetry. Thus, the youths, trying to escape, throw the boat on the water just as easily as if it were a box of bees;[26] on Pylades' shield land a forest of enemy arrows; a thousand lances and swords fall on Oreste; Oreste's breathing becomes so heavy that it turns into black, thick vapor. Unfortunately, this epic scene, while extolling the young men's superhuman strength, is largely inconsequential to the development of the plot, since both men are ultimately overpowered and taken prisoner just as in Euripides. The exposition is a mere poetic tour-de-force, displaying the author's stylistic prowess and rhetorical ability through which he hoped to win renown.

Predilection for verbal rhetoric also led to profuse expression of sentimentality, whereby characters dwelt at length on pledges of love and friendship, passions and inner thoughts. A comparison of the episode of the letter in these same two plays illustrates the point. Briefly, Iphigenia wants the letter delivered to Argos and agrees to reveal its contents to Pylades so that he will be able to deliver the message should the letter be lost at sea. In Euripides, the young priestess gives a brief summary of the letter's content (770–785), bringing about the immediate recognition of the two siblings: Orestes realizes that Iphigenia is his presumed-dead sister. In Rucellai, instead, the recognition happens very slowly, as Pylades reads the whole letter (4.169–285), stopping here and there to allow for expressions of amazement and surprise. The prolonged reading is punctuated by the repetition of apprehensive "alas," by commonplaces of fraternal love, cherished memories, and pledges of loyalty and affection. Thus, a scene that Aristotle admired for its dramatic intensity and considered among the "best" examples of tragic *agnitione*,[27] is reduced to a protracted affair weighed down by sentimental recollections and wringing emotions.

A modern reader or spectator may not appreciate these protestations, for they tend to delay the development of the plot and lessen the purported intensity of the characters' emotions. Partiality for sentimental effusion, however, met with the approval of contemporary audiences who were well accustomed to the poetics of the heart, promoted in part by the prevailing influence of Petrarchism. Undoubtedly, the urge to rival their counterparts and excel in the art of poetry incited playwrights to exhibit both their understanding of human passions and the stylistic virtuosity to express it. Consider, for example, Tasso's keen perception of Alvida's despair as she learns that Torrismondo no longer loves her and has abandoned her:

> . . . E Torrismondo è questi,
> questi, che mi discaccia, anzi m'ancide,
> questi, ch'ebbe di me le prime spoglie,
> or l'ultime n'attende: e già se'n gode;
> e questi è il mio diletto e la mia vita.
> Oggi d'estinto re sprezzata figlia
> son rifiutata. O patria, o terra, o cielo,
> rifiutata vivrò? Vivrò schernita?
> Vivrò con tanto scorno? Ancor indugio?
> Ancor pavento? E che? La morte o'l tardi
> morire? Ed amo ancora? Ancor sospiro?
> Lacrimo ancor? Non è vergogna il pianto?
> Che fan questi sospir? Timida mano,
> timidissimo cor, che pur agogni?
> Mancano l'arme a l'ira, o l'ira a l'alma?
> Se vendetta non vuoi, né vuole Amore,
> basta un punto a la morte. Or mori, ed ama
> morendo; e se la morte estingue amore,
> l'anima estingua ancor, ché vera morte
> non saria, se vivesse amore e l'alma.
> (*Torrismondo* 5.1.101–20)

[. . . And this is Torrismondo! / It is he who sends me away, or rather kills me; / he who had the first spoils of me / now can't wait for the last; and already he rejoices; / and this man is my delight and all my life. / Today, the despised daughter of a deceased king, / I am rejected. O native land, O earth, O Heaven, / shall I live rejected? Shall I live scorned? / Shall I live with such shame? Do I still delay? / Am I still afraid? Of what? Of death, or of dying too late? / Do I still love? Am I still sighing? / Still weeping? Is it not a disgrace to weep? / Why all these sighs? Timid hand, / most hesitant heart, what are you waiting for? / Is anger lacking weapons, or the soul anger? / If you do not wish vengeance, and Love does not wish it, / all death requires is a moment. Die, then, and love / while dying; and if death extinguishes love, / let it extinguish also the soul, for it would not be / real death if love and the soul should live on.] (trans. Passaro).

Alvida's state of mind is skillfully conveyed in its progressive stages, beginning with the apprehension that she has been deceived and forsaken, to the realization that she is all alone in the world, to the confusion as to what to do, and finally to the decision to end her life. The description is complemented by stylistic signifiers that point most incisively to her deep-seated emotions: the anaphoric insistence of "questi," for instance, reveals Alvida's unconscious reluctance to let go of her only reason to live; the series of rhetorical questions point to her state of confusion; and the hammering alliterations of "amore . . . morte . . . O mori . . . ama . . . morendo . . . alma . . . anima" in the last lines underscore her final resolve to commit suicide.

Surely audiences appreciated the playwright's deep understanding of the character's fluctuating emotions and the stylistic versatility articulating it. However, dramatists had to be careful not to be taken with their own linguistic prowess and forget that verbal expression must correspond to the characters' competence to verbalize their thoughts. Disregard for congruence between a character's speech and deed or state of mind often led to a serious flaw of characterization. This was particularly apparent in despondent characters who, like Alvida, expressed their anguish with studied eloquence. It is indeed incongruent for someone so distraught as Alvida to articulate her despair through select figures of speech, such as anadiplosis ("questi / questi"), anastrophe ("d'estinto re sprezzata figlia"), chiastic *reduplicatio* ("rifiutata vivrò? vivrò schernita?" and several others with "ancor"), *equivocatio* ("l'arme a l'ira, o l'ira a l'alma"), *bisticci* ("morte . . . amore . . . Or mori"), and the internal and external rhymes of the last four lines. The inconsistency is especially detrimental to dramatic theater, as it tends to undermine the sincerity of the characters' emotions, and, by extension, the premise of realism upon which the world of the stage is predicated. As a result, theater fails in its purpose to involve the spectators who, questioning the character's credibility vis-à-vis his or her emotions, remain largely indifferent to the purported drama taking place on stage.

Whether the playwrights' unusual emphasis on emotions reflected an understanding of human psychology unknown to the ancients, as Leopardi noted,[28] or a mellowing of the age, as some scholars have suggested,[29] is not as relevant to our discussion as the fact that it reflected Petrarchism, a living literary tradition. It is beyond the scope of the present argument to consider the merits or the shortcomings of Petrarchism other than to note that whereas its influence on poetry might have been meaningful, it could hardly have been effective on an action-based genre such as theater. At its best, its dwelling on the characters' emotions succeeded in stifling dramatic action; at its worst, language took an importance all of its own, ignoring the necessary correspondence between words and deeds. Predilection for verbal communication is most damaging to theater, for it encroaches upon the basic function of the stage to represent dramatic action. In the absence of significant stage action, spectators cease to be viewers and become mere listeners left to their imagination to construct events evoked by the spoken word. In this theater of words, representation takes place mostly in the mind of the spectator, reducing the actual stage to an ostentatious prop.[30]

This may very well be our reaction, but it was hardly the concern of contemporary audiences who seized every opportunity to attend a dramatic performance either at court or in the private residence of local nobles. Spectators found delight and intellectual challenge in the world of words they came to hear and to imagine. For playwrights and spectators alike, the emphasis was not so much on the plot, but on innovations and on the language in which it was cast. For their part, dramatists promised story lines told in beautiful language and in the style of Dante, Petrarch, and Boccaccio, whom Giraldi called eternal and bright lights of the sweet and vulgar tongue.[31] The poetics of verbal communication articulating this promise reflect an esthetic ideal that inspired writers to aim for new rhetorical heights while emulating their own literary tradition. It is reasonable to assume that the spectators took pleasure in their ability to identify literary allusions to the great poets of the past and appreciated ingenious variations on established themes and stylistic patterns. They surely recognized Ugolino's expression "Tu vuo' ch'io rinovelli / disperato dolor" [you want me to renew / despairing pain][32] in Massinissa's refusal to recall old wounds "per non rinovellar vechio dolore" [in order not to renew past pain] (*Sofonisba*, 425). And, how could they not recall Petrarch's "di me medesimo meco mi vergogno" [I am ashamed of my self][33] when they heard Sofonisba's promise to speak frankly "benché meco medesma mi vergogno" [although I am ashamed of myself] (460).[34] Very likely, audiences relished their privileged roles as judges of literary style and poetic talent, while playwrights sought acclaim and asked to be considered worthy of, or superior to, their counterparts both living and dead. Such was the taste of a society schooled in the humanist tradition of *studia litterarum* and of *bene dicere*.

Contemporary Spatial Setting and Courtly Ambiance

Excessive preference for verbal rhetoric was but one of the features, albeit a major one, of Renaissance culture reflected on the stage, for tragedy came "clothed" in other living traditions that also conferred a unique cultural stamp upon theater. We need only to look at the setting of numerous plays that, though set in ancient times, are cast in a modern, courtly atmosphere. It is not unusual for playwrights adapting mythological plots to refer to characters as knights and barons, and to allude to dramatic action as taking place in castles or fortresses, all icons of Medieval and Renaissance culture. In some cases, as in Rucellai's *Oreste*, the scenic space is actually dominated by a structure that looks like a Renaissance fortress. The modernity of this scene is particularly striking when one compares it with its Greek counterpart. In Euripides the action takes place before the imposing structure of Artemis's temple. In the Italian version, the shrine takes on the appearance of a fortress with high walls, immense turrets, a deep moat, iron doors, and a drawbridge suspended by huge chains (1.93–94, 113–18). This attempt to transpose myth into a familiar cultural milieu must have appeared obvious to spectators who surely knew enough Greek history to recall that the ancients, as Machiavelli pointed out, were not known for building strongholds and were even reluctant, at times, to build walls around their cities.[35]

This intent to project myth in a contemporary milieu is equally apparent even when the castle is not shown, but simply referred to as an extension of the dramatic space. Such is the case in Anguillara's *Edippo* where a messenger tells how Polyneices sent one of his captains to take over the castle in which Oedipus was being held captive. He describes the castle as having five heavily defended ramparts each guarded by valiant knights all faithful to the castellan, who refused to surrender the fortress to anyone other than the lawful king of Thebes (4.2, p.103). The castellan, the fortress, the ramparts, Polyneices's intent to force the day ("tentar la Fortuna") with four hundred men in order to take control of the fortress ("insignorirsi del castello") convey to the scene a strong sense of Renaissance reality. The modernization is especially apparent when one views the scene against the simplicity of the Greek version where Oedipus is said to live in a plain "house" where his sons "shut him up / behind the bolts."[36] For contemporary audiences the realistic description of the castle cut across the barrier of time and myth, enlivening the representation with a sense of cultural immediacy relevant to their own living experiences. Undoubtedly, most of them were well acquainted with castles and fortresses and could easily complement with their imagination whatever features the messenger's description might have left out. They could also place in contemporary context the castellan's refusal to surrender the stronghold to Polyneices's forces. Renaissance history abounded with episodes of loyal castellans who risked their lives rather than surrender the fortress in their charge, as well as of those who sold out to the enemy at the first sign of danger or profit. The 1499 heroic stand of Caterina Sforza's castellan Dionigi Naldi was definitely fresh in the minds of most spectators. Like the mythological castellan, Naldi ignored the enemy's threats, declaring that he was not afraid to die by the enemy's sword, but only of being hanged for treason.[37]

The vestige of contemporary realism investing mythological characters and events was not confined to the spatial and historical realities of Renaissance castles and castellans. The presence of barons and knights or the mere allusion to their existence in the world of myth also underscores the acculturalization process. In Anguillara's *Edippo*, for example, *cavalieri* of great virtues are said to be everywhere in the kingdom. The male chorus refer to Creon as a "cavalier d'onor" (3.2, p. 61), and Oedipus remembers that he once fought and killed four honorable knights (3.2, p. 64), one of whom turned out to be his own father, King Laius. Overwhelmed by the discovery and the sense of guilt, Oedipus decides to become an knight-errant in order to expiate his sin. He sounds much like a despondent knight of the chivalric tradition, when he exclaims:

> Vo' per castigo andar del mio peccato
> Di guerra in guerra, e guadagnarmi il vitto
> Con l'arme in man, se ben servir dovessi
> Per privato guerrier.
>
> (3.4, p. 75)

[As a punishment for my sin I want to go / fighting from war to war. I shall earn my living / with my sword in hand, even if I have to fight / as a common knight.]

When he finally realized that he had married his own mother, Jocasta, he felt so shamed and so dishonored that he could never again see himself in the company of "uomini d'onor" (3.5, p. 84). And, the Princess of Andro (a character of Anguillara's invention) commends the "cavalieri de la corte" for foiling Ismene's suicide attempt and for making sure that two priests stayed by the girl's side (5.3, pp.131–32).

These knights or men of honor are more than mere mythological figures with modern appellation. They are often said to exhibit qualities reminiscent of knights from the courtly love tradition. Second Messenger, for example, describes Polyneices as "affabil, liberal, cortese, e intero" (5.2, p. 104). In Dolce's *Medea*, both Medea and King Creon refer to Jason as *Cavaliere*. Medea, in particular, speaks of him and his deeds as if he were a villainous knight of King Arthur's court. He should not have forgotten, she reproaches him, "la mia verginità, di cui facesti / Insieme col mio honor dolce rapina" [my virginity of which you made, / Together with my honor, sweet theft]. And may it please God, she curses him, that you die before staining your name "di perfido, d'ingrato, e di crudele" [with perfidy, ungratefulness, and cruelty] (2, p. 17). In her desperate attempt to convince him to come back to her, she appeals to his sense of "cortesia." His rejection of her, she says with bitterness and sarcasm, is her reward ("guiderdone") for having helped him in obtaining the Golden Fleece and in eluding her brother's vengeful pursuit. For his part, Jason sees himself as a Cavaliere of noble lineage and intends to treat her with the honor and the dignity becoming a knight of his rank. Accordingly, he offers her his protection "per bontà, per amor, e per pietade" [out of kindness, love, and compassion] (2, pp. 18–19), all qualities reminiscent of the knights that populate the chivalric world of Boiardo and Ariosto.

To be sure, *Medea* does not list dramatis personae with the designation of Baroni or Cavalieri, nor do they appear on stage as extras. They are simply alluded to as members of the kingdom's ruling aristocracy. Actually, they are mentioned only once, in act 4, where Nuntio tells Medea that Jason's royal wedding was attended by the most distinguished barons in Corinth (4, p. 32). But even a simple allusion is enough to suggest a world inhabited by kings, barons, knights, and, of course, the fair Lady in distress, Medea. The mythological *illud tempus* of the stage was thus cast with an aura of Medieval courtly life whose values and ideals still fascinated the poets and the courts of Renaissance Italy. The introduction of these living traditions was not intended to modernize, transform, and adapt myth to Renaissance culture, but to make the remote world of the stage come to life. In this way the presentation became more meaningful to contemporary audiences, while preserving its essence and ancient *auctoritas*.

The sense of cultural proximity was perhaps more immediate when barons were actually seen on stage, as in Rucellai's *Oreste*. Here, King Toante goes about the city of Tauris accompanied by his barons. The entourage is actually listed as dramatis personae with a speaking part, albeit a small one: one baron has a two-line response in act 3 and a short comment in act 5.[38] Their presence on stage is a clear innovation from the Greek original, which does not list royal attendants as actual characters. Though the barons' contribution to the development of the plot is minuscule and could have been achieved easily by other characters such as herdsmen, the nonclassical designation of their names stands in obvious contrast with ancient characters with whom they come to coexist, adding an aura of contemporaneity to the mythological background of the action.[39] Also, their role as a royal following addresses a question of princely decorum and courtly realism, since it serves to underscore the majesty of the characters whom they escort. It would have appeared unseemly to a Renaissance audience for a prince to come and go, as does king Toante, all alone without a courtly entourage. Giraldi argues for the need to have numerous actors on the stage, not only because a small cast might prove tedious to the spectators, but also because of princely decorum. This was especially true of his times, says Giraldi, when one saw the courts of great princes crowded with a multitude of nobility.[40]

The question and the cultural relevance of princely decorum is all too apparent on the dramatic stage, especially when dealing with the representation of royalty. It was not unusual for spectators to behold kings and queens entering the stage with unusually large retinues all robed in superbly embroidered costumes. In the 1585 performance of Giustiniano's *Edippo,* Pigafetta tells us that Jocasta and Creon entered the stage with an "appropriate" train of attendants and that Oedipus was accompanied by an escort of twenty-four soldiers all in exotic Turkish uniforms,[41] which, incidentally, was equal in number to Duke Ercole's armed guard.[42] Between actors, chorus, escorts, and other extras, Angelo Ingegneri counted 108 participants. They were so beautifully and expensively dressed, Ingegneri observes, that after the performance many noblemen approached the players to ascertain that the costumes were as sumptuous as they appeared from afar.[43] The majesty and the opulence of this Renaissance performance contrast sharply with the simplicity of the Greek myth. In Sophocles, Oedipus emerges from the central door of the royal palace either alone or with a small escort. Unfortunately, we lack credible accounts of Greek performances to speak with certainty about the size or the attire of the retinues that accompanied royal characters onto the stage. However, considering that at a Dionysian festival a playwright presented four plays in a day (three tragedies and a satyr-play), it is reasonable to assume that the representation did not last long and that there could not have been much time for pageantry. Whatever

Drawing by Giovan Battista Maganza per *l'Edippo tiranno*. New York, Scholz Collection.

Andrea Palladio. *Teatro Olimpico.* Designed by Vincemnzo Scamozzi. Vicenza, Italy. (Foto Alinari/Art Resource, NY)

pageantry there might have been, it could not have been significant because of what Ingegneri called the "rozzezza dei tempi" [coarseness of the times].[44]

This is not to suggest that classical drama represented royalty without an appropriate entourage; there are enough textual indications to conclude that kings and queens appeared on stage with their attendants, handmaidens, soldiers, and bodyguards.[45] However, there are no indications suggesting that Greek or Latin dramatists ever crowded the stage with supernumeraries. To the contrary, they tended to use extras rather sparingly. Even then, details imbedded in the discourse of the characters reveal that the function of these extras was not always limited to decorum, often they had specific, though silent, theatrical roles. In *The Phoenician Women,* for instance, attendants carry onto the stage the bodies of Jocasta and her two sons; in Æschylus's *The Eumenides* local citizens serve as jurors at Orestes's trial; and in Seneca's *Oedipus* soldiers carry out the king's orders to arrest Creon. Of course, neither the small number of these characters nor their dramaturgical usefulness takes away from their function as royal entourage; it simply points to the stage economy of ancient drama and, by contrast, to the large and ostentatious escorts with which Italians dramatists chose to represent royalty.

The sumptuous staging of royal processions, which in classical times was either substantially limited or simply alluded to for the spectators to imagine, is largely a Renaissance novelty. In antiquity, Oedipus's story, for example, could not have been cast in so much elegance not only because of the "coarseness of the times," as Ingegneri suggested, but also because of its inherent realism, as critics of the 1585 representation of Giustiniano's *Edippo* pointed out at the time. Sperone Speroni, objecting to the lavishness of the performance, noted that the old king had little to celebrate and could hardly afford to appear in ostentatious costumes, since he and his people were desperately trying to figure a way out of a devastating pestilence.[46] But Renaissance audiences, accustomed to ceremonial entrances and the magnificent style of contemporary rulers, undoubtedly expected to see Oedipus in princely splendor. Speaking of the spectators' aesthetic expectations, an anonymous witness of the 1568 performance of *Alidoro* noted that

> a' tempi nostri (non so per qual cagione) le cose sono cresciute in tanto lusso, e i gusti sono divenuti tanto delicati, che non si può recitare poema cosí esquisito, che gli spettatori, poi che n'hanno udita ben picciola parte, non cerchino nuovi e variati diletti.[47]

> [I do not know why, but in our times things have grown in so much luxury, and aesthetic taste has become so refined that it is difficult to represent a great play, because the spectators, after familiarizing themselves with the plot, tend to look for and expect to find new and different delights.]

Oedipus's lavish stage presence certainly rivals or excels these expectations, as the king seems to step out, as it were, from his mythological *illud tempus* and come to life as a magnificent lord of the Renaissance. Stately pageants, besides impressing aesthetically minded audiences, underscored the royal dignity of the character. In his defense of *Didone*, Giraldi argued that large casts not only provided for a lively representation, they also mirrored the princely custom of great retinues. It would be indecorous, states Giraldi, for a king to appear in public with a diminutive retinue. Ingegneri shared this view and added that it would be unrealistic for a prince to go about without the appropriate entourage.[48]

The notion of princely decorum and the ostentation upon which it was predicated had the specific, if unspoken, purpose of enhancing one's reputation. Wealthy sponsors were so intent on displaying their munificence, and thus their power, that they paid little attention to the high cost of the production: the more lavish the performance, the more prestige it conferred upon its patrons. Reputation was so intrinsic to Renaissance culture that people would go to great lengths to protect or enhance the integrity of their name. This was especially true for ruling princes whose political longevity often rested on their reputed ability to defend their states. Machiavelli underscored repeatedly the importance of princely reputation, noting that a ruler's failure or success to preserve his state often depended on how weak or how strong he was perceived to be by friends and foes. It is in this contest that Giraldi's King Sulmone, afraid of being perceived as a weak ruler, insists on displaying his power and resolve to the world by executing the alleged traitor Oronte (*Orbecche*, 3.3.1680). And Speroni's King Eolo is deeply troubled by the infamy of his children's incest, and fears posterity's harsh judgment (*Canace*, 1939–58). Concern with one's reputation was so paramount that Italian and foreign rulers so feared the slanderous pen of Pietro Aretino that only the dauntless ignored his threats to smear their good name.

This Renaissance emphasis on honor often informs the thought and deeds of mythological dramatic characters, such as Eteocles and Polyneices. In Euripides' version of the Oedipus myth, Jocasta does not give a reason as to why the two brothers imprisoned their father; she simply says that they shut him up so "that this fate might be forgotten / which needs too much intelligence to explain it" (*The Phoenician Women*, 63–65). In Anguillara's rendition of the myth, the young princes prevent their father from leaving the city because they fear that news of the tragic story (the patricide, the incest, and the eye-gouging) would spread from court to court, tarnishing forever the House of Thebes. The gentleman-messenger, relating the events and the reasons that led to the king's demise, reports that following thoughtful consideration the brothers agreed that great "ignominy" would befall the royal family if they allowed the blinded and broken old king to wander from city to city recounting his shameful deed:

> Si consigliar di non voler lasciare
> Vedere in quella forma il padre al mondo,
> Per fuggir l'ignominia, che potea
> Nascer dal farsi tal veder per tutto.
>
> (*Edippo*, 4.1, p. 98)

[They decided not to allow the world / to see their father in that condition / in order to avoid the ignominy which might / rise from being seen like that (disfigured) everywhere.]

They justified their decision to lock him up, the messenger continues, by invoking the good of the state, piety, and honor. Specifically, they argued that their action would appease Apollo and thus arrest the spread of the plague; that their compassion prevented them from letting Oedipus become a wandering beggar; and that his begging would bring general opprobrium to the court and the dynasty ("troppo n'andria del nostro onore"). Thus, deaf to their father's pleas and indifferent to possible censure by local nobles, they ordered that he be locked in the castle (4.1, p. 99).

Renaissance audiences surely identified with the importance that the mythological brothers placed on reputation. Undoubtedly, many were reminded of actual events from their recent past, such as the bloody episode that brought shame to the court of Ferrara. It was only at the turn of the century that Duke Alphonse went out of his way to protect the honor of the Este family, which was stained by the bloody quarrel between his younger brothers Giulio and Ippolito. The animosity between the two siblings led to a grisly incident when Cardinal Ippolito, ever jealous of Giulio's handsome looks, ordered his men to kill Giulio and carve out his eyes. The victim barely survived the attack, and lost one eye and was severely disfigured. No one better than the duke understood the deleterious impact on the Este reputation and the serious political repercussions that could follow should the truth be known. In a personal note to his sister Isabel, he expressed his apprehension about the shame that the news of the affair could bring upon the family honor. Such was his anxiety that he asked her to destroy the note and proceeded immediately to mount an all-out diplomatic effort to control the damage. The official version practically exonerated the young cardinal, stating that the attack was perpetrated by servants moved either by personal revenge or by the mistaken belief it would please Ippolito.[49] Most governments saw through the distorted account, and the Este, like the two Greek brothers, were widely censured for their cruelty.

Brigands and Pirates

The similarities in the two episodes help to bridge the gap between the illusion of the stage and the real world of the spectators, as it points to a striking parallel between the present of the audience and the distant, fabled past of the characters. Fictional characters come to life also by sharing, to some extent, in the hopes and fears of contemporary audiences. Consider the reasons that prompt Rucellai's Pilade to ask Ifigenia to disclose the content of the letter she wants him to deliver to her brother Oreste, prior to the recognition scene. In the Greek play, Iphigenia agrees to reveal the message, admitting the possibility that the letter could be lost at sea as a result of a storm. In the Italian version, however, it is the ever-present fear of unpredictable Fortune and the dread of piracy and brigandage that prompt the disclosure. Pilade, reflecting a prevailing Renaissance view that assigned Fortune a significant role in the course of human events, wants to know the contents of the letter so that he may be able to deliver the message should adverse Fortune cause the letter to be lost in a ship to wreck. When Ifigenia points out that she would not expect him to fulfill his pledge under circumstances beyond human control, Pilade reminds her of the constant and widespread danger of piracy and brigandage:

> E come le marine, i liti, e i porti,
> Isole, fiumi, laghi, ponti e passi,
> Tutti son corseggiati da pirati,
> O'n preda di ladroni, e rubatori.
>
> (4. p.113)

[(you know, Iphigenia) how the shores, the beaches and the ports, / islands, rivers, lakes, bridges, and passes / are all plundered by pirates, / and preyed upon by brigands and thieves.]

Lest anyone believe that Pilade's fears are an isolated instance, we need to recall that in *Torrismondo* Alvida and Frontone were captured by Norwegian pirates and later escaped from Goth corsairs who were also "accustomed / to preying on the vast fields of the waves" (4.5.57). And in *Sofonisba*, the chorus laments the suffering and devastation visiting the city of Cirta thus: "so much plunder, / So much violence, so many wrongs / So many wounds and deaths" (622–24). The violence of this fictional account could easily apply, comments Beatrice Corrigan, "to many scenes then still fresh in Italian minds: notably to the siege of Prato in 1512, which had ended in a massacre shocking even in that age of atrocities."[50]

The immediacy of these foreboding events tends to revive the characters of ancient drama, making them come alive in a contemporary world where it was indeed dangerous to travel by land or by sea. The dreadful specter of pirates ravaging the coasts and of murderous thieves operating around bridge crossings and through the countryside surely struck a chord in the hearts and minds of the spectators. Sixteenth-century audiences were all too familiar with horrifying stories of pirates and brigands. Many were surely familiar with that scene in act 3 of Machiavelli's *Mandragola*, where a lady, fearing that the Turks may come back to plunder again the coasts of Italy, expresses women's fear of being impaled by Turkish pirates. Such fears were founded on the harsh reality of the times, for, as Machiavelli wrote in a 1499 letter, people everywhere talked about the frightful plundering and preying by the Turks.[51] Aretino, too, reflected a general fear of pirates when in 1537 wrote that the French and the Turks "fanno tumulto in terra e in mare" [work havoc on land and at sea].[52] Pirates or corsairs, such as Giovanni Grimaldi, Battista Aicardo, Francesco Draperio, Paolo Fregoso, the abbot of Farfa, the French pirates out of Marseille and Toulouse, the Moors, the Turks, the Knights of Saint John of Jerusalem, terrorized seafarers and coastal villages throughout the Mediterranean. The seas belonged to them and no one was immune to their lawlessness. Merchant ships often sailed in large convoys with armed escorts in order to defend against the threat of pirates who often reached even the powerful.[53] They did not hesitate, for instance, to seize, torture, and hold for ransom the papal emissary, the Franciscan Alvarode Quiñones, who was on his way to see the Emperor Charles V. Judith Hook tells how the Moorish corsairs who captured him held him until payment was made.[54]

This atmosphere of violence and unsafe seafaring conveyed a contemporary quality to the fear of pirates expressed by the stage characters: Pilade's fear evoked the spectators' own fears. His dreadful prospect of being "dispogliato" (robbed; 4, p. 114) while traveling on land is equally real to audiences who knew that their roads and bridges were infested by ruthless highwaymen.[55] Travelers everywhere were easy prey of notorious armed bands, and women were particularly vulnerable to mistreatment and rape. The story of a noblewoman who was seized and raped while traveling through the Rimini territory was undoubtedly a vivid reminder of the danger of land travel. Detailed accounts tell how Sigismondo Malatesta brutally raped the woman and, because she resisted him, allowed forty of his men to rape her.[56] Ariosto painted a frightening picture of murdering outlaws roaming the countryside of Garfagnana. Even he, the governor of the territory, would not stray from the safety of his residence, declaring wise those who did not wander away from the castle.[57] One of the most widely feared outlaws was the priest Don Niccolò de' Pelegati of Figarolo who, according to Burckhardt, "took part in many assassinations, violated women, carried others away by force, plundered far and wide, and infested the territory of Ferrara with a band of followers in uniform, extorting food and shelter by every sort of violence."[58]

The evocation of existing, genuine anxieties such as these conferred upon the genre a contemporary quality that freed it from the bounds of mere imitation and made it come to life in a new sociohistorical context. The new "clothes" in which playwrights dressed tragedy were easily recognized by Renaissance audiences, who saw aspects of their own culture represented on stage. They were hardly troubled by the incongruity that their own living realities should inform characters and situations of long ago. They simply attributed the anachronism to the illusion of theater and went on to appreciate all that was emotionally and intellectually relevant to them. Tragedy was thus shedding its classical image and was slowly assuming a modern identity. It came to be known appropriately as the Italian Renaissance tragedy, for it was the living traditions of that period that brought to life the ancient genre and its characters. On the stage, audiences saw the reflection of their society in its customs, its taste, and its anxieties. Future generations of playwrights both from Italy and abroad saw its limits and its merits and learned what to avoid and what to improve upon. Unquestionably, Renaissance tragedy is a rich field of study for scholars intent upon understanding the spirit and the cultural priorities of a society that gave a great impetus to modern civilization.

3
Their Gods, Our God: Christian Religion in the Tragic World of Myth

IN THE WORLD OF TRAGEDY, UNLIKE THAT OF COMEDY, CHARACTERS inevitably come to experience adverse situations that are beyond human control and understanding. Whether oppressed by powerful tyrants or fated by divine plan, they find themselves suffering helplessly or struggling hopelessly against inexorable forces. Their course of action is limited: they can bear alone the harshness of their fate, like Oedipus, or turn scornful of the oppressor and, like Dante's Capaneus, rise defiantly above their suffering. Where the oppressor is another human being, typically rulers whose might places them beyond the reaches of the law, victims can appeal to the deity for justice. Naturally, divine response and the way in which it manifests itself vary according to the conception that humans have of their godhead, that is, according to the religion they profess. In the world of ancient tragedy, where gods were seen as superior beings constantly mingling with mortals and taking sides in their quarrels, divine intervention manifested itself through natural disasters, disguised gods, oracles, and other similarly ineluctable forces. In dramas cast in the Christian world, such as the sacred plays of the Middle Ages, the deity was equally present, of course in its Christian essence. Reflecting popular beliefs in divine omnipresence, angels and demons were common fixtures on the early Italian stage. Pitchfork-bearing and fire-breathing devils were as real to Christian spectators as angry Furies were to ancient audiences. As the Italian stage evolved into the more secular drama of the Renaissance, the divine assumed a less conspicuous role, a reflection of the growing belief in a deity somewhat removed from the affairs of the world. Accordingly, the divine no longer manifested itself through the actions of celestial creatures, but mostly through the beliefs and invocations of the characters, who conceived it as the unfailing judgment awaiting humans in the hereafter. This physical absence notwithstanding, there were stage representations in which the resolution of the plot was ultimately resolved by direct divine intervention.

The notion of the deity mostly removed from earthly activities is rooted in the Renaissance celebration of human nature as capable of determining its own destiny. Humanist ideals inspired individuals to consider themselves responsible for their own actions and free to realize their physical and intellectual potential. They believed in their ability and prerogative to explore their world and improve upon it.[1] They also saw themselves as capable of managing the course of human events, at least on a fifty-fifty basis as Machiavelli argued. At the same time, they were fully aware that on Judgment Day, as Savonarola and other vociferous preachers never tired of reminding their audiences, they would have to answer for their deeds. But if, on the one hand, elevating God above worldly concerns and thus establishing the centrality of humankind on earth may be seen as the most acclaimed achievement of Renaissance thought, on the other hand, it would ultimately prove to be an instrument of its undoing. It was an ideal that was bound to crumble against the harsh reality of human limitations, as faith in one's intellectual and physical abilities was hardly adequate to deal with devastating events such as plagues, wars, rebellions, and similar calamities. Renaissance confidence in human *agere et intelligere,* which promoted the exalted view of the individual as an earthly god, was shattered by events that proved too overwhelming for any human being to bring under control. The devastation of the 1527 sack of Rome, for instance, pointedly underscored human inadequacy and helplessness. A disillusioned Francesco Vettori, having lived through the atrocities and the sacrilege perpetrated by the imperial forces on the city and its sanctuaries, wrote that henceforth he would try to live out the rest of his life without ever again engaging in the useless task of pondering on the nature of things or speculating on what ought to be.[2] Such was the effect of the sack that, in the opinion of many, it shattered forever the Renaissance belief in the individual's ability to determine and control the course of worldly affairs.[3]

Though awareness of the crisis surfaced in many writings of the period, the dramatic stage served as a most effective forum for stressing its actuality and bringing it to the collective consciousness of contemporary audiences. In a seemingly contradictory representation of the divine, theater dramatized the notion of a deity that, on the one hand, left humans free to determine their affairs and, on the other hand, intervened decisively whenever efforts proved inadequate. The idea of a deity somewhat removed from the world made it easy for Renaissance playwrights to follow the Aristotelian precept that the plot should evolve according to its own internal dynamics and arrive at a resolution with no interference from the supernatural. Not surprisingly, in the world of cinquecento tragedy, most victims are left to endure their misfortunes alone. However, the divine was never so removed from Renaissance culture and, inherently, from the playwrights' consciousness, as to exclude its active presence in the world of tragedy. When divine intervention happened, it happened swiftly and decisively, especially when the dramatic situation reached a crisis beyond the characters' human control. Admittedly, divine interference, normally signified through the deus ex machina expedient, was not a common occurrence on the dramatic stage of the Renaissance. Martelli's *Tullia* and Aretino's *Orazia* are the two most celebrated instances of ex machina resolutions. We shall discuss in detail the ideological and dramaturgical ramifications of this expedient in both plays, dwelling on how it reflects the bankruptcy of some cherished ideals of Renaissance Italy. Perforce, the discussion must proceed from a clear understanding of the role of religion in the world of cinquecento tragedy and how playwrights reconciled ancient religions with Christian beliefs.

The rare presence of supernatural beings in cinquecento tragedy is especially noticeable if we recall the frequency with which angels and demons appeared in sacred plays. One of the reasons behind this change was the secular nature of the new theater, which dealt more consistently with contemporary cultural issues. The retreat or removal of the divine from the represented world of the stage may be seen, at least in part, as the reflection of the growing cultural emphasis on human ability to shape the course of earthly events. The fact that humanist and neoplatonic ideals raised the individual to some sort of *deus in terris* undoubtedly contributed to the belief that the divine had a limited role in controlling or resolving earthly issues. Another reason may be found in the assimilation of ancient dramaturgical precepts that cautioned against undue reliance on divine intervention. In his *Poetica,* Trissino states that a good dramatic resolution must issue from the action itself and should not be imposed by the gods through the ex machina expedient.[4] Most recently, scholars have proposed a third reason, namely, a lack of religion on the part of the characters and, inherently, of the playwrights who create them. Marvin Herrick, whose influential work on Italian Renaissance drama has served for years as a point of reference for modern English-speaking readers, noted that in "breaking away from the popular *rappresentazioni sacre* the neoclassical dramatists of Italy also broke away from the Christian religion, at least in tragedy." Before denouncing "this lack of religious feeling [and] moral conviction," he points out that the characters "almost never invoke the Christian deity, the only one that their authors could have believed in."[5] This view must be taken to task, for it is too broad and can hardly stand against the overwhelming textual evidence that points to a strong presence of religion in the world of tragedy. In addition, it fails to recognize that in many instances the invocations or religious beliefs of a mythological character are pagan in name only. And, not least important, it ignores dramas cast in the Christian setting where the divine is very much in the thoughts and in the invocations of most characters.

Religion in Christian and Mythological Settings

With few exceptions, Italian Renaissance drama is cast in the world of ancient myth, where one cannot reasonably expect mythological characters to invoke the Christian deity. Where tragedies are set in a Christian milieu, we find overwhelming evidence that characters express Christian beliefs and plead constantly for divine comfort and justice. It suffices to look at Dolce's *Marianna,* one of the few dramas that may be said to take place in a Christian setting. The characters' numerous appeals to the divinity not only give proof of intense religious fervor, but also leave no doubt as to the essence of the deity being invoked. Marianna, for example, invokes God at least ten times, calling Him "giusto Dio . . . Re del Cielo . . . Dio clemente e giusto," and other equally pious appellatives. Herod, the cruel tyrant who orders the execution of his wife and children, invokes God no fewer than eight times. And the chorus, whose views often reflect those of the playwright, mentions or invokes God at least fourteen times. Most of the other characters, including Plutone and Gelosia from the prologue, name God several times, often pleading for His forgiveness and justice. They also refer to Hell at least five times and to Paradise once. In the whole play, there are no fewer than seventy holy references, many of them ardent invocations.[6] Consider Herod's plea for divine mercy, as he implores God to prevent Marianna's death:

> Pietoso Dio che sei nimico espresso
> De l'opere crudel, fa', tua mercede,
> Che questa crudeltà non sia adempita.
>
> (5.2951–53)

[Compassionate God, you who are the declared enemy / of all cruel deeds, intercede, merciful one, / so that this cruelty may not be carried out.]

Lest there be doubt as to whether the deity invoked is indeed Christian, we need only to recall the chorus's praise of God for having delivered the children of Israel from Egypt (1.749), or Prologue's description of Jerusalem, where the action takes place:

> E' la città dove l' figliuol di Dio,
> Alor ch'egli vestì l'umana spoglia,
> Sparse ne' cuor de' suoi più cari eletti
> Il seme de la santa alma dottrina
> Ch'e' credenti la via del ciel aperse.
>
> (95–99)

[It is the city where the Son of God, / when He took on His human nature, / infused in the hearts of his followers / the seed of the holy doctrine / which opened the way to heaven for the faithful.]

Strong religious sentiment such as this may also be found in tragedies where the setting is not expressly Christian. In *Rosmunda*, for instance, the young heroine argues that she owes obedience not to king Alboino but to the Lord that rules the universe (410). Falisco believes that the ungrateful are most displeasing to God (576); Serva announces that God has put an end to Rosmunda's suffering (1164); Nutrice wants the maidens to pray for divine help (1122); and the chorus pleads for divine compassion (307–39). Throughout the text, there are more than twenty pious references, and all the characters, except for Alboino and the messenger, mention God's name at least once. Although the essence of the deity they invoke is not specifically identified as Christian, there is no question that it is the same Godhead that the playwright and the spectators believed in. Just like contemporary audiences, the chorus implores God and, for some critics anachronistically, His compassionate Mother (549–50).[7] Nutrice prays for divine help to do righteous deeds and instructs Rosmunda's maidens to pray for God's help in their pious undertaking (1123). Rosmunda, happy with the final outcome of the action, reiterates her belief that God often helps humans with their good deeds (164), and thanks Him thus:

> Tu se' pure Dio in ciel come ogniun crede,
> Et hai la cura de le cose umane
> E porgi aiuto a l'opere piatose!
>
> (1223–25)

[You are indeed in heaven as everyone believes, / and you care about human things / and lend us Your help with our pious deeds.]

3: Their Gods, Our God

The young maiden of the chorus, fearing the loss of her chastity and her honor at the hands of the enemy, implores God's help and, in a tone that critics have described as Catholic,[8] declares herself ready to die rather than submit to such an outrage:

> Io non recuso di morir, Signore,
> Pur ch'io salvi l'onore
> Sacrato insin dalle mie prime fasce,
> Al sancto matrimonio per cui nasce.
>
> (336–39)

[I do not refuse to die, O Lord, / in order to save my honor / consecrated since my first swaddling bands / to the holy matrimony for which it is destined.]

This open and frequent expression of religious piety not only informed cinquecento tragedy, it was also an effective dramaturgical expedient in that it helped to draw the spectators into the dramatic action. It invited them to share in the tragic experience of the victims, who sought strength and redress in religious beliefs similar to their own. Indeed, as audiences shared the characters' convictions and emotions, they were more likely to forget that the representation was just a fiction and allowed themselves to become more involved in the development of the action. This is not to suggest that communality of religious beliefs was a sine qua non of theatrical experience, but only that it contributed to the sense of realism with which playwrights sought to bring the world of the stage ever closer to the world of the audience. However, although the realistic representation provided by communality of religion was easily achieved in dramas cast in a Christian culture, it presented serious obstacles when dealing with plots based on mythological sources, which, as we know, constitute a large part of Renaissance dramatic production. The contrast between the beliefs prevailing in ancient plays and those of the intended audience could undermine the favorable disposition of the audience toward the representation. Perhaps unwittingly, Christian spectators would tend to withhold their sympathy from characters who placed their faith in promiscuous and petty gods. Even the most sophisticated and tolerant spectators would understandably persist in regarding the action as distinctively fictional and look upon it as an imitation of a distant world bearing little resemblance to their own.

The dilemma was especially serious for Renaissance authors who insisted on verisimilitude as a means of involving the audience while at the same time looking to ancient theater for inspiration and *auctoritas*. Following the poetics of "dressing" classical tragedy in contemporary attire, most playwrights opted to endow pagan gods with Christian attributes. In this way, they preserved the mythological atmosphere while proposing a notion of the divine closer to their own. They were most careful not to limit the presence of the divine, which was a major force in the universe of mythological characters. In *Adriana*, for example, the divine is so prevalent that scores of gods are mentioned dozens of times. Designations such as Jupiter, God, gods, Mars, Phoebus, Prometheus, Heavens, Saturn, and similar appellatives appear in almost every page of the text. This overwhelming presence of religion is perhaps better appreciated in adaptations that allow for a comparison with the ancient versions. In Rucellai's *Oreste*, epithets, such as "Giove, Dio, dii, dèi, dea, Cielo," and other similarly holy attributes, occur at least four times as often as in the Greek original. And in Anguillara's *Edippo* references to the deity are so common that its classical sources cannot sustain the comparison.

Admittedly, pious references per se, though denoting a strong presence of the divine, do not always reveal the extent of the individual's faith or the essence of the deity invoked. That is, the simple mention of God does not imply religious belief, it can merely reflect a cultural formality. Only through a close look at the language in which characters articulate their appeals may we determine the true extent of their religious feeling. Mythological characters populating Renaissance tragedies naturally appeal to Apollo, Artemis, Zeus, and to legions of other immortal beings that ruled their world. However, these appeals often reveal a religious sentiment that is more intense and more pious than the one expressed by their Greek and Roman counterparts. In Sophocles' *Oedipus the King*, for example, Oedipus does not implore divine help, but questions his fate and laments the gods' cruelty and lack of compassion. He blames Apollo for bringing "my sorrows to completion" (1331), sees himself as "godless" (1360), and feels "hated by the gods" (1517) because he is "the most cursed, whom God too hates / above all men on earth" (1345). Seneca's Oedipus also blames the "cruel gods" for the plague of Thebes, and believes that its many victims "glut the greedy anger of the gods" (1.91, 218), "Who'er ye be" (2.275).[9] This view of an unpropitious and even hostile deity contrasts sharply with the devout tone with which the Italian Oedipus mentions the name of God almost every time he speaks. Anguillara's Edippo is happy and thankful that "by the grace of God" his sons have been model children. He exhorts them to harbor in their hearts "the fear of God" and to follow the example of their "santa" mother in doing virtuous deeds that are "pleasing to God" (1.2, pp. 16–18). And finally, with dramatic irony, he prays that the wrath of God may befall those who satisfy their sinful lasciviousness upon their own flesh and blood:

> Mandi Dio l'ira sua, la sua vendetta
> Contra ciascun, che con le proprie carni
> Cerca sfogar la sua lascivia ingiusta.
>
> (1.2. p. 19)

[May God send His ire, His vengeance / against those who, with their own (relatives), / try to satisfy the incestuous lust of the flesh.]

Evidence of strong religious feeling is also found in Rucellai's *Oreste*, where the young protagonists appeal to a deity considerably more benevolent than the ancient prototype. In Euripides, Orestes and Pylades prepare to enter the temple determined not to fail Apollo's oracle, for only "a coward turns away" (115). Failure would further provoke the wrath of the frightful Furies who would undoubtedly continue to torment young Orestes. In the Italian version, instead, Pilade exhorts Oreste to do the will of God, not out of fear of incurring His wrath, but out of faith in His compassion and unfailing help:

> Obbediam pure al gran voler di Dio,
> Ché chi lui segue, al fin conduce ogn'opra,
> A Dio, che scorge il nostro amor di sopra,
> Nostro pronto obbedir sí forte aggrada,
> Ch'ad ogni passo n'aprirà 'l cammino.
> ....
> De i buoni e giusti ha Dio mai sempre cura,
> E gli uni e gli altri con pietà riguarda.
>
> (1.100–107)

[Let us, indeed, do the great will of God, / for those who follow Him always reach their goals, / to God, who sees our love from above, / our obedience is so pleasing / that He will guide us through our path. / ... / God always has care of the good and the righteous, / and looks upon them all with piety.]

The question may arise as to the essence of the deity these characters invoke, for the "Dio" or the "Giove" mentioned or worshipped may refer equally to the Christian God as well as to a pagan deity. In standing literary tradition, it was not unusual for Christian authors to invoke the powers of the gods or refer to the Christian godhead as Jove without ever implying belief in the ancient deities. Renaissance Petrarchist poetry in particular is awash with references to mythological divinities, such as Apollo, Diana, Juno, Mars, Minerva, Venus, and other gods. The practice was in fact so common that it led some scholars to view it as yet another pagan element of the age. This view did not win notable critical endorsement mainly because it failed to recognize that poets invoked the gods not in their essence, but only in their form. If mythological divinities reappeared in art and in poetry, observes Eugenio Garin, they reappeared in the authentic beauty of ancient myths.[10] Indeed, devout Christian poets, such as Petrarch, Poliziano, Bembo, and many others who in their poetry often invoked mythological deities and referred to the Christian God as Jove, could hardly be attributed pagan sentiments. After all, before them, Dante, in the *Divine Comedy*, the most Christian of poems, did not hesitate to invoke the gods of Homer and Virgil or refer to Christ as "Highest Jove."[11] This is not to say that all the mythological deities mentioned in the literature of the Italian Renaissance and, especially in the ancient world of tragic theater, are actually Christian, but that one must examine the particular reference or invocation to determine the essence of the deity invoked.

Naturally, mythological characters invoke the deities of their world; however, the language they use often points to a religion that is more Christian than pagan. Edippo's God is clearly more Christian than the cruel and vindictive deity that "hated" the Oedipus of Sophocles and Seneca. The pious tone of his invocations undoubtedly reminded contemporary audiences of their own prayers to their own Godhead. They surely recognized the designation of Christ in Altile's reference to Heaven as the place "whence descended the true man" (*Altile*, 2557).[12] Also, like Oreste and Pilade, they, too, would have done the will of God out of love of Him who sees "our love from above" (1.103). Contemporary audiences certainly shared the counselor's conviction that upon death humans owe their flesh to the earth, and their souls to God (*Adriana*, 4.3.3–4). Lest these pious allusions be taken as isolated instances reflecting the beliefs of individual characters, we should consider the religious beliefs spoken by various choruses, keeping in mind that the chorus tends to reflect the concerns and the ethos of the stage audience, and, at times, the authors' point of view. The chorus of women in Dolce's *Giocasta*, for instance, address Bacchus as the "Santo" Rector of Thebes, the "Padre" to whom they consecrate ("consacriamo") their hearts, since they cannot offer sacrifices or give gold and silver (2. p. 50). In an admonition that could easily pass for a Christian sermon, they caution against the assumption that earthly events can take place outside the will of God. It is foolish to believe, they warn, that

3: Their Gods, Our God

> 'l gran Padre eterno
> Che là su tempra e move
> Ad uno ad uno i bei lucenti giri,
> Non abbia di quaggiù tutto 'l governo
> A tal, che non si trove
> Poter che sanza lui si stenda, o giri.
>
> (3. p. 75)

[The great eternal Father / who from above tempers and moves / one by one the beautiful, shining stars, / does not have on earth all control / such that there is no / power that rules or moves without His wish.]

Though omnipotence is inherent to almost any divinity, one cannot overlook the devout language which is reminiscent of Christian phraseology commonly found both in liturgy and in literature. The chorus's "bei lucenti giri," for instance, echoes the "santi giri" with which Dante refers to the motion of the universe.[13] The definition of the deity as the mover of the universe, common in neoclassical drama, is also reminiscent of Dante, who ends the *Comedia* by referring to God as "l'amor che move il sole e l'altre stelle" [the Love that moves the sun and the other stars].[14]

Equally telling is the religious tone in Anguillara's *Edippo* where both male and female choruses articulate through their prayers a notion of the divine that is fundamentally Christian. In terms that could have been employed easily by contemporary audiences, they invoke the "beati spirti" in Heaven, appeal to the "padre del Ciel" to make his "santa volontà" manifest and call for a prayer so that "onnipotente Dio" may reveal His will to them (2.3. pp. 24–25). Echoing Edippo's allusion to his own misdeed as sin and to himself as a sinner,[15] the choruses caution against considering earthly possessions the ultimate good ("sommo bene"), for it can all be lost in an instant. They believe that "Sol chi si fonda in Dio, / Può dir d'avere un fin stabile, e fermo" [only those who rely on God / may count on a definite outcome] (3.5. p. 87). The depth of their religious sentiment is especially apparent in their prayers for divine intervention to prevent the ominous fight that is about to take place between the rival brothers Eteocles and Polyneices. On the eve of the battle, the people of Thebes are urged to worship God at the temple and to fast until sundown (4.3. p.108), while men and women from various choruses plead with the King of Heaven on their knees and kiss the ground as a sign of humility and helplessness:

> Coro di uomini: Tu, Re del Ciel, provvedi,
> Poi che bastar non può consiglio umano,

	A riparar al mal troppo vicino.
Coro di donne:	Tu, Signor, che ne vedi
	Nel cor, non far, che ti preghiamo in vano:
	Piovi il favor su noi santo, e divino.
Coro di uomini	Col cor, col volto, col ginocchio chino
e di donne:	Ti supplichiam . . .
	In segno d'umiltà, baciam la terra.

(4.3. p. 111)

[*Chorus of men*: Thou, King of Heaven, intercede, / since human ability is inadequate, / to prevent the approaching danger. *Chours of women*: Thou, Lord, that know / our hearts, do not let our prayers be in vain: / let your divine and holy help rain upon us. *Chorus of men and women*: With our hearts, our appearance, and on our knees / we beg you . . . / In sign of humility we kiss the ground.]

Such expressions of religious ardor, especially by fasting, genuflecting, and kissing the ground, are more peculiar to Christian worship and are rarely found in classical drama. Similar piety is definitely not to be found in the Euripidean prototype *The Phoenician Women*, where the women of the chorus are mostly concerned with the here and now of their existence. They are not particularly concerned with Oedipus's "sin" or tragic experience; instead, they are in awe of his heroic deeds and thus beg Pallas to make them proud mothers of sons as noble as Oedipus (1061–62). Recounting the founding of Thebes, they invoke Epaphus, one of Jupiter's natural offspring, to protect them from the destruction that the brothers' rivalry was sure to bring upon the city. They do not appeal to the god's compassion, but to his ability to do all that he wishes: "Epaphus, send us the goddesses of the torch, / defend this land, for the gods all things are easy" (684–86). The detached tone of this invocation begs comparison with the devout appeal in the Italian version, where the chorus implores the intervention of Holy concord, who, nourished in the bosom of the great God of Gods, "per riposo di noi discendesti in terra" [descended on earth for our sake] (*Giocasta* 4, p. 89). Worthy of note in this invocation is the allusion to the coming of Christ suggested by "scendesti in terra," an expression typically found in Christian prayers. This idea of God as the father of benevolent, celestial forces is also found in *Oreste* where the chorus voices the belief that *Pietas* and *Fortitudo* were conceived in God's bosom (2. 55). Always speaking for the collectivity, the chorus recalls the Biblical reminder that after death humans will return to dirt, dust, and smoke (2.484–85).[16]

While convictions such as these suggest that the deity informing the world of cinquecento tragedy was basically Christian, they should not be seen as evidence that Renaissance dramatists attempted to convert the mythological world to Christianity. They simply sought to "clothe" the old with the new, without ever intending for the modern to blot out the ancient from which they drew both inspiration and prestige. They aimed for a theatrical representation in which the new existed alongside the old, a representation that would speak to the contemporaries with the authority of the ancients. Thus, in *Edippo*, where references to Dio and Jove appear side by side, it is not surprising to find Christian and pagan terms in the same phrase, such as the chorus's reference to "i santi servi di Giove" [the holy servants of Jupiter] (4, p.108). And, while Rucellai's Oreste professes beliefs that could easily be considered Christian both in tone and substance, his sister Ifigenia identifies herself as the daughter of a direct descendant of Jupiter "Re de gli uomini e padre de li Dèi" [king of humans and father of gods] (*Oreste*,1. 261–62). Faithful to her pagan convictions, she also swears by "quella Dea ch'adoro' [that Goddess I so much adore] (2.169). This coexistence is perhaps most obvious in *Orbecche*, where Nemesi, herself a mythological goddess, speaks of the divine in terms befitting the Christian God. Though in her lengthy peroration she refers to the deity as Giove or Dio indiscriminately (1.1.97–197), her descriptions of the divine often evoke the Catholic notion of God. Attributes such as "Creatore eterno . . . alta providenzia . . . divina giustizia . . . bontà del Fattor . . . providenzia eterna," are all patristic designations of the divine.[17] Also, her description of the Godhead as the source of all good, who in His wisdom allows humans to suffer so that they may enjoy eternal happiness (1.1.105–26) is a fundamental tenet of the Christian faith. These beliefs notwithstanding, Nemesi is still the goddess of revenge, whom Prologue describes as powerful, terrifying, and burning with rage (89–91). True to her role, she orders the Tartarean Furies to plot a revenge against Sulmone, insisting that it be far more ferocious than those taken on Tantalus, Thyestes, and Athamas (1.1.193–96).

The coexistence of Christian and pagan elements make it tempting to see Nemesi, as well as other characters who express this coexistence, as an anachronism: a Christian voice in pagan clothing. More appropriately, she may be characterized as a hybrid who expresses her views in terms essentially Christian, while remaining a pagan goddess. She represents an instrument of divine justice that speaks to both the stage and theater audiences in ways that are congruent with their respective beliefs. For the fictional community of the stage, she is Jupiter's terrifying agent of revenge; for the spectators, instead, she is a reminder of God's just wrath. In this sense, the pagan and the Christian elements, existing side by side, are not contradictory but complementary. They combine to articulate the theatrical metaphor wherein representation points to reality and the new is heard through the authoritative voice of the past.

Notably, the two religions never merge into a single notion of the divine and are generally associated with specific dramatic roles. Usually the chorus and helpless victims tend to invoke a deity that is essentially Christian; villains and fearsome tyrants, instead, appeal to the more earthly gods of mythology. Thus, in Dolce's *Thieste*, the ferocious Atreus calls on the gods of revenge, while the grieving Thieste pleads with a compassionate deity ("celeste pietate," p. 28) to end his suffering. The distinction is dramaturgically significant in that it allows the playwright to direct the spectators' response toward that which should be followed or eschewed. Undoubtedly, spectators instinctively feared and rejected the world of violence which Atreus and his vengeful gods signify. Conversely, they sympathized with Thieste, since they too believed in the same caring and just deity. They also shared the chorus's belief that God's justice, though late in coming, will not leave unpunished Atreus's unspeakable crime:

> L'Almo Fattor del mondo
> Giusto e pietoso Dio,
> Non lascierà giamai
> Senza giusta vendetta
> Questo peccato rio,
> Ch'ogni peccato altrui vince d'assai,
> Sta pur l'empio Tiran lieto e giocondo,
> Degno gastigo aspetta;
> Se ben l'ira del cielo
> Non vien con molta fretta.
>
> (5.5. p. 39)

[The High Maker of the world / just and loving God, / shall never let go [unpunished] / without just revenge / this evil sin, / for it far surpasses the sins of others. / Let the impious Tyrant be happy and cheerful, / for worthy punishment awaits him, / though the wrath of heaven / does not come with much haste.]

The religious essence of this conviction is particularly relevant when compared with the notion of the divine prevailing in the Senecan source, where the "gods have fled" and Thyestes is left to experience his tragedy all alone. His heartrending plea to the "avenging gods" to hear his grief and answer his need for justice is more a cry of impotence and despair than a true act of faith in divine assistance: "Ye too, ye gods, wherever ye have fled, / Hear what a deed is done!" (5.5.1149–50). This sense of aloneness and impotence in a world where the gods are absent or, at least, indifferent to human need for compassion and justice, while accentuating Thyestes's drama, puts in relief the deep piety of Dolce's Thieste and the chorus. It especially underscores these characters' belief in a removed, but not aloof, deity, whose just wrath will eventually but inevitably befall the godless.[18] In this, they join Edippo, Giocasta, Marianna, Oreste, Rosmunda, and all the other characters and choruses from the tragic stage of cinquecento Italy who share their beliefs. To a varying degree, they all believe in a deity that manifests its presence not in the physical world but in the heart and mind of the individual, not through tangible intervention, as in the world of myth or in the *sacre rappresentazioni*, but through the beliefs and invocations of the faithful. It is in their faith that God exists, that He comforts them and gives them hope. He is the universal law that guarantees the righting of all human injustice, albeit in the hereafter, by punishing the wrongdoers and rewarding the deserving.

The Deus ex Machina Expedient: Martelli's *Tullia* and Aretino's *Orazia*

It must not have been difficult for contemporary audiences to recognize that the notion of deity prevalent in the world of the tragic stage was similar to their own. They too believed in a deity that let humans resolve their own affairs, reserving judgment for the afterlife. However, as the ideals of human greatness and ability to manage worldly events began to wane, the people of the Renaissance began to turn to the divine to fill the void. They pleaded for Heavenly intervention whenever they were confronted with misfortunes that were beyond their ability to control. Thus, the deity that had been relegated to the distant celestial spheres so that humans might rule their own world was now invoked to turn its benevolent gaze downward upon its terrestrial creatures. This shift in perception of God's role in the world enhanced the standing of the Church, which, paradoxically, emerged stronger than it had been at the head of the coalition forces against the imperial armies of Charles V. It can fairly be argued that the military catastrophe culminating in the sack of Rome was a providential misfortune because it led Rome to rediscover its true might in spiritual leadership. In this renewed and more appropriate role, the Church welcomed and espoused the awakened need for the divine. The abating faith in human self-sufficiency, compensated by the growing belief in a godhead still *absconditus* but apt to intervene in the affairs of the world, found its representation on the dramatic stage by means of the deus ex machina. To be sure, this dramaturgical expedient appears in only a few neoclassical dramas, but such rarity should not be interpreted as lack of ideological relevance. Instead, it must be seen as the early manifestation of a growing religious sentiment that culminated in the Counter-Reformation. It is also a reflection of the poetics of the time that discouraged the use of divine forces in the resolution of the tragic plot.

Contemporary aversion to the ex machina device was such that Giraldi was criticized even for the simple use of the gods in his *Didone*. In his defense, the playwright justified the use of divine characters, noting that they were essential to the normal development of the action and that they were not used to bring about the dénouement of the plot. Embracing Aristotle's prevailing view against the use of divine intervention, other than "for matters outside the drama,"[19] he reiterated that the solution of a dramatic conflict should result from the natural development of the plot and not from the sudden and arbitrary introduction of the gods.[20] This general disinclination toward the introduction of divine forces on the tragic stage makes it unlikely that playwrights would use the expedient carelessly, thereby inviting the critics' censure and jeopardizing the audience's approval. It is more likely, instead, that they employed the ex machina not so much as a mere theatrical feat, but as a signifier of certain religious convictions that were beginning to permeate a culture whose failed ideals left a great void to be filled.

From this perspective, the ex machina characterizing plays such as *Tullia* and *Orazia* is the manifestation of a rising belief in divine intervention in earthly matters, especially where human efforts proved inadequate in influencing the course of events. In both plays, in fact, the gods appear in order to preserve the integrity of the sociopolitical order threatened by developments that elude the control of those who initiated them. The circumstances that eventually lead to divine intervention in *Tullia*, for example, are set in motion by the ambitious Tullia and her husband, Lucius, who, intent upon seizing the throne, assassinate the reigning rulers. The usurpation and the mindless ferocity of the murders so offend the people of Rome that they rise up in arms against the bloodthirsty couple. As the rebellion threatens to drag the city into further bloodshed and ultimately undermine the very stability of the state, a helpless and fearful Lucius desperately pleads for immediate, divine intervention: "Hear my prayer, O Lord, and render vain / the furor and the arms of the incensed crowd" (p. 110). The deity responds to the impending disaster through the irate voice of Romulus, son of Mars and Father of Rome. After chastising the people for attempting to arrogate to themselves Heaven's prerogatives to depose rulers and dispose of kingdoms, Romulus, who appears as a beam of light, orders the mob to go home so that Lucius may reign in peace until his destiny is fulfilled. The play ends with the chorus reminding both the stage and the hall audience that divine laws rule the world or "everything within us, as it is said" (p. 111).[21]

Romulus's interference may appear gratuitous, since it does not seem warranted by the play's internal dynamics. Had the play attracted meaningful public attention, that is, performances or discussions, those who criticized Giraldi's use of the gods would have undoubtedly denounced Martelli's divine intervention as formally unfounded and arbitrary. They would have argued that the plot reached its natural conclusion with Lucius's successful seizure of the throne and that the conflict issuing from the people's reaction is an unnecessary appendage. Textual evidence, however, shows that the playwright did not go against prevailing dramatic poetics, for the role of religion in the world of *Tullia* is so prevalent that it justifies the gods' interference. A close look at the text reveals that the divine is an intrinsic element of the play's world and that its intervention is therefore consistent with the natural development of the plot.

Religious references are so frequent that it is not uncommon for characters to mention God by name or attribute a half dozen times in a single speech. For instance, at the end of the play, Lucius, in assuring his friends that the gods are on his side, refers to the divine at least fifteen times in less than fifty lines (pp. 109–10). Also, their prayers and invocations denote a conception of the divine as a supernatural force having an active role in the affairs of humans. It is this religious conviction that leads Lucius to believe that it was God who willed his return from exile in order to reclaim the throne. He says that the Corinthian high priest advised him to leave for Rome right away because Heaven was most propitious to "your wishes" (p. 32). Also, Tullia, in the exposition of the antefactum, recalls that it was God who gave the throne to Tarquinius (Lucius's father), whom the ruling usurpers assassinated. Both Tullia and Lucius, as if orienting the audience toward the final appearance of the semigod, suggest that the gods will ultimately restore the kingdom to them, for they are the rightful successors (pp. 32–38). Lucius begs God to make it so that his cruel adversary loses the kingdom (p. 91). And, as the enraged crowd threatens the stability of the state, Lucius implores Jupiter to intervene, reminding the deity that He promised the kingdom to Tarquinius, that He gave him the sign to come to Rome to reclaim the throne, and that He should now make good on His promise:

> Tu promettesti al mio buon Padre il regno . . .
> A me in Corinto non un solo segno
> Desti . . .
> Finisci i danni miei; sostien, ch'io viva
> Ne la mia patria, e nel mio Regno in pace.
>
> (p. 110)

[Ye promised the kingdom to my good Father . . . / In Corinth Ye gave me more than one sign . . . / End my trials; allow that I live / in peace in my homeland and kingdom.]

This belief in a deity actively involved in earthly matters is also shared by the people who accept with the utmost reverence Romulus's injunction and return quietly to their homes. The spectators, too, dazzled by the luminous god and with his thunderous warning still ringing in their ears, leave the theater pondering the ideology informing the resolution of the dramatic conflict and the crowd's immediate acceptance of it. They, too, must pay heed to the admonition against subverting the order that only the divine can alter.

For some scholars, Lucius and Tullia's successful drive to the throne poses a serious moral dilemma, for, in their view, it represents a reward for the unspeakable atrocity the couple displayed in the senseless mutilation of the king's corpse. Cut into pieces, the old man's body was thrown in the street for the people to behold and for animals to feed upon, leaving his spirit to wander without a resting place (pp.104–5). Readers have questioned the ethical basis for allowing these murderers to enjoy the fruits of their crimes with the added blessing of the gods. Others, however, have defended Martelli's decision on grounds of verisimilitude, noting that it reflects real life instances wherein evildoers often go unpunished.[22] Be that as it may, these arguments are not truly pertinent to the play's ideology, for they proceed from a code of ethics that exists outside the realm of the text. Seen on the basis of textual evidence, the issue emerges not so much as a matter of morality, but rather as a question of political theology. Romulus's admonition that only God can dispose of rulers and the chorus's reminder that God governs the world according to His inscrutable plan both point to the notion of a deity that is ready to intervene whenever humans attempt to interfere with the predetermined course of its providential plan. Pointedly, it is not Lucius's desperate appeal that prompts the god's sudden appearance, but the threat that the mob poses to the stability and the integrity of the state. The role of the divine, then, is not to reward the ambitious and bloodthirsty couple, who in due time ("destinato giorno," p. 112) will answer for their misdeeds, but to preserve order and save Rome from certain ruin. It is not mere coincidence that the intervening deity is none other than Romulus, the Father of Rome.

A similar concern informs the ex machina resolution of the tragic conflict in Aretino's *Orazia*. Here, it is Minerva who appears at the end of the play in order to preserve the integrity of the state. The divine Voice (of Minerva) is heard ordering a rebellious Orazio to submit to the supremacy of the state and accept its tribunal's judgment against him.[23] Several critics have condemned this reconciliation of the dramatic conflict as unnatural; others, pointing to its departure from Aristotelian precepts, have called it unnecessary, a defect, and, merely theatrical.[24] These objections, arising from the traditional aversion to ex machina resolutions of the tragic plot, need not be so rigid as to overlook evidence pointing to the deity as a major internal force driving the dramatic action. *Orazia*'s plot not only develops in a highly religious environment, it is also determined by religious convictions, at times. It suffices to recall that the proud and uncompromising Orazio, whose obstinacy intensifies the dramatic conflict, is a devout hero who will bow only to divine will. It is natural, then, that in the end the gods intervene to force him into submission, defusing the confrontation that threatened his life and the integrity of the state.

Orazio's initial refusal to acknowledge Rome's authority over himself leads to a serious dilemma that cannot not be resolved without undermining either the supremacy of state or the integrity of his heroism. For if, on the one hand, the state allowed Orazio to place himself above the law, it would de facto renounce its sovereignty; on the other hand, if the valiant warrior were to submit meekly to the state's punishment, nominal as it may be, he would no longer be true to his titanic character.[25] His defeat of Rome's enemies and his intolerance of any assault on his valor (he kills his sister for accusing him of cruelty toward the enemy) make him a hero of truly monumental proportions. Such a characterization would be seriously flawed if he were to submit to a power less than divine. It is therefore to the deity that he ultimately bows his head, solemnly proclaiming "I fear Jupiter" (5.2804). In submitting to a higher power, writes Hegel, a tragic hero retains the integrity of his character, for he continues to adhere to his essential pathos, while his will is "broken in its bare obstinacy by a god's authority."[26]

Of course, the ex machina would not have been necessary had Aretino adhered to Livy's account of the episode, as some have suggested.[27] In the Latin original there is no need for divine intervention because Horatius recognizes the authority of the people of Rome, thus precluding any possibility of rebellion on the part of the young hero. But then, the play would have resulted in a mere dramatization of the traditional conflict between the state and the individual. The playwright chose to go beyond the source and, by elevating Orazio from a plain hero to a tragic character, added a significant religious component that redefines the ideological base of the story. Divine intervention, far from being sprung on the stage for "theatrical effects," is the logical development of a dramatic action that is strongly influenced by the religious atmosphere arising from holy ceremonies, pious invocations, and references to the city's temples. The most significant of these symbols is undoubtedly the towering temple of Minerva. It is to the goddess that Orazio offers the spoils of war and hangs them on the door of her temple. The shrine so dominates the dramatic space that it tends to convey religious connotation to all the deeds that take place within its sphere. Thus Orazio's murder of Celia, besides being a crime against the state, is an affront to the goddess under whose eyes it was committed. In fact, the gods, said to be indignant, look upon the prideful hero with disdain and swear to avenge the misdeed (5.2431–37). It should come as no surprise, then, that it is the deity that ultimately imposes the punishment and forces Orazio to accept it. Significantly, the order to "bow" in submission not only resolves the confrontation between Orazio and the state, it also serves to appease divine anger. The intervention, then, has the dual function of preserving the political stability of the state, inherent in the inviolability of its laws, and of allowing Orazio to expiate his "sin" against the gods.[28] This double role is clearly defined by Minerva's admonition that humble obedience cleanses the sin [and] preserves the law (5.2771). From this perspective, divine mediation is not unwarranted or unnecessary, as some have suggested, but immanent both to the spiritual welfare of the individual and to the political integrity of the represented world. Religion, says the patrician Spurio, is the ladder through which "il mondo ascende al cielo" (humans ascend to heaven) (2.711–12). And, for the high priest Marco Valerio, the well-being of the state is better guaranteed by the observance of religion than it is by the might of the sword:

> Il valore de l'asta e de la spada
> E 'l timore de i riti e de le pene
> Non tiene in alto le cittade magne,
> Come la riverenza e l'osservanza
> De la religione e de gli Iddii.
>
> (1.404–8)

[The valor of the lance and the sword, / and the fear of the laws and of punishment / do not sustain great cities / as (do) the reverence and the observance / of religion and of the Gods.]

What emerges from this notion of religion and from the mediating role of its deity is the expression of an ideology fundamentally Counter-Reformist to the extent that it proposes the divine as the ultimate guarantor of sociopolitical stability. Pointedly, the deity usually intervenes when events threaten the political order underpinning the stability of the state and only after human efforts have proven inadequate to control them. In the metaphor of theater, it may be argued, the recourse to the ex machina expedient reflects the growing awareness of human limitations and, implicitly, the need to rely on the help of a superior power. More specifically, it suggests that in the cinquecento, as reliance on the divine replaced beliefs in the self-sufficiency of humans, the Church began to assume the prominent role of interpreter of Heaven's will. It was from this position of relevance that it renewed the call for the return to more Christian ways and for the strict observance of religion. Thus, not with the strength of its sword, which had been blunted forever by the imperial armies in 1527, but armed with the menace of God's wrath, the Church proposed itself both as mediator in worldly affairs and as the guardian of divine laws. The fearful demons of the Middle Ages would be replaced by fearful Inquisitors, who, intolerant of dissension, succeeded in frightening into submission commoners and princes alike. Admittedly, it is somewhat premature to speak of the Counter-Reformation in the first half of the cinquecento, but one can already see the budding that will come into full bloom in the second half of the century. Seen in this cultural context, the ex machina might not have been a favorite dramaturgical device, but it must have made a lot of sense to contemporary spectators, especially to the intellectual elite who could see on the stage the reflection of the *forma mentis* that was beginning to shape their culture.[29]

In this sense, the dramatic stage was a viable mirror that reflected for the spectators the dramatization of ideals and religious beliefs informing their lives. For us readers, it is a window into the cultural dynamism behind the evolution of Renaissance thought. The high frequency of religious allusions on the part of dramatic characters, while revealing, on the one hand, a strong presence of the divine in the world of theater, on the other hand, points to audiences religious enough to appreciate and presumably share the same religious beliefs. Contrary to traditional critical views, the divine was indeed an intrinsic part of neoclassical drama. And if it was not always clear whether its essence was Christian or pagan, it was not due to the lack of religious feeling, but, at least in part, to the dominant mythological setting that tended to attenuate the expression of religious feelings in Christian terms. To a lesser degree, it was also due to the notion of the deity as a monitor rather than an active participant in the affairs of humans. But this idea was not so absolute as to preclude the growing belief in the divine as the determining force in resolving human predicaments too great for the individual to manage. The notion of the godhead as sometimes involved and sometimes uninvolved in the resolution of worldly matters was not a contradiction, as it may seem, but the reflection of the changing perceptions that Renaissance society had of religion and its godhead.

4
The Nature of Kingship: The Debate on Machiavellism

> Tous ces crimes d'Etat qu'on fait pour la Coronne,
> Le Ciel nous en absout, alors qu'il nous la donne."
> —Corneille, *Cinna*

TAGEDY IS ABOUT WICKED KINGS, SAID ISIDORE AND OTHERS AFTER him.[1] Lady Tragedia herself exemplifies the idea in her prologue to Dolce's *Marianna*, where she declares that unlike Comedy, she brings grief and tears. Appearing in dark clothes with a crown on her head, a scepter in one hand and a drawn sword in the other, she tells the audience that she brings on stage the horrible deaths of cruel tyrants and of unfortunate kings and queens.[2] Royal victims and villains populate the tragic world of ancient drama and are especially common on the Italian Renaissance stage. In some instances, grief and tears result from the senseless deaths of young lovers, who, like Romeo and Juliet, kill themselves because of a tragic error. In Groto's *Adriana*, Latino poisons himself on the mistaken assumption that Adriana is dead; when she awakens from her faked death and finds her lover dying, she kills herself (4.8).[3] In some other instances, tragedy brings on stage the heroic deaths of unfortunate rulers, mostly queens, who decide to end their lives rather than live in shame or in servitude. Trissino's Sofonisba and Giraldi's Cleopatra, for example, choose to die rather than be taken captives to Rome. The most common tragic plot, however, is woven in murder and bloodshed perpetrated by cruel tyrants. Their wickedness ranges from Alboino's macabre pleasure to force and watch Rosmunda drink from her own father's skull to Sulmone's dismemberment of Orbecche's husband and children to Herod's execution of Marianna and the children.

A primary function of this savagery is to arouse fear in the hearts of the spectators and involve them emotionally in the dramatic action. While scholars have long recognized the dramaturgical effect of stage bloodshed, the ethos of the tyrants perpetrating the violence has gone largely unnoticed. One cannot dismiss these cruel characters as simply deranged, for it would trivialize the ideological thrust of the individual play and seriously undermine the genre, which is traditionally based on the actions of kings and princes. Nor can one dismiss their bloody deeds as slavish and fashionable imitation of Seneca or as mere dramatic means intended to rattle the nerves of the spectators, as has been suggested.[4] Instead, stage tyrants must be seen as heads of state whose official acts tend to define a notion of kingship that sanctions their violent behavior. As many of these rulers either die a horrible death or live to regret their atrocities, one must consider the impact that their demise might have on the political philosophy informing the nature of kingship. More specifically, we must determine whether and to what extent such a demise signifies the repudiation of the ideology that stage tyrants represent. Only after understanding the tyrant's rationale for using violence, on the one hand, and the reasons for his death, on the other, can we begin to appreciate the ideology dramatized in a particular play.

The principles underpinning the notion of kingship prevailing in cinquecento tragedy are usually expressed as the king defends his actions against the advice of his counselor, captain, or courtier.[5] Typically, after the king voices his resolve to punish an alleged perpetrator against the crown, the counselor attempts to dissuade him from using violence. Against the king's argument that the use of force is necessary in order to assert royal power and reputation, the counselor suggests that a show of compassion may earn the prince a nobler reputation. When the king points out that the threat and use of force likens him to God, who with His thunderbolts reminds humans of His power, the counselor counters that God is also caring and forgiving. Confuting the idea that a ruler should be feared by his people, the counselor argues that higher glory is attained from the love rather than the fear of one's subjects. And against the tyrant's insistence that kings can do as they please because they are and have always been above the law (*legibus soluti*), the counselor points out that kings are subject to the ups and downs of Fortuna and ultimately to divine justice, just like any other human. As the debate continues to articulate similar differences, it becomes clear that the two characters stand for the dramatization of competing notions of princeship: one based on humanist ideals, the other on traditional precepts informing Machiavellian theory. The dynamism inherent in this debate ultimately appears to settle on the emerging reason of state ideology, which tends to assimilate the best aspects of both sides.

4: THE NATURE OF KINGSHIP

The debate must have had a sobering impact on the spectators, who could not help but view the stage events with an eye to their own reality. The experience reminded them, if obliquely, that their well being was tied directly to the ethos and the political fortunes of the ruling prince. But, whereas the debate reflected the playwright's view of the changing trends in the political philosophy of Renaissance Italy, the political import of the activities surrounding the performance itself went beyond the author's intent. As it usually happened, the day, the pageantry, the guest list, the time, and the place of the representation were all at the discretion of the local ruler or sponsor, who viewed the event as an opportunity to celebrate his power and the traditions upon which it rests.

THE MACHIAVELLIAN NOTION OF KINGSHIP AND THE TRAGIC STAGE

Throughout most of the cinquecento, Machiavelli's precepts on princeship dominated all forms of political debate both in Italy and abroad. He was such a pervasive presence in Renaissance political discourse, writes Peter Donaldson, "that nearly all political discussions had to take account of his work and orient themselves in relation to it, whether by absorbing him, or defending him."[6] Political perspectives might vary from author to author, but in the end they all converged on the Machiavellian ways and means of acquiring, retaining, and governing a state. One of the most discussed aspect of his theory was the notion that princes may do whatever is necessary in order to defend and preserve the welfare of the state. That a prince engage in deception, intimidation, and even murder for reasons of state was not an original Machiavellian suggestion. Machiavelli pointed to several historical, mythological, and biblical figures who perpetrated violent crimes in the name of the state. One of them was Moses, who in order to see "his laws and institutions go forward, was forced to kill a great number of men."[7] Machiavelli's novelty was simply to yank the concept of reason of state away from the ethical anchors to which quattrocento humanists had tied it. Fearing unrestrained tyranny, the humanists insisted that a prince strive to behave with honor, honesty, liberality, and other noble virtues extolled by Cicero, Seneca, and other ancient writers.[8] Against this idealism, which had been greatly undermined by the harsh historical realities of the time, particularly by Charles VIII's shocking invasion of Italy in 1494, Machiavelli forged a political theory based largely on a flexible notion of princely *virtù*.

Without repudiating classical virtues, he argued that a virtuous prince had to be willing and ready to engage in fraudulent and violent behavior if and when the circumstances made it necessary and the interests of the state warranted it. More specifically, a prince should be able to take on the cunning quality of the fox and the fierce nature of the lion when "necessità" and/or *utile* required him. Thus loosened from fixed moral standards, Machiavelli's idea of *virtù* generated a controversy that was to engage political thinkers from diverse cultures and ideologies. Treatises on kingly virtues and on the duties and prerogatives of rulers contributed to a vast production of political writings known as reason-of-state literature, following Botero's influential treatise *La Ragion di stato* (1589).[9] Many writers rejected Machiavelli's political realism as immoral, and some, such as Reginald Pole, went as far as to consider it the work of the devil or the Antichrist. Others sought to subordinate his teachings to religious morality, according to personal beliefs and prevailing cultural trends. Renaissance Italy did not experience the political challenges and anxieties that eventually brought about civil wars both in England and in France. Nonetheless, it was in the middle of the debate that did not take place on the battleground, but on the field of literature.

Although political treatises were the appropriate literary genre for arguments concerning statecraft, the dramatic theater was without doubt a unique forum for such a topic. True to the time-honored tradition that tragedy should represent the actions of royalty, Renaissance tragedy dramatized possible worlds in which the role of the king was central to the development of the play and the political philosophy informing it. Most playwrights built their tragedies around the Sophoclean conflict between the interests of the state and the rights of the individual. In the name of the state, stage tyrants did not hesitate to take whatever measures necessary against individuals whose actions threatened the integrity of the state and, inherently, the common good. Though individual tragedies distinguish themselves by virtue of their peculiarities, they all seem to center the ideological conflict on 1) the nature and extent of the king's authority, 2) his unique notion of the state or the common good, and 3) the means he might employ to defend it.

Kings thought of themselves as having absolute power and could do anything they wished. They were the law, for, according to tradition, their wish had the force of the law: "quod principi placuit, legis habet vigorem." As for the concept of common good, there was no question either on the stage or in the auditorium that the individual's rights and interests were subordinate to the sovereignty of the ruler, the ultimate and legitimate custodian of the public good. In Dolce's

Giocasta, the diviner Teiresias, arguing that it is just that one individual suffers for the "comun ben" or common good, calls upon Creon to sacrifice his own son Menoeceus in order to save Thebes (3.1, p. 67). And in *Marianna,* 4. 2754, the royal counselor reminds Herod that the Roman Consul Torquatus placed the common good above all personal interests when he ordered the execution of his own son. Machiavelli, too, praised Torquatus's deed. He also praised Romulus's murder of Remus, a crime that he found totally justified on the grounds that it was perpetrated for the common good.[10]

The idea of public good, though clearly defined and championed by political counselors, was often sacrificed to the ambitions of those in power both in the fiction of the stage and in real life. The line between private and public interest was often blurred in the minds of many rulers, who tended to identify the common good with their own *utile.* Their personal honor, power, wealth, aims, and ambitions were all expressions of the state. In a world constantly threatened by territorial disputes, expansionist designs, armed invasions, conspiracies, and other destabilizing forces, the continued welfare of the state often depended on the prince's ability or reputation to protect it. Urbino was one of those principalities. Its existence as a political entity rested on the military and diplomatic prowess of its ruler Federico da Montefeltro, who defended it successfully against the expansionist ambitions of the its neighbors and especially from the Pope's claim that the duchy was Church territory.[11] The "good" of the state was so inextricably joined to that of its ruler that the two entities were considered one and the same: the prince was the state and the state was his. This form of identification is best captured in Louis XIV's expression "l'état c'est moi." Rulers could do anything they wished, for, in the words of King Polifonte, laws and justice

> non hanno sopra i principi potere
> chè mal si converria, s'essi le fanno,
> ch'essi a l'opera lor fosser soggetti.
>
> (*Merope,* 956–59)

[have no power over ruling princes. / It would be ill conceived for kings to be subject / to the laws which they themselves make.]

This unique notion of the state informed the behavior of many stage tyrants, who viewed the common good as that which was good, or *utile,* for them. Torelli dramatizes this concept in his *Merope,* where king Polifonte plans to wed Queen Merope both out of love and for the good of the state. He believes that nothing should happen to a great king that is not tied to the common good (706). And in Dolce's

Ifigenia, the diviner Calcante tells Agamemnon that in order to obtain favorable winds for the Greeks to sail for Troy he must sacrifice his own daughter, Iphigenia, to the gods. As the king agonizes over the choice between the good of the state and his paternal love, Menelaus advises him to spare the girl and kill the diviner, instead. He brushes aside Agamemnon's objection that it is not just for a king to kill those he governs, noting that "just" is that which brings *utile*. Relieved, Agamemnon accepts his brother's morality of the *utile*, fearing only that if the truth were revealed it would undermine his leadership (p. 16). Dolce returns to this Machiavellian notion of "necessity" in *Medea*, where Creon, considering Medea's presence a menace to the stability of the kingdom, banishes her from Corinth, citing *utile* and the law as the basis for his decision (p. 13). The royal decree appears to articulate a genuine concern for the welfare of the state, were it not for the courtier's harsh assessment of kingship. When Medea's nurse wonders how Creon, himself a father, could order a mother away from her own children, Balio, the courtier, explains that the love for one's children is superseded by one's political ambitions. Rulers do not hesitate to kill their own children in order to feel secure in their reign. As for the law, Balio continues, they have total disregard for it, especially when pursuing their own *utile* (p. 6).

Of course, the stage view of a kingship that sanctioned the tyrant's bloody deeds, placed him above the law, and made no distinction between his interests and those of the state was deeply rooted in Seneca's tragedies. This does not mean that its widespread representation on the tragic stage of the Italian Renaissance was a servile imitation of the Ancients, as some have suggested. It was, instead, an attempt to show kingship in its nakedness and to debate the soundness of its ideological underpinnings, especially the unrestrained use of force. Though the stage arguments articulating the debate reflected various theories and ideals, many of them took issue against or inspiration from Machiavelli. Alboino, for instance, evokes Machiavelli's *Prince*, chapter 17, when he argues that a king should found his rule on cruelty, for it stirs fear in the subjects and incites them to obedience (*Rosmunda*, 349–52). Oronte seems to recite from *Prince*, chapter 25, when he says that Fortune beats those who fear her, but is beaten by those who stand up to her (*Orbecche*, 2.3.726). Dell'Anguillara's Oedipus, echoing *Prince*, chapters 17 and 19, advises his sons against taking the women of their subjects because it can easily earn them the contempt and the hatred of the people (*Edippo*, p. 19). And Polifonte's view that a king should use force when reason fails, and resort to fraud where the use of violence is not possible (*Merope*, 971–74) echoes precepts from *Prince*, chapter 18.

4: The Nature of Kingship

Giraldi's *Orbecche*

Among the better known tragedies of the Italian Renaissance, Giraldi's *Orbecche* offers the best dramatization of the debate on kingship. For one thing, it features king Sulmone, the bloodiest and most wicked ruler in all of cinquecento tragedies. It also casts the outspoken, royal counselor Malecche, whose aversion to tyrannical rule tends to underline and counterbalance Sulmone's wickedness. The two characters emerge as the horns of the debate with the counselor advocating a benevolent form of rule and the king insisting that true princely power is rooted in the use of force. For Sulmone there is no limit to the type or degree of force a sovereign may use against those who threaten the integrity of the crown. He considers kingship a license or a cover for rulers to do anything they wish. Echoing the view of King Atreus, his Senecan counterpart, that "kings do as they will" (*Thyestes*, 2.1.215–45), he dismisses the counselor's warning that his bloody deeds might tarnish his princely reputation. Kings, he argues, cannot be blamed for their actions, for all royal acts are covered by the exculpatory mantle of kingship:

> . . . Che biasimo puote
> Avere un Re di cosa ch'egli faccia,
> Le cui opere tutte sotto il manto
> Real stanno coperte?
>
> (3.3.1720)

[What blame can / a king receive for the things he does, / since his deeds are all covered / by the regal mantle?]

The deeds in question are Sulmone's murders of Orbecche's husband and their children. He believes that the offspring from his daughter's furtive marriage to the presumed commoner Oronte threaten the integrity of the state. The children's plebeian origin would forever stain the honor of the royal house, undermine their claim to the throne, and perhaps arouse expansionist ambitions in the hearts of neighboring lords. His concern is so real that he is most eager to appease and forgive his widowed and childless daughter in the hope that she will consent to a political marriage with their traditional enemy and neighbor the great king Selino. The noble and worthy progeny springing from such a princely union would guarantee the future of Sulmone's dynasty (5.2.2821–24). These hopes undoubtedly had a familiar ring to contemporary audiences, for they too viewed marriage as a means to strengthen or legitimize one's power and prestige. Speaking of the rise of Western monarchies, Perry Anderson notes that dynasty was the ultimate instance of legitimacy and that marriage was "the supreme device of diplomacy."¹²

Sulmone's concern for the survival of his dynasty underscores the coincidence between the king's interests and those of the state. He had always wanted to make peace with his archenemy Selino in order to ensure the survival of the royal dynasty and bring peace to his people (3.2.1431–33). Reflecting the largely accepted Machiavellian precept that a ruler's primary duty is to "maintain" the state, no one in the play seems to question the king's political aims and the means to realize them. Questions do arise, however, about the ethos that determines his insistence for vengeance and the excessive cruelty with which he carries it out. His motives for seeking revenge against Oronte appear to be primarily personal: he feels betrayed by a foundling whom he raised at court as one of his own. In his eyes, the young man is an ungrateful opportunist of vile stock who took advantage of his trust and goodwill. But there are also political imperatives that demand Oronte's punishment. His secret marriage to Orbecche is a serious attack upon the honor of the royal house and a lasting stain on the integrity of the dynasty (3.3.1661–65). Accordingly, Sulmone intends to devise a punishment that will show what happens to those of ignoble, ill-conceived breed ("mal nata prole," 5.1.2442) who dare to undermine the reputation of the king.

Malecche, questioning the need for the punishment, argues that despite the allegations Oronte is actually a noble young man, albeit not of birth. In his attempt to convince Sulmone to accept Oronte as a worthy son-in-law, the old counselor points out that the young man is of exceptional virtues. He has shown great ability both in handling important matters for the state and in fighting against Selino's armies (3.2.1343, 1598). True nobility, Malecche continues, lies in one's natural virtues rather than in riches and noble birth. Voicing a concern frequently found in other cinquecento tragedies, he warns the king not to value individuals for their wealth and power, for in a world ruled by whimsical Fortune today's rich may be tomorrow's poor, just as yesterday's beggars may become tomorrow's rulers:

> Onde spesso si vede che quei c'hanno
> L'arche travi d'argento e gravi d'oro
> Divengono mendichi e ch'i mendichi
> Son alzati a gli scettri, a le corone.
>
> (3.2.1358–61)¹³

[Hence one often sees that those who have / the coffers full of silver and heavy with gold / become beggars, and the beggars / are elevated to the scepters and the crowns.]

Contemporary audiences undoubtedly shared Malecche's argument, since his ideas on nobility and Fortune are rooted in their own culture. His concept of nobility echoes the humanist belief that nobility resides in one's own virtues and may be acquired only through one's worthy deeds.[14] His reference to Oronte's heroism in war and wise management of state affairs evokes the prevailing view that individuals are measured by their *agere et intelligere*, that is, their physical and intellectual endeavors. Also, the allusion to Fortune's capricious undoing of the rich and powerful is not a mere literary commonplace, for the Renaissance attributed great importance to the role of Fortune in human affairs. Machiavelli, for one, conceded that Fortune controls almost half of all worldly events, leaving to humans the control of the other half. Fickle Fortune and a liberal ideology praising individuals for their personal abilities rather than their birth made it possible for commoners to aspire to higher rungs on the social ladder.[15] The path for such a climb had already been charted both in history and in literature. Undoubtedly, audiences recalled with ease Machiavelli's stylized portrait of Castruccio Castracani, a mere foundling (incidentally, Oronte, too, is a foundling) who through his personal abilities (*virtù*) and the help of Fortune became the acclaimed ruler of fourteenth-century Lucca. Audiences were also all too familiar with examples of baseborn individuals who became princes in their own right: the shepherd boy Antonio Campano became bishop (1462); Adriano Castellesi of Corneto, though of humble birth, rose to the cardinalate (1503) and became "one of the richer member of the college";[16] and the Florentine chancellor Bartolomeo della Scala (1428–97) was a miller's son. Who in the Renaissance could not recall the peasant origins of the Sforza and the mercantile background of the Medici!

If the resonance of living realities in Malecche's argument wins the audience's approval, it does not move Sulmone from his resolve to punish the "vile traitor" Oronte. The question of vengeance, as noted above, is both personal and political. On the personal level, the king might have been able to forgive the perpetrator or, at least, reduce the punishment. There is a moment, albeit but a moment, when he appears to entertain a change of heart, as he doubts his courage to go through with the execution of his plan: "What do you fear, my soul? what frightens you so?" (3.3.1674). However, political considerations, namely, the need to uphold the honor of the royal family, to preserve the integrity of the state, and to bring peace to his people, compel him to act, and act decisively. He must not appear fainthearted or incapable of defending the state. On at least two separate occasions, he voices the Machiavellian belief that a ruling prince must guard against being perceived as weak and irresolute by either friend or foe. In his view, to let affronts against the crown go unpunished is to reduce the royal court to a barrack and the king to the most vile of men:

> . . . i Re sarian da meno ch'i più vili
> Uomini ch'abbia il mondo e le lor corti
> Verrebbero da men che le capanne.
>
> (5.1.2455)

[Kings would be less than the most vile / men in the world, and their courts / would be considered less than huts.]

And so, after a brief hesitation reminiscent of Atreus's "Why hesitate? . . . Wherefore, my soul, / Art Thou afraid? Why fail before the deed" (*Thyestes*, 2.1.276, 326–28), he decides to vindicate his honor. With as much force as the gravity of the offense requires, he intends to show the world the resolve of his might: he will wash the stain on his royal honor with the blood of the "vile" Oronte and his children (3.3.1680).

From this perspective, Sulmone's decision to murder and dismember the victims issues not from a bloodthirsty nature, but from the dictates of power. In the eyes of the audience, his violent behavior falls within the established tradition of vengeance, a commonplace in ancient literature, particularly in drama and in epic poetry. One needs only to think of the Homeric stories about avenging heroes and vindictive gods, of Æschylus's revenge-driven *Oresteia* and, not least, of Seneca's tragedies. But it would seriously simplify the ideological significance of the play to believe, as has been suggested, that the bloody deeds in *Orbecche* are a plain imitation of this tradition.[17] Sulmone's revenge differs substantially from his vengeful counterparts in that he is not driven by fate as Orestes, by spite as Medea, by an inconsolable grief as Achilles, or by a savage urge to retaliate as Atreus. Nor should one reduce the function of the horrific in the play to a mere "dramatic device intended to sharpen the emotional impact made by the tragic spectacle."[18] Sulmone's explicit motives for using violence clearly point to a reason of state ideology that recognizes a prince's need to vindicate the dignity of the crown. This is not to say that his actions proceed from a purely political necessity, for, again, in the tyrant's mind there is no distinction between his personal *utile* (or need of vengeance) and that of the state. He repeatedly stresses the need to avenge the honor of the crown so that *he* will appear strong and decisive, and thus discourage others from doubting *his* resolve (3.3.1665). For him, then, violence is not just a personal thing, but also a means of projecting political power.

Without questioning the right of a ruler to appear strong, Malecche argues that political power can also be projected, perhaps more effectively, through the exhibition of a prince's personal virtues. He advises the king to pardon Oronte's alleged affront to the crown, noting that "il perdonare è da Signor gentile" [to forgive becomes to a noble lord] (3.2.1172).[19] In a tone reminiscent of Castiglione's courtier, whose role is to show the prince how much honor will come to him from the justice, the liberality, the magnanimity, and other virtues that are proper to a prince,[20] the counselor insists that true princely qualities are not vengeance and brutal force, but compassion, prudence, and the control of one's passions:

> Mostrar senno, valor, pietà, clemenzia,
> Non pur opera istimo di Re invitto,
> Ma d'uom ch'assimigliar si possa a Dio.
>
> (3.2.1257–59)

[To show wisdom, valor, pity, clemency, / is not, I believe, the behavior of an invincible king, / but of a man who can be compared to God.]

He exhorts his lord to follow the example of the great king Pisistratus, who chose to forgive rather than seek vengeance against the enamored young man who dishonored the royal family by forcibly kissing the king's daughter in public (3.2.1306). Most spectators undoubtedly recalled Dante's use of the episode as an exemplum of gentleness for the wrathful to contemplate.[21] Malecche's suggestion that virtuous kings resemble God and the religious connotation inherent in the exhortation to emulate Pisistratus not only underscore the merit of humanist princely virtues, they also point to a notion of kingship anchored on Christian morality.

The lines of the contemporary political debate on the nature of kingship are clearly drawn here between the humanist notion of a kingship, somewhat Christianized, and the traditional tyrannical ruler revisited and in part reproposed by Machiavelli.[22] The personal virtues and qualities that Malecche advises Sulmone to embrace are those normally proposed in mirror-of-princes literature or advice-books for Renaissance rulers. Machiavelli, as noted earlier, rejected the strict adherence to these virtues as being too idealistic, noting that there are times when a prince must proceed skillfully and resort to least admirable methods, such as the use of force and deception. Sulmone's exhibits great ability at both duplicity and violence, putting into practice Machiavelli's precept that a prince should be willing and able to be sly like fox and fierce like a lion.[23] His decision to kill his base-born grandchildren, for instance, is necessitated by the fear that they could someday ascend the throne, thereby lowering the dignity of the crown and jeopardizing its stability. Thus, they must perish, lest they be a lingering reminder of the outrage (3.3.1684–89).[24] The decision is both practical and necessary. It is necessary because it preempts future challenges to the stability of the throne by unworthy claimants who might find favor with the people. It is practical because, by murdering Oronte and the children all at once, it eliminates the eventuality of having to kill them later one at a time, thus avoiding the risk of being perceived as a bloodthirsty king. In his reasoning, Sulmone seems to follow closely well-known Machiavellian precepts. Advising the new prince how to solidify his power in a newly conquered state, Machiavelli insists on the need to eliminate the family of the previous ruler, for, once his line is extinguished, there is no one left to be feared, since nobody else has any credit with the people. He also warns that a prince who must engage in acts of violence should do them all at once so as not to do them over an extended period of time and risk earning the reputation as a bloodthirsty ruler.[25] The wisdom of this advise is concisely stated in a maxim from a Machiavellian who warns that "if you injure your neighbor, better not do it by halves."[26]

Sulmone also proves to be a skillful Machiavellian dissembler as he beguiles Malecche by falsely promising to forgive the alleged offenders. He orders the old courtier to take the royal ring to Oronte as a token of his good faith and as a sign of his intent to appoint him successor to the throne (3.2.1629–34). The insidious ploy is intended to guarantee that the victims do not attempt to escape and that, unsuspecting, come to him to meet the violent fate he has devised for them. He sustains the dissimulation by repeatedly making ambiguous statements about his royal word of honor and his affection for his daughter and the children. For example, he swears to Malecche that he has always kept his word "quando ad altrui con fé legata i' l'abbia" [whenever I gave it in good faith] (3.4.1850). The statement is clearly devious, since only he would know when and whether he gives his word in good faith. In equally dissembling terms, he tells Orbecche that his affection for her and the children is such that he is about "a fare oggi di voi quel che far voglio" [to do with you all that which I want to do today]. He adds slyly that he loves them "non men da me che siate voi amati" [not less than I should love you] (3.4.1886–94). Only the spectators understand the tragic irony informing Sulmone's wily words and his murderous intentions.

The purpose of the deception is to prevent the intended victims from escaping and to inflict a punishment that fits the deceptive nature of the crime like a Dantean *contrappasso*. Oronte is considered a "traitor" for allegedly having betrayed the king's trust; now, it is his naive trust in the king's plot that brings him to his own death. Sulmone explains to Allocche that he planned his scheme so that

> . . . simil fosse
> La vendetta a l'oltraggio. Egli l'ingiuria
> Mi fece allor che per lo più fedele
> L'avea de la mia corte, et io ho voluto
> Che la fé istessa lo conduca a morte.
>
> (5.1.2511–15)

[vengeance would correspond to the injury. / He offended me while I held him as the most faithful / in my court. And so, I wanted that / faith itself leads him to his death.]

Sulmone is proud of his scheme because it produces a fitting punishment worthy of a true king.[27] In his view, the gruesome killings represent a rhetorical expression of power meant to enhance his reputation as a capable ruler determined to defend his honor and his crown. On more than one occasion, he stresses the idea that he intends the punishment as a show of force for the world to behold or, in his words, "dimostrare il poter nostro al mondo" [to demonstrate our power to the world] (3.3.1680). Reiterating this same concept, he later tells his minions Tamule and Alloche that he meant the unusual punishment to show others what happens to traitors.[28]

This rhetorical intent is of paramount importance if we are to understand the political ideology that undergirds Sulmone's use of violence against his helpless victims. His reluctance to forgive stems largely from the belief that a show of compassion would earn him the reputation of a weak and vulnerable ruler. Echoing Machiavelli's advice against appearing cowardly or indecisive,[29] he fears that rulers who do not show a forceful resolve to avenge an affront open themselves to further attacks (3.3.1715–16). Like Seneca's Nero, who believes that "the people scorn the feeble" and that the subjects "must fear" the prince (*Octavia*, 2.2.434–38), he is convinced that indecisive princes are perceived as the most "vile" of men (5.1.2445–56). Taking issue with humanist ideology and deriding those who hold that it is better to be loved than feared, he reaffirms his belief in the traditional theory that a prince's political power is based on fear not on love. In words reminiscent of Machiavelli's *Prince* and of reason of state authors, such as Botero and Tassoni, he argues that no prince should mind being called cruel.[30] Dismissing as idle the suggestion that a king should strive to be loved by his subjects, he insists that a king should fear above all not being feared by his people (5.1.2468). He reiterates his conviction that those who avoid being feared are bound to lose the state because, he believes, hate and power go hand in hand:

> Abbiami in odio pur, pur che mi teman
> Tutti i sudditi miei. Nati ad un parto
> Son, come due fratelli, il regno e l'odio,
> E chi non cerca esser temuto, cerca
> Lasciare il regno tosto e venir servo.
>
> (5.1.2482–86)

[Let my subjects hate me as long as they all fear me. / Like twin brothers, hatred and royal rule / were born at the same birth. / And he who does not wish to be feared, will loose the kingdom and become a slave.]

Clearly, the emphasis here is not so much on the actual use of force, but on the fear that the threat of violence generates in the hearts of friends and foes alike. Rhetoric of force is indeed an effective means of reducing violence in that it earns the prince so fearsome a reputation as to discourage all attempts upon his authority. It is in this context that Machiavelli discusses in detail how Cesare Borgia had Remirro de Orco cut in half and placed in the town square with a wooden stake and a blood-stained knife by the corpse.[31] Sulmone utilizes the rhetorical force of this precept as he shows the limbs of his victims to Orbecche and, inherently, to the stage audience, fulfilling his promise that his punishment would be a spectacle for the world to behold. Such staging of violence effectively projects the power of the king who exhibits both the ability and the determination to destroy those who dare to challenge his rule, including members of his immediate family. A wise show of force keeps the subjects in great awe and fear of the their ruler, just as the fear of thunderbolts reminds humans of God's power. In Sulmone's view

> Un Re dovrebbe esser terribil sempre,
> E lo dimostra chiaro il Re del cielo,
> Il qual, mentre serbar vuol la sua altezza,
> Tien ne la man il fier fulmine ardente.
>
> (5.1.2474–77)[32]

[A king should always appear terrible, / as demonstrated by the King of the heavens / who, wishing to maintain his dignity, / holds in his hand the fierce thunderbolt.]

The association of kingship with the divine evokes the notion of *imitatio dei*, a commonplace in ancient drama and a recurring topic in Renaissance political treatises. In the ongoing debate between

4: THE NATURE OF KINGSHIP

Machiavellian theory and the humanist conception of princeship, the principle was largely inconsequential because, since God could be perceived both as compassionate and fearful, the divine could be used conveniently *utramque partem*. In *Orbecche*, Malecche exhorts Sulmone to be compassionate and forgiving like God; Sulmone, for his part, insists that kings should be fearsome like God. The question was of major interest to Counter-Reformation writers on reason of state theory, who tended to anchor political theory to moral or religious principles. Giovanni Botero, in his seminal treatise *Ragion di stato*, argued that religion is the foundation of kingship and that the power of the ruler proceeds from God.[33] He believed that kings, in addition to being pious and observing of God's law, should possess secular qualities, such as a sense of justice, liberality, valor, wisdom, and other similar virtues. Above all, they should establish a reputation as strong and fearsome rulers through the sporadic but convincing use of violence. In this respect, notes Botero, princes would be just like God who with his display of thunder and lightning instills terror and fear in the hearts of mankind:

> Prudentemente severo fia colui che con poche esecuzioni ed asprezze terrà il popolo in ufficio e si farà tener per terribile, imitando in ciò Dio, il quale con tuonare spesse volte cagiona negli animi degli uomini paura e terrore senza danno; ma acciochè i tuoni non perdano il credito per non far mai colpo, tra mille tuoni saetta qualche volta, e per lo più qualche cima d'albero o giogo di monte. (*Aggiunte*, 2.434)[34]

> [Prudently severe is he who, with few executions and roughness, holds his people in line and in fear of him. In this he imitates God who, by thundering frequently, stirs fear and terror in the hearts of men without actually hurting them. But in order for his thunderbolts not to lose their credit by never striking a target, once in a thousand such thunderbolts He strikes the top of a tree or the peak of a mountain.]

Thus, not only did Botero appreciate, like Machiavelli, the importance of a fearful reputation as a rhetorical means for reducing violence, but also, like Sulmone, he linked a king's behavior to Divine deeds. The idea is significant because it represents not so much the assimilation of Machiavelli, but rather the attempt to anchor Machiavellism in religious morality. Botero and other Counter-Reformation political theorists tried to correct or reject Machiavelli, but they often found themselves at little variance with basic Machiavellian precepts, including the need for the prince to be able and willing to practice dissimulation and violence. This compatibility tends to vindicate Machiavelli's rejection of humanist idealism and upholds, to a great extent, the validity of many of his precepts that deal with what he calls the "verità effettuale della cosa" [actual truth of the thing] or Realpolitik.[35] Sulmone's murders and display of the victims' limbs evoke Machiavelli's story of Remirro de Orco's dismemberment, Botero's "few executions," and God's thunderbolts—all meant to foster the rhetoric of fear that keeps friends and foes from doubting a ruler's power and resolve.

These similarities notwithstanding, Sulmone is not the ideal representative of the emerging concept of princeship. Though appearing to prevail over Malecche's humanist position, his notion of kingship is ultimately rejected, as signified by his violent death. Pointedly, the champion of an ideology grounded in deception and violence is himself victim of deception and violence. He is dismembered in the same way and with the same knife he dismembered his victims. And, like them, he fell victim to deception, as Orbecche, in order to kill him, led him to believe that she had already forgiven him. Ironically, he fell at the hands of the one who, in his mind, was to guarantee the prosperity of the state and the future of the dynasty. These ironies and parallels tend to turn upside down Sulmone's notion of kingship, causing the spectators to dwell on the dynamics that bring about the king's demise and on the ideological implications it articulates.

If the king appears at first to be on the winning side of the issue, as he carries out the punishment according to kingly prerogatives, his victory is a victory of sorts. In the end, he dies victim of a grieving and despondent Orbecche who, with the same dagger used to kill Oronte and the children, severs his head and hands and carries them out of the palace for the stage audience to behold. In the chorus's frantic description of the slaying, the emphasis is mostly on the violence: the furious slashing, the cutting of limbs, the gushing of the blood from the butchered body. This gruesome death stands as poetic justice that points back to Sulmone's own brutality: he died the same savage death he gave others (5.2.2853–64). His end recalls and validates Creon's conviction that "the king who holds his throne with cruel sway / must fear the fearful; on its author's head will fear return" (Seneca, *Oedipus,* 3.1.753–56).

The context of fear in which Creon's wisdom places Sulmone's death must not be taken as an indictment of politically motivated violence, which Machiavelli recognized and Counter-Reformist authors on reason of state doctrine endorsed as a basic tenet of political rhetoric. It is instead a denunciation of Sulmone's own monstrous nature, the unrestrained ethos that he exhibits in the sadistic pleasure with which he killed Oronte and the children. The audience surely took notice that Sulmone, instead of having his sentence carried out by others, as do most kings in Italian Renaissance drama, chose to cut his victims to pieces with his own hands, as if to satisfy the savage craving of a wounded ego. According to the messenger's account of the ghastly scene, he fell on the mangled children like a lion falls on its bloodied prey, laughing at Oronte's wailing (4.1.2270–2300). Such wanton brutality is not the outburst of a man gone temporarily mad, but further evidence of a consistent pattern of a bloodthirsty disposition that other characters experienced and/or denounced. At the beginning of the play, Nemesis refers to him as a "fierce tyrant" who dared to place himself on the same level with the gods (1.1.178), and the ghost of his adulterous wife remembers him as a most cruel husband (1.2.234). Orbecche, in particular, puts in perspective her father's monstrous character by recalling his slaying of his incestuous wife and son, and the subsequent, unwarranted slaughter of many innocent people. Pointedly, she comments that if one could find any justification for any killing, nothing could justify Sulmone's murder of his own brother, a most gentle human being (2.3.760–65). Given this violent temperament, it is not surprising that the tyrant's dying wish be yet another "vendetta," this time against Orbecche as she frantically slashes at his helpless body. It is also a fitting paradox that the last word of so cruel a man be a pusillanimous cry for help and mercy: "Oimè, pietade!" (5.2.2835–43). Cruelty, vindictiveness, and cowardice are all qualities repugnant to civilized standards of human behavior and make Sulmone abominable in the eyes of both the stage audience and the spectators who, perhaps unwittingly, are gratified by his gruesome death.

It would reduce the play's ideological stance if we were to dismiss Sulmone's violent death as yet another example of Senecan revenge, whereby characters quench their thirst for personal justice by delighting in the suffering of their victims. Far from the calculating and sadistic planning of classical avengers such as a Medea or Atreus, Orbecche's revenge is the spontaneous, irrational reaction resulting from unbearable grief. Her agony is so overwhelming that, unable to bear it, she stabs herself there and then with the same dagger that killed her children, her husband, and her father. Sulmone's death, instead, must be seen in the context of his savagery, which goes beyond any ideological justification and needs, therefore, to be contained. The first to condemn his cruelty are the chorus and semichorus, who call his death a just and deserving retribution willed by divine justice. Reacting to the messenger's description of the king's butchery, the chorus inveighs against the "impious" tyrant and warns that he shall not escape the certainty of God's immense justice (4.1.2430–39). Not long after this ineluctable foreboding, Sulmone meets his grim fate. The semichorus, watching Orbecche slaying her father, judges the killing righteous and suggests that God could not have been more pleased by the death of so evil a tyrant: "a Dio non s'offre vittima più grata / D'un malvagio Tiran com'era questo" [one does not offer God a more guilty victim / than an evil tyrant as was this one] (5.2.2867–68).[36] In this condemnation, one must see the rejection of unrestrained kingship and the predisposition toward a political ideology moored to moral and religious values.

Sulmone's demise, just like Alboino's death, Eolo's denunciation of the cruelty of kingship, and Herod's repudiation of his royal actions, represents not so much an indictment of a ruler's determination to preserve the state, but the censure of a behavior loosened from all moral principles. The political orientation of *Orbecche* points to an ideology that embraces the pragmatic appeal of Machiavellian realism while it recognizes the need to anchor princely behavior to ethical canons. This is not a vindication of the humanist idea of princeship, for, as we noted above, Machiavelli clearly showed its inadequacy against the historical realities of the time. It is instead an attempt by Counter-Reformation writers to assimilate Machiavelli and fasten his flexible notion of *virtù* to prevailing principles of religious morality. After all, as Botero argued, religion was the "foundation of the state," royal power proceeded from God, and kings were ultimately accountable to God's justice. This emphasis on religion is by no means a repudiation of the traditional notion of kings and royal prerogatives, for they are still considered *legibus soluti* in their dutiful endeavors to "maintain" the state. Most reason of state authors agreed that when necessitated by reason of state princes may employ not-so-honorable means such as force and fraud, provided that the nature and extent of their actions do not offend society's moral and religious values.

What is significant in this notion of kingship is that it reconciles relevant aspects of humanist idealism with key precepts of Machiavellian realism, and anchors them to religious morality. The ethos arising from such a combination tends to subject kings and their actions to divine laws, to human judgment, and to the vicissitudes of life. Accordingly, rulers are reminded that, like all other humans, they are subject to God's justice as well as to the whimsical doing of Fortune. The rich and powerful in particular, Malecche warns Sulmone, must be mindful of the instability of Fortune, which doles out favors in such a way that "oggi sono / D'uno e diman d'un altro" [today they are enjoyed / by one individual, and tomorrow by another] (3.2.1355). This sense of instability is perhaps best expressed in *Rosmunda*, where the chorus comments that heaven may cause rulers to lose or regain their kingdoms "in men 'dun ora" [in less than an hour] (145–48).[37] This sense of vulnerability undermines the traditional notion of godlike kings, as it underscores the precarious nature of their human condition: they, too, must fear the ups and downs of life and the ineluctable retribution of divine justice. In the absence of these restraints, rulers run the risk of going astray and, like Sulmone, ruin both themselves and the state. In this sense, the violence-ridden world of the stage emerges as an exemplum of a calamitous notion of kingship, whereby unbridled despots wantonly bring suffering upon the community. Inherently, it suggests that the political stability of a state depends largely on the cultural and religious ethos which determines the ruler's actions and motives. In the words of *Merope*'s nurse, without the rule of just princes cities and kingdoms are "inutili cadaveri, e vili ombre" [useless cadavers and vile shadows] (1960–65).

Theater as Rhetoric of Power

Stage representation of kings perpetrating violence undoubtedly had a strong cathartic effect on the spectators. On the one hand, they were frightened by the vivid reminder that they themselves could be ruled by equally fierce despots; on the other, they rejoiced in their good fortune to live under a benevolent lord. It was not uncommon for spectators to receive assurances that they were watching atrocities perpetrated long ago and far away from the safety of their seats. In *Orbecche*, Prologue tells the audience that the horrible events of the stage take place not in peaceful and prosperous Ferrara, which is governed by a most wise signor, but in a distant land, once happy and now cast into misery and despair.[38] The distinction between the "here and now" of the auditorium and the "there and then" of the stage allows the audience to see the theatrical experience as a contrast between the possible world of the play and the real world of the audience: the first, violent and threatening; the second, peaceful and safe. And so, the experience takes on the form of a realistic and meaningful event as it moves from the fearful reminder of how terrible life could be under an ungodly tyrant, such as Sulmone, to the comforting awareness of being governed by a most magnanimous lord, such as Duke Ercole. Spectators know that if they live safely in such a great city as Ferrara, it is

> Mercé de la giustizia e del valore,
> Del consiglio matur, de la prudenza
> Del suo Signor.

[Thanks to the justice, the valor, / the mature wisdom, and the prudence / of its Lord.]

The message is both one of relief and foreboding, for, while reassuring the spectators in their present fortune, it carries the veiled threat that the fearful world of the stage could conceivably become their real world should they forget that they owe their good fortune to the ruling prince. The barely suggested yet unmistakable specter of tyrannical rule tends to awaken in them a sense of gratitude toward their benevolent lord and urges them to renew their oaths of loyalty to him. This in turn legitimizes and further solidifies the lord's power. It is reasonable to assume that the spectators appreciated the intimidation inherent in the theatrical metaphor, for cinquecento audiences were all too familiar with the rhetoric of fear that often informed state celebrations or the traditional staging of moral or religious allegories. Suffice it to recall that the representation of "evil" as a means of orienting one's attention toward "good" had long been the basic function of *sacre rappresentazioni*. By dramatizing the devil's deeds and the horrors of hell, sacred plays had for centuries scared audiences into stricter compliance with religious norms and into a more pious, submissive behavior. One might say that the sacred theater was to religion what the secular stage was to political power: a rhetoric of intimidation meant to remind all subjects of the prince's political power and resolve.

The function of theater as a rhetoric of political power is especially apparent when one considers the cultural and political context in which dramatic plays were written and performed. Students of theater have noted the control that sovereigns, as both sponsors and censors, exercised over the written text and its production. As we saw in the first chapter, some have argued rather tenuously that most dramatists, being aristocrats, academicians, courtiers, or otherwise dependent on the court for their livelihood, had vested interests in promoting the political system under which they wrote and prospered. Equally tenuous is the argument that, since the works were often commissioned by and/or dedicated to a prince or a member of the nobility, authors tended to reflect their patrons' ideology. In reality, playwrights did, at times, take the opportunity to praise their worthy sponsors in the dedicatory letter and/or in the prologue; however, it can hardly be said that the dramatic text itself was a celebration of power.

The political instrumentation of drama was usually confined to the extratextual activities that marked the performance, namely, daylong festivities, decorum, pageantry, selection of guests, seating arrangements, and other pertinent activities. The event provided amusement for the audience and the opportunity to celebrate the sponsor's power and wealth. Normally the ruler would make his long-awaited entrance accompanied by important guests. He would then take his seat on a raised platform at the center of the hall, or center stage, as it were, holding the attention and the admiration of the spectators, who were seated around the lordly dais according to their rank. It was easy for them to watch the play and behold, at the same time, the prince and his entourage, who offered themselves "come spettacolo"[39] It helps to picture the performance as having two stages: a virtual stage (the platform) occupied by the prince of the "good" and real world, and the actual stage dominated by the threatening world of the representation. Shifting their attention from the stage to the platform, spectators would inevitably note the prince's reaction to the performance, which would influence their own response. Paraphrasing what Stephen Orgel says of Queen Elizabeth's presence at a theatrical performance, we may say that cinquecento spectators watched both the play and the prince at the play. Their response was not just to the drama, but to the relationship between the stage and its primary audience, their lord.[40]

As noted earlier, plays were performed for the benefit of select and invited spectators who were, ipso facto, members of the ruling class. The invitation to attend a performance was for them an honor and a formal recognition of their noble status. In turn, their presence was a show of loyalty that confirmed the host in his prestige. In the process, they all became participants in the exercise of power. The festivity, then, provided the opportunity for ruled and rulers to convene in the celebration of the traditions that sanctioned their social and political status. Through the display of power and munificence, the prince seemed to say to *his* audience that the elegance, the amusement, and the honor bestowed upon them was all his doing, and that their privilege was bound inextricably to the political fortunes of his rule: they would rise with his prosperity or fall with his demise. In support of this phenomenon, Attolini cites Paruta, who in his *Della perfettione della vita politica* (1579) writes that spectacles and public celebrations tend to awaken a desire for glory in the hearts of the people and ultimately involve them in the preservation of customs and symbols that celebrate political power.[41]

From this perspective, then, the spectators' theatrical experience grew out of both the play's ideological debate and the pageantry that accompanied the performance: the first was the intent of the playwrights, the latter was the wish of the prince. Unquestionably, theater was an effective instrument of political power that rulers used to affirm their legitimacy and influence. However, as we saw, its rhetorical purpose was intrinsic to the pomp characterizing the performance, not to the written text. Playwrights regarded their work as literary accomplishments rather than a means of propaganda celebrating the existing political order, as some critics have suggested. They were primarily interested in artistic achievement, while dramatizing significant cultural realities of their times, such as the ideological debate on the nature of kingship.

5
Tragic Heroines: The Debate on the Emerging Question of Women

VICTIMS OF TRAGEDY GENERALLY FALL INTO ONE OF TWO MAJOR categories: those who fall because of their unwitting errors (Oedipus, Othello), and those who refuse to accept a life inconsistent with their ideals (Antigone, Andromaque). Most heroes of the Italian tragedy in the Renaissance belong to the second category, since they choose to die rather than live under demeaning conditions. In many a tragedy, action typically arises from the tension between the wishes of those in power, often the king, and the individual's refusal to abide by such wishes: Sofonisba refuses to be taken to Rome by the victorious Romans, Rosmunda defies Alboino's orders and buries her father, Orbecche rejects her father's wishes to marry Selino and to live in the world of man's brutal power and politics. Though the victims' refusal does not take the form of an epic deed, the choice to commit suicide rather than compromise the integrity of their principles elevates them to tragic stature. Protagonists who are simply executed without a struggle also rise to heroic dimension by virtue of the inner strength and the *fortitudo* with which they face death. In death they all rise above their oppressors and, at the same time, enhance the righteousness of their beliefs.

It is interesting that these victims are usually women and that, with the exception of Tasso's *Torrismondo*, most original Renaissance dramas feature the heroine's name as their titles: *Sofonisba, Rosmunda, Tullia, Orbecche, Orazia, Canace, Marianna, Adriana, Merope, Acripanda.*[1] Such exclusive emphasis on women as tragic heroines is unusual for a genre that traditionally included men as well as women in the roles of dramatic figures, from Oedipus to Antigone, from Agamemnon to Electra, from Thyestes to Phædra. The choice to dramatize situations dealing with passions or ideals peculiar to either male or female characters may reveal a playwright's personal preference and ideology. However, when the whole genre seems to concentrate on one gender, then it tends to call attention to a specific cultural dilemma that is of great concern to the playwright and, by extension, to the society that the theatrical audience represents. It is a common feature of tragedy to dramatize cultural crises, especially between humans or between certain groups of humans and the social or cosmic world.[2] From this perspective, then, the stage represents the forum from which tragedy "speaks to audiences about themselves and their problems."[3] In the case of the Italian tragedy in the Renaissance, it calls attention to the quarrel between men and women, one of the most divisive and widely debated issues in Renaissance society. Joseph Kennard points out that the dispute was "a vital question in the literature of the time," and goes on to credit Giraldi for having brought it "on to the tragic stage."[4] Giraldi was indeed an outspoken critic of woman's low status in society and his views on the subject surfaced in most of his plays, making the issue a relevant theme of the dramatic stage. However, in all fairness, earlier playwrights, such as Trissino and Rucellai, had already called attention to the question of womankind.

The dispute is most apparent in the paradox of representing women as both victims and heroines. Victims, to be sure, not of their own errors, but of a patriarchal society that treats them as inferior and subservient beings. In tragedy, the role of the patriarch is commonly associated with those in power, normally a king who, usually for reasons of state, demands that his queen or his daughter live or behave according to his wishes. Tragedy starts as these women, expected to be submissive, weak, and intellectually limited, refuse a world that denies them the ability to think and hence the dignity to live in freedom. The behavior articulating this refusal represents a serious threat to the stability of the social order that, in turn, moves to crush them swiftly and inexorably. The noble cause of their death, the courage, the resolve, and the equanimity with which they endure their fate are all heroic virtues that challenge the traditional view of woman as inferior to man and as subservient to his needs and sociopolitical interests. The audience, then, is given to witness a dramatization of the debate between the traditional and the evolving notion of womankind. One should not expect the outcome to resolve the issue. First because it will be partial to the playwright's ideological preference, and second because it will not satisfy all points of view, as often happens in major cultural debates. However, it will have the desired effect of bringing the question to the fore and dramatically reminding the spectators of the need to address the problem. Thus, the dramatic stage emerges not merely as a mirror of reality, but as an active instrument of culture forcing a dialogue on the true human worth of woman and on her rightful place in society.

The Traditional Notion of Womanhood

A full appreciation of the debate and of the dramatic situation facing the female tragic figure must perforce take into account the misogynist tradition in which it is deeply imbedded. The Middle Ages inherited and embraced the ancient view that women were mentally, morally, and physically inferior to men. Medieval *florilegia* listing women's bad qualities and denigrating anecdotes, as well as literary writings such as Boccaccio's *Corbaccio*, inevitably found their way into later literature. Common sources of misogyny were Galen's speculations on the physical and physiological peculiarities of women, Roman laws excluding women from public office and denying them equality under the law, and patristic literature that, recalling Eve's sin, perpetuated the view of woman as the source of evil.[5] Female inferiority was particularly institutionalized in the family, which assigned them a largely servile role: obedience and dedication to the husband, childbearing, and housekeeping chores. These are the three qualities that make a good wife, wrote Francesco Barbaro, echoing the prevailing notion of woman.[6] As women could perform such a restrictive and subservient role without much need for education, their learning was generally limited to the reading of the Bible and the exemplary lives of saints.

The conventional view of woman as morally and intellectually inferior did not go unchallenged either in literature or in real life. The *Decameron* features numerous female characters who denounce the unfairness of the laws and the social customs by which they are required to live. Suffice it to recall the story of Madonna Filippa who, charged with adultery, reminds the judge that the law against adulterous women is unjust because it was enacted without the consent of those [women] who are supposed to obey it.[7] The legal suit that Lusanna brought against Giovanni Della Casa in Florence (1455), insisting on the legality of their marriage, is one example of a woman's courageous attempt to challenge the system and, in the words of Eugene Brucker, its "elaborate mechanisms designed to control and discipline members of her sex and class."[8] Treatises in praise of women, although written in many cases to please female patrons, contributed to keep the issue in the cultural foreground.[9] A considerable impetus to a serious reconceptualization of womankind came from the humanists who, dwelling on the human condition and on the *intelligere* ability of mankind, placed woman on the same spiritual and intellectual level as man. Savonarola, echoing St. Paul's view that all humans "are all one in Christ Jesus" (Galatians 3:28), preached that before God "non est masculus neque foemina" [there is no distinction between man and woman].[10] And Agnolo Firenzuola, in his treatise on women's beauty, argued that if humanity were divided into two equal parts (men and women), one part would be "tanto buona quanto l'altra, tanto bella quanto l'altra" [as good as the other, as beautiful as the other].[11] Speaking of this growing reaction against the traditional view of women, Silvia Ruffo-Fiore, notes that "many Renaissance humanists began to defend women and to assert their essential goodness and intellectual acumen as comparable and even exceeding at times that of men. Thus they advocated their equal right to education in negation of the medieval principle of *mulier taceat in ecclesia*."[12]

As the underpinnings of the traditional notion of woman were coming under attack, a cultural debate began to grow, especially when the defenders of woman could counter the speculative arguments of her detractors with concrete examples of scores of real women who had demonstrated unusual abilities both in public and in private life. If Catherine of Siena, Joan of Arc, and Christine de Pisan were lonely stars in the past, there were many other women in prominent social and political positions who were living legends in their own time. The deeds and reputation of well-known women such as Isabella d'Este, Barbara of Branderburg, and Caterina Sforza left no doubt as to women's ability to govern, to maneuver in the crafty arena of politics, and to appreciate the fine arts. In the literary field, women poets such as Veronica Franco, Gaspara Stampa, Vittoria Colonna, and Veronica Gambara earned the respect and the admiration of renowned male counterparts. Ariosto, praising the many virtues of Isabella d'Este, says that "her intellect shines in the light of day and in the darkness of night."[13] It was perhaps the high regard enjoyed by these and other well-known women that led Jacob Burckhardt to assume that "women stood on a footing of perfect equality with men" and to warn against the "sophistical and often malicious talk about the assumed inferiority of the female sex."[14]

It is none too surprising that if the public recognition and appreciation of female excellence emboldened the defenders of woman, it also caused both secular and religious misogynists to dig in their heels to attack. The Church, especially the Church of the Counter-Reformation, reiterated its unyielding position by defining woman in terms of the traditional feminine virtues of chastity, piety, dedication to the family, and by referring in its reformed liturgical texts to the *infirmitas, imbecillitas,* and *humilitas* of the female sex.[15]

Modern feminists writers, such as Gaia Servadio, believe that the Church of the Counter-Reformation revived the Medieval view of woman as symbol of sin.[16] But dominant as the Church was in the cultural life of Renaissance Italy, it could not silence the debate that by now had become a battle between the sexes. Treatises, letters, sonnets, speeches, and pamphlets openly praising or vilifying women kept the dispute in the cultural forefront of the times. Views on either side of the issue were also expressed within the context of larger works, such as narrative poems, short stories, and comedies.[17] Even the visual arts expressed symptoms of the controversy, as some artists continued to portray woman in her traditional role, while others depicted her in new and significant functions. Andrea del Sarto, for example, portrayed Mary Magdalene, a woman, disputing with the Doctors of the Church. Michelangelo rejected the moral inferiority of the female sex by having Adam, not Eve, as was the convention, pick the prohibited fruit of knowledge. He also, defied the ecclesiastical aversion against female priests by portraying women as celebrants at the altar.[18] The polarization of the two extremes of the debate may best be observed, on the one hand, in Ariosto's praise of women for having excelled in whatever art they showed interest, and, on the other, in a sign at the entrance of a public park near Pesaro which read: "Ad oche, a donne, a capre questo giardin non s'apre" [this garden is not open to ducks, women, and goats].[19]

The Stage View of Women

One of the most significant forums for the debate on women was undoubtedly the dramatic stage on which playwrights portrayed woman's efforts to assert her independence from traditional male dominance and from the cultural prejudices that for centuries vilified the female sex. Tragedy is truly an effective vehicle for dramatizing ideas and attitudes because it tends to involve the audience through live voices, shocking deeds, and stirring human emotions. Surely, Italian Renaissance tragedy is not just about the battle of the sexes or the "querelle de femmes," though it contains catastrophes arising from unbridled passions of the types for which tradition tended to blame women as the source.[20] It specifically represents aspirations and ideals that the characters, through their words and deeds, humanize and cast in the context of the living culture. The life that theater brings to the dispute about women is noticeably observed, albeit from a male

Michelangelo Buonarroti. *The Sacrifice of Noah*. Sistine Chapel, Vatican City. (Foto Alinari/Art Resource, NY)

point of view, in the complaints that female characters commonly voice about their condition and the cultural prejudices that malign them. The most common grievance is that women are more wretched and less free than any "other animal on earth" and are despised by all, including their own fathers. Orbecche and Dolce's Medea, among others, curse their own gender as the source of their suffering. Orbecche specifically laments that nothing makes her more unhappy "che l'esser donna" [than my being a woman].[21] Admittedly, this dispiriting view calls to mind Euripides' Medea who also sees women as the most unfortunate creatures required "to buy a husband and take for our bodies / A master" (*Medea*, 231–34). But, the fact that the complaint is rooted in ancient tradition should not lead one to view Orbecche's dejection as a trite literary commonplace void of genuine grief. To the contrary, the longstanding tradition lends validity to the heroine's regret, as it tends to underscore the universality of woman's affliction. The Italian Medea distinctly reflects contemporary thinking when she refers to husbands as woman's own curse, in that they have absolute power over her life and treat her not with love but with harshness and cruelty.[22]

This bleak view is not unique to a love-scorned woman such as Medea, who is fatally bent upon vengeance and destruction. Several other heroines voice similar complaints, especially about the

Michelangelo Buonarroti. *The Original Sin: Adam and Eve picking the fruit of knowledge.* Sistine Chapel, Vatican City. (Foto Alinari/Art Resource, NY)

oppressive male power that denies them the right and the capability to think and act freely. In Orbecche's opinion, women, unlike every other animal on earth, are not free, and are severely punished if they attempt to act of their own free will (2.916–21). Faced with her father's decision to force her into a political marriage, she recalls, as does Dolce's Medea, the Euripidean topos of "buying" husbands with silver and gold, and censures the current custom of preferring a gold-laden husband over a husband of gold (2.872–73).[23] She speaks for most of her dramatic counterparts when she complains that

> Com'a perpetuo carcere dannate,
> Sotto l'arbitrio altrui sempre viviamo
> Con continovo timor, né pur ne lece
> Volger un occhio in parte ove non voglia
> Chi di noi cura tiene.
>
> (2.900–904)[24]

[As if born in an eternal prison, / we live always under male control and / in constant fear. Nor are we permitted / to direct our stare at something or someone without the consent of / those who control us.]

Raphael. *Original Sin*, **detail of vault. Stanze di Raffaello, Vatican City. (Photo Vanni/Art Resource, NY)**

Orbecche's dismal portrait of woman's condition, far from being a self-pitying observation, evokes reality as contemporary audiences knew it and were about to be vividly reminded of it by the tragic

Andrea del Sarto. *Dispute over the Trinity.* **Galleria Palatina, Palazzo Pitti, Florence. (Foto Alinari/Art Resource, NY)**

death of the poetess Isabella Morra in 1546. Her brothers, having discovered her (platonic?) relationship with the poet Diego Sandoval De Castro, killed her, her teacher (the go-between), and eventually Sandoval himself.[25] Orbecche's view echoes also the general attitude of the period as reflected in treatises on female virtues and housewifery that recommended, among other things, that a wife follow her husband like a shadow and that, like a mirror, smile when he smiles and appear sad when he is sad.[26]

This notion of woman as brainless and infantile is expressed on stage also by male characters even as they attempt to come to her defense. Arguing in favor of a female character, they often suggest that transgressions by the weaker sex are not to be taken seriously, since women lack the wisdom to act sensibly. For instance, Falisco dissuades the victorious Alboino from punishing Rosmunda who, in a deed reminiscent of Sophocles' Antigone, has violated the royal degree prohibiting the burial of her father, the defeated King Comundo. Falisco, echoing Aeneas's view that there is no glory in killing a woman, advises the king against punishing Rosmunda. After all, he argues, "le donne son donne" [women are women] (466).[27] Dolce's Jason shares this patronizing attitude toward the weak sex as he, in accepting Medea's apologies for being angry at him after he abandoned her, readily forgives her because "essendo donna, sei di scusa degna" [being a woman, you are to be excused] (p. 23).

The picture of woman ruled by passions and vagaries and, therefore, incapable of sound judgment, is also colored by her alleged cruelty and deceitfulness. Rucellai's Toante, having been deceived by Ifigenia, inveighs against all women: "Ah! deceitful and false female sex, / You conceal evil thoughts with your beautiful words!" (*Oreste*, 5.297–98). Giraldi's Octavius, having been deluded by Cleopatra who kills herself instead of going to Rome with him as she had promised, calls women nest of deception (*Cleopatra*, 5.6.2901). For Lamanno women are infernal furies (*Altile*, 5.4.3090). And the chorus in *Orbecche*, shocked by the ferocity of the heroine's bloody attack upon her father, can hardly believe that there could be so much violence in a human being, "especially in a woman" (5.2.2846). The same disbelief was voiced by contemporary critics, who accused Giraldi of misrepresenting woman's compassionate and delicate nature. Recalling Alberti's and Castiglione's views of woman, they argued that women, unlike men, do not possess warrior-like qualities, but passions, piety, and domestic sweetness. This was indeed the image of woman that Renaissance Italy had and preferred to have, and any departure from it represented an assault on the idealization of woman as well as on her practical, auxiliary role in man's human, social, and political activities.[28]

Perhaps the most obvious stance against womankind is exhibited in Speroni's *Canace*, where a servant enumerates the bad qualities of "femminil natura," as if he were reading from a medieval *florilegium*. With reference to Canace's secret pregnancy, the servant declares woman "meno intera" (incomplete) and endowed with a feeble mind that causes her to fall into errors much more readily then men. He believes that they are fickle, artful in hiding their propensity to sin, and oblivious to the consequences of their whimsical actions (1075–95). The misogynist atmosphere informing the play is particularly evident in King Eolo's decision to put to death Canace for her incestuous relationship with her own brother. The fateful decree also applies to the nurse for having conspired to conceal the crime. The order is blatantly prejudicial, for, while prescribing the immediate execution of the two women, it merely threatens to punish the equally incestuous son, who, though forgiven, ultimately chooses to kill himself. Also, while the king eventually acknowledges his error and barely mourns the death of his daughter, he is overwhelmed with grief by the news of his son's death and breaks down in a long, inconsolable lament: "Son, where are you? Who took you away from me?" (1971). Eolo's grief, arising more from the loss of his son than that of his daughter, though conceivably the expression of closer emotional ties with the young man, is undoubtedly the manifestation of a cultural bias in favor of the male born. Alberti's Giannozzo reminds us of this cultural prejudice as he prays God for a marriage full of happiness, harmony, moral integrity, and the proverbial "molti figliuoli maschi" [many male heirs].[29]

The high value that patriarchal society places on offspring, especially male heirs, has a bearing on the importance of woman as a childbearer. Though many scorned the idea of marriage because they could not suffer the inconveniences of having a wife, they acknowledged with reluctance the importance of her procreative ability. If one could have a family without having to take a wife, wished in vain Pietro Lauro, it would be better living without one.[30] Procreation was the most common means for man to consign to posterity his worthy accomplishments and to guarantee the stability of the existing sociopolitical order: male heirs would continue to uphold the laws and honor the institutions upon which stood patriarchal rule. Orbecche recalls that Sulmone had placed in her womanhood his hopes for the survival of the kingdom and the dynasty. The king was in fact very happy when he believed, rather naively, that his daughter was ready to consent to a political marriage, whence a princely male offspring would carry in perpetuity the name of the royal family (1.441; 5.2822–23). Groto's Orontea makes an equally telling statement when she counsels Adriana to accept the prearranged marriage so that there may be an heir to the throne. The queen hopes that her daughter's children will some day take revenge upon their enemy, thus vindicating the integrity of the kingdom and the honor of the dynasty. When Adriana, pondering her mother's advice, wonders if the weight of the war has come to rest all on her shoulders, her mother quickly adds that she is indeed "the state's only hope" (3.1.165).

Female reproductive power was not just a means to the political ends of the patriarchal family or the state, it was also woman's potential threat to established authority. Rosmunda makes this point as she begs Falisco not to deliver her father's skull to the bloodthirsty Alboino, arguing that the dead cannot bring harm to the living. She offers her own head, instead; for, although a woman, she is the real threat. In a warning reminiscent of Caterina Sforza's reply to the conspirators who threatened to kill her children,[31] Rosmunda reminds Falisco that from her womb could soon be born those who would avenge Comundo's death:

> Benché femmina sia: da questo ventre
> In brevissimo tempo nascer ponno
> Molti vendicator del sangue nostro.
>
> (295–97)

[Although I am a woman, from this womb / in a short time can issue / many avengers of our blood.]

The same concept is echoed in Martelli's *Tullia*, where the chorus dissuades a despondent Tullia from committing suicide on the grounds that her death would only please the enemy. She must live, the chorus tells her, for, although a woman, widowed and alone (they were unaware that her husband was still alive), she has the capacity to give birth to many who could exact just revenge upon her enemies (p. 88). The menace resonates loud and real in the minds of those who have reason to fear for their personal safety as well as for the stability of the order that empowers them. It is out of this fear that Sulmone murders Orbecche's children, that Eolo prescribes the death of Canace's infant, and that Marianna's Herod orders the execution of his own children. Fearing that with the passing of time the children's hostility toward him would become more open and daring, Herod decrees their immediate death, thus removing the threat both to the safety of his person and to the integrity of the throne (4.2673–82).

Woman's awareness of her ability to threaten a male-dominated order represents an assertion of her self-worth and of her potential to influence a world that persists in restricting her role to servile functions. But this capability, though acknowledged and appreciated both in the fictional realm of tragedy and in the real world of the audience, does not enhance appreciably the status of woman, since it points only to her "animal" function, her childbearing. Most heroines know that in order to achieve full human dignity they must impugn the misogynist contention that women are intellectually limited, and thus incapable of exercising responsibly the freedom to think and to determine the course of their own lives. Hence, *Rosmunda*'s female chorus claims intellectual virtue on the grounds that all humans were created in God's image and endowed with "alta mente" [high intelligence] (333–34). And Adriana, while conceding to her menacing father that he may well mutilate her body and take the life which he gave her, declares that no physical force can shake "la mente invisibile, immortale" [the invisible and immortal mind] (3.2.53). Giraldi's Cleopatra, too, calls attention to her acumen, as she scoffs at the traditional belittlement of female intelligence. She proudly points out that Octavius underestimated her perceptive ability by assuming that she, being a woman and thus "priva d'ingegno" [devoid of intelligence], could not see the deception behind his empty promises. But, whereas he failed to deceive a woman, she retorts proudly, a woman shall now outwit him:

> Ma se saputo non hai tu ingannare
> Una donna . . .
> Vedrai tu, ch'una donna avrà saputo . . .
> Ingannare te . . .
>
> (5.2)

[But if you did not know how to deceive / a woman . . . / You shall know how a woman succeeded . . . / In deceiving you . . .]

And "La Tragedia a chi legge," appended to *Orbecche*, addressing the criticism that Giraldi misrepresented the conventional notion of woman by endowing the female characters of his tragedies with too much wisdom, points out that women are as intellectually capable as men: "come l'uomo la donna" [like man like woman] (3213).

But mere claims of intelligence were bound to have little impact on a culture whose institutions had grown so accustomed to the notion of female intellectual inferiority that systematically excluded women from the decision making process. While most women accepted with resignation their traditional role, the better educated and the more daring denounced institutionalized misogyny, exposing by words and/or deeds the fallacy of its assumptions. Those of authentic awareness and strong character, such as the ideal women of the tragic stage, refused to renounce their human dignity, insisting on the right to be free to choose and to influence the course of their own lives. They are not the female warriors of Ariosto and Tasso, for they do not claim superior physical strength or blinding beauty in their endeavors to assert their self-worth. To the contrary, they concede physical inferiority and other peculiarities of the female sex, but stand firm on their claim to intellectual ability and to the right to make their own choices. They may be feeble, fearful, light-minded, delicate, frivolous, and however else tradition has chosen to portray them,[32] but they are not so weak as to lack the *fortitudo* to refuse to live by the will of others and in conditions of servitude. Thus, Rosmunda exhorts her ladies-in-waiting that although they are "weak and timorous women" they should be ready to die at the hands of the enemy (186). And Dolce's Polissena tells Ulysses not to hesitate to kill her; for, although she is a woman, and thus considered timid, carefree, and "with a zest for life," she is not afraid to die (*Hecuba*, p. 20). Marianna, noting that it is not at all commendable to go on living in shame, praises Cleopatra for having embraced death rather than live captive in Rome (1.371, 666). Adriana, after lamenting her despairing condition, invites other women (those same women who at the end of the play see themselves as "imbecilli e stanche" [feeble of mind and body]) to refuse to live in a world of harsh fathers, uncaring mothers, unfaithful lovers, prideful husbands, unjust rulers, and men—the mortal enemies of women (3.3.11–27).

The choice to die is not a cowardly act revealing one's inability to endure the adversities of life, but the ultimate sacrifice of those who refuse to abdicate their human dignity and live in abject servitude. Thus, Sofonisba's decision to commit suicide is not the despairing act of a forlorn lover, as has been suggested,[33] but the triumph of an individual's will to remain free or, as she puts it, "fuggir la servitude" [to escape servitude] (1804). And Adriana, in response to her father's ultimatum to either accept the yoke of marriage or fall to the fatal blow of his sword, offers her neck rather than take the husband he has chosen for her (3.2.46). The list of women who preferred to die rather than live according to others' wishes or under conditions irreconcilable with their ideals is long and dates back to the heroines of myth and legends. Lest we believe that the stage is merely dramatizing legends from the distant past, we need only think of the exemplary courage and the ultimate sacrifice of real women, such as Joan of Arc, Anneken Jans, Elisabeth Dirks, and other female personages of that historical period. Notable is the courage of Princess Evdokia's ladies-in-waiting. Having encouraged her husband Prince Vladimir of Starista to drink the poison as ordered by Ivan the Terrible, the princess and her daughter chose to die with him by the same poison. When the ladies were shown the corpses and threatened with the same fate unless they begged for the tsar's mercy, they refused. They defiantly told Ivan that they preferred to die and "be with God in Heaven, cursing you until the Day of Judgment, rather than remain under your tyrannical rule."[34] They were promptly given to the dogs and their bodies were left for the birds and wild animals to feast on.

It is this rejection of life, a rejection grounded on the unambiguous awareness of moral superiority, that ennobles and elevates a character to tragic stature. True tragedy happens as individuals of indomitable spirit resolve to engage in a mortal conflict with the forces (social, political, cultural, religious) that repress the liberation of the human spirit from earthly restraints. The tragedy of the protagonists of Renaissance drama lies not so much in the discovery or loss of happiness, as in many of their ancient and modern counterparts, but in the lopsided clash between their resolve to live with human dignity and the might of a misogynist culture equally determined to repress it.

Naturally, this notion of tragedy excludes those who, shying away from conflict, invoke death as a refuge from all human misery. Tragedy is also absent in protagonists such as Rosmunda who, like Racine's Andromaque, desists from her initial refusal to live under conditions she despises, thus compromising the tragic moment.[35] By consenting to marry Alboino in order to kill him, Rosmunda turns her moral cause into material gain, thus reducing her story to a dramatic predicament cast in violence and murder. She rises to tragic heights only in her initial resolve to die rather than submit to the rule of her mortal enemy. However, she ceases to be a tragic figure the moment she accepts the nurse's pragmatic advice and devious suggestion that being married to the king will enable her to protect her people and take her revenge upon the bloodthirsty Alboino. At best, she is a Machiavellian virtuoso capable of seizing the moment and adapting to changing circumstances. One should caution that, although the implication here is that dying would have elevated Rosmunda to tragic stature, death in itself does not a tragedy make. Tragedy lies in the unwavering rejection of a world that is fundamentally incompatible with one's own values and ideals. The refusal inevitably dooms the characters who ultimately emerge as tragic figures, rising above those same forces that destroyed them.

Dying in order to remain free is not as paradoxical as it may seem, for it is inherent in the supreme sacrifice of martyrs and patriots who die for their beliefs and ideals. Giraldi's Cleopatra, expressly wishing to emulate Sofonisba, who preferred to die rather than live prisoner in Rome, chooses death as the best means of attaining freedom. She believes that by dying more honorably than she lived, "meglio procurar la libertade / Saprò con la mia morte" [I will more readily obtain freedom / with my death] (5.2.2725–40). Dolce's Marianna invokes this noble decision as an inspiring deed, and acclaims the Egyptian queen as magnanimous of thought and deed or in her own words, "generosa reina" (1.369).[36] Death as an honorable medium of achieving freedom surely reminded contemporary audiences of Cato of Utica, who took his own life rather than surrender his "precious" liberty to Caesar's dictatorial rule. Dante elevated him to eternal fame as the one who thought that death "for freedom was not bitter."[37] Of course, freedom through death must be taken as the vindication of the uncorrupted will, which the living elevate to a paragon of honorable and righteous behavior. Giannozzo Manetti makes this case by pointing out that in committing suicide both Socrates and Cato were sustained by hopes of immortality.[38]

Tragic victims thus know that whether by execution or by their own hand their sacrifice is not only an heroic alternative to tyranny, but also a means of achieving lasting fame. Sofonisba is fully aware that her suicide will win her wide renown, for she believes that one should strive either for an honorable life or for an honorable death (1789–90). Similarly, Medea argues that a woman should seek "onorata morte" rather than live in shame (p. 8). And Acripanda believes that "bel morire" or dying well happens when one exits this life and begins to live after death (2.1, p. 75). In many tragedies, this aspiration to high honors is fulfilled almost immediately after death, as heroines are given state funerals and are memorialized through magnificent burial chambers or other monuments. Herod, for example, ordered that Marianna's corpse be embalmed with the best essences, lest time decompose it, and be placed in the sepulchers of the ancient kings (5.3275–80). In the case of Aretino's Celia, a divine voice (ex machina) prescribed that the girl be buried in a stately tomb of beautiful and colorful stones. In addition, the people of Rome decreed that the state sponsor a yearly commemoration of her death (*Orazia* 5. 2614–19, 2789–92). Less typically, tribute was sought in literature, wherein heroines may live through the ages, always in memoriam of the bravery with which they vindicated their convictions. Aretino's Nutrice believes that Celia's epigraph will be written in "indelible ink" so that posterity will always remember and tell her story (3.1739–43). And in *Adriana*, Prologue tells the audience that the tragedy was inspired by a story that the playwright found written on "marble stones" (78). Echoing this theme, the play ends with Adriana's dying wish that some day a compassionate author will write about her tragedy. Accordingly, she begs Mago to see that her story is written in stone and placed inside the tomb. She then pleads with the Heavens

> che qualche autor, mosso a pietà, negli anni
> avvenir, la riduca in forma, ch'ella
> possa rappresentarsi a' fidi amanti,
> che de' caldi sospir, de le pietose
> lacrime loro, ornin la nostra morte,
> e da la nostra tomba questo loco,
> prenda, e conservi eternamente il nome.
>
> (5.8.63–69)

[that some author, moved to compassion, in the years / to come, may dramatize it so that / it may be represented to true lovers, / who, with deep sighs and moving / tears, will honor our death. / And that this place from our tomb / may take its name, and preserve it in eternity.]

Notably, it is not just any death, but "bel morire" that is commonly invoked as an heroic and noble ideal. Sofonisba equates dying well with some sort of rebirth, as she believes that "ben morendo quasi si rinasce" [dying well is almost a rebirth] (309), and Orbecche, echoing a Petrarchan conceit, tells her nurse that a timely death is a gift from the heavens (2.1.408). More specifically, Dolce's Hecuba, paraphrasing Rosmunda's Nurse (*Rosmunda,* 60–61), comforts her doomed daughter by telling her that death is beautiful when it brings honor to one's life; but it is least desirable, she adds, when it causes grief to the living:

> E veramente è bella quella morte,
> Che rende honor a la passata vita:
> Ma non si dee morir; quando il morire
> A se porge diletto, ad altri danno.
>
> (*Hecuba*, p. 21)

[And truly beautiful is that death / which renders honor to one's past life. / However, one must choose not to die, / when dying brings pleasure to oneself and damage to others.]

Besides concern for the welfare of others, dying well is also defined by the demeanor that victims show in the face of death. The act of dying either quietly, like Sofonisba who serenely ingests the fatal poison, or violently, like Orbecche who stabs herself, was considered "beautiful" if the victim approached the final hour with courage, composure, and determination. Such was Marianna's behavior, as she was forced to watch her children being strangled. The messenger reports that the queen stood grief-stricken but immobile, as if she were "a marble statue or a painting" (5.3141–43).

The wish and the resolve to die well was not a mere topos peculiar to mythological characters and ancient historical figures, but a common Renaissance ideal. According to Nancy Lee Beaty, *ars moriendi* literature, already popular in the Middle Ages, became a rich tradition in the Renaissance, which saw a great number of tracts published on the subject.[39] Petrarch's *Triumph of Death* celebrated the motif by portraying female protagonists who demonstrate their heroism by dying well. Beautiful death is also a recurrent theme in his *Rime*, where it is not uncommon to hear the poet longing for "bel morire" or simply praising the sweetness of death. Both in Petrarch and in most *ars moriendi* treatises, the beauty of death was often seen in its merit to deliver humans from earthly trials and tribulations, while the victims' virtue was reflected in the equanimity with which they met their fate. However, with regards to the heroines of the Renaissance stage their willingness to die does not proceed from the Stoic conclusion that the pleasures of life are illusory and thus not worth pursuing, but from the wish to live in freedom and with dignity. Theirs is not a disengagement from the world, but an heroic stand against a world that prevents them from experiencing life to their full potential. Thus, Sofonisba dies "contenta" (1853) not because life is not worth living, but because she refuses to live without the freedom she has so much cherished. And Marianna obediently offers her head to the sword of the executioner as an act of defiance against a "godless" king who has sentenced her to die (5.3180, 3207).

Courage, defiance, and especially rational control of one's passions were all basic qualities of the ideal hero as evinced in the literature of the time. Humanist and Renaissance literary texts provide legions of examples praising humans' ability to control their impulses or "rebellantis motus animi" by subjecting their passions to their will. Thus, Salutati writes that to be led by the senses is not peculiar to men but to beasts, and Bandello praises some of his characters for their ability to conquer their passions.[40] Heroic attributes such as these were mostly associated with man, since woman was typically considered weak and intellectually incapable of controlling her emotions. However, the mental and the emotional composure characterizing the heroines of Renaissance drama threatened to undermined this elitist notion, as it tended to raise woman to the heroic stature of man. Clearly, their resolve and equanimity placed them in the tradition of brave women, such as Lucretia, Virginia, Dido, and versions of Cleopatra, who chose to die or were killed because of their passions or convictions. However, unlike some of these classical counterparts, they did not sacrifice their lives for "their men or for their chastity,"[41] but for freedom and the human dignity it confers. And it is largely in the nobility of this cause that the novelty of the heroines of the Italian tragic stage lies.

It is indeed the cause for which they die and the equanimity with which they face death that earn these tragic victims the admiration of both the stage audience and the viewing public. The spectators' admiration grows as they anxiously wonder whether the "weak" and "frail" heroine will ultimately break down and give in to hysterical lamentations, thus reducing the dramatic tension to a pathetic scene. With reference to this anxiety, Ian Maclean notes that apprehension mounts as "the fear and irresolution which the doomed heroine might be expected to show is transferred to the onlookers." However, as she remains collected and unwavering in her decision, the anxious audiences, having experienced what Maclean calls a "reversal of emotions," are left in awe before such resolve and outward control of emotions, especially in a woman.[42] This is the sort of apprehension that the spectators experience in *Marianna* as they listen to the lengthy and moving report on the queen's death. As the messenger relates to Herod how Marianna was made to witness one by one the executions of her two children and of her own mother, a solicitous public anxiously waits to hear whether the grieving queen ultimately lost control of her emotions and gave in to despair or continued to stand there like a marble statue. The audience in *Orbecche*, too, wonders whether in the concluding scene the heroine, dagger in hand, will join her dead husband and children or will simply lack the resolve to commit the ultimate act. The exemplary courage and composure with which these heroines finally meet their fate inspire praise and admiration in the hearts of spectators who did not anticipate so much heroic virtue in a woman. For the audience, it begs the question whether women are not as capable of heroism as men. After all, the willingness to die and the strength to sustain suffering are intrinsic to the notion of heroism and the heroic act and not to the gender of the victim, be it on the battlefield or on the home front.

Admittedly, not all tragic victims provoke the same *admiratio*, for, as noted above, not all engage in a fatal clash against a tyrannical world. Some heroines, such as Canace and Marianna, are simply victims of an intransigent and abusive patriarchal culture. However, to the extent that they are innocent and powerless victims of cruel punishment, they all arouse pathos in the hearts and minds of those who witness or learn about their suffering. Ironically, among the first to express compassion are often those same kings who decreed or otherwise allowed the executions. It suffices to recall Herod's uncontrollable grief upon realizing that his wife and children were innocent victims of his blinding jealousy and murderous rage. His anguish resonates in his repeated invocation of Marianna, as he, like a man gone mad, asks:

> Ah, Marianna mia, dov'ora sei? . . .
> Ahi, Marianna mia, non mi rispondi? . . .
> Ahi, Marianna mia, dove sei gita?
>
> (5.3233–45)

[Ah, my Marianna, where are you? . . . / Ah, my Marianna, why don't you answer me? . . . / Ah, my Marianna, where have you gone?]

He would kill himself if he could join her in heaven, but he acknowledges, just as Shakespeare's Othello will acknowledge, a century later, that he would be cast to the deepest corner of hell.[43] He will pay homage to her memory by embalming her body and preserving it in the royal burial grounds. Echoing the sorrow of other murderous husbands and fathers of drama, he is fully aware that the most poignant memorial is his painful and indelible sense of guilt that will always torment him (5.3235–85).

While such heartrending grief may arouse compassion in some spectators, it does not lessen the sense of horror that the king's cruelty generated in the hearts and minds of the audience. It actually intensifies the already apprehensive atmosphere, for remorse, by its very nature, calls attention to the source of its contrition, thus evoking images of the victim and her ghastly death. Thus, as the object of pathos oscillates from the dead victim to the repentant murderer, the spectators find themselves fully drawn into a rather unusual theatrical experience: they are moved to pity the victim, on the one hand, and to fear and pity the grieving tyrant, on the other. It is indeed an anomaly for a merciless, bloodstained character to inspire terror and compassion at the same time. The paradox is inherent in the role of the king who is called upon to judge and punish his own wife or daughter. As the spectators instinctively begin to juxtapose theatrical fiction with the reality of their world, the paradox emerges as symptomatic of the dilemma confronting a patriarchal society whose stability demands that its male members oppress the women they love. In this larger context, the stage heroines come to symbolize the victims of cultural misogyny, and the kings its standard bearers. The seemingly anomalous role of kings as cruel but repentant tyrants is actually a dramatization of their evolution from champions of misogyny to its most passionate critics. The blame they place on their fateful deeds is a most forceful repudiation of the austere patriarchal rule that gives men total sway over the life of women. The denunciation is especially effective because the grief articulating it tends to engage the spectators, earn their sympathy, and predispose them favorably towards the dramatized viewpoint.

To an audience undergoing a cathartic experience, the play's emotional conclusion, whether inspired by the repentance of the wicked king or by the agony of the dying heroine, constitutes a passionate appeal to denounce gender prejudice. As the spectators leave the theater with the vivid memory of the king's grief and of the cruel fate endured by the heroine, they are certain to conclude that misogyny is an insidious, cultural prejudice to be shunned. The heroine's *fortitudo* in the face of death surely caused them to question the traditional notion of the "inconstant" female, while the moral strength of her refusal to live in a world that refuses to acknowledge woman's intellectual ability impugned basic tenets of misogyny. Indeed, the nobility of her cause, her resolve, and her exemplary behavior undoubtedly strengthened and raised to higher consciousness the argument of those who believed that woman's moral and intellectual inferiority is not natural, but ideological and cultural. For the presumably well-read spectator of the time (Renaissance theater audiences of Italian tragedy generally came from privileged social classes) the validity of the argument was also borne out by the growing number of female poets whose writings earned the respect of their male counterparts. Arguably, these early women of letters paved the way for writers such as Moderata Fonte and Lucrezia Marinella, who would try their hand at treatises on love, woman's beauty, and similar topics traditionally discussed by male authors. Displaying an amazingly wide knowledge of the classics, they attacked with authority misogynist assumptions, dispelling myths and prejudice and providing for the first time a woman's perspective on female topics such as woman's looks, behavior, duties, virtues and vices.[44]

Theater's Ambivalent Endorsement of Women

As the debate thus shifts from the fictional world of the stage to the actual reality of the audience, theater has partly fulfilled its function as a forum for dramatizing cultural crises. Through his art, the playwright has entertained the spectators while calling attention to a divisive cultural and moral issue. It would be naive to persist in the argument that theater, and art in general, merely mirrors the culture in which the playwright lives, for it often proposes solutions, points to alternatives, or simply occasions a dialogue that helps chart a course out of a crisis. These representations definitely go beyond a simple reflection of the crisis, for they suggest the recognition of woman's mental ability and freedom of choice upon which human dignity rests. The treatment of the issue, the responses of various characters, and the strong moralizing of the choruses leave little doubt as to the plays' didactic purpose. The author's ideological preference is intentionally left unstated, lest the spectators resist it as too self-assertive and partisan. The choice of theater, among other art forms, as a vehicle of expressing views is particularly effective mainly because, as Giraldi recognized, playwrights through their "artificio" are able to reach, delight, and instruct even the least responsive of spectators.[45] Indeed, stage representations tend to draw the audience into the dramatic action, capture the *benevolentia* of the audience, and predispose it favorably toward the author's point of view.

The intent to predispose the audience is often evident at the beginning of the play, when spectators are asked for their undivided attention and emotional approval. Usually through Prologue, playwrights, having mentioned the tragic events about to be represented, exhort the public to respond to the dramatic action with "a few tears" (Dolce's *Ifigenia*, p. 53). In some cases, as in *Adriana*, playwrights attract the spectators' attention by promising an experience so moving as to provoke in them "un'Etna di sospiri, e un mar di pianto" [an Ætna of sighs and a sea of tears] (Prologue, 6). A show of compassion, they believe, is a clear sign of appreciation for the play's action and its author's art. Interestingly, this appeal is most often directed to female spectators. In Dolce's *Medea*, for example, Prologue thanks the Venetian ladies for the many tears they have shed in appreciation of the author's other plays, and asks them to honor the present tragedy with an equal profusion of tears. He proceeds to warn them not to be easily moved by Medea's false protestations, for nature was more than generous in bestowing on womankind a great ability to deceive through facile tears and other affectations:

> Deh non vi movan le parole false;
> Che ben sapete, quanto la natura
> Fu di doglie, di pianti, e di sospiri,
> Di fallaci querele, e di lamenti
> Al sesso Feminil cortese e larga:
> Come ne gli occhi, e ne la bocca vostra
> Stanno a voglia di voi lagrime e riso.
>
> (*Medea*, p. 3)

[Do not let (Medea's) false words move you, / for you know how lavish was nature / in endowing the female sex with (deceitful) cries, sighs, / false complaints and laments. / (You know) how easy it is for you (women) to will a smile on your lips / and tears in your eyes.]

The appeal is contradictory, to say the least, for while it asks the ladies in the audience for their "tearful" appreciation of the representation, it emphasizes the shallowness of woman's emotions, especially the insincerity of her tears. This dim view of woman is hardly mitigated by the fact that it refers to a fictional and proverbially vengeful character, for although the caveat proceeds from Medea's false "words," it comes to rest on the deceptive nature of the entire female sex.

Further evidence of this ambiguity is discernible in *Orbecche*, where Prologue invites those spectators who are not used to bloody violence to leave the theater. The rhetorical plea is of course directed to the ladies in the audience who are "accustomed / to playing and frolicking / and by nature sweet and delicate" (40–41).[46] Their blithe and gentle disposition, Prologue states, could not endure the violence of the events to be shown on stage. This traditional notion of womankind, reminiscent of Boccaccio's characterization of his female audience in the *Decameron*, is in obvious contrast with the representation of Orbecche as a woman of unusual emotional, mental, and physical strength. The contrast is first brought to the surface in the third scene of act 2 where Orbecche seemingly invites a comparison between strong and courageous women, such as herself, and the prevailing treatment of women as grown up infants who are denied the ability and the freedom to think and act independently. Also, her hacking of Sulmone's body stands in vivid contrast with Prologue's view of women as "sweet and delicate." Her savage attack on her father was so shocking to Renaissance audiences that it prompted a strong censure from those who argued that such violent behavior was not becoming to a woman, especially a princess. Giraldi answered his critics by declaring that women are equal to men ("La Tragedia a chi legge," 3211–23). This defense, though contributing to the playwright's reputation as a "feminist sympathizer,"[47] is clearly inconsistent with the patronizing and rather demeaning way in which he characterized his female spectators and woman in general.

It must be rather perplexing for the spectators, as they, on the one hand, are urged to admire the woman of the stage for her *fortitudo* and her claim of human dignity, and, on the other hand, are reminded that women are light-minded and easily ruled by passions rather than reason. It likely occurred to most spectators that this contradiction evoked the same ambivalence exhibited by other defenders of women, such as Ariosto and Castiglione. They, too, praised woman for her virtues and accomplishments, while lapsing, at the same time, into prejudicial comments that betrayed the insincerity of their "feminist" views,[48] *ante litteram* of course. Boccaccio is perhaps the most obvious example of this ideological quandary. Though a pioneer of feminism both through his *De mulieribus claris* and the portrayal of emancipated female characters in the *Decameron*, Boccaccio was also capable of fierce vituperation of woman. The rabid misogyny of his *Corbaccio* was to become a rich source of misogynist labels and clichés for future detractors of woman.[49] A case-by-case study of writers with ambivalent views on women would probably serve to explain their double stance in terms of individual life experiences: an unloving mother, a scornful lover, a disagreeable wife, and so on. However, it is more to the point to argue that the ambivalence persisting in avowed defenders of womankind points to an ideological uncertainty deeply rooted in the culture. Renaissance society, while experiencing the growing presence of exemplary women both on the political stage and in literary forums, was unable and unwilling to free itself from traditional beliefs and to acknowledge woman's human and intellectual worth.

From this perspective, the paradox emerges as symptomatic of the ideological ambivalence at the heart of patriarchal culture and the misogyny it breeds. The dilemma is already inherent, as pointed out, in the fateful role of the stage king as the *pater familias* who finds himself in the oxymoronic situation of having to kill and to mourn those he loves. His plight generates an equally ambiguous reaction of pity and fear in the hearts of the spectators. As their experience gains relevance outside the illusion of theater, Herod's or Eolo's tragedy emerges as a reminder of the predicament facing a culture that promotes the value of woman as one's mother, wife, and daughter while, at the same time, relegates her to institutional mediocrity. Undoubtedly, men of reason and goodwill, aware of the historical evidence of women's accomplishments, were sincere in their wish to renounce gender prejudice, recognize woman's intellectual ability, and accord her full social citizenship. But the re-conceptualization of woman inherent in such recognition is more easily professed than practiced, for it is one thing to denounce prejudice, and quite another to live free of it. Even for the most fair-minded individuals, it was, and continues to be, too great a leap to embrace a concept of womankind that would cause them to re-think all they have learned from books and from life. Whether consciously or unconsciously, most men sense a serious threat to the stability of a social order grounded on institutions traditionally dominated by men.

If this observation identifies the sociological source of the ambivalence, it does not circumscribe the relevance of the theatrical experience which lies in affecting a way out of a cultural crisis as much as in merely reflecting it. Indeed, tragic theater did more than simply dramatize the debate on women. It came out clearly against misogyny by showing the falsehood of its prejudicial assumptions. And though the denunciation was somewhat mitigated by the playwright's ideological ambivalence, it is a vivid reminder of the painful toll that misogyny exacts on its victims and on those who practice it. The audience leaves the theater with the indelible memory of the suffering that the heroines of drama endured with resolve and equanimity. Etched on their hearts is also the sorrow of the men who, having realized the harm they caused both to themselves and to the ones they love, denounce patriarchal culture and the cruel role it imposes on them. The ideological appeal and the emotional impact defining the theatrical experience will most likely cause spectators to dwell on the harmful effects of misogyny and thus start the process that may someday bring about a new notion of womankind. It is through this seminal power that theater, and literature in general, intervenes in the making of social history.

Part II

Theatrical Innovations

6
The Evolving Concept of Stage and Dramatic Space

Le parole son l'ombra de le cose, / E le cose il model de le parole

[Words are shadows of things, / and things are models for the words]

—Orazia

WITH FEW EXCEPTIONS, THE BODY OF EXISTING CRITICAL STUDIES on the Italian Renaissance tragedy examines the genre in terms of its literary form and content, treating theater as any other work of literature either in prose or poetry. Though the approach has yielded significant results, its scope is rather limited because it tends to focus mostly on the written text, ignoring the theatrical features that distinguish the genre. A stage piece does not consist of just a verbal code, it is also informed by a theatrical text that is expressed through sounds, movements, gestures, appearance, diction, tone of voice, spatial dimensions, and similar stage peculiarities.[1] These signs, either independently or with the complement of verbal constructs, help to color, underscore, and even define themes and authorial points of view, which in their totality inform the playwright's ideology and the work's poetics. Besides producing meaning, they also predispose the audience to a favorable reception of the representation by capturing their attention and drawing them closer to the action. By engaging the spectators sensorially, through sight or sound, theatrical percepts tend to establish, among other things, a strong sense of spatial proximity between the audience and the stage. The resulting feeling of nearness and immediacy creates an atmosphere of anxiety and suspense that helps draw interest toward what is signified on stage.

Unlike written or verbal discourse, stage signs communicate through a series of systems (acoustic, visual, and oral) that involve both the cognitive and the sensory perception of the audience. Notably, these systems often occur in sequence, reinforcing messages already transmitted by other systems, sometimes cryptically.[2] Communication signified by the distant sound of a horn, for example, does not take place instantaneously, as, say, in a dialogue, where the interlocutor hears the words, sees the speaker's gestures, and receives the message all at the same time. Here, reception often occurs in successive phases: the sound of the instrument; the disheveled appearance and excited voice of the character, typically an anxious messenger, who bursts into the scene with information about the sound; and finally the actual explanation. The time span between the audible, the visual, and the verbal is filled with dramatic suspense, which, in turn, prompts the audience to listen with heightened attention to the much-awaited verbal contextualization. Meaning may also be generated by the architectural setting of the stage as well as by the relationship between dramatic spaces. The sight of a royal palace or a temple dominating the stage, for instance, immediately suggests to the audience that the dramatic action will develop within a semantic field that is primarily political or religious. This initial perception prompts the spectators to anticipate the representation of events or verbal explanations that will determine the thematic relevance of the space(s). Similarly, contrasting spaces tend to foreshadow the unfolding of episodes that will articulate a thematic clash. Thus, the contrast between a deed that occurs in the interior space of a residence and an event that takes place out in the street elicits a comparison between what is considered public domain and that which is private.

This unique fashion of producing meaning and conveying it to the audience is so intrinsic to theater that no dramatic work can be fully appreciated without a critical evaluation of its semiotic text, often referred to as the performance, or the spectacle, theatrical, or nonverbal text. Admittedly, a thorough analysis of the semiotic text of a Renaissance drama is practically impossible mostly because of lack of evidence. As of yet, we have no significant documentation regarding the stage production of Renaissance tragedies either because the representation was not recorded or because the play was not performed.[3] Short of actually producing a play, one has no definite way of analyzing all the auditory and visual percepts that inform a live performance. Even then, analysis could not be complete because important sensorial signs are inevitably lost once the spectacle is over, unless it is documented on film.[4] The only reliable, albeit limited, document is the play text, where one may find enough stage directions to attempt a virtual reconstruction or production.[5] Granting, then, that a close reading of the written text can approximate staging, the reader attempting a reconstruction still faces the problem of recovering relevant dramaturgical instructions or didascalia, as they are often called, which in Renaissance drama are typically embedded in the speech of various characters throughout the play. As this tedious task often yields too few details to allow a complete evaluation of the various semiotic codes, it is important to proceed with caution and not speculate where concrete evidence is lacking.

Readers must make a serious effort to identify whatever theatrical signs a close reading of the written text may yield and re-create a virtual representation that can inform an overall analysis of the work. Only with the complement of the spectacle text, unfortunately not always fully recoverable, can we consider a play in its entirety. To ignore this intrinsic aspect of drama is to take the theater out of the genre and reduce it to a simple literary text, perpetuating the humanist view of tragedy as a poem to be read rather than performed. Also, considering the majestic setting of tragedy, the artistic talent, and the great sums of money necessary for its production, it would ignore the importance that Renaissance culture placed on spectacle both as rhetoric of power and as a measure of refined esthetic appreciation. Ultimately, we would not be able to appreciate the poetic message in all its nuances, since it would lack the additional connotation that spectacle and pageantry confer upon the staged events that typically inform the noble action and the princely characters of tragedy.

Although during the Renaissance the written text was considered the major component of the play, the performance text became more and more important in response to rising esthetic expectations of cinquecento audiences. Spectators demanded that theatrical representations reflect and even surpass the prevailing taste for pageantry and spectacle. Playwrights sought the help of painters and architects, such as Peruzzi, Aristotile da Sangallo, and Vasari, for the design and construction of elaborate scenes and for the staging of special effects. Experts were engaged for the selection of elegant costumes, as the spectacle of stage pageantry grew more popular with spectators eager for visual gratification. But theatricality, in the Barthian sense of "theater minus the text,"[6] did not become so overwhelming as to suffocate the drama, for while the display delighted the audience, its semiotic nature or referentiality enhanced the literary text by encoding it with specific meaning. The semantic field of an action or of a speech act normally expands to include the added connotations that pertinent spatial or sensorial signs confer upon it. The concept is quickly grasped if one considers that a simple blasphemy may become a flagrant desecration if spoken in front of or inside a religious shrine. Similarly, a murder, in addition to being an atrocious crime, becomes a contemptuous challenge to society's basic tenet of law and order if committed in public or within the spatial boundaries of a symbol of justice, such as a police station or a courthouse.

Spatial context is so essential to the production and/or the definition of meaning that it is unquestionably the most basic element of the nonverbal text. The first space to appear before the eyes of the spectator is the all-encompassing stage set, that is, the mimetic space with all its physical structures, such as buildings, arches, doors, streets, exits, and other similarly visible features. Clearly, the reader perceives the scenic space in a totally different way, for in order to visualize the set he or she must first reconstruct the scene by piecing together spatial signs scattered throughout the text. Thus, only after reading all or most of the play can readers become virtual spectators and begin to imagine and experience what actual spectators apprehend instantaneously long before the action begins. But whether the stage set is apprehended by sight or by imagination, it is the main point of reference for readers and spectators alike. The scenic space is of major semiotic importance, for it frames all the stage acts and signs, and serves as a decoding center for events occurring outside the playing area.[7] As spectators behold the scene throughout the representation, they cannot help but correlate its physical appearance with the events taking place within it. Stage setting, then, tends to define and contextualize the dramatic action, reinforcing it visually and conferring upon it specific meaning.

Though we lack sufficient documentary evidence to determine with certainty the layout of the typical tragic scene, most plays provide enough references to buildings, their specific locations, and other architectural features to allow an approximate or virtual reconstruction of the stage set. The character reciting the prologue usually provided a general description of the scene. Besides addressing pertinent issues, such as the question of poetics, Prologue identified for the audience the city in which the action was about to take place. Often, just before leaving the stage where the action was about to begin, he would point out the street or buildings from which the characters were about to enter the stage. In *Marianna*, for instance, Prologue tells the spectators that the city shown in perspective on the backdrop is Jerusalem and that the tragic deeds will unfold inside the Castle, which, we presume, is visible on one side of the stage. Other buildings, such as the king's palace and Solome's residence, are identified later on the course of the play as characters note rather casually that either they or others are about to go in or come out of this or that particular palace. A common clue suggesting that a space is visible to the spectators is the use of the deictic "questo" [this], as in

Marianna's expression "questa regal casa" [this regal house] (1.231) indicating the royal palace. Another clue is the adverb "dentro" [inside], which characters in *Marianna* often use to underscore the vicinity of a building. Speech acts, such as Berenice's "Andrò dentro" [I shall go inside] (1.482), Marianna's "io vo dentro" [I am going inside] (1.696), Solome's "Tornerò dentro al mio tranquillo albergo" [I shall return inside my tranquil house] (2.857), and Herod's order to Berenice "vanne dentro" [go inside] (2.1385), establish the adverb "dentro" as a spatial marker of a structure that is near or within sight of the audience. The meaning of "dentro" becomes particularly clear when it is corroborated by other spatial clues, such as "ecco" [look!] or motion verbs such as to enter, to exit, to come. Throughout the play there are enough clues imbedded in the discourse of the characters to warrant the safe assumption that at the lowering of the curtain, as was the stage practice then, the spectators beheld a scene with Jerusalem painted on the backcloth and an imposing castle partly shown in perspective (since it is not used as an exit). Next to the castle and on a more realistic scale stands either Solome's residence or the royal palace. Either way, both residences should be represented in verisimilar dimensions as part of the proscenium or playing area, since their respective entrances are used as exits.

In plays where there is no prologue, as in those adhering closely to Greek tradition, the description of the scene is usually provided by one of the first characters to appear on stage. In the opening lines of *Tullia,* for example, Lucius tells his brother Demaratus that they have now arrived in Rome and points to the Ariccia forest and the Aventine hill, two Roman landmarks presumably depicted on the backdrop. He also identifies one of the buildings as the royal palace where the action will take place. "Questa è la trista casa" [this is the sad house], he tells his younger brother, where now lives the murderer of their father King Priscus. Thus, the scene, fully visible to the spectators throughout the representation, consists of a backdrop featuring the city of Rome, with the Ariccia forest and the Aventine hill recognizable in the distance. The playing area is flanked by the royal palace on one side, and, as we learn later, by Tullia's residence on the other. The entrances to the two buildings serve as functional exits.

Such a set was quite an innovation with respect to the typical scene in ancient theater, which normally consisted of the facade of a palace and/or a temple. The structure, generally facing the theater audience, had a main entrance and one or two side doors. In some cases, the entrance's double doors would remain open to show a bloody event still unfolding inside.[8] In Æschylus's *Agamemnon,* it is

View of remains of Theater at Priene. Samsun Kale, Turkey. (Photo Vanni/Art Resource, NY)

through the open door that the audience, having heard Agamemnon's agonizing cries for help, see the bodies of Agamemnon and Cassandra with a bloodied Clytemnestra standing over them (1343–90). And in the opening scene of Euripides' *Iphigenia in Tauris,* the open doors allow the audience to see the blood dripping from the altar where Iphigenia had performed a sacrifice of what was most likely a human victim.

All doors were of realistic dimensions and were therefore used as exits. The forward part of the wings had openings that served as streets or roads used by characters approaching or leaving the scenic space, such as messengers or foreign visitors. In some instances, besides the statues of various gods in the front or on the sides of the royal palace or the temple, there might also be a stone altar to the right of the stage, as in Sophocles' *Oedipus the King*.[9]

The Italians did not follow this traditional form of stage setting, partly because by the time they began to emulate ancient theater, they had already acquired a new notion of theatrical space. Though it is difficult to establish with certainty how and when new ideas began to have a measurable impact on the physical structure of

6 : THE EVOLVING OF STAGE AND DRAMATIC SPACE

Baldassarre Peruzzi, *Prospettiva per Scena Comica.* **Architectural design, plate XLI, sixteenth century. Gabinetto dei Disegni e delle Stampe. Florence. (Foto Alinari/Art Resource, NY)**

the stage, we can say with confidence that it was Vitruvius's *De Re Architectura* that provided the impetus for innovative approaches to the architecture of the dramatic scene. The treatise deals with architecture in general; however, the few comments and references that the Roman author makes to stage architecture inspired all sorts of discussions and speculations, which ultimately led to the creation of a modern stage. Following its rediscovery in 1414 (for it was somewhat known during the Middle Ages), the Latin manuscript generated great interest among Italian humanists and other European students of antiquity.

The numerous editions, commentaries, illustrations, reprints, and translations that make up the work's editorial fortunes from 1486 (when it was first printed) to the end of the sixteenth century support the notion that it sparked discussion on stage design in much the same way that Aristotle dominated discussion of dramatic theory.[10]

Basttiano da San Gallo. ***Urban Scene for Theatre*, c. 1535.**

Leon Battista Alberti was one of the first authors to offer an important view on the physical structure of the stage. Inspired by Vitruvius's writings, he suggested that the scenic space include the residences of private citizens.[11] This inclusion of urban space and other novel ideas proposed by other Vitruvian commentators, such as Perruzzi and Prisciano, formed the basis of Renaissance stage architecture.[12]

The Notion of Scenic and Dramatic Space

The author chiefly responsible for the propagation of the new concept of theatrical space was unquestionably Sebastiano Serlio, who discussed and sketched the prevailing ideas in Book II of his *Architettura* (1545). His drawings of the four dramatic scenes (comic, tragic, pastoral, and satyr) and the brief comments accompanying them became so popular that within seventy-five years Book II "had appeared in all the major languages of Europe."[13] The most important feature of these sketches was the use of perspective, which allowed for the representation of streets and various types of buildings, depending on the type of scene. The tragic scene, for instance, consisted of temples, palaces, and stately private residences flanking both sides of the stage. Adorned with arches, columns, and other architectural

6 : The Evolving of Stage and Dramatic Space

Sebastiano Serlio. *Scena tragica.* **Bibliotheque de l'Arsenal, Paris. (Giraudon/Art Resource, NY)**

decorations, these buildings flanked a wide street that vanished into the city projected in perspective on the backdrop.[14] Characters no longer exited through the back of the stage, but through the doors of the lateral buildings.

This concept of space reinforced the idea that the stage represented a whole city of which the playing area was but a street or a square, albeit an important one. The notion per se was not new, for in the past, too, the scene framing the dramatic action was understood to be an area of the city. Sophocles's audiences, for example, were fully aware that the royal palace in front of which Oedipus's tragedy was represented was in the city of Thebes. The location is often referred to by euphemisms, such as the house of Cadmus, and its people as "sons and daughters of old Cadmus" or simply men of Thebes. But, whereas in classical drama the city existed primarily as a verbal allusion or construct, in the Renaissance stage it was a visual percept framing the dramatic action for the duration of the play. As a permanent fixture of the scene, the city constantly reminded the audience that the stage was but a small section of a wider space. It also predisposed them to entertain the illusion that dramatic characters were "real" individuals who belonged to a larger community, where they lived as normal citizens.

These innovations had a significant impact on the concept of dramatic space, which now could be thought of as extending beyond the confines of the visible stage and still be perceived as an integral part of the scenic space. The houses and the streets featured on the backdrop did not represent dead space, but an implicit visual allusion to a lively city teeming with people whose activities could and did have a direct bearing on the action unfolding on stage. Offstage sounds and voices heard on stage and in the auditorium sustained the illusion of a lively city. Similarly, characters claiming to be coming from or going to buildings, streets, squares, and similar offstage spaces conferred a sense of living reality upon the urban setting pictured on the backdrop. In this way, the city represented in perspective is part of the dramatic space, which includes, roughly speaking, any area where events relevant to the plot are perceived by the audience as taking place at the time of the action. This element of contemporaneity is fundamental to the concept of dramatic space because where the action is already concluded there is no drama. The prevailing notion of dramatic space as an "imaginary stage," or a "spoken space,"[15] must be taken a step further, then, as to exclude any place where actions, regardless of their relevance to the plot, have already taken place. This includes all locations informing the antefactum as well as spaces where events have just been concluded. Thus, in *Orazia*, the field in which Horace defeated the Curiaces is not a dramatic space because the deadly contest is actually over when the theatrical action begins. By the time the audience learns about the outcome of the duel, the battle site is deserted and, as far as we know, void of any drama.

Of course, contemporaneity alone is not enough to characterize a space as dramatic. The unfolding event must also enter the consciousness of the audience and draw them close, in spirit of course, to the space where it is occurring. In *Adriana*, for instance, a disheveled and breathless messenger arrives on stage to report on the raging battle being fought somewhere outside the city gates. Though the battle is happening at the time in which it is reported and is instrumental to the development of the plot, the battlefield is not a dramatic space to the extent that the message does not engage the spectators sensorially: they cannot hear or see the raging fight. They are spatially too far removed to feel emotionally drawn to the fighting and respond to its ferocity and mayhem. At best, then, the battlefield both here and in *Orazia* is a spatial referent that serves to contextualize the deeds reported verbally on stage.

Ultimately, I believe that no space can be truly dramatic if the audience is not drawn to experience the event contained or identified with that space. A condition necessary for such experience is spatial proximity, that is, it must be within earshot of the audience. In some instances, the mere sensation of being near the location where the action is taking place is sufficient. In Euripides' *The Phoenician Women* (105–81), for example, Pedagogue and Antigone standing on a rooftop behold the distant and dusty battlefield where the gathering armies are readying for battle. Though the field is far away, their description of the soldiers' armor and movements is so vivid that, like a camera zooming in on the maneuvers, it gives the audience the sensation of being very close to the action. In either case, spatial closeness, as J. L. Styan points out, helps create an atmosphere of intimacy and immediacy between the auditorium and the stage, compelling the audience to call "upon otherwise untapped sources of sympathy and response."[16] Spectators may perceive spatial proximity either sensorially (audibly and/or visually) or through a witness who observes and describes the deed as it takes place offstage. In *Marianna*, King Herod, consumed by the suspicion that his two sons may some day usurp the throne, refuses all their pleas of loyalty and orders their immediate arrest. Fearing for their lives, the boys run away from the soldiers who pursue them somewhere off stage. Perhaps for reasons of decorum, Dolce chose to represent the ensuing brawl indirectly, that is, through the vivid account of the chorus who is in the privileged optical position to see what the audience cannot:

> O crudeltate immensa!
> *Ecco* le spade ignude,
> *Ecco* come ambedue
> Si difendon da molti,
> Benché inermi e garzoni.
> Ma lassa, che valore
> A troppa forza cede.
> *Ecco* come son cinti d'ogn'intorno,
> Et *ecco* che son presi.
> O lagrimoso giorno!
>
> (4.2651–60)

[Oh, what an immense cruelty! / There, with their swords drawn, / look at how the two / defend themselves against many / although young and unskilled. / But, alas, that valor cedes to greater force. / Look at how they are surrounded / and, there they are captured. / Oh what a day of tears!]

The description, which is typical of the *hic et nunc* technique (to be discussed in the next chapter), is so graphic and compelling that it engages the spectators both on the emotional and the sensorial level. Emotionally, it urges them to feel the same sense of cruelty and grief expressed by the young maiden of the chorus as she reacts to the sight of the boys fighting in vain but heroically against their ineluctable fate. Sensorially, the sounds of crashing sword blades and the repetitive use of the deictic "ecco," which stresses motion as well as temporal and spatial proximity, invite them to "see," as it were, the gestures and movements characterizing the commotion. Spectators have the sensation that the dramatic space has expanded beyond the physical limits of the stage, allowing them to experience an event that is actually taking place out of their visual range.

The effect is undoubtedly more direct when dramatic space is signified by sound, which not only tends to invade the stage and auditorium, but also startles the audience. Noise, such as human screams, the shrill sound of a trumpet, or the thud of a heavy object, bursts into the theater as if by shattering the stage's visual barriers, and brings with it the space in which it occurred. Also, since the meaning of stage auditory signs is not always clear, it tends to puzzle the spectators, who must wait for additional clues or verbal explanations. The growing anxiety hastens the feeling within the audience that the scene has expanded to include the space associated with the sound. This potential for expansion is by no means limited to nearby places, since the spectators can have the sensation of being *near* a place that is actually far from the stage and the auditorium. A battlefield, a town square, or a city street not represented on stage may be viewed as dramatic spaces as long as the events they contain are perceived by the audience as taking place at the time of the representation. In *Tullia*'s last scene, for instance, the Roman people have risen against the murderous usurpers of the throne. The spectators do not see the mob approaching the royal palace. They simply hear the growing uproar of a gathering crowd. Nonetheless, the clamor connotes dramatic space to the extent that it suggests that something pertaining to the action is happening somewhere. Although the *somewhere* is far off stage, the noise tends to bring it close to the audience, who cannot help but wonder what is going on *out there*. This anxiety and the resulting

6 : The Evolving of Stage and Dramatic Space   141

sense of proximity tend to predispose the audience to behold in their minds' eye the staging grounds of the unfolding event. As the fracas erupts onto the scenic space, evoking the streets whence it comes, the whole city, ever present on the backdrop, becomes a virtual stage.[17] Thus conceived, dramatic space allows the virtual representation of all sorts of happenings and activities, reinforcing the illusion that theater involves an entire community and not simply the individual characters directly participating in it.

The notion that dramatic spaces could exist beyond the physical limits of the stage greatly enhanced the function of the scene as the play's semantic center. The stage was no longer just the playing area where most of the action took place or where messengers came to recite long monologues recounting how a particular event had taken place. Though still essential to dramatic representation, these stage functions became increasingly less dominant as dramaturgical innovations redefined the concept of scenic space. The growing preference for showing rather than telling diminished perceptibly the role of the messenger. Also, the practice of representing or "showing" dramatic events as unfolding in visually inaccessible spaces decreased the importance of the stage as the playing area. The innovations came to underscore the function of the stage as a decoding center for all dramatic events, especially those taking place on "stages" outside the viewing area. It was here that events, in particular those signified by sounds, were reported or explained before they could acquire specific meaning and connotation. Indeed, only after being properly decoded on the scenic space and fully appreciated by the audience could dramatic deeds take their appropriate place in the context and in the evolution of the plot.[18] Thus, the commotion that the spectators hear in *Tullia*'s final act acquires the specific meaning of a popular revolt only after the messenger enters and explains to both the stage and theater audiences that the people of Rome are clamoring for the death of the usurpers and the revenge for their slain king.

Brief as a messenger's or an eyewitness's account might be, their roles as dramaturgical expedients remained fundamental to theater, since verbal explanation was generally necessary to the semantic realization of most theatrical signs. Without the spoken word, the street noise in *Tullia* would never acquire its specific meaning nor would the audience in *Marianna* appreciate the squabble between Herod's boys and the soldiers. The need for verbal complement, however, in no way reduces the importance of the semiotic text, which has a language of its own, though one that, admittedly, is not always sufficient for full communication. Undoubtedly, readers would have no difficulty understanding the meaning of a dramatic event following a character's description of it. However, their appreciation of the episode would be left wanting, since they, unlike the actual spectators, could not experience the semantic and aesthetic import that the semiotics of the stage confer upon the dramatic event. Relying solely on the suggestive power of the written word, readers could not benefit from the additional, performative language that is often expressed, as in *Tullia*, through the messenger's sense of urgency, his disheveled appearance, and his frightened tone of voice ("pauroso, e travagliato in vista" [p. 108]). Nor could they appreciate the connotations that the scenic space suggests to spectators beholding its scene. The audience not only hear the explanation of the event, they also behold the royal palace that witnessed the slayings that led to the murderous events of the play. The building stands as a visual reminder of the atrocities committed within its walls and as a signifier of a political power that proclaimed and perpetuated its legitimacy by means of murder: King Priscus was assassinated, with his wife's consent, by Servius who succeeded him on the throne; Servius and his wife were slain, with their daughter Tullia's approval, by Lucius, Priscus's son and Tullia's husband; now, Lucius's life is threatened by the rioting masses. Against such a sanguinary spatial context, the uproar, which the messenger described as an uprising, emerges as a violent outburst of the people's rage against a kingship characterized by usurpation and bloodshed.

Undoubtedly, dramatic space tends to define rather sharply the semantic field of events that take place within its boundaries. A backdrop featuring a city, for instance, implies that events informing the dramatic action concern to some extent the entire stage community. Conversely, a scene dominated solely by a royal palace, as in *Canace* or *Torrismondo*, denotes a dramatic situation articulated by events dealing primarily with the private affairs of the king, the royal family, and/or the throne. The imposing structure of a temple overlooking the scene reminds spectators that events must also be viewed from a religious point of view. Of course, the shrine's deity and/or the specific appearance of the temple will determine the type and the extent of religious significance. The forbidding temple in *Iphigenia in Tauris*, for example, clearly suggests the bloodthirsty nature not so much of King Thoas but of the deity Artemis. However, the fortress-like features (turrets, moat, drawbridge, etc.) that characterize the same temple in *Oreste* tend to place events in a context that is more secular than religious, as they suggest the overbearing presence of a bloodthirsty tyrant for whom religion is but an instrument of power.

Meaning may also be generated by the opposition between visible and sensorially perceived spaces. Consider the contrast in *Tullia* between the royal residence and the streets of Rome: the first is visible, the latter is signified audibly; the first is at the center of the scenic space and of everything that happens in the representation; the latter lies in the background, out of sight of the spectators, who are reminded of its existence only when the threatening sounds of revolt burst onto the scene. The palace stands tall before the audience as an unyielding symbol of the political power and the murderous ambitions it breeds. The streets, unseen and distant, connote the milieu of the powerless, who have but a negligible role in both the constitution and the exercise of power. Their remoteness underscores in particular the irrelevance of the people's voice, which proves inconsequential in the final resolution of the conflict. The binary opposition palace/streets, visible/hidden, near/far emerges, thus, as a signifier of an ideological clash between the ruled and the rulers, between a corrupt yet legitimate state and its civic-minded citizenry. Significantly, the clash does not reach the spatial level, since divine intervention prevents the people from invading the palace. The aborted attempt emphasizes the people's inadequacy to influence the nature of kingship, which is the exclusive prerogative of the divine. In the words of the intervening deity, only God has "la cura de' Regi, e degl'Imperi" [full authority over kings and kingdoms] (p. 111).

As the representation nears its conclusion and the curtain is about to rise, the semiotics of the stage speak a language of images that only onlookers can experience. The calm that now reigns on stage reaffirms in the minds of the spectators the perception that the popular revolt has failed and that order has been reestablished. With the uproar fading into silence, the streets cease to exist qua dramatic space. Similarly, the people, their presence no longer evoked by sound or space, vanish both from the play's ideological clash and from the audience's theatrical consciousness. Thus fades the spatial dynamism articulating the play's conflict, and the entire stage text is reduced to the scenic space, which remains the sole center of attention and thematic relevance. The spectators behold the dominating structure of the royal palace as the unmistakable symbol of the prevailing supremacy of kingship. As they leave the auditorium, they take with them sensorial images of political power, arrogance, cruelty, bloodshed, revolt, and suppression. And whenever they ponder their theatrical experience, these plastic images will stand out as points of reference and recollection. For some time to come, these and other similarly indelible images will help them recall the contrast between the futility of the people's outrage and the unbridled ambitions of unscrupulous tyrants. In sum, they will continue to represent the basic themes informing the play's ideology. Thus, the theatrical text not only produces meaning, but also facilitates the retention of meaning, as the plasticity and the dynamism of the stage sign tend to leave an indelible impression on the minds of the spectators. Of course, the written word, too, produces meaning and suggests images; however, the resulting experience is limited, since it happens only on the intellectual level without the full participation of the senses and is thus void of all the emotions inherent in sensorial perceptions.

Aretino's *Orazia*: A Case in Point

Among the tragedies most suited for a critical approach based on the function of dramatic space and spatial dynamics, *Orazia* is perhaps the best choice because it is arguably one of the most innovative tragedies of the Italian Renaissance both thematically and dramaturgically. The play did not always enjoy critical acclaim. Many of Aretino's contemporaries dismissed it as the self-serving work of a debauched, unscrupulous, low-life writer. Aretino was indeed all that and more: he was "il flagello dei principi" [the scourge of princes]. With his libelous pen, he threatened to undo the reputation of prelates and rulers who ignored his requests for favors and gifts. He was feared by Charles V, despised by Francis I, honored by Clement VII, and paid by those who wished to preserve or improve their reputation. With the passing of time, however, the question of his moral character gave way to critical objectivity, allowing readers to focus on the merits of the work rather than on the flaws of its author. Beginning with Pierre Louis Ginguené, who early in the nineteenth century suggested that the play rivals Shakespeare, critics continued to praise the work, some judging it the best tragedy of the Italian Renaissance and others even calling it a great tragedy.[19]

Critical attention focused on the play's ideology and encouraged scholarly investigations on this or that theme, on one character or another, depending on individual preferences. Scholars raised questions about Aretino's use of the ex machina device and about the tragic nature of the play's conflict. Some critics, comparing Celia's drama to that of Antigone, have identified the play's central theme as a Sophoclean conflict. Others, focusing both on Nutrice's advice that Celia resign herself to her fate and enter the college of the goddess Vesta (the modern equivalent of a nunnery) and on Publio's acceptance of God's providential plans, have insisted on the play's Counter-Reformation ideology. Several critics have called attention to the play's political themes, arguing that Popolo's belief in the people's right to elect kings reflects Aretino's republican tendencies.[20] Still others, in particular Pierre Larivaille, see the work as a propaganda piece celebrating the authority of the Holy Roman Empire in the face of the Lutheran rebellion and other challenges. The strength of this last argument lies both in the play's conclusion, in which the authority of the state is restored by divine will, and on extratextual evidence, namely, the author's wish to be made cardinal.[21]

Though these critical approaches reveal *Orazia*'s thematic wealth and diversity, they often stand in contrast with one another, causing the reader to question their validity. It is immediately clear, for instance, that the Sophoclean conflict pitting Celia's private grief against the public joy arising from Rome's victory is fundamental to the play's structure. However, its overall importance is seriously compromised when one considers it against the Counter-Reformation notion of resignation expounded by Nutrice. These two points of view exclude each other, as the theme of resignation or renunciation proposed in one reading negates the emphasis that the other reading places on the assertion of the rights of the individual. Similarly, the suggestion that the play reflects Aretino's republican preferences is cogent to the extent that the Popolo's views of kingship evoke democratic ideals. However, against the political absolutism inherent in the judges' belief that kings rule by "disposizion celeste" and are "quasi Numi terrestri" [quasi-terrestrial gods] (4.1951–59), the idea of republicanism becomes difficult to sustain. The conflicting nature of these critical views does not diminish the importance of the various themes; it reveals, instead, the narrow scope of the critical approach that tends to focus only on selected aspects of a particular issue, such as the view or the role of a single character. An approach with a wider scope would undoubtedly place specific topics in a fuller context and take into account all the pertinent arguments and contradictions that an overall view of the play might yield. Only then can one reconcile the different interpretations and see the various themes not in conflict with one another, but as distinct aspects of the play's ideology.

Such a comprehensive view requires that we consider *Orazia* not just as a written, literary work, as has been done in the past, but also as a stage piece articulated by its nonverbal, theatrical text. The complementary nature of the two texts will permit a broader perspective of the play, allowing for a reading inclusive of all the themes and arguments informing the work's ideology. The most important element of theater semiotics is the all-encompassing scenic space, which, like a narrative frame or "cornice" such as in Boccaccio's *Decameron* or Chaucer's *Canterbury Tales,* defines the entire dramatic action. From the beginning of the play, scenic architecture sets the semantic parameters that determine or connote the meaning of all the deeds shown or reported on stage. Both readers and spectators view the set as the spatial context in which events find their meaning and place in the story. Readers, however, do not always have an immediate mental view of the stage; they must read on until sufficient details are given as to the shape of the set. In fact, those attempting a virtual representation of *Orazia,* as proposed here, have little knowledge of the scenic space when the play begins. Unlike the actual audience, who behold the scene the moment the curtain falls, they must wait until much later in the play before they can begin to envision the layout of the scene. The only spatial reference given prior to the representation is provided by Prologue who, pointing to the city depicted on the backcloth, explains that it is Rome, where the action will take place: "Ecco là Roma" [there you see Rome] (20). Besides this initial spatial reference, readers have no clear idea regarding the physical appearance of the stage or where the characters stand as they take part in the action. As the plot unfolds, they learn of temples and buildings and arches, but still lack spatial data confirming the exact location on stage or whether these structures are part of the scenic space. For instance, when Celia faints and Nutrice tells Ancilla to go into the house to get scented water and vinegar (2.1210), there is no specific indication to help determine whether the house is visible from the auditorium. Only in act 4, when Littore announces that the trial against Orazio will be held "on this street" (4.2265), that is, where Celia was killed, do readers learn that the scene is a major street in the city of Rome. As to the direction of the street, it is safe to assume, following Serlio's precepts and drawing of the tragic scene, that it runs perpendicular to the auditorium, vanishing into the city in the background.[22] It is at this point that readers can begin to visualize the scenic space as consisting of the city with its uneven chimneys and variously colored rooftops looming in the distance and a main street flanked by stately buildings adorned with columns, arcades, and other architectural decorations.

One of these buildings is the temple where Celia goes to pray. When she arrives in front of the shrine, she tells Nutrice "Ecco il tempio u' gir soglio" [here is the temple where I normally come to worship] (1.664–68). The spatial indication is clearly meant for the spectators (or the readers), for the nurse would surely know about Celia's favorite temple. The demonstrative "Ecco" and her invitation to Nutrice to go inside leads to the assumption that the temple is situated on the street from which the two women are seen to go in and, later, come out (2.1137). Additional evidence that the temple

6 : THE EVOLVING OF STAGE AND DRAMATIC SPACE 147

is visible from the auditorium is offered by Servo, who has come to display the spoils of war, that is, armor and clothing items that the victorious Orazio took from the vanquished Curiaces and offered to Minerva. For purely didascalic purposes, Servo explains that he is hanging the spoils of war on the door of Minerva's temple which is, he points out, "questo qui" [this one here] (3.1325). The deictics "this" and "here" leave no doubt that the structure is visible from the hall and that it is indeed situated on the street. Also, since both stage and theater audiences can see Servo place the trophy on the door and then go through it into the temple, just as Celia and Nutrice before him, it is safe to assume that the entrance is of realistic dimensions and thus a practicable or actual exit. The shrine, then, must be the first building on either side of the playing area.

Another building represented on the scene is the residence of the Oratii, presumably situated across the street from the temple. Of all the verbal allusions to the house, one in particular places it within the confines of the stage. The reference is in act 3 when Orazio, having killed his sister Celia, tells the crowd (identified with the character Popolo) that he is going home to take off his armor. Soon afterward, commotion and loud voices announce that the soldiers have entered the house and arrested the young hero. Orazio's father Publio, who remained outside (on stage) talking to Popolo about his daughter's murder, is puzzled that he did not see the soldiers approach the house. The only way they could have entered the house, Publio is forced to conclude, is through "the back door" (3.1675), for if they had come through the front door he and the bystanders (and consequently the audience) would have seen them coming and taking Orazio away. The observation supports the assumption that the front of the house is on the street of the scene and that it is visible to both stage and theater audiences. Publio confirms this location in act 5 when, fearing that news of Ancilla's suicide might further incite the crowd against Orazio, he bids Nutrice go back inside the house ("ritòrnati dentro," 5.2363) The bidding "ritòrnati dentro," unlike equivalent expressions, such as "ritòrnati a casa" [go home] where there is no particular sense of spatial proximity, strongly suggests that the house is indeed very close and in the scenic space. Its door, then, is the entrance which throughout the representation is repeatedly used as an actual exit. This means that the structure must be of realistic dimensions, its location fixed at the front end of the stage across from the temple.

Thus the scenic space, which the actual spectator beholds and the virtual spectator or reader is finally able to visualize, consists of the city of Rome in the background and a major street with the temple of Minerva on one side and the house of the Oratii on the other. It may help to conceive of the stage set as a magnified section of the city that allows the spectator to zoom in, so to speak, and behold urban spaces characteristic of the whole city. Minerva's temple, then, is the concrete representation of several other shrines alluded to throughout the play, such as the temple and the college of Vesta, which Celia could enter as a vestal virgin (3.1350), or the temples of Jupiter Stator and Jupiter Feretri, which, according to Spurio, are located on the Palatine and the Campidoglio, respectively (2.726–27). These diagetic, spatial references constitute the physical context of all the religious beliefs expressed by various characters and all the references to the scores of religious ceremonies that, on this particular day at least, seem to engage the entire city. In short, the temple is a semiotic expression of the religious fervor permeating Roman society. The patrician Marco Valerio gives voice to this religious sentiment when he asserts that great states are not founded upon the might of the sword, but upon the observance of religion and reverence for the gods (1.408).

The residence of the Oratii, too, must be seen as a physical representation of all the houses painted on the backcloth. Its appearance, the domestic activities taking place inside, and the constant entering and exiting of its residents convey a strong sense of realism. Spectators cannot help but assume that similar human activities enliven the houses that they see depicted on the set. In their theatrical experience, the rooftops, suggested by the set's pictorial images and mentioned by several characters throughout the play (5.2499, 2754), are more than a mere abstraction. They represent living spaces where many of the play's characters work and live with their families.

This spatial setting is appropriately complemented by the presence of a city street where citizens gather and interact, weaving and strengthening the public fiber of the community. Just as the house and the temple are physical representations of similar spaces constituted either verbally or pictorially, the street, too, represents other streets frequently mentioned in the play (3.1434, 4.2265, 5.2504). By its very nature, it also implies the existence of other city places to which it leads and from which it can be reached. It is a small window to the city to the extent that it allows spectators to follow, virtually of course, the whereabouts of the characters: they may follow Valerio as he leaves the stage to go to the main forum in order to see the ambassadors of war, or fetial priests, as they are called (1.383), or go with Publio to Porta Capena where a joyous celebration is taking place (3.1291–98), or join the Duumviri (the two judges) who intend to go to the royal palace in order to hear the king's instructions

(4.2199). Spectators can also entertain a mental image of the nearby square from which a noisy crowd is approaching the street (4.2146–47) or visualize Littore (a soldier-messenger) returning from the royal palace with the king's decree (4.2243). These and other references to various parts of the city further stress the illusion that the picture on the back of the stage represents the whole city. Publio reinforces the sense that the dramatic action involves the entire community when he argues that all Romans should plead for Orazio's pardon, including

> Le case, i tetti, gli edifici, i fori,
> Gli acquedutti, le mete, le colonne,
> I templi, gli archi, i teatri, le moli,
> I colossi, le terme, i simulacri
> Et insieme co i sette colli altieri
> Gli intrighi che in le vie rompano i passi.
>
> (5.2499–504)

[The houses, the rooftops, the buildings, the forums, / the aqueducts, the *metae* (obelisks), the columns, / the temples, the arches, the theaters, the monuments, / the great statues, the thermae, the *simulacra* (sacred statues) / and together with the seven proud hills / the street obstacles (or distractions) that hinder (slow down) one's walk.]

Spatial designations and the phenomena characterizing them invite the audience to look beyond the physical barriers of the scene and imagine a city with all its temples, streets, squares, public buildings, and private houses, all teeming with the daily lives of its residents (and characters) going about their affairs. For both the virtual and the actual spectator, it is the mental picture of a world where an entire community lives and defines itself through its civic and religious activities. The scenic space is the window to this world, as well as its center, where many of the city's events, in particular those informing the dramatic action, are shown or reported. The character playing out or discussing these events on the stage, then, is not a mask, a mere voice in a fictitious world, but a "true" citizen whose life does not begin and does not end in the playing area of the stage. The scene is but a small part, a metaphor of a cosmos whose spaces connote not so much the edification of princely power, reflected in the imposing royal palaces that often dominate the stage of tragedy, but the celebration of a society that defines itself through its religious places, the privacy of the home, and the rule of law as interpreted and enforced by the people in the public forum of the street.

Spaces are not mere symbols, they are also semantic fields that confer particular meaning to events taking place within their boundaries.

In this sense, spatial context is fundamental to the appreciation of drama in that it helps to shape the spectators' perception of the tragic deed according to the nature of the space containing it. The temple of Minerva, then, while a symbol of religious faith, as suggested by Celia's worship and Orazio's offerings, gives special meaning to the murder of Celia in that it took place within its sacred confines. Had it taken place elsewhere, Popolo would have viewed it only as a crime against the laws of the State and prosecuted accordingly. But, since it desecrated the holy grounds of the temple, it is also a blasphemous affront to the divinity. In fact, the killing so offended the gods that they swore to avenge the death of the young girl. Popolo is convinced that the gods look upon Orazio disapprovingly and that they have sworn "vendetta" for the death of the innocent girl (5.2434–37). Given this indignation, we should not be surprised that at the end of the play it is the gods that impose the resolution of the tragic conflict. A divine voice, presumably that of Minerva, orders the reconciliation between Orazio and Popolo, and the burial of Celia as prescribed by religious rites.

The significance of the tragic deed is further defined by the Oratii's residence, which, by all spatial indications, is situated across from the temple's columns where the killing took place. The death of the young girl threatens the extinction of the Oratii family, practically decimated in just one day. The house now stands almost void of life following the death of the two young Horatii on the battlefield, Celia's murder, and the suicide of the maiden Ancilla. Orazio, the sole surviving sibling, is taken away from the house, as he is arrested and taken into custody. The empty structure, then, emerges as a spatial context that raises the girl's murder to a grievous attempt against the integrity of the family. Ironically, Orazio is the only man potentially capable of guaranteeing the continuity of the family name (Publio is too old), but this possibility is in serious jeopardy, as his fate rests in the hands of the people, represented by the Duumviri prosecuting the case.

The people's insistence that Orazio be tried and sentenced, albeit lightly, is due in part to the public space in which the crime was perpetrated. Had the killing taken place inside the house, it is conceivable that the people would have considered it a family matter and perhaps would not have invoked the full weight of the law. In fact, Ancilla's suicide does not become an issue in the play primarily because it is kept within the confines of the house. However, since the murder took place on a public street, it becomes an arrogant challenge to the moral sensitivity of the community. For Popolo, the misdeed, although "understandable," as it was committed in a moment of rage, is nonetheless a "nefarious" act that offends the sense of measure of a society that cannot comprehend why a young virgin "Per piangere lo sposo . . . / Sia suta condannata a sì gran pena" [for having mourned her loved one . . . / should pay with her life]. Nor can the people understand how the girl's sorrow could have possibly diminished the public "letizia" or happiness arising from the victory celebration (3.1598–1604). This public indignation changes the role of Popolo from simple bystander to the voice of justice, the champion of the desecrated values who insists on a sentence meant to vindicate the moral integrity of the community and the spirit of the law.

Besides contextualizing and defining the action, space often generates meaning, especially through its dynamics, that is, the relationship between two or more spatial signs. The rapport between the street and the Horatii's house, for instance, is characterized by a dichotomy of open and closed spaces suggesting a clear demarcation between public and private. The street is the domain of the people, where events of common interests take place; the house is the private and inviolable space of the individual citizen. In the open streets, the people celebrate their victory; in the intimacy of the home, Celia is alone with her personal sorrow. Here they brought her when, overcome by anguish at the news of the death of her betrothed, she fainted on the street. Publio, mindful of the distinction between public and private domain, saw to it that the girl's personal sorrow did not clash with the crowd's euphoria. This distinction emphasizes the contrast between the emotional isolation of Celia and the unrestrained happiness of the people. The antithesis closed/open, inside/outside, then, is not only a sign of the demarcation, but also of the delicate balance between public interest and the right of the individual. Such harmony allows Celia to give free expression to her sorrow in the privacy of her house, while the people scream their happiness in the open streets.[23] However, when this spatial distinction is ignored, order is undermined and conflict ensues between the interests of the individual and the good of the community.

On the spatial plane, the conflict happens when Celia leaves the privacy of the home and invades with her personal grief the happiness of the people on the street. No longer able to contain her pain, she throws herself into the crowded street demanding "tanto spazio" [as much space] as necessary to wash with her tears Curiace's blood-stained vest, which she had made for him and is now being displayed as evidence of Orazio's triumph (3.1438–39). Soon afterwards, as if to counterbalance this spatial intrusion, the public (the State through its soldiers) break into the Oratii's home in order to arrest the young fratricide. The commotion signifying the struggle between Orazio and the soldiers not only accentuates the clash between the spaces, it also points to the ideological polarity pitting the State against the individual: on the one hand, the individual's right to immunity from harm within the sanctuary of the home; on the other hand, the State's prerogative to affirm its sovereignty anywhere within its boundaries.

Admittedly, the conflict arising from the State's rejection of Orazio's prideful contention that as the savior of Rome he is above the law and, therefore, not accountable for his crime, could be easily resolved by crushing Orazio's resistance. However, such a course of action on the part of the State would bring about the extinction of the Horatii family. The survival of the family is the most compelling force driving Publio, perhaps the most important and definitely the most visible character on stage. His role in the play both before and after Celia's murder is to represent, preserve, and enhance his family reputation.[24] His passionate and untiring plea for his son's life, hardly attributable to paternal love (considering the little grief he expressed for the death of his other children), underscores his determination to see the Horatii name live on through time. After all, according to the divine Voice, the future of the Horatii race rests with Orazio, whose offspring will produce many soldiers and great leaders, including the famous Orazio Coclite, who alone will one day defend and hold Rome's "most strategic bridge" against the invading Etruscan forces (5. 2775–82). Rome would be unquestionably deprived if the last of the Horatii were to succumb to the blindness of its justice, the family forever extinguished.

At this point, the controversy signified semiotically by the encroachment of one dramatic space upon another, emerges as a serious dilemma threatening the integrity of the social order. On the one hand, the State would embark on a path of self destruction if it undermined the family, the very soul of its existence. On the other hand, it could not survive as a sovereign entity if it were to allow families or individuals to rise above its laws. A satisfactory resolution of the impasse requires the mediation of other forces or institutions with a stake in the preservation of the social order. One such force is institutionalized religion, which stands to lose influence and prestige as religious ardor and activities would undoubtedly diminish in a destabilized society. It is no coincidence, then, that it is the divine Voice that in the end imposes a compromise meant to preserve the integrity of the existing order: Orazio will accept the sovereignty of the State by submitting to a punishment that will cleanse him of his excessive pride, but spare his life; the State must see to the burial of the dead and erect pillars (Livy's *pila Horatia*) in memory of the fallen

6 : The Evolving of Stage and Dramatic Space

Oratii. This ex machina intervention is hardly capricious or dramatically unwarranted, as some critics have claimed,[25] for religion is one of the most relevant themes of the play, as evinced by the community's pious celebrations and by the characters' expressed religious beliefs. Spatially, its importance is signified by the temple that, together with the Horatii residence and the city street, constitutes the major signs of the play's semiotic text. Pointedly, just as religion does not figure in the conflict public/private, State/individual, the temple does not enter into the spatial opposition house/street, inside/outside; it simply stands as a disinterested witness to their reciprocal encroachment. Its interests lie mostly in the vindication of its desecrated space and in the observance of its rites, such as the burial of the dead.

The intervention preserves the integrity of the constituted order by bringing together society's major institutions, that is, the play's basic themes: God, family, and country. Semiotically, the reconciliation is signified by the restoration of the spatial balance between the home and the street, the private and the public. It is in the open space of the public street that at the end of the play all the characters representing or personifying the various themes come together: Publio and Orazio as representatives of the family; the Duumviri as officials of the State; and Popolo as the ultimate custodians of society's civil and moral values. Here, the individual parties resolve their institutional differences and rejoice as one people in the reestablished civic harmony found in the observance of the values of society's basic institutions. Notably, Voice addresses the entire community from the temple's rooftop, proclaiming the importance of its sacred space and emphasizing the principle that the deity reigns above all human concerns. As the play ends, the audience beholds a stage whose spatial signs and the themes they define have reclaimed their original integrity: the people crowd the street, Publio eventually retires into the sanctuary of his home, and the Voice vanishes after booming its divine decree from the rooftop of its shrine.

The decisive role of the deity and the spatial harmony that now reigns on the stage point to a manifestly Counter-Reformist ideology in so far as they allude to religion as the guarantor of peace and stability. The theme is especially underscored by the temple's imposing structure, which dominates the scenic space and, at the same time, tends to define the play's poetic message. It is important to point out that although the shrine is the most predominant and concrete spatial sign, it is the entire spatial context that signifies, complements, and reinforces the message. Throughout the play, spatial signs and spatial dynamics not only help to determine the semantic relevance of dramatic events, they also allow the viewer or reader to observe seemingly contrasting themes as integral elements of the same ideology. This is true not only of *Orazia* but of any stage drama, for the complementary function of the theatrical text, of which space is a fundamental component, tends to expand and define the semantic field of the verbal/written text, allowing the audience, be it actual or virtual, to attain a comprehensive understanding of the play's art and ideology.

7
Representing the Unrepresentable: The *Hic et Nunc* of Tragedy

THE GROWING NOTION THAT DRAMATIC SPACE WAS NOT CONFINED to the visible scene led to the assumption that the action could be represented in any place where events could be sensorially perceived as happening there and then. This heightened the potential of theatrical representation because it facilitated the showing, albeit indirectly, of events that were materially impossible to show on the stage, namely, huge crowds or scenes offensive to the prevailing social decorum. In particular, it made it possible to bring violent and tragic acts within the sensorial apprehension of the audience without violating the Horatian precept against the staging of bloody events. Spectators could experience horrifying, dramatic events that were unfolding at the time without actually seeing them. In most cases, the experience was facilitated by the account of an eyewitness who described the tragic deed while it was taking place somewhere offstage but within his or her sight. The immediacy of the description engaged the spectators in the drama that was unfolding often within earshot of the auditorium. This rendered ineffectual the traditional function of the messenger as the narrator of events that had already taken place somewhere away from the playing area. Playwrights with a keen sense of the stage replaced the messenger who told a story of horror with the eyewitness who called attention to the horror of the story as it was developing. The resulting sense of spatial and temporal proximity to the action, the very essence of the dramatic *hic et nunc*, allowed the dramatist to draw the spectators into the tragic experience, hold their attention, and tap their emotional resources.

We may better appreciate the dramaturgical import of this technique if we place in the context of the theater poetics of the time, especially within the notion of catharsis as understood by Renaissance authors. They all agreed that a basic aim of tragedy was to arouse pity and strike fear in the hearts of the spectators; however, there was no consensus regarding the way in which to stir these emotions. The showing of ghastly acts, the most obvious means of frightening an audience, was particularly problematic, since the representation of violence was traditionally considered indecorous. Classical tragedy shied away from staging gory scenes, and both Aristotle and Horace declared their aversion to the representation of bloodshed.[1] Playwrights and theorists, such as Bartoli and Piccolomini, suggested that the messenger narrate the tragic deed so that the spectator might "see" the event in the theater of the mind. This alternative found support among those who, like Castelvetro, feared that violent scenes could not be faithfully staged and would therefore undermine theater's claim to realism.[2] But the reliance on the messenger's narration tended to relegate theater to a "talky" and static presentation void of meaningful dramatic action. Tragedy risked becoming a tedious, verbal account of a dreadful event that took place at another time, in another place, leaving the spectators largely uninvolved. The need to involve the audience remained perhaps the most arduous challenge facing Renaissance dramatists, one that they knew they had to overcome if their plays were to have the desired impact on their audiences. More specifically, the question was how to expose the audience to the tragic action in a way that would excite their emotions.

Of course, the most direct way was to stage the action so that the spectators might actually see the killings and other atrocities, as was later done in "tragedies of blood" by Elizabethan dramatists such as Marlowe and Webster.[3] For the Italians of the Renaissance, however, the choice was not so simple. Though violence was widely practiced both by rulers of state, who used it as a rhetoric of power, and by private individuals seeking to settle their affairs by force, playwrights were fully aware that the sight of bloodshed would prove offensive to the refined taste of contemporary audiences. They also knew that it ran counter to the classical precept of decorum, which limited the extent to which violence would be acceptable on the stage. Murder and bloody scenes, although mentioned by Aristotle as factors contributing to the spectators' tragic experience, were not recommended by Horace. For the Latin poet, it was both distasteful and unrealistic ("incredulus odi") to stage episodes in which humans were literally dismembered and their limbs roasted and served for dinner or where children were slaughtered and thrown onto their father's feet, as in Seneca's most gruesome tragedies *Thyestes* and *Medea*. This notion of decorum had strong roots particularly in the Greek theater, which provided a stage tradition relatively free of "indecorous" atrocities. In *The Medea*, for instance, Euripides spared the audience the repugnant ferocity of Medea by having the crazed mother kill her children off stage (5.1379). And in *Orestes*, he has Electra refuse to dwell on the grisly deeds of the house of Atreus "in the interests of decorum."[4]

Social decorum and stage propriety were not so rigid as to preclude Italian dramatists from representing death on stage. Admittedly, these scenes were seldom violent, as most deaths were brought on quietly and slowly by poison. Trissino's Sofonisba, for example, is helped onto a chair as she senses the slow approach of death caused by the poison she had taken earlier. After a rather serene death underscored by a simple and soft "Io vado, adio" [I depart, farewell] (1904), she is gently covered and, still on the chair, is carried somberly inside the palace. Unlike Sofonisba, Giraldi's Didone is brought on stage following her suicide attempt. After showing faint signs of life by trying to raise her head and turning her eyes (5, p. 125), she dies rather quietly, and, like Sofonisba, is placed on a "royal" chair and taken inside the palace. Groto's Adriana, on the other hand, kills herself in plain view of the audience. She punctures her heart with a pin that she found by chance on her dress. Her act, however, is so furtive and her death so serene that the scene is not at all violent. In fact, the magician and the minister, both on stage, assume that she died of the poison that, she falsely told them, she had drunk earlier. Only after Ministro examines her body does he realize that she pricked herself to death (5.8.101).

Of course, observance of decorum was not written in stone and was eventually challenged by those who, like Giraldi, thought of appealing to the taste of their contemporaries by representing ghastly scenes featuring human limbs still dripping with blood. Such is the scene where Giraldi's Sulmone presents Orbecche with a tray containing her husband's and her children's body parts. Whatever the horror this scene might generate within the audience, we should note that it shows the result of a brutal deed rather than the deed itself, which is appropriately narrated by the messenger. A true representation of violence, instead, is the suicide that she commits in plain view of the audience. But, either because of the negative criticism it received or because the author preferred dramatic plots with happy endings, the show of blood characterizing *Orbecche* was not repeated in Giraldi's other tragedies. Indeed, direct representation of violence remained sporadic in Renaissance theater. The gruesome events and the ghastly details that populate many tragic plots continued to be reported on stage by means of the traditional messenger.

Barring blood and dismemberment from the stage, playwrights could have focused their attention on the dramatic conflict in the mind of the character, thereby shifting the drama from the tragic deed to the psychological torture of the personage, as it was masterfully accomplished by Racine a century later. But in Italy no serious attempt was made to develop character, since, in keeping with the prevailing understanding of Aristotle, characterization was considered less important than plot and theme. Playwrights focused instead on developing well structured, complex, and bloody plots as a means of inspiring fear and terror in their audiences. Many playwrights wove their plots with narrative accounts of unspeakable atrocities, looking to Seneca as the authoritative source of grisly details of bloodshed and human dismemberment.[5] But even narrations of the most heinous crimes could not (and cannot) be expected to arouse a strong emotional response for the simple reason that they represent descriptions of recollections of events that took place in a world far removed both in space and time from the spectators. The dramatic force of the tragic deed, it must be noted, does not lie solely in the cruelty of the act or in the suffering of the victim, but in the apprehension it generates within the audience. A story about a violent death might simply inspire sympathy for the victim and hatred toward the murderer. By contrast, its direct representation would be so vivid, so immediate, and so gruesome that it would tend to obscure the line between fictional and real, causing too great a shock for the audience to bear. We recall that a spectator actually fainted during the 1541 performance of *Orbecche*.

Dramatic Limitations of Stage Narrative: The Role of the Messenger

Spatial and temporal distance between the occurrence of a tragic act and the reporting of it on stage has the effect of shielding the audience from the immediacy of the horrifying experience and, inherently, from a meaningful emotional impact. We may see the inefficacy of this dramaturgical technique in Speroni's *Canace*, where prince Macareo learns from a messenger that Canace, his twin sister and lover, has committed suicide and that their child was slaughtered, as decreed by King Eolo, the young lovers' father. Upon receiving the fatal news, a grief-stricken Macareo stabs himself, according to what we learn, again, from a messenger reporting the suicide to the murderous king. From a theatrical standpoint, the play is rather static, since little or nothing happens on stage other than the messengers' reports of what has taken place somewhere inside the palace. In the narration, the tragic events, cruel and unspeakable as they indeed are, lose much of their dramatic force vis-à-vis the audience, who

7: Representing the Unrepresentable

perceive them as far removed both in time and space. The narrative is also devoid of dramatic suspense, since it merely confirms what the spectators already know. Long before the messenger's report, they hear Eolo prescribing the victims' death and the manner in which they were to die: Canace was to stab herself with a knife provided by the king; the nurse was to drink poisoned wine, also provided by the king; and the child was to be killed and left in the forest for the wolves, the crows, or the dogs (1397). The spectators can hardly be apprehensive about a story whose outcome they anticipate and whose drama has already been played out in the past and far away from the auditorium.[6]

The effect is much the same when the tragic event is set to happen in the future, as in Euripides' *Iphigenia in Aulis*. This play, too, lacks dramatic suspense to the extent that the tragic deed does not take place during the representation. As the play ends, Iphigenia is seen walking in the direction of Artemis's altar into the grove where, according to chorus, she "shall drip / With streams of flowing blood / And die" (1514–15). With respect to the audience, then, the deed will have no dramatic impact, since it will happen beyond the boundaries of the play's time span, that is, after the spectators leave: there is no drama in an empty auditorium.[7] Thus, removed both spatially and temporally from the tragic deed that is to take place after the performance is actually over, the spectators can hardly be expected to project their sentiments into the ominous future of the young heroine and participate in her agonizing final moments. At best, they may leave the theater somewhat apprehensive about her impending death, and hope that she is spared by some sort of divine intervention, as in fact happens.[8] But, once they have left the auditorium, the intervening spatial and temporal remoteness will most likely cause them to forget all about the young princess's fate as more immediate and mundane concerns vie for their attention.

Of course, the concept of remoteness, and inherently of proximity, assumes a different connotation if the play is read rather than represented. Readers, being in the privileged position to apprehend the action through their imagination and at a leisurely pace, may choose to dwell at length on a particular event or on the agonizing experience of a tragic character. Without sensorial precepts to orient their response in a specific way, they can let themselves be drawn into the action regardless of whether it has already taken place or has yet to happen in the future. Also, free from the constraints of the temporal sequence in which events are represented on stage, they can go back and forth on the written page and/or focus on specific aspects of the play.[9] But, unlike the reader who relies on the suggestive power of the written word and is somewhat free to envision or dwell on selected aspects of the narrated event, the spectator is obliged by theatrical conventions to accept the illusion that the action is actually unfolding in a specific manner, at that particular time in or near that space signified by the stage. In other words, the spectator's apprehension of the tragic deed is largely dictated by the stage representation, including the scene and all the audiovisual signs that go into the dramatization of a literary text. This peculiarity distinguishes the theater from other literary forms insofar as it brings the imitated action physically close to the spectators, placing them in the midst of the dramatic event both spatially and temporally.

The sense of being close to the action while it is unfolding is a necessary condition in fulfilling one of drama's fundamental functions, that is, to arouse the spectators' emotions.[10] The importance of proximity, clearly underscored in Horace's view that what strikes the ear moves us far less than what passes before our eyes, was first recognized by Trissino, himself a dramatist and a commentator of Aristotle's *Poetics*. Commenting on the concepts of pity and fear, Trissino stressed the notion that we feel most vulnerable to human ills not so much when we hear about them, but when we see them happening near us.[11] The potential impact of this psychological observation could not be fully appreciated as long as playwrights persisted in conceiving and representing stage events not as developing there and then, but as having taken place in the past somewhere offstage. With the action mostly narrated, the force of tragedy came to rest not so much on representation but on the expressive power of the word, as in ancient drama.[12] For a generation of dramatists schooled in the example of the ancients, it proved difficult to break away from a tradition that provided both inspiration and authority.

We should point out here that the reporting of a tragic event by means of a messenger did not always result in static or "talky" scenes. Though devoid of the drama that had already been played out, oral expositions could be rather moving and even theatrical, especially if expressed in highly kinetic or motion-suggestive language and complemented by appropriate mimetic articulation. One needs only to recall the scene in *Rosmunda,* where the servant rushes onto the stage to report how the terrible Alboino had forced young Rosmunda to drink out of her father's skull:

> E' dixe: Ecco la testa di tuo padre:
> Bevi con epsa e teco ti rallegra.
> La misera, condotta in questo loco,
> Piangendo *refuggia* sì duro bere;

7: Representing the Unrepresentable   161

> E quanto più *fuggia*, tanto più forte
> Instava con minacce alte e superbe.
> Finalmente expugnata, ben tre volte
> Con le *tremanti* man volse pigliare
> L'amara taza, e tante volte abasso,
> Vinte da la pietà, cascor le mani.
> Alfine el Re la prese et a la bocca
> Di lei la pose; onde sforzata e vinta,
> D'indi beveo più lagrime che vino.
>
> (1009–21)

[And he said: Behold your father's skull / drink from it and be merry. / The wretched girl, brought to this place, / crying, refused so repugnant a drink; / and the more she turned away from it, the more forceful / would he become with his cruel threats. / Finally subdued, three times / with trembling hands she tried to raise / the bitter cup; and as many times the hands, / Overcome by grief, slumped down. / At last, the King took it and to her mouth / he placed it; thus weary and subdued, / from it she drank more tears than wine.]

The dramatic force of this narration issues in part from the use of Alboino's own words, which convey a strong sense of realism and immediacy, causing the audience to feel as though they can almost hear the drunken king. The scene's major impact, however, rests largely on the kinetic intensity of the language that sets it in motion.[13] The verbs "fuggia" and "refuggia" vividly depict the girl's pathetic struggle to pull away repeatedly from the wine-filled skull. The trembling hands, with which she tries time and again to bring her father's skull to her lips, are a poignant and graphic reflection of her mental and physical anguish. One can almost see the king staggering toward his weeping young queen, seizing her head, and forcing her to drink from the nefarious "cup." The rising tension is further intensified by the way the servant tells her story. Her admission that she was terrified by what she saw leads us to assume that she punctuates her verbal description with gestures, intonation, facial expression, and, intrinsically, a sense of fright and urgency. We must imagine the servant not merely reciting, but acting out the terrible scene, which, in turn, allows both the stage and the theater audiences to appreciate the girl's drama.

Unfortunately, the degree of appreciation can only be limited, for it is acquired indirectly through the mediation of the messenger, whose point of view is undoubtedly biased in favor of her queen. Also, the very act of recalling an event that has already taken place renders its narration devoid of whatever element of suspense the episode might have created had it been told while it was happening. Thus, kinetic language and fine acting notwithstanding, the exposition of the girl's ordeal is not immediate enough to elicit a strong emotional response from the spectators who feel removed from a gruesome deed that has *already* happened somewhere *off* stage and is now being recalled for their information.[14] For the spectators to be drawn close to a character's dramatic experience, the action must not be a story about suffering, but the representation of suffering itself. It is not difficult to imagine the emotional intensity that Rosmunda's drama would arouse were the audience exposed to the gruesome episode while it was taking place. But Rucellai, like several other early dramatists writing in the first quarter of the century, did not believe it appropriate to represent violent scenes. In fact, as in the case of Rosmunda, he chose to represent Alboino's murder at the end of the play by means of narration. We can well imagine the chilling fright that would settle on the entire auditorium if the servant described the bloody episode as it was taking place. The spectators would see the great river of blood, wine, and foam that, according to the servant, was spewing out of Alboino's pierced breast, while his severed head rolled onto the floor with its eyes turning and its teeth chattering.[15]

The Immediacy of the Tragic Here and Now: Giraldi's *Orbecche* and Aretino's *Orazia*

There is no question that stage violence was a most effective dramaturgical means to draw the audience into the dramatic action. Undoubtedly many dramatists were confounded by the apparent paradox inherent in the *Ars poetica,* where Horace warns against representing bloody and horrific episodes, while suggesting that tragic deeds are most impressive when performed before the unfailing scrutiny of the spectator's eyes ("oculis subjecta fidelibus"). But, playwrights with a keen sense for the theater worked around this apparent contradiction by opting to place a character in a position whence to describe the action as it was taking place out of the spectators' view. The technique does away with the traditional messenger, who normally reports what has already happened offstage and is therefore the pivotal element of narration drama. Instead, it relies on the eyewitness, a character who sees and describes the tragic deed as it unfolds somewhere behind a column, in an entrance way, on a street offstage, or in any nearby place hidden from the spectators' view. Unlike the messenger's report, which may be affected by the process of recollection or other factors, the eyewitness's description, being immediate and spontaneous, tends to have a considerable emotional

7: REPRESENTING THE UNREPRESENTABLE

impact on the audience. The observer's graphic description of a live event allows the dramatist to represent the "unrepresentable" in all its dynamism, in the theatrical present, just a few feet away from the audience.

In most instances, the technique consists of three dramatic sequences, not always occurring in the same order. In the first sequence, the victim, normally at the moment of being murdered or otherwise harmed, is heard denouncing the misdeed with agonizing cries for help and/or desperate calls for human or divine revenge. Originating from behind a column or somewhere backstage, these distressful calls tend to draw the spectators into the action, causing them to listen intently for other sounds that may shed light on what is happening. In the second phase, a character witnessing the event proceeds to describe it while it is taking place. The effect is a vivid and dramatic portrayal of what the eyewitness is seeing at that particular time not far away from where he or she is standing. The spatial and temporal proximity resulting from this exposition generates a tense atmosphere both on the stage and in the audience, causing characters and spectators alike to follow with suspense the event as it continues to unfold somewhere beyond the boundaries of the scenic space. Finally, in the last sequence, the perpetrator comes back on stage to confirm and justify his or her crime, thus corroborating the witness's account of the deed. Inevitably, the sight of the murderer, often stained with the victim's blood, tends to intensify the terror that the victim's cries and the witness's exposition have already instilled in the hearts of the spectators.

An early use of this technique, in somewhat elementary form, can be seen in ancient tragedies, where a bloody deed may be signified simply by the victim's pleas issuing from inside a house or palace. As there is no character witnessing the deed, it usually falls on the chorus to interpret the event for the audience.[16] In Euripides' *Medea*, for instance, the revenge-crazed protagonist kills both of her children. Apprehension and terror rip through the auditorium when a child's voice pleading for help is heard coming from within Medea's palace. The spectators learn of the children's fate when they see and hear the woman-chorus debating whether she should enter the house and try to defend the children from their murderous mother (1276). The suspense continues to mount until the chorus tells a grieving Jason that his children are dead, "and by their own mother's hand" (1309). Though the scene successfully creates an atmosphere of deep apprehension through the children's screams, it fails to expose the audience to the live drama taking place just beyond the scenic space. Horror and suspense would surely turn into cathartic fear and pity if an eyewitness were to describe Medea's savagery and the boys' struggle to live.

A more developed form of the technique is found in Æschylus's *Agamemnon* (1255–1390), where the prophetess Cassandra predicts the violent death of Agamemnon as well as her own. The exposition, however, is an elementary form of the eyewitness sequence in that it is a prophecy, not a description, of a misdeed about to be committed. Also, her vision is not a clear account of the tragic event, but an obscure allusion to the killings that will soon take place inside the place. The details of her prediction are so cryptic that a confused man-chorus confesses to be totally lost and "bewildered in a mist of prophecies"(1112–13). However, immediately after Cassandra enters the palace, the puzzle begins to unravel as Agamemnon's cry is heard from within: "Ah, I am struck a deadly blow and deep within!" The dreadful scream arrests the spectators' attention and slowly draws them into the action by causing them to wonder where the voice came from and to listen anxiously for sounds that may reveal what is happening. Ultimately Clytemnestra confirms the king's death as she stands over his corpse (and Cassandra's) and defiantly admits: "I stand now where I struck him down"(1379).[17] In the end, the spectators are not exposed to the bloody killings and decorum is tastefully observed. However, the eyewitness sequence, as characterized by Cassandra's baffling prophecy, is too rudimentary for the audience to fully appreciate the drama unfolding a short distance from their seats.

The dramaturgical importance of this technique, even at its most rudimentary stage, cannot be underestimated, for it represents a valid attempt to bring the tragic deed within the sensorial perception of the spectators without exposing them directly to its violence. Unfortunately, though several examples might be found in ancient theater, only a handful of Renaissance playwrights, notably Giraldi and Aretino, recognized and exploited its potential.[18] Giraldi was one of the first major dramatists to use this technique in his *Orbecche*, where semichorus, instead of the customary Senecan messenger, describes king Sulmone's murder at the hands of his own daughter, Orbecche. The scene is reminiscent of Agamemnon's murder in Æschylus's *Agamemnon*, albeit much innovated and arguably more dramatic. Its effectiveness lies mostly in its greatly developed eyewitness sequence. Unlike the Greek version where the tragic deed is predicted to happen, in *Orbecche*, the woman-semichorus witnesses and describes the slaying while it is taking place. Consequently, her exposition, unlike Cassandra's puzzling references to the murders, is a clear and vivid account of Orbecche's violence and of the king's last agonizing moments. Briefly stated, the episode begins as the king shows Orbecche the platters containing the head and limbs of her husband and children. The grieving mother and widow draws the knives stuck in their limbs and approaches her murderous father in a seemingly submissive way. The apprehensive Sulmone tells her to put down the knives and asks her to follow him inside, where he will show her his fatherly love and royal graces. As they enter the palace, and are thus offstage or at least out of sight of the audience, the young princess in the frenzy of despair falls upon the king with both knives.[19] Just as in Æschylus, the audience does not see the stabbing, but can hear the king describe his own death through screams of pain and vengeance:

> Ai malvagia, ai crudele, oimé ch'io moro,
> Oimé che posto m'ha il coltel nel petto
> La scelerata figlia! oimé aiutate
> Il vostro Re, soldati. A che tardate?
> Pigliatela, uccidetela . . .
>
> (5.2.2830–34)

[Ah! wicked, ah! cruel woman, alas I'm dying, / alas she has driven a knife into my chest / the evil daughter! alas help / your king, soldiers. Why the delay? Seize her, kill her . . .]

The king's cries for help have the dramaturgical function of directing the audience's attention to the dramatic space where an act of extreme violence is taking place. They also set up the mechanism by which spectators will be able to follow the act as it unfolds. In fact, the screams prompt the arrival of semichorus, whose primary function is to observe and describe the grisly dismemberment that follows. Indeed, though semichorus rushes onto the stage following the king's pleas for help, her function is not to intervene and affect the outcome of the action, but to witness Orbecche's bloody rampage and relate it to an audience already in shock:

> *Semicoro*: Che grido, oimé, che voce è questa orrenda
> Del Re Sulmon? La figlia col coltello
> Che tenea ascoso ne la destra mano
> Gli ha dato in mezzo il petto, mentre ch'egli
> La voleva abbracciare, e li dà morte.
> Ma questo non le basta, anco lo *sgozza*
> Con un altro coltello.
> *Sulmone*: Oimè, pietade!
> *Semicoro*: Egli è del tutto morto. Oh quanto sangue
> *Versa* d'ambo le piaghe! Ma che veggio?

> Puot'esser tal furore in petto umano?
> E spezialmente in una donna? Il capo
> Gliele *leva* dal collo e da le braccia
> Ambo le mani.
>
> (5.2.2836–48)

[*Semicoro*: What scream, alas, what horrific voice is this / of King Sulmone? His daughter, with the knife / which she held hidden in her right hand / stabbed him in the chest, while he / was trying to embrace her, and gives him death. / But this is not enough for her, for she is also cutting his throat / with another knife. / *Sulmone*: Alas, have pity! / *Semicoro:* He is dead beyond doubt. Oh, so much blood / is flowing from both wounds! But what do I see? / Can there be such furor in a human being? / And especially in a woman? The head / she severs from his neck, and from his arms / both hands.]

Semichorus is clearly terrified at the sight of so much blood and bewildered by the fact that a woman could perpetrate such a nefarious crime. The apprehension renders her testimony particularly effective, as it helps to heighten the spectators' anxiety and draw them closer to the action. Lest the audience doubt the veracity of semichorus's exposition, Orbecche herself confirms that she has in fact taken revenge on her murderous father. She reappears from the palace holding the bloody knife and carrying his head and hands still dripping with blood (5.2.2886–88).

The horror of this spectacle undoubtedly intensified the apprehensive atmosphere first created by the dreadful silver vessel containing Oronte's and the children's body parts. It is reasonable to assume that the spectators were quite shocked by gruesome sight and the gory testimony of human savagery reminiscent of Seneca's *Thyestes*.[20] However, the dramatic intensity of the scene is somewhat weakened because it grows out of a human drama already concluded and described earlier in all its grisly particulars by a frightened messenger (4.1.2121–2324). Though no spectator can remain untouched by Orbecche's heartrending wailing as she stares at the vessel, the scene does not generate as much dramatic tension and suspense as when the dying victims themselves are heard crying for help or pleading for mercy. For, a victim's agonizing sounds fill the air with a momentous sense of urgency, provoking in the spectators deep fears as well as a disturbing awareness of their inability to respond to the call for help. The audience, then, is not merely watching a horrifying scene, but is also drawn into the role of apprehensive bystander sharing, as it were, in the victims' suffering. In the case of Sulmone's death, it is the victim himself who taps the spectators' emotions with imprecations and desperate pleas for help. Although it is difficult to feel pity for such a monstrous and sadistic man, the audience cannot remain indifferent to the lacerating moaning of a dying human being just a few feet away from them. Even the spectators most aware of theatrical illusion cannot help but feel some degree of compassion.

Sulmone's appeal for help would have a temporary and limited impact on the audience, as was the case in several ancient tragedies, were it not for the eyewitness, whose vivid description brings before the mind's eye of the spectators all the ghastly details of the tragic moment. The motion verbs articulating semichorus's exposition goad the audience to visualize Sulmone as he opens his arms to embrace Orbecche, while she proceeds to stab him and cut his throat ("sgozza"). Spectators can also envision the pool of blood spreading ever wider as it continues to flow out ("versa") of Sulmone's body, which lies lifeless at the feet of his frantic daughter. The movement suggested by the highly kinetic verb "to raise" ("leva") also provides a sharp image of the girl furiously hacking the corpse, setting in motion (in the imagination of the spectator) the savage cutting off of the head and the hands of the dead king. Thus, the scene derives its dramatic force not from the actual sight of violence, but from the agonizing cries of a dying man, the graphic and passionate exposition of the eyewitness, and the appearance of a blood-stained Orbecche confirming the deed. The sense of immediacy and suspense arising from these dramaturgical sequences contribute to a powerful dramatization that would be difficult to achieve through other means. Exposition through the traditional messenger, for instance, would present the deed as removed from the audience in time and space, ultimately weakening its emotional impact. Direct stage representation also would be less effective, as its horrifying butchery would offend the audience's sensitivity and inevitably condition their emotional response.

In addition to protecting the spectators from the sight of bloodshed, indirect representation is particularly effective in prolonging suspense and intensifying dramatic tension. The audience feels drawn progressively closer to the drama unfolding in its presence, albeit out of its sight, as each of the three *hic et nunc* sequences raises the level of anxiety both on the stage and in the auditorium. In the first sequence, the victim's pleas or imprecations startle the unsuspecting audience, stir their fears that an act of violence is been perpetrated upon an other human being, and baffle them as to what exactly is taking place. In the second sequence, the witness's mimetic and oral exposition, while shedding light on the nature of the tragic deed in progress, heightens the spectators' apprehensions. Indeed, the exposition can be so graphic, moving, and horrifying that it causes the spectators to experience, within the limits of the theatrical of course, both the victim's suffering and the killer's violence. The last sequence reinforces the growing sense of fear as the spectators behold with shuddering repugnance the bloody murderer.

Though all three sequences are important to the effective use of the technique, the exposition phase is perhaps the most essential. Here, the eyewitness functions like a mirror reflecting the hidden action on stage, allowing the audience a virtually visual experience of it. For the reflection to be effective, however, it is not enough that the description be accurate, it must also be compelling both through its verbal depiction and through the eyewitness's reaction inherent in his/her appearance, diction, movement, and other similarly perceptible signs. In other words, the reaction expressed verbally and mimetically must be congruent with the horrific and/or pathetic quality of the event described. Otherwise, the sequence (and implicitly the playwright) fails in its primary purpose to inform and move the audience. What rouses the spectators' feelings of pity and fear is not just the atrocity of the crime, but also the disturbing cries of the victim and, in particular, the reaction of the character witnessing it. For, if witnesses describing a gruesome deed are not manifestly affected by the atrocity, they cannot be expected to communicate persuasively the full extent of what they see. In the scene of Sulmone's murder, for instance, besides the victim's poignant cries for help and revenge, we hear and see semichorus visibly terrified by the ferocious spectacle before her eyes. The horror articulating her description of the king's death is so intense that it increases the spectators' level of anxiety and receptiveness, causing them to feel as though they would have experienced the same horror had they witnessed the same atrocity.

Admittedly, a staged event constitutes the highest level of direct representation and may be the ultimate expression of the tragic here and now. However, it is important to stress that its effect on the audience rests not so much on its visual impact, but on the congruence between the deed and the word that complements it. The spectators must somehow appreciate the correlation between the event they are witnessing and the state of emotions, intentions, and motives of the characters directly involved in it. In this respect, direct representation operates on the same dramaturgical assumptions as indirect representation: it too needs the appropriate characterization and the realistic exposition of the distress and pathos that define both deed and characters. Giraldi himself points out that actions alone are not enough, for a murder in itself will not inspire pity or fear unless someone, using "appropriate words," arouses these passions in the hearts of the spectators.[21] Unfortunately, he failed to heed his own advice when he, espousing Seneca's penchant for atrocities,[22] attempted to intensify the terror in his audience by having Orbecche kill herself on stage in plain view. This dramaturgical feat was rather daring for the times, and Giraldi was widely criticized for going against established norms of stage decorum. Though he managed to silence his critics,[23] the scene would remain a weak attempt to win the audience's sympathy toward the tragic victim.

The failure stems mostly from the lack of realism inherent in the incongruence between the suicide and Orbecche's excessive concern with both the rationalization of her action and the rhetoric in which she cast her sorrow. Her long dissertation on the motives for her vengeance is so punctuated by stylistic feats, rhetorical exhibition, and Petrarchan conceits that it tends to shift emphasis away from her anguish, thereby weakening the dramatic tension generated by the heartrending grief that led her to murder her father. We listen to the young heroine as she, holding Sulmone's head and the knife still dripping with his blood, gives voice to her despair:

> Or *godi*, traditor, de' tuoi misfatti,
> *Godi*, via più d'ogni *dur* Scita *crudo*
> E più *fier* d'ogni *fiera*,
> . . . .
> *Sazio* ti sei del sangue mio innocente:
> Et io mi son del tuo colpevol *sazia*,
> Ma con cagion più giusta. E 'n che t'aveva
> Offeso Oronte *mio*, crudele, et *io*?
> . . . .
> O *sol* che *sol* il mondo orni et illustri.
>
> (5.3.2896–2912)

[Now delight, oh traitor, in your misdeeds, / delight, [oh you] much more unfeeling than any cruel Scythian / and fiercer than any wild beast, / . . . / You sated with my innocent blood: / and I sated with your guilty [blood], / but with a more just cause. And how did / my Oronte offend you, oh cruel hearted man, and how did I? / . . . / O sun, that alone adorn and shine.]

The rhetorical virtuosity characterizing this short sample of Orbecche's long speech, which ranges from *repetitio* (godi . . . godi) to assonance (dur . . . crudo) to "bisticcio" or pun (fier . . . fiera) to *redditio* (Sazio . . . sazia) to internal rhyme (mio . . . io) and to the Petrarchan pun (sol . . . sol), is so inconsistent with the distraught state of mind of a grieving mother that the audience may understandably question the sincerity of her despair.[24] Giraldi would have done well to heed

Trissino's admonishment that true sorrow does not produce studied language.[25] Just like events represented by a witness's description, direct representation, too, must be grounded on realistic characterization, for it is not the crime per se that frightens and moves the spectators, but the extent to which it can happen in the real world and to real people like themselves. The degree of such realism lies largely in the congruence between the deed and the personages involved in its execution and/or exposition.

It is partly because of the incongruence between word and deed, between representation and characterization that *Orbecche*, undoubtedly Giraldi's best play and, for reasons of poetics, one of the most discussed dramas in the Italian Renaissance, has not been considered a truly great tragedy. Paradoxically, Giraldi failed exactly where he hoped to involve the audience.[26] He believed that the immediacy of direct representation with its shocking sight of blood and death would generate an overwhelming emotional response from the spectators and guarantee their participation in the dramatic action. But the terror he intended to provoke by showing Orbecche's bloody suicide fails in its purpose mainly because it shows a lack of realism in the heroine's character. Her preoccupation with adorned speech has the unintended effect of deemphasizing her grief and, implicitly, of minimizing the impact of her violent death. Style and polished speech might earn her the admiration but not the sympathy of the audience, who remain emotionally alien to her drama. Simply stated, the public cannot be expected to feel pity when Orbecche herself seems concerned with the elegance of her discourse. The ultimate effect of the suicide scene, then, is to relax that wrenching hold on the spectators' emotions that the indirect representation of Sulmone's death had so effectively gripped. This tends to lessen the dramatic intensity of the tragic deed, giving it a pure "entertaining" dimension and eventually reducing it to a mere bloody spectacle. In the end, one wonders whether a brief, pithy speech or an altogether silent gesture signifying a definite refusal to go on living would not have rendered the suicide much more forceful, Orbecche more tragic, and the play a better tragedy altogether.

The dramatic weakness of the suicide scene reinforces the view that it is not so much the sight of blood and violence that arouse the spectators' emotions, but rather, as we noted earlier, the realistic characterization of both the crime and the characters involved. A grisly sight, such as in Seneca's *Medea,* where the title character kills her children in plain view of the audience, is indeed shocking. But, in and of itself a murder does not bring about the cathartic fear and pity that is tragedy's primary aim. In fact, the audience barely notice

Medea's killings, as the children utter no sounds: they simply die.[27] Nor is there any attempt by an eyewitness to call attention to the agony and the struggle that is normally associated with a violent death. Pointedly, the poignancy of Sulmone's death lies entirely in the cries of the dying man and in the eyewitness's vivid and horrifying account of the murder. The sight of the hands and head that Orbecche severed from the corpse and carried back onto the stage though a terrifying spectacle, does not add to the drama; it simply presents evidence of the butchery that took place inside the palace. That the display of bloodshed is not necessary for the effective representation of violent acts is perhaps best illustrated in Aretino's *Orazia*, where the scene of Celia's murder is accomplished without the exhibition of gory details. The episode begins when a grief-stricken Celia accuses her victorious brother Orazio of excessive cruelty and, implicitly, of having murdered her betrothed Curiace. The enraged young hero grabs her by the hair, drags her behind a column, and kills her under an archway.[28] The deed is bloody, but its representation has none of the ghastly particulars that characterize *Orbecche* and other "bloody" tragedies of the Renaissance.

Aretino's accomplishment in *Orazia* resides not so much in the plot, taken almost literally from Livy's *Ab urbe condita* (1.23–26), but in his theatrical mastery. Skillfully, he stages most of the action and leaves to narration only those events that cannot or need not be represented, such as the mortal duel between the Curiatii and the Horatii brothers.[29] As for Celia's murder, Aretino opted against the show of violence in the Livian source, where the deed takes place in the street before the huge crowd accompanying the victorious Horace. He chose instead, most likely for reasons of decorum, to represent it indirectly. In the play, Orazio warns the crowd to stand back while he drags Celia to her death (3.1576). The warning must be taken as Orazio's resolve against any attempt by the crowd to interfere with his act, not as his intent to hide his crime from them. In fact, those close to the archway do witness the killing. The need to take the action behind the column, then, is but a dramaturgical pretext meant to shield the theater audience from the sight of violence. This is not to say that they are spared the violence, the struggle, and the agony informing the deed. The young maid Ancilla, a character in the appropriate optical position to see what is happening behind the column, describes the event so vividly as to draw the spectators into the unfolding drama. Actually, dramatic tension begins to rise both on the stage and in the auditorium when a despondent Celia confronts a proud Orazio and contemptuously reminds him that nothing can erase the memory of her Curiace even if "nel core /

Mi porgi il ferro" [you plunge your dagger in my heart] (3.1564–65). She could not have been more prophetic.

The audience grow increasingly more apprehensive when they see an enraged Orazio grabbing Celia by the hair and furiously pulling her behind the column away from the safety of the crowd. While the forceful act seizes the spectators' attention, the actual time it takes Orazio to drag the girl off the stage allows for dramatic tension to increase, adding suspense to an already foreboding atmosphere. From a psychological standpoint, these ominous few moments can seem an eternity to a perturbed public who cannot help but wonder where Orazio is taking Celia and what will become of her. Their fears intensify as they hear Celia invoke the memory of her Curiace, whom she is about to join: "O mio consorte, / Colui che a me ti tolse, a te mi manda" [Oh my betrothed, / He who took you away from me, sends me to you]. In the minds of spectators her fateful end is but certain when they hear the finality of Orazio's pithy sentence: "E così sia" [And so be it!] (3.1572–73). Consternation turns into terror as they hear Ancilla describe the killing:

> Per le trecce dorate, per le chiome
> Bionde e sottili egli l'*ha presa* e *tira*
> ....
> Oimè, oimei, oimè, sotto a quell'arco,
> Risospingendo ognun col guardo indietro,
> La *trascina* il crudele e forse adesso,
> Oimè, le *toglie* la vita. O Nutrice,
> Non andare sì oltre, ch'ecco il crudo
> Che il fier coltel, che *goccia* di sangue,
> *Ripone* ardito in la guaina sua.
>
> (3.1569–80)

[By her golden braids, and by her hair / blond and fine he has grabbed her and pulls her / . . . / Alas, alas, alas, under that arch, / with his fierce glance pushing back everyone, / the cruel man drags her, and perhaps now, / Alas, takes her life. Oh, Nutrice / do not advance further, for, the cruel man / replaces the cold dagger still dripping with blood in its sheath.]

Ultimately, Orazio himself confirms the murder when, again in plain view, he defends his righteous deed before a horrified crowd and tells both Ancilla and Nutrice to assist Celia, who is dying of a fatal wound in the heart, just as she ominously intimated a few moments earlier.

The scene is thus accomplished according to the three dramaturgical sequences: the victim's cry of resignation, the eyewitness's account, and the perpetrator's own admission. However, though

Orazio's closure and the confrontation leading to the tragic deed are important features of indirect representation, there is no question that the scene's dramatic force rests mostly on Ancilla's graphic and moving description. Indeed, the maiden's exposition, articulated by a horrified expression and vivid details of Orazio's rage, serves as a mirror through which the spectators may "see" the unrepresented deed. Their minds' eye is stirred by the suggestive power of action verbs ("tira . . . trascina . . . toglie . . . goccia . . . ripone") that, like strokes of a painter's brush, impress indelible images of violence in the minds of the audience. The verb "goccia," in particular, not only implies that the victim has been stabbed, it also suggests the ghastly audiovisual image of a bloody blade with blood dripping and splashing on the bloodstained pavement. The image is sustained and reinforced by "ripone," which prompts the spectators to visualize Orazio standing over Celia's lifeless body and decisively pushing his dagger back into the holder. They can "hear" the cold sound of steel as the weapon slithers and settles harshly into its sheath, underscoring the finality of the tragic act.

If the maiden's highly kinetic speech paints brisk images of violence, her bewilderment underscores the agony that makes the event dramatic. Her terrified reaction colors her exposition so poignantly that it heightens the sense of urgency already gripping the audience. Through her eyes, they can "see" the horror of the sight that she is beholding. The extent of her shock is especially signified by the repeated "Oimè," which seems to choke all her efforts to call for help, as if she were paralyzed by the violence before her eyes. This inability to express her thoughts accentuates the depth of her pathos which, as Frye suggests, is usually increased "by the inarticulateness of the victim."[30] Whether by word or by gesture her grief is so compelling that it tends to transport the spectators into her terrified perspective whence to "witness" the murder. Undoubtedly, the description tends to orient their emotional, rather than intellectual, response because, as they "watch" with her, they cannot help but feel the grief and the terror permeating the tragic deed. In their minds loom long Ancilla's horrified expression and the dreadful image of Orazio's dagger dripping with Celia's blood.

The effectiveness of the maiden's exposition underscores the fundamental importance of the witness's role in the indirect representation of seemly or otherwise unrepresentable scenes. Where the eyewitness sequence is lacking or is not fully developed, the technique fails in its primary purpose to arouse the spectators' emotions, leaving them unaffected by the violence and the drama taking place a short distance away from them. Such is the case in Corneille's *Horace*

(1640), which, incidentally, dramatizes the same story as Aretino's *Orazia*. In the French version, as in its counterpart, the fratricide takes place out of the spectators' view, following an ominous confrontation between the siblings. However, though the spectators actually see Horace unsheathing the murderous sword and chasing his sister Camille offstage, the haste in which the deed is accomplished precludes the use of the eyewitness sequence. The scene reaches its dramatic climax as Horace, outraged by Camille's deathly wish to be the cause of the extinction of Rome and all its people, dashes toward her with the obvious intent of silencing her forever. Immediately afterward, the spectators learn of her fate as they hear a fatally wounded Camille cry out from behind the curtains: "Ah! traître!" (4.5.1321). The very next lines are spoken by Horace, who, back on stage, confirms the murder by proclaiming it a just and swift punishment (4.5.1322–23). In the first line of the following scene, he tells an alarmed Procule that he performed an act of justice (4.6.1324).

The basic purpose of this scene is to inform the spectators that a tragic deed has taken place and to generate the continuum of the action. The effect is somewhat similar to that of a narrated event, with the difference that here the audience can actually hear the victim's last words as well as the perpetrator's admission to the crime. But, Corneille makes no serious attempt to create an atmosphere of apprehension within the auditorium. There is no eyewitness, there is no exposition of the bloody deed, and there is but a faint attempt to represent Camille's agony. There is only her execration of her killer. But, a simple "Ah traître!" is hardly enough to draw the spectators into the action and allow them to experience the suffering of the dying victim. It cannot be denied that the utterance is agonizing enough to perturb the audience; however, there just is not enough time for their shock to evolve into an appropriate emotional response. Her death is confirmed too soon after her last words (in the next line, to be exact) for fear and suspense to intensify in the hearts and minds of the spectators and allow them to share, always within the illusion of theater, in the tragic experience. The time compression in which the scene is played out, for the episode is accomplished in just three consecutive lines, tends to diminish the dramatic importance of the deed, reducing it to a pretext for the development of the plot and the play's ideology.

There is no question that the absence of the eyewitness sequence weakens considerably the scene. Without the eyewitness's exposition reflecting the hidden stage-action into the auditorium, the audience cannot "see" the fatal stabbing, the blood, and the agony of the dying victim. Though the spectators are cognizant of Horace's deadly

7: Representing the Unrepresentable 175

rage and Camille's drama, they remain emotionally removed because there is neither the time nor the dramaturgical opportunity to feel the full impact of the tragic deed. Procule's mild reproof that Horace should have treated Camille more mercifully is hardly a serious attempt to provoke the audience's pity. Sabine's harsh words and wish to die so that she can rejoin her dead sister-in-law could have provided the dramaturgical opportunity to elicit the spectators' pity for the young victim and their indignation toward the murderous brother:

> A quoi s'arrête ici ton illustre colère?
> Viens voir mourir ta soeur dans le bras de ton père,
> Viens repaître tes yeux d'un spectacle si doux
> Ou si tu n'es point las de ces généreux coups,
> Immole au cher pays des vertueux Horaces
> Ce reste malheureux du sang des Curiaces.
>
> (4.7.1335–40)

[What stops your noble rage? / Come and see your sister dying in your father's arms, / come and fill your eyes with such a sweet sight / or if you are not quite tired of these generous blows, / sacrifice to the dear fatherland of the Horaces / these unhappy remains of the blood of the Curiaces (herself).]

But this scathing denunciation of her husband's sense of pride and duty, sustained through the entire scene, hardly dwells on the pathos of the dying Camille. At best, it is a passionate attack on the ideological imperatives of raison d'état with its claims of priority over the needs and interests of the private individual. Sabine's wish to join Camille in death, passionate as it may be, stalls on a long-debated moral and political issue, thus stopping short of stirring the audience's sentiments and emotionally drawing them into the action. Therein lies the major difference between the two otherwise similar scenes in the sister tragedies *Orazia* and *Horace*.[31]

The comparison clearly underscores the significance of the role that the character-witness plays in indirect representation. More specifically, it shows that the effectiveness of this dramaturgical technique lies both on the vivid exposition of the tragic event and on the sense of temporal and spatial proximity that it conveys to the audience. As we saw in *Rosmunda*, description alone, graphic and moving as it may be, lacks the living drama that typically articulates an event that is developing there and then. Indeed, a narration of a drama that has taken place *in the past* and *away* from the audience cannot be expected to generate a significant emotional response.

Nor can proximity in and of itself elicit such a response. As shown in *Horace*, the mere sense of spatial and temporal nearness does not cause sufficient apprehension to stir the audience's sense of fear and/or pity. It must be complemented by an eyewitness's description and commentary. His or her account, however, must be congruent both verbally and mimetically with the dramatic nature of the deed represented. As we saw in *Orazia*, the dramatic impetus of Celia's murder issues mostly from the spatial and temporal proximity that the eyewitness's vivid and the kinetic description brings ever so close to the audience. Where congruence between word and deed is lacking, as in Orbecche's suicide, the witness looses credibility and the exposition fails in its intended impact on the audience.

In its fully accomplished form, then, the *hic et nunc* technique is a dramaturgical expedient that affords an effective substitute to the direct staging of violence at a time when bloody and gruesome scenes were not considered an esthetically viable form of theater. Its basic structure combines the traditional practice of verbal reporting with the growing tendency for stage representation. As we have seen, the tragic deed that the spectators are given to contemplate is almost entirely built on verbal constructs: the victim's last utterances, the eyewitness's description, and the perpetrator's admission. However, the picture emerging from these attestations no longer resembles the mostly informative and static descriptions that often result from the long and wordy monologues found in traditional plays. Here, instead, noises, mournful sounds, horrified gestures, and kinetic language all tend to cause the spectators to sense and "visualize" that which is happening just a few feet away from them. The inherent sense of immediacy and urgency confers upon the scene the atmosphere of a living drama, raising the representation to a higher level of realism and, thus, narrowing the gap between the fiction of the stage and the reality of the auditorium. Indeed, the feeling of spatial and temporal proximity, which a fully developed *hic et nunc* technique obtains, not only brings the hidden scene to the fore, but to life as well, allowing the audience to experience the horror and the pathos normally associated with tragedy.

8
The Theatrical Language of Sounds and Movements

THEATRICAL INNOVATIONS SUCH AS THE CONCEPT OF DRAMATIC space and the *hic et nunc* technique contributed significantly to the growing notion of drama as an art form suitable for stage representation. The fluidity of the dramatic space and the immediacy of the events associated with it helped to create and sustain the illusion that a stage representation was a live and realistic imitation of human actions. The effectiveness of these novelties rested largely on the sensorial percepts that often informed and articulated them. It was the language of loud noises, of the characters' motions, and of other similarly lively signs that prompted audiences to suspend disbelief and allow themselves to be drawn into the tragic experience. In this chapter, discussion will focus on the semiotics of theater, particularly on sounds or voices as well as on the characters' physical movements on stage. The emphasis will be on the dramaturgical effectiveness and the thematic import of sensorial signs, both visual and auditory. I intend to argue that in either function theatrical signs are a viable means of communication and may communicate in varying degrees. A sign may signify a message that requires verbal explanation, such as the sound of a mysterious noise, or it may complement a spoken statement, in the same way that tears add to one's words of pain or joy. In some instances, it may even communicate independently of verbal discourse; a hearty laughter, for example, needs no verbal "aid" to express a person's apparent happiness.

Playwrights and stage theorists shared the notion of signs as an effective means of theatrical communication and expressed it in various ways in their plays or in their critical writings. Sebastiano Serlio, perhaps better than any other Renaissance theorist, underscored the communicative virtue of signs, as he discussed scene setting, particularly where and how to place statues, pictures, and other stage properties. He considered it appropriate for the backcloth to represent painted images of people or animals in an inactive position, such as the picture of a sleeping person or dog. However, he cautioned against the existing practice of painting figures of characters engaged in live activities, such as a woman looking out of a balcony or standing in a doorway, because they do not move and yet they suggest motion.[1] The suggestion is especially significant because it reaffirms the ancient notion of tragedy as imitation of action and, at the same time, stresses the novel understanding of nonverbal language as a valid means of theatrical communication. More specifically, while Serlio echoes Aristotle's definition of tragedy as an imitation through action rather than narration, he goes beyond the Aristotelian precept that representations be accomplished "by means of language rendered pleasant at different places in the constituent parts by each of the aids [used to make language more delightful]."[2] The implication, here, is that the basic purpose of appearance, tone of voice, gestures, noises, decorum, and other "aids" is to render verbal language more "pleasant" and "delightful."

To be sure, Serlio's view that painted human figures communicate the idea of motion or lack thereof does not deny the complementary function of the Aristotelian "aids." It merely argues against the presumed, absolute dominance of verbal language by suggesting that visual signs (images) can produce meaning of their own and may exist, therefore, either as reinforcement of word-pictures or independently of verbal discourse. The point may be seen at work in Celia's death scene (*Orazia*, 3), where the language of theater semiotics shows both its complementary and independent communicative functions. The sight of Orazio's dragging Celia offstage and to her death speaks eloquently in and of itself of Orazio's murderous intent. Here, the image alone is an independent source of meaning, as it conveys the message without the need of verbal qualifiers. The characters' movements and their overall body language are so expressive that the spectators need no verbal explanation as to the meaning of the action. By contrast, Nutrice's despairing gestures, horrified facial expression, quivering voice, and stammering speech, as she witnesses Celia's death, serve to reinforce her verbal description of the murder. Without the aid of these signs, Nutrice's word-picture of the scene would lack the necessary sense of urgency for the spectators to appreciate the full extent of the drama taking place behind the curtains.

Whether theatrical signs produce their own independent meaning or merely reinforce verbal discourse, they are such an intricate part of theater that no discussion of a play can be complete without taking into account their function. Visual and audible percepts not only enliven the stage, they also help to stress specific viewpoints or themes, which are often fundamental both to the understanding of

8: Theatrical Language of Sounds and Movements 179

a play's ideology and to the full appreciation of its representation. Accordingly, we must consider signs in all the connotations that their context(s) may confer upon them. Orazio's arrest may serve to illustrate the multifunctional nature of theatrical signs. The audience first learns of the incident when Popolo, hearing loud voices coming from within the Oratii's residence, concludes that the young hero has been arrested. As both spectators and stage characters presumably turn their heads in the direction of the noise, a puzzled Pubblio concludes that the soldiers had to come in from the back door, since he was standing in the front of the house all along (*Orazia*, 3.1672–75). Though the spectators do not see the actual arrest, the visualizing power of the voices undoubtedly allows them to imagine the physical struggle between the troops and the recalcitrant young hero. On the dramaturgical level, the fracas tends to create tension on stage and in the auditorium, as both audiences grow apprehensive about the events unfolding behind the scenic space. On the semantic plane, it points to the conflict between the State and the individual, which is one of the major themes of the play. Spatial context reinforces this idea of conflict, as the soldiers' forceful entry into the Oratii residence articulates the spatial contrast inside / outside, public domain / private space. Within the ideological framework, the soldiers' entry constitutes an invasion of the individual's right to privacy. On the literary level, the commotion signifying the arrest emerges as an indication that the Renaissance view of tragedy was evolving from the traditional literary art form toward a more theatrical, performative, spectacular genre suited for stage representation.

Though the meaning of nonverbal signs depends on the context(s) within which they develop, their most peculiar and immediate function is to engage the eyes and ears of the spectators, reinforcing the idea that the representation is a realistic imitation taking place before them, there and then. In theater, it is not enough to declare that a story is unfolding. Spectators need to sense that it is unfolding in the active present (not in the static present of narration or painted characters) in order for them to feel drawn into the action and experience its drama. The visualizing dramatist brings about this sensation by providing a lively blend of sights and sounds, which tend to rouse the spectators' interest and hold their attention on the action developing on stage. Let us consider the example of a messenger hurrying onto the stage. First, the sound of running steps preceding the character's appearance has the powerful effect of subduing the auditorium into apprehensive silence, as it causes both the theater public and the stage characters to turn their heads toward the direction of the sound. When he or she finally appears, the audience is absorbed by the phenomenon itself as it dwells on his or her facial expression, demeanor, type and condition of clothes, manner of speech, and other details that might be considered significant. After the initial sensorial impact, these phenomenal instances eventually settle in the minds of the spectators as signifiers of a particular event. Indeed, as spectators apprehend these phenomena and ponder their significance, they begin to perceive the nature of the message long before they hear it spoken. The words, which the messenger finally speaks, confirm or amplify their initial suspicions. Paradoxically, it is verbal language that renders the sign "pleasant" and "delightful," and not the other way around.

Notwithstanding the importance of theater semiotics both as dramaturgical expedient and as means of communication, early Italian dramatists did not rush to exploit its full potential. They were too rooted in the poetic and rhetorical standards of both their own culture and ancient drama to venture boldly into an area of the genre not sanctioned by literary tradition. Innovations in the tragic theater of the Italian Renaissance came slowly and sporadically, making it difficult to gauge or trace the unsystematic pace of its progress. Certain tragedies written in the first half of the cinquecento, such as *Orbecche* and *Orazia* for example, were more suitable for stage representation than others composed toward the end of the century, such as Tasso's *Torrismondo* (1587) and Torelli's *Merope* (1589).[3] Part of the reason for this apparent anomaly may be found in the evolution of two distinct notions of tragedy, which divided dramatists between those who followed the literary or Grecian mode of tragedy and those who, with a penchant for the stage, introduced innovations that rendered their plays better suited for representation.[4] However, it must be added that the latter did not set out to revolutionize traditional drama, which continued to be a source of authority and imitation. They simply introduced changes that reflected the growing view of the genre as a theatrical art form animated by lively gestures, motions, sounds, and similar stage activities. Although they were not always successful, their creative efforts reveal a determination to realize on stage their idea of theater as the live and realistic imitation of human actions. Evidence of these efforts may be seen by comparing and contrasting ancient tragedies with Renaissance imitations of them and by discussing important differences between cinquecento dramatizations of the same story, such as the myth of Dido from Virgil's *Aeneid*. In the ensuing pages, we shall discuss Dido's tragic end as dramatized separately by Pazzi, Giraldi, and Dolce, but first let us compare Rucellai's *Oreste* with its Euripidean source, *Iphigenia in Tauris*.

8: Theatrical Language of Sounds and Movements

Dramaturgical Elements in Rucellai's *Oreste*: Sounds, Retardation Technique, and Movements

Though it would not be difficult to make several such comparisons, we prefer to focus our attention on Rucellai's *Oreste* and its source Euripides' *Iphigenia in Tauris*. Rucellai's play is especially appropriate for our consideration for two significant reasons. First, it is one of the few dramatic imitations written in the early part of the century, just as enthusiasm for Greek tragedy was beginning to find its place on the Italian stage and in its culture.[5] Second, its innovations make it stand out as an exemplary adaptation and not as a slavish imitation or mere reelaboration of its source. Admittedly, the plot follows rather closely Euripides's story of Orestes and Pylades, who travel to Tauris (modern Crimea) to steal the statue of Artemis in order to return it to Athens. The boys are caught before they can accomplish their mission and are brought to the priestess Iphigenia, who must prepare them for immolation to Artemis, a fate prescribed for all foreigners who happen on the shores of Tauris. Iphigenia eventually recognizes Orestes as her long-lost brother, and the three young Greeks ultimately escape from Tauris. Notwithstanding this close adherence to the original source, there are major thematic and dramaturgical differences that underscore Rucellai's preference for innovations and signal an important development in the evolution of Italian drama.[6]

The use of sounds and physical movements is of particular interest not only because it reveals Rucellai's independence from the source, but especially because these sensorial signs tend to enliven the action, redeeming it from the narration of the Greek source and rendering it more theatrical. We will discuss both of these dramaturgical features, beginning with the function of noise as observed in the capture scene of the first act and in the last act where Iphigenia, feigning the need to wash the prisoners and Artemis's statue, goes to the shore and escapes with both the statue and the prisoners.

In the classical source, the capture of Orestes and Pylades is mostly narrated and presented as far removed from the audience both in time and space. A messenger arrives unexpectedly on the scene and reports that local herdsmen have apprehended two strangers hiding by the rocks on the seashore. The spectators gather that the captives are the two youths who, at the beginning of the play, faced with the difficult task of breaking into the temple, decided to go hide somewhere on the shore until nightfall and attempt the break-in under the cover of darkness or "under the night's dim eye" (*Iphigenia*,

Iphigenia in Tauris. Pompeii. (Foto Alinari/Art Resource, NY)

112–20). In the Italian adaptation, instead, the boys are forced to abort their plan and go into hiding because of the sudden sounds of a horn and loud human voices. Pilade succeeds in convincing Oreste to get away from the temple only after asking rhetorically "Non *vedi* quanta gente si raccoglie? / Non *senti* tu le *grida*, e'l *suon* del *corno*" [Can you not *see* all those people gathering? / Can you not *hear* the *voices* and the *sound* of the *horn*?] (1.174–75).[7] Soon afterward, loud voices coming from the beach below startle both the public and the stage audience. Only at this point in the representation does a messenger arrive on stage to explain that a local herdsman sounded the alarm because he saw two strangers lingering suspiciously around the temple and that the shrill cries issued from the fracas marking their capture (1.435–545). Clearly, sound is a deterring factor informing Rucellai's rendition of the episode, which, unlike its Greek source, is rather lively and suspenseful. Audible signs not only serve to generate the action, as they cause the boys to run back to the shore, where they are eventually apprehended, they also create an atmosphere of tension and suspense both on the stage and in the auditorium.

8: Theatrical Language of Sounds and Movements   183

A basic function of the loud noises is to free the action from the verbal constructs of the original version and thrust it more toward a theatrical realization. In Euripides, the boys discuss the danger of scaling the temple's high walls or of forcing the "brazen locks" in plain daylight, and come to the logical conclusion that the best strategy is to hide until dark. The sequence develops entirely on the discursive plane, reducing the stage to a mere platform from which the characters talk about the action. The only movement in the whole scene is their exit, which, we suppose, they execute rather calmly, as Orestes agrees to wait until dark: "Yes, let us go and find a hiding-place" (119). In Rucellai, instead, the youths' decision to withdraw to their ship on the shore below is determined not by verbal arguments, but by the alarming sound of the horn and the excitement it generated among the gathering crowd. Also, their exit is definitely more theatrical than their Greek counterparts', since they face the immediate threat of converging crowds. They act out their exit, retreating very carefully as not to raise suspicions about their actual intent or give the impression that they are afraid. They drew back, says a woman of the chorus, like lions who have sensed the presence of hunters:

> Come'e' s'avvider ch'eran discoperti,
> Si ritrasson guardando verso noi
> Come leon c'han visto i cacciatori.
>
> (1.442–44)

[As soon as they realized that they had been discovered, / they retreated, looking at us / like lions who have noticed the hunters.]

Audible signs have also the dramaturgical function of expanding the dramatic space to include the "somewhere" offstage signified by the commotion. The blare of the horn and the loud human voices indicate clearly that dramatic events relevant to the plot are taking place in areas beyond the scenic space, promoting the illusion that the whole town is a stage and that all its citizens are on it. They also foster in the audience the sensation of being so close to the action as to be able to appreciate it whether or not it takes place on the scenic space before them. For, in addition to signifying and expanding dramatic space, noise also bridges the distance between the "somewhere" of the action and the spectators, provoking in them a sense of being spatially close even to events that unfold out of their sight. At times, this sense of proximity may be achieved through the eyes of a character-witness, as in the instance where Pilade notices the people gathering in the distance and exhorts Oreste to behold ("vedi") them. We would expect the exhortation to rouse Oreste's anxiety as well as the curiosity of the spectators who, like the boys, turn their heads in the direction of the noise. As they cannot see beyond the physical limits of the stage, the young men's eyes become the visual medium through which they may behold, within the illusion of theater of course, the unseen space and the action associated with it. Thus, they watch and wait with anticipation for the crowd to converge in front of the temple, on stage, and shed light on the meaning of all that noise. Rucellai masterfully exploits this state of rising anxiety by retarding the arrival of the messenger with news of the commotion, thus leaving the audience suspended in anticipation and wonderment.

The audience remains in suspense through two lengthy scenes totally unrelated to the mysterious noise. In the first one, Chorus launches into a sixty-two-line tirade against human sacrifices to the gods; in the second, Ifigenia recounts how she, a Greek princess, wound up in Tauris (1.243–400). Abruptly, distant sounds deliver the stage from Ifigenia's static narrative, filling it with live action again. The young priestess interrupts her story to ask in horror "Ma che *strida* son quelle?" [But what are those shrill sounds?] (1.401). No sooner than she hears the strident sounds coming from the shore below she inquires about a woman coming toward them, causing both the stage audience and the spectators to look in the direction of the sea-path. Just as with Pilade's exhortations "senti" and "vedi," in the earlier instance, here too, sound combines with sight to make the unseen event sensorially accessible to the spectators, allowing them a more immediate and tangible perception of the action. The theatrical quality of this scene is particularly obvious if compared with the original source, where the action is all spoken until a maiden notices and describes a herdsman "running, stumbling, from the beach!" and wonders aloud "what can have happened there?" (236–37). Like the shrill voices in Rucellai, the maiden's urging to look toward the sea-path enlivens the stage, delivering it from Iphigenia's static narrative. However, her pointing to the herdsman is but a meek dramaturgical attempt to give the audience a sense of being near the beach and the event unfolding on it, for the absence of perceptible noises signifying the uproar undermines any illusion of proximity.

The importance of sound lies also in its inherent tendency to stir anxiety in the hearts of the spectators by alerting them to an occurrence beyond the scenic space without immediately identifying its referent. More specifically, it serves to arrest the attention of the audience and to hold it in suspense until the event it signifies is explained on stage. Of course, the meaning of many sensorial signs is somewhat determined by specific contexts and existing cultural codes. In most cultures, a deafening crash, the clamor of a horn or of human voices can signify either the presence of danger or a festive occasion. However, those who abruptly hear the loud noise are left wondering whether it has to do with a celebration, a rebellion, or a disaster of some kind. In the absence of an immediate and specific referent,[8] sounds tend to signify undefined meanings that inevitably create uncertainty as to what is happening or what may happen next. The tension arising from this apprehension continues to intensify until the sign's referent is identified and the phenomenon explained.

Rucellai exploits this theatrical function of sounds rather effectively as he allows the clamor of the horn (absent in the Greek version) to remain a source of anxiety for a considerable length of time. Spectators wait in suspense for several scenes before they learn from a woman of the chorus or messenger that the horn had signaled the sighting of two strangers moving stealthily around the temple. But prior to this revelation, they hear the screams (also lacking in Euripides), which not only raise their anxiety, but also force them to pay close attention to the events on stage, hoping for hints that may help alleviate their anxiety. Undoubtedly, they are all ears when the woman-messenger finally tells how the boys were first spotted near the temple and then apprehended on the beach. She adds that the capture was a remarkable feat, marked by fierce fighting and alarming screams.

The novelty and the effectiveness of this retardation technique becomes especially obvious when we compare the capture scene with its original version. In Euripides, the messenger is first seen coming, then arrives on stage and immediately reports that the boys were taken into custody, all in the time span that it takes to recite nine lines (*Iphigenia*, 236–345). The scene develops so swiftly that there is hardly enough time for the events to generate any meaningful suspense within the audience. In Rucellai, instead, the pace of the dialogue indicates that plenty of time elapses between the shrieks, the arrival of the messenger, and the final explanation of the noise. Admittedly, Ifigenia's suspicion that the sounds may mean that herdsmen "fatto aranno" [must have captured] a new prey down on the shore below (1.402) directs attention to a possible referent, reducing the need for alarm and speculation on the part of the audience. However, the author is careful to present it as mere probability ("fatto aranno"), leaving a trace of doubt in the minds of the spectators. The uneasy feeling that has already begun to invade both the stage and the auditorium intensifies as the spectators suddenly hear the sounds of rushing footsteps, announcing the arrival of the messenger. When she finally erupts onto the stage, the spectators behold a visibly agitated woman, drenched in sweat, and still out of breath. The urgency signified by her disheveled appearance commands absolute silence and the undivided attention of both the public and the stage audience. Anxious to learn the meaning of all those disquieting signs (the voices, the horn, and the shrill cries), they are emotionally primed to hang on to the messenger's every word. But her immediate words tend to heighten the seriousness of the noise rather than explain its meaning. Here, Rucellai masterfully suspends the audience in anxiety, as he chooses to retard the messenger's account for at least fifty lines. Imagine the spectators' frustration as the messenger, instead of telling the story, dwells on its wonderment, insisting that the episode she is about to describe is full of "meraviglia." Ifigenia expresses everyone's growing impatience as she, in a clearly exasperated tone, enjoins the messenger just to tell the story: "Tell it; what great thing can this be?" (1.448). Though the messenger begins to narrate the story immediately following Ifigenia's bidding, she does not get to the explanation of the shrieks until some forty lines later when she starts to describe the noisy struggle between the boys and a group of local herdsmen (1.484).

This retardation technique is also most effective early in the last act, where a deafening thud issues from within the temple. The noise is part of Iphigenia's scheme to escape from Tauris, taking along the statue and the two boys. In the Greek original, the young priestess tells King Thoas that she must take Artemis's statue to the shore in order to cleanse it, alleging that the presence of the murderous prisoners defiled it. She explains that at least one of the captives is an unworthy sacrificial victim, having slain his own mother. She leads the king to believe that the wooden idol showed her displeasure with the impurity of such an offering by turning away from the prisoners and even shutting her eyes, so as not to look at them (1165–67). A skeptical Thoas finally agrees to let her take the statue and the prisoners to the shore and, in secrecy, wash them all with sea water. The entire incident is verbally represented, and its dramatic quality is articulated mostly by the characters' dialogue and the various dramaturgical "aids," such as tone, diction, expression, appearance. Though in the Italian version the episode is practically the same, its exposition is markedly different. Rucellai introduces the element of noise, which not only renders the action more lively, it also casts it in a cloud of mystery, tension and suspense, which ultimately affect the audience's reception of it.

Long before Ifigenia comes out of the temple carrying the idol, a deafening crash and a frightening scream issue from within the

8: Theatrical Language of Sounds and Movements 187

temple, startling both the stage and the theater public. The king, who was leisurely waiting in front of the temple for the sacrificial ceremony to begin, expresses the bewildering and frightful effect of the earsplitting loudness as he asks his retinue:

> Ma che *stridore* spaventoso e strano
> Esce dal fondo abisso de la terra
> E col *rimbombo* i nostri orecchi *intruona*?
>
> (5.33–35)

[But what a fearful and strange shrill sound / issues from the deep bowels of the earth / and with its boom deafens our ears?]

As the noise invades the entire auditorium, it breaks the scene's physical barriers, expanding the dramatic space into the temple's interior, the staging grounds of the noisy event. Though the happening remains visibly inaccessible, the noise brings it within the sensorial perception of the spectators, causing them to fix their eyes on the shrine's entrance and wait anxiously for signs that may shed light on the mysterious occurrence.

This theatrical rendition represents a significant departure from the Greek original where the event is practically a verbal construct. Although the action is narrated in both the original and the adaptation as having already taken place, Rucellai's introduction of the noise alters radically the way in which the audience perceives it. In Euripides, the spectators, like the stage audience leisurely waiting out in the temple's courtyard, have no prior knowledge or suspicion of what is actually happening inside the temple other than the assumption that Iphigenia is preparing the two captives for the sacrificial offering. In Rucellai, instead, the thunderous noise subverts that assumption, alerting the spectators that something unusual is taking place. Not knowing what the "something" is, they are left guessing as to what is going on and what may happen next. Just as in the capture sequence, here, too, their suspense grows as they wait for a messenger to arrive and explain what occurred inside the shrine. A horrified woman-messenger, looking like an "infernal fury," arrives immediately after Toante has called attention to the noise; however, she is so frightened and so hysterical that instead of telling what happened, she keeps on talking about how terrible the sound was and what foreboding it conveys for the entire kingdom. The suspenseful effect of this retardation on both the spectators and the stage characters is expressed in the frustration with which Toante finally orders her to tell what she saw and "dimmel tosto" [tell it fast] (5.45–66).

When, finally, the messenger begins to tell the long-awaited story and the audience is about to relax, Ifigenia rushes out of the temple, interrupting the narrative and causing everyone to turn in her direction. Dramatic tension rises again, as the stage audience runs toward her to hear her version of the incident. The interruption, the change of narrator, and the inherent retardation should not be seen as a capricious toying with the spectators' anxiety, for it is a skillful expedient meant to underscore the shift from the mere facts of the story, narrated by the messenger, to the sinister omens that the young priestess is about to reveal. The heightened suspense helps prime both the public and the stage audience to listen very carefully to Ifigenia as she predicts deadly plagues and devastating earthquakes, unless the statue and the prisoners are taken to the shore and cleansed properly (5.125–33).

Interestingly, tension and suspense not only tend to create an atmosphere of apprehension, they also cause characters to behave instinctually, providing insightful hints as to the true nature of their personality. In Euripides, for instance, King Thoas's reaction to Iphigenia's omens stands in sharp contrast with that of his Italian counterpart. In the Greek play, where the incident does not generate a great amount of tension, the king receives the maiden's omens with obvious skepticism, asking how she knew that one of the prisoners was an unworthy sacrificial offering, how a divinity could be so easily defiled, and whether it was necessary to take the statue out of the temple. Only after a series of questions spanning over sixty lines does he allow the priestess to do "everything the Goddess wants" (*Iphigenia*, 1158–1220). Though clearly fearful of the dire predictions, Thoas remains calm and in control of the situation and of himself. By contrast, the reaction of his Italian namesake is immediate, uncritical, and fearful. Rucellai's Toante is so apprehensive that, trembling with fear, he quickly lends credence to Ifigenia's scheme and declares himself ready to carry out her wishes and to take whatever remedy is needed against so much evil (*Oreste*, 5.134–35). The innate cowardice, which he managed to hide so well behind his savage taste for violence and bloodshed, is especially revealed by the quickness with which he wants to run into a safe hiding place. Pointedly, this aspect of his character is expressed vividly not so much by speech as by his body language and physical movements on the stage.

Unlike noise, movement often does not create suspense because it is visually perceptible and is generally observed in association with its referent, thus communicating its meaning directly and immediately to the audience. There is no need for messengers to explain it, nor can it serve to build tension by means of retardation expedients.

Like noise, however, it too animates the action and enlivens the stage. In Rucellai's play, the dramaturgical relevance of movement is particularly obvious in two separate sequences: in the squabble between Pilade and Oreste (act 3), and in the commotion that follows the king's order to all Taurians to go and stay inside (act 5). The reasons for the young men's squabble arise from the episode of the letter that Ifigenia wants delivered to Argos. In Euripides, prior to the recognition scene between Iphigenia and her brother, Orestes, the priestess artfully obtains the king's pardon for one of the prisoners. Orestes decides that he will stay behind to be sacrificed, while Pylades should go free and deliver the letter. Pylades protests his friend's decision, but his protestations are of no avail and are quickly dismissed by an unyielding Orestes. The whole argument is thus contained in a simple exchange of points of view between the two companions. In Rucellai, instead, the verbal contention turns into a physical wrangling, as words give way to a tug of war over the dark robe which must be worn by the sacrificial victim. Both men pull and tear at the fatal cloth, each claiming it for himself. The quarrel goes on for about forty lines punctuated by pushing and shoving:

> Oreste: Lasciala a me, che fui primo a pigliarla.
> Pilade: Che vuoi tu farne? oimè, oimè, lasso!
> Oreste: Così far voglio, e così far m'aggrada.
> Pilade: Tu perdi il tempo in van; che fai, che pensi?
> Oreste: Orsù, deh leva omai di qui le mani.
> ....
> Oreste: Che di' tu? che fai tu? che furia è questa?
> Pilade: Lascia la vesta a me; la vesta è mia.
> Oreste: La vesta è mia, la vesta a me fu data.
>
> (3.256–95)

[*Orestes*: Let me have it, I was the first to grab it. / *Pylades*: What do you want to do with it? alas, alas, poor me! / *Orestes*: This is what I want, and this is what I like to do. / *Pylades*: You are wasting your time. What do you think you are doing? / *Orestes*: Now then, get your hands off this. / . . . / *Orestes*: What are you saying? what are you doing? What fury is this? / *Pylades*: Let me have the robe; the robe is mine. / *Orestes*: The robe is mine, the robe was given to me.]

As speech yields to physical action, the stage comes to life involving and entertaining the spectators both sensorially and intellectually. The message, which in the ancient source was mostly verbal, here is cast in both words and gestures, wherein gestures complement and stress linguistic communication. The emotional intensity informing the youths' intimate relationship is so high that it cannot be contained by calm and thoughtful linguistic discourse. For over two hundred lines (3.256–4.86), the two friends evoke sweet childhood memories, declare themselves ready to die for one another, embrace, kiss, and shed tears of love and sorrow. Pilade, in particular, is so despondent that he requests another cape for himself because he cannot go on living, he says, without his "better half" (4.52). He vows to end his life after making arrangements that his ashes be placed in Oreste's urn so that the two may rest together in a single sepulcher (4.87). But, these protestations, though many and protracted, prove insufficient to fully express the intensity of the boys' emotions and are ultimately complemented with the language of physical gestures and movements. Though less articulate and more instinctive, the noisy disagreement is an eloquent manifestation of the boys' feelings and convictions. Its visual expression more than complements the verbal inadequacy frustrating the characters' need to express their deeply felt emotions and stresses the depth of their friendship.

Understandably, theater scholars may view with raised eyebrows the introduction of physical squabbling on a tragic stage, since histrionic wrangling is more suitable to comedy. However, the noble ideals of unconditional fraternal love, undying loyalty, and self-sacrifice, which inform the friends' disagreement, confer upon it a somber mien becoming the noble genre. The gravity of the dispute is also underscored by the dark color of the cape, a visual reminder of the death that awaits the unfortunate "winner." Besides its function as a visual, dramaturgical expedient meant to stress the action and give physicality to the characters' emotions, the squabble also reflects a major difference between Rucellai's characters and their Greek prototypes: the first are passionate and hardly able to verbalize or control their bursting emotions; the latter are composed and almost cerebral in the expression of their thoughts. In Euripides there is no squabble, and the disagreement is sustained through calculated and rational arguments. The two friends, in fact, do not appear bound by as much affection and loyalty toward each other as they are by common political interests. Pylades' reason for wanting to stay behind stems primarily from his fear of what people might think should they see him safely back in Argos. They may spurn him "as one who betrayed a friend," and may even say, he tells Orestes, that "I had wished or even caused your death / To benefit, as husband of your sister, / By my inheritance—to win your throne" (678–83). This fear notwithstanding, he quickly accepts the bidding to go back and marry Electra (Orestes' other sister) and "through your children / Build up once more the house of Agamemnon" (698–99).

The effect of stage movement as a signifier of a character's personality traits or inner thoughts may best be observed in the character difference between King Thoas and his Italian parallel Toante. Although differences between the two versions of the Taurian king may be noted in several instances, the flurry in the scene following the goddess's alleged displeasure with the victims is undoubtedly the most revealing. In *Iphigenia in Tauris*, it is the rapid exchange of short lines, characterizing the stichomytic structure of Iphigenia's dialogue with the king, that connotes agitation and liveliness on stage. The conversation on the need to keep all citizens off the streets, while the priestess goes to the shore to wash the statue and the prisoners, consists of a fast repartee of one-line exchanges, which, though seventy lines long (1157–1226), conveys a strong sense of urgency and quick action. But there is hardly any action on stage. There is only the idea of movement, which is verbally created as the young priestess urges the king to order all Taurians to stay indoors. It is clear that a herald will carry out the king's orders and that people everywhere will be running inside for cover; however, on stage there is no appreciable physical activity for the audience to behold. In Rucellai, on the other hand, this same scene is characterized by both emotional excitement and hasty physical movement, as suggested in part by the use of *reduplicatio*, or repetition, a widely used rhetorical figure in *Oreste*. Here is Toante shouting orders, following Ifigenia's warning to keep everybody inside:

> Andiam via tosto, andiam via tosto, andiamo,
> Andiam via, fuggiam via, entriam là dentro,
> E voi, Olimpia, prendete le chiavi,
> Ch'in la più scura parte io vo' serrarmi.
>
> (5.145–48)

[Let's go away quickly, let's go away quickly, let's go / let's go away, let's flee, let's enter there, / and you, Olimpia, get the keys, / for I want to lock myself in the safest corner.]

The performance suggested in this speech act prompts one to visualize a stage in general disarray, with people running in all directions. The scurrying effectively shows a stage audience in absolute panic. Most frightened is Toante, who is running and screaming over and over the only command his fear-gripped mind is capable of articulating. He trembles with fear so much that, unlike his circumspect prototype, he accepts without questions the girl's story about the goddess's displeasure. His only concern is to find a secure place in which to hide. This instinctual reaction shatters in an instant the carefully fashioned image of himself as a cruel tyrant and externalizes his true cowardly nature. The savage king, with a professed bestial lust for human dismemberment and bloodshed, is actually a wretched coward.[9] This basic personality trait stands him in stark contrast with the kingly demeanor of his Greek counterpart and accounts for the different conclusions of the two plays. In *Iphigenia,* a wise Thoas follows Athena's admonition and, swallowing his pride, calls off the chase in the belief that there is no "dignity in challenging a God" (1480). Order is thus reestablished and the Taurian kingdom returns to its original status of normalcy. *Oreste,* instead, ends with Toante frantically cursing the gods, extolling human strength above divine reliance, and inciting his people with lures of gold and riches to pursue the fugitives and avenge their king. The stability of the kingdom is thus thrown further into a chaotic spin, as the coward king tries recklessly to reassert his old, tyrannical image.

The stage action ends, leaving the spectators with the task of placing such a roaring finale in the larger context of the play. As the process brings them to reflect upon the entire theatrical experience, they most likely revisit, perhaps subconsciously, those moments that startled them, raised their anxiety, held them in suspense, and brought them close to the dramatic deed. It is a mental process that Anne Ubersfeld aptly calls "resémantiser," by which the spectator, after recalling the semiotic text turns "au sens, à l'idée [as] le sémiotique s'ouvre sur le sémantique" [to the meaning, to the idea (as) the semiotic calls forth the semantic].[10] Thus, they will hear in their minds the sound of the horn and the subsequent shrieks and associate them with events surrounding the boys' capture. The deafening thud and the shrieks issuing from within the temple will elicit in them visions of bloodshed and human sacrifices. Vivid images of the squabble over the brown cape will return, evoking the depth of the boys' friendship in the face of certain death. And the sight of Toante scurrying ignobly to safety will surface to underscore the king's cowardice. Spectators will juxtapose this lasting impression of Toante to the boisterous image he attempts to resurrect in his final speech and see him as the contemptible bully he truly is. Unlike his wise and god-fearing prototype, Toante is a godless coward who craves human butchery and rules by means of fear and violence.

While this thematic novelty points to Rucellai's independence from the ancients, the novel use of sensorial precepts reflects his view of the genre as a literary form rooted in performance. Readers can stage the text in their imagination and apprehend emotionally and intellectually the story and the drama of the characters. They can also contemplate the poetic message and the moral or political ideology that informs it. However, their experience cannot be much different than reading a prose account of a dramatic story with a lesson for them to ponder. They cannot feel the sensorial impact that the stage movement, the sound of the horn, the shrill cries, and the deafening thud produce on the spectators. Only a live audience may appreciate the full potential of these signs both as dramaturgical expedients and as a means of communication. To merely imagine the noises and the characters' gestures and movements is to reduce significantly much of the tension and suspense that they generate in the hearts of the spectators. It also reduces the memorable impression that these signs etch in the minds of the spectators regarding the events they signify. Like milestones, they help recall themes and characters, allowing their semantic peculiarities to resurface and contribute to the spectators' apprehension of the play's ideology and to the enrichment of their theatrical experience. From a theater so conceived, Rucellai emerges as a worthy emulator of the classical canon, and as a playwright who viewed drama as a genre destined primarily for the stage before a live audience.

Three Dramatizations of Dido's Death: Pazzi, Giraldi, and Dolce

The story of Virgil's Dido, the Carthaginian queen who committed suicide after her lover Eneas abandoned her (*Aeneid*, 4), offered Renaissance playwrights the unique opportunity to bring to the stage an original dramatization of a popular classical myth, instead of the usual imitation of ancient plays.[11] Alessandro Pazzi De' Medici wrote *Dido in Cartagine* (1524) at a time when Italian tragedy was still in its infancy and writers were discovering and beginning to appreciate Greek tragedy through translations and imitations. It is not clear to what extent Pazzi's play influenced future Renaissance dramatizations of the story, namely, Giraldi's *Didone* (1541), Dolce's *Didone* (1547), and Etienne Jodelle's *La Didon se sacrifiant* (1558–1560?). Robert Turner, in his comparative study of the four plays, suggested that Giraldi was at least aware of Pazzi's work, that Dolce had a general knowledge of both Pazzi's and Giraldi's tragedies, and that Jodelle wrote his *Didon* under the influence of the Italians.[12] Focusing on the plays' sources (besides the *Aeneid*), on their adherence to established dramatic principles, and on select peculiarities characterizing individual plays, he judged Giraldi's *Didone* the best of the other two Italian versions, Jodelle's better than Giraldi's, and Pazzi's worthless, or, in his words, "comme n'ayant aucune valeur."[13] Be that as it may, my intention here is not to question Turner's critical assessment or the criteria underpinning his conclusion, but only to make two observations. First, a playwright's awareness of previous dramatizations inevitably inspires a sense of competitiveness with his predecessor(s), resulting in a work that revealed his own sense of theater as well as the prevailing taste of his audiences. Second, Turner's critical parameters underscore how traditional criticism has focused on the literary aspects of drama, ignoring its theatrical dimension.[14]

Admittedly, all three Italian dramatizations, the focus of the ensuing discussion, exhibit limited theatrical qualities, as they are too rooted in the verbal expression of Dido's regrets and forlorn passions, which, though highly fitting to poetry, are ill suited for stage representation.[15] The episode that the playwrights dramatize with a varying degree of theatrical emphasis is the death scene in the last act when Dido, having seen Eneas sail away from Carthage, climbs on the pyre built in an inner courtyard of the palace and kills herself with the sword Eneas left behind. Though the three versions follow closely the Virgilian story, the particular treatment of the harrowing details surrounding the queen's death reflects the individual author's view of the genre, his sense of stage representation, and the inherent dramaturgical impact on the audience. Pazzi's rendition of the scene is rooted in verbal discourse, as the episode is mostly narrated by Barce, the nurse of Dido's dead husband, Sychaeus. However, though the queen's death is reported as having taken place, the scene features a series of sensorial sequences that can be fully appreciated only through a stage representation. One such instance is the propagation of scented smoke on stage and, presumably, throughout the auditorium. As the sacrificial priestess prepares the pyre, a woman of the chorus notices that from the altars around the pyre "fumar si vedono dei solenni odori" [one can see smoke of solemn odors] (p. 114). We must take this observation as a stage instruction indicating that smoke arising from burning incense or other matter normally associated with solemn functions, begins to permeate the air on stage. It is reasonable to assume that the smoke eventually makes its way into the theater as to affirm the credibility of the chorus and, at the same time, secure the spectators' participation in the experience. The sense of realism created by the sight and the smell of actual smoke is likely to draw the spectators closer to what is happening beyond the scene and cause them to grow anxious as to its meaning and what may happen next.

Equally theatrical is the chorus's description of the Trojan fleet as it begins to sail away from Carthage:

> Spumar l'onda marina
> dalli agitati remi
> si scorge, e i bianchi veli
> che egualmente via portan gli alti legni.
> Diresti una cittade
> di mille torri piena
> pel verde mar natare
> et sparir da tuoi occhi a poco a poco.
>
> (p. 115)

[One sees the sea waves foaming / under the forceful roars, and the white sails / which equally push the tall ships. / You would say a city / dotted by a thousand towers, / floating on the green sea / and slowly disappearing from your sight.]

Though paraphrasing the Virgilian narrative, the description is quite original both in its comparison of the fleet to a floating city and in its theatrical representation of the faraway action.[16] In a technique somewhat reminiscent of the *hic et nunc*, the audience gets to visualize the action through the chorus's colorful account of tall, white sails spread on the background of a green sea. The comparison of this image to a city of thousand towers (not in the *Aeneid*) adds a sense of corposity to the chorus's verbal description, making it easier for the spectators to picture in their minds the unfolding event. Also, the use of kinetic verbs, such as the "foaming" of the waves, the "agitation" of the roars, and the sails "pushing" the tall ships away into the horizon tends to make the image come to life. The idea of lively activity suggested by these verbs not only helps to visualize the action, it also gives the sensation that the event is developing nearby, narrowing the spatial gap between the auditorium and the dramatic space on which the event is taking place. An important detail, present in Virgil but with significant theatrical impact here, is the breaking of dawn, which allows the chorus to see and describe the events unfolding on the sea below. In Virgil, the detail serves to measure the passing of time and as a touch of realism meant to explain how Dido could see the fleet sailing away. In Pazzi, the transition from the darkness of night to the light of day has the added dramaturgical function of actually rendering the stage illumination progressively brighter, as the chorus indicates:

> Già la rosata aurora
> spegne con l'altrui luce
> del cel li lumi spessi
> che cedon com'è justo al vicin sole.
>
> (p. 115)[17]

[Already the rosy dawn / effaces, with the light of the other (planet, the sun) / the dense lights of the skies / which give way, as it is natural, to the rising sun.]

This sensorial experience reinforces in the spectators the sense that they are witnessing the action in the making and lessens, therefore, their natural resistance to be drawn into the fictional world of the representation. Another theatrical instance that further indicates that the play is meant for the stage is the commotion that news of the queen's death produces on stage. In the *Aeneid*, the poet narrates that a loud scream issued from within the palace. As Fama spread the fateful news, Virgil continues, the city began to mourn the queen, filling the air with great lamentations (4.665–68). Pazzi dramatizes the episode by having Barce announce that the queen has stabbed herself to death. While the old nurse is talking, the chorus hears "strida" [shrieks] (126) that prompt her to exhort all the women of the chorus to run toward the palace: "corriam ch'i' sento il romore / che di questo m'accerta" [let us run, for I hear a noise / which confirms this (the suicide)] (127). These references to noise and movement must be construed as stage cues calling for the characters to rush toward the palace, and for the production of sounds loud enough to be heard in the auditorium, lest the chorus's observations prove insignificant. We must also assume that the spectators see the women run toward the main entrance of the palace, which, according to previous spatial indications, may be either on one side of the stage or facing the auditorium.

A theatrical element not present in Virgil, but reminiscent of Seneca's *Thyestes,* is Pazzi's decision to have King Iarba's messenger bring on stage Pygmalion's head and hands for Dido to behold. Now that the king has avenged the death of Dido's husband, Sychaeus, he expects her to honor her pledge to marry him, a promise she never meant to keep. Nuntio's observation that the queen appears reluctant to look in the vase containing her own brother's limbs, underscores the theatrical nature of this scene. Puzzled by Dido's aversion to approach the dreadful vase and look at the body parts of the man she wanted dead, the messenger observes rhetorically: "Adunque ti turba / vedere justa vendetta del tuo Sicheo?" [Then, it perturbs you / to behold the just revenge of your Sychaeus] (120). Though the question calls attention to Dido's state of mind, it is an important stage direction in that it instructs the actor playing Dido's role to show by means of physical movement, gestures, and facial expressions that she is visibly perturbed.[18] Without the use of words, but only through body language she must express repugnance toward

8: Theatrical Language of Sounds and Movements   197

the savagery, satisfaction for the revenge, disgust at the thought of having to marry her old enemy, and her determined refusal to go on living.

This reliance on nonverbal means of communication reinforces the argument that the play is best suited for the stage, where it can best express its full text. Notwithstanding Pazzi's emphasis on the literary aspects of his tragedy, most notably versification (the play is written mostly in stifling hexameters), it is clear that only spectators may experience the full theatricality of the play. Readers may stage the text in their minds and, inspired by the suggestive power of the word, envision the action and the theatrical signs articulating it. But, imagined movements, smells, and sounds cannot have the same impact as when perceived sensorially. Unlike the spectators, the readers cannot appreciate in its entirety the simulation of daybreak slowly filling the stage or the smell and the sight of the spreading smoke rising from the pyre and the altars around it. Nor can they hear the alarming sounds or sense the conflicting emotions that Dido expresses through her body language upon seeing the horrifying vase. With regard to this last instance, the reader has only Nuntio's verbal observation "turba" to imagine the loathing, the pleasure, and the despondency that the spectator may observe in Dido's expressive gestures. One should caution that this theatrical aspect of the play does not make Pazzi an active promoter of the notion of drama as a theatrical genre, nor does it say that his *Dido* is an easily stageable play. It only shows that even though Renaissance authors were steeped in the art of verbal rhetoric and considered tragedy a literary genre mainly to be read, there was a tendency even among early playwrights to write with an eye for the stage, where audiences could hear and see the plays acted and recited.

The extent to which Pazzi's awareness of the stage influenced other dramatizations of Dido's myth is a matter that awaits a definitive study. We know that Giraldi was aware of *Dido in Cartagine*. However, there is little evidence, at least from the theatrical perspective, that he imitated, adapted, or improved upon Pazzi's play. The plot of his *Didone* is significantly different from that of Pazzi's play, and the cast is practically doubled. Also, he placed a much stronger emphasis on the characters' inner thoughts, as can be surmised by the many and lengthy soliloquies. These variations account, in part, for the length of the play which is almost twice as long as Pazzi's *Dido*.[19] But, of particular interest to us is the emphasis that Giraldi placed on the theatricality of his play, which is mostly on Dido's death scene. There is no smoke to smell or dawn to behold or tall ships to imagine sailing away on the green sea. Lively action, engaging the eyes and ears of the spectators, begins to unfold at the beginning of act 4, where Dido faints following a long (257 lines) and heated confrontation with Eneas. We can well imagine the commotion on stage, as the ladies of the chorus scatter to take her inside the palace, while Achates presses a reluctant Eneas to get away (4.1, p. 95). But true dramatic action starts in the third scene of the last act, when Anna, Dido's sister, calls Barce's attention to a messenger emerging from the palace, "visibly perturbed, shaking his head, and slapping and waiving his hands" (5.3, p. 118).

The sight alarms Anna and Barce so much that they want to run immediately to him to learn the reason for his grieving gestures. They check their instinctive curiosity and choose, instead, to hide and listen to his lamentations. This decision sets in motion a retardation technique meant to raise dramatic tension and hold in suspense the two women and the entire audience. As the messenger continues his lament without revealing its source, the women, overcome by anxiety, approach and press him for details. The delaying expedient grows more exasperating, as the messenger, ignoring Anna's pleas to tell what happened, dwells on the tragic nature of the event rather than on narrating it. To a large extent readers could experience the same effect as the spectators, since for the most part the suspense is verbally created. After all, the primary purpose of the scene is to prepare us, readers and spectators alike, for the dreadful news of how Dido climbed on the funeral pyre and fatally stabbed herself. However, their experiences of the last scene where the ladies bring Dido on stage to die, differ considerably, for, while the readers apprehend it as a conceptual statement, the spectators view it as a lively, physical action. The scene, which Mary Morrison rightly called a spectacle and a "moving finale,"[20] begins to unfold as the royal maidens appear on stage carrying the dying queen. The grieving women, observes Messo, have placed her on the royal throne and "la portano quì tutte piangendo, [. . .] / Eccole" [weeping, they are bringing her here . . . / Here they come] (5.4. p. 124). The action, which readers can only see through their minds' eye, unfolds vividly before the eyes of the spectators. The deictic "eccole" causes everyone in the auditorium to turn in the direction of the maidens who, still wearing black headbands or veils, have begun to walk onto the stage, as in a funeral procession (p. 125). A sense of gloom grips the entire audience as the auditorium slowly fills with the pathetic wailing of all the characters on stage, especially the inconsolable Anna, who faints while attempting to stab herself. As with the fainting of Dido in act 3, here too, we would expect the spectators to feel the tension rising in the auditorium as the ladies-in-waiting rush to prevent Anna from the fatal deed. The play ends as a cortege of grieving characters solemnly carry away their dead queen and her lifeless sister. The somber mood of the emptying stage tightens the emotional hold on the spectators, leaving them to reflect on the entire theatrical experience.

The dramatic force of this scene lies not so much in the grim details, which follow rather closely the Virgilian source, but on the emotional impact arising from the visual apprehension of them. Following Anna's repeated "Oimè,"[21] the readers can imagine her sorrow, but, unlike the spectators, they cannot hear her grieving voice nor see her despairing gestures. They can imagine, too, Dido's repeated efforts to rise and speak, but only the beholder can experience the dramatic impact of such an emotion-wrenching sight. From this theatrical perspective, the critical view of the play as a "pedestrian imitation" of its source is yet another indication of the limitations of literary criticism in its persistence to consider theater merely as a literary text. For, if the story is a faithful reproduction of the Virgilian myth, as Philip Horne has suggested,[22] its theatrical dimension is a novelty reflecting Giraldi's own creativity and sense of drama. His grasp of the dramatic moment is especially apparent when we recall the conclusion of Pazzi's *Dido*, where the episode is entirely narrated. The comparison is not meant to establish the literary or theatrical superiority of one play over the other, but only to observe that Giraldi's decision to represent rather than tell the fatal event points to his keen understanding of what is dramatic and the impact that its representation may have on the audience. The decision also speaks of his dramaturgical ability to tap the spectators' emotional resources, draw them into the action, and move them to pity the tragic victim. This he accomplished without recurring to the terrorizing tactics of exposing the audience to the sight of Senecan atrocities, as he did in his *Orbecche*, the play that set the example for many of the bloody tragedies in the second half of the cinquecento.[23] *Didone*, unlike its sister tragedy, spares the audience the sight of gruesome details, relying only on the pathos of the heroine's last agonizing moments as the means to rouse the spectators' emotions and elicit their compassion for the dying queen.

Blood and horror, instead, are the attractions that Dolce promises in his *Didone*. In the prologue, Cupid tells the audience that he has come to make sure that Dido's city "bathes in her blood" and that old men, women, and children "go prey to swords and flames." There is little lively action on the stage, as the plot develops mostly on verbal accounts, arguments, and lamentations all leading to the climactic death scene of the last act. As in the previous dramatizations of the myth, the particulars surrounding the queen's demise follow closely the source, except for the addition of Anna's own hanging. However, this ghastly deed is not shown but simply reported, as are Dido's horrifying encounter with Sychaeus's bloody ghost (3, p. 16) and her suicide (5.3, p. 36–37). The representation of the bloodshed that Cupid promised in the prologue begins in the last act when Prefetto and Consigliero see Nuntio coming out of the palace carrying a bloodstained sword. The image acquires shocking intensity as a horrified Prefetto asks about the victim of that blood "ancor stillante, e caldo" (still dripping and warm) (5.3, p. 35). The description is clear enough for the readers to picture it vividly in their minds; however, only the spectators can appreciate its full force, as they hear the words and see red liquid dripping on the floor while a rising, faint vapor suggests that it is still warm. This gruesome sight causes the spectators to grow tense and apprehensive, since they are still uncertain as to the nature of the crime and the name of the victim.

Through the customary retardation technique, Dolce continues to hold the audience in suspense by having Nuntio talk about how he is going to tell a most dreadful story, and then claim that he cannot speak, such was the horror. Finally, he describes the event, including the horrific sight of Dido soaked in her own blood, still foaming, bright red, and warm (5.3, p. 37). He has barely finished reporting what he saw, when Consigliero calls attention to a loud noise, followed immediately by the appearance of Bitia frantically pulling her hair and beating her chest with her hands (5.3, p. 38). Bitia's dreadful appearance engenders great apprehension both on stage and in the auditorium, as it gives rise to all sorts of ominous conjectures. The fear that something terrible has happened is soon confirmed by Bitia's account of Anna's own hanging from a window. Notably, the dramatic effect of this sequence lies entirely on the theatrical manifestation of Bitia's grief and not on the hanging per se. With respect to the spectators' apprehension of the action, the suicide, pathetic as it may be, is practically void of drama, since it happened in the past, away from the scene, and thus outside the audience's sensorial perception.

The horror promised in the prologue is mostly narrated and therefore of scarce theatrical relevance. The experience of the spectator is not significantly different than that of the reader, since both must stage the narrative of the atrocities in their minds. However, spectators do appreciate, in ways not consented to the reader, the shocking sight of the bloody sword and the dreadful appearance of Bitia with her disturbing moans and wild gestures. Dolce's choice to horrify the spectators by exposing them to these fearful theatrical occurrences underscores his intent to draw them into the action and move them to pity the tragic victims. Also, the novelty of these events points away from a possible influence by the story's previous dramatizations, where neither Bitia nor the bloody sword are featured. One would expect that Dolce, writing two decades after the first dramatization of the Dido's myth, would place more emphasis on showing rather than telling, as to reflect the growing importance of the stage in the theatrical consciousness of Renaissance dramatists and their audiences.[24] Paradoxically, the theatrical dimension of Dolce's play is not as extensive as that of Giraldi's version, which, in turn, is less than that of Pazzi's *Dido*.

This seemingly anomalous decrease in stage emphasis should not be taken as a decline in theatrical awareness, but as an indication of the playwrights' artistic preferences and agonistic aim to distinguish themselves from their counterparts. It further reveals that the notion of theatricality was not predicated on the number of events shown or on the stage percepts and props employed, but on the nature of the event the playwright chose to emphasize. Thus, while Pazzi made the most extensive use of the stage, none of the details he showed bears directly on the most dramatic moment of the story, namely, Dido's suicide, which is simply told, just as it is in the Virgilian narrative. The representation may fill the spectators with great sensorial gratification, but it does little to arouse their emotions and move them to pity the tragic heroine. Though Pazzi clearly espouses a notion of tragedy as a literary form suited for the stage, he reveals a weak sense of drama, which partly explains his limitations as a tragedian. Giraldi, on the other hand, opted to stage the death scene "with true dramatic flair,"[25] exposing the spectators to the living drama of the dying queen. Dolce, too, chose to expose the spectators to the tragic deed of the story. However, unlike Giraldi, he focused not so much on Dido's heartrending last moments, but on the horror that the sight of the bloody sword might produce within the audience. Disturbing and frightening as the grim image of the sword dripping with warm blood might be, it can only elicit a limited emotional response, since the spectators view it as a sign of a drama already lived out outside their sensorial perception.[26] Thus, if Giraldi's *Didone* is considered the best of these three rather average dramatizations,[27] it is due, at least in part, to its emphasis on the audible and visible anguish characterizing the live drama of its fateful queen. He seems to have understood better than his counterparts that the successful staging of Dido's story hinged on drawing the spectators into the action by arousing not just their "maraviglia" and/or horror, but also, and especially, their compassion for the tragic victim. It is largely this sense of the dramatic stage and the appropriate characterization that ultimately distinguish the three tragedies and their respective authors.

Though the playwrights of the Italian Renaissance did not always exhibit a keen grasp of the tragic moment and the ability to stage it, they all subscribed to the notion that drama should be written for the stage. A dramatist, wrote Trissino, had to envision the characters' costumes and gestures,[28] that is, a stage where the literary text could find its full expression before a live audience. In order to predispose the spectators to a favorable reception of their plays, authors had to engage them both emotionally and intellectually so as to secure their attention and interests. While narrative and poetry appealed to the spectators' imagination and, through it, stirred their emotions, the language of theatrical signs appealed directly to their senses, allowing them to see and hear dramatic deeds being imitated there and then on the stage in their presence. The narrative of the traditional messenger, vivid and articulate as it might be, could only recall for the audience the liveliness, the immediacy, the tension, and suspense that theatrical signs brought to life on the stage for the audience to experience directly. Undoubtedly, there was a growing sense of appreciation for the stage as an intrinsic constituent of drama, but the recognition of theatrical language both as a means of communication and as a dramaturgical device could not guarantee the production of great dramatic works. The failures and the successes of the Italian Renaissance dramatists must ultimately be attributed to their creative talents or limitations, for artistic excellence issues not from one's knowledge of the rules and precepts informing art form, but from one's poetic ability to create.

Conclusion

THE PRECEDING DISCUSSION CONFIRMS OUR NOTION OF CINQUE-cento tragic theater as a window into significant cultural aspects of Renaissance Italy. Through the dramatic stage we can see what theater audiences and, by extension, the people of the Renaissance valued and what concerned them. It allows us a glimpse of the cultural realities that dramatists infused into the ancient genre in order to make it relevant to their audiences both aesthetically and ideologically. But whereas theater is for us a mere window, and a narrow one at that, for Renaissance audiences it was a mirror of their culture. On the stage they saw their customs, recognized their religious beliefs, experienced their fears, and witnessed debates on social prejudice and political ideology. They also appreciated the artistic creativity of the playwrights and of the stage directors or "architects" whose stagecraft and ingenuity satisfied and even challenged prevailing aesthetic taste.

We noted that the function of theater as a reflection of traditions and changing realities was the result of an evolving process that started at the turn of the sixteenth century when classical theater entered the aesthetic and literary consciousness of Italy. Enthusiasm for the classics fostered the discoveries of ancient plays, encouraged their propagation through translations, and inspired several close imitations of them. This purely academic enthusiasm for the classics soon gave way to the growing insistence that theater be relevant to the times, just as it had been for the Greeks and the Romans. Thus, playwrights proceeded to "clothe" the characters of classical tragedies with distinctive elements of their own culture. Ancient kings appeared in sumptuous attire typical of Renaissance princes, and royal retinues were so elegant and so large that clearly reflected contemporary customs and taste. Mythological characters spoke a language reminiscent of Dante and Petrarch, another sign that tragedy was shedding its ancient image and assuming a modern identity.

Scholars have complained about the obvious anachronism that characterizes many a Renaissance tragedy. But, as we saw, it was a peculiarly convenient notion of realism, one that allowed playwrights to claim the *auctoritas* of the ancients and, at the same time, view historical facts and traditions in the context of contemporary decorum and reality. Thus, since in their times it was considered indecorous and unrealistic for a prince to go about without a worthy escort, it was perfectly normal for them to represent a mythological king with soldiers in contemporary, sumptuous, and, at times, exotic uniforms. The anomaly did not deter dramatists from their determination to enliven ancient theater with their own customs and, in the process, reduce the temporal and cultural distance between the fiction of the stage and the reality of the auditorium. To the spectators, a mythological king, say, resembling a Renaissance prince in both manner and appearance was undoubtedly more real than a character wearing a mask symbolizing a king. They simply viewed the incongruence as inherent in the illusion of theater and went on to appreciate all that was emotionally and intellectually relevant to them.

In keeping with this determination to enliven the ancient stage with their own realities, playwrights did not hesitate to have mythical characters voice religious beliefs and invocations that in speech and tone reminded the spectators of their own Christian sentiments. Contemporary audiences certainly believed in the religious conviction of Adriana's counselor that upon death humans "owe their bodies to earth, and their souls / to God" (*Adriana*, 4.3.3–4). Undoubtedly they found little difference between references to Juno as "the Regina delle stelle" or to Venus as "Santa Madre d'Amore" (Dolce, *Didone*, 1, p. 9) and the appellations they commonly reserved for the Holy Virgin. Also, it was not unusual for playwrights to set mythological events in Medieval or Renaissance spatial settings. Kings such as Edippo, Toante, and Creonte lived or stayed in castles featuring deep moats, drawbridges, high walls, and ramparts manned by valiant knights. In some instances, the action took place in a distinctively courtly atmosphere as the cast of characters included barons and knights either present on stage or said to participate in events somewhere in the world of the play.

It was against this contemporary background that dramatists informed their plays with social and political issues of great importance. The use of the deus ex machina was more than a mere dramaturgical expedient; it was also a sign that religion was beginning to assert itself once again as one of the most dominant forces in Italian culture. And the king of the tragic world was more than just the tyrant of old. Through his role playwrights dramatized the symbol of an ideology too rooted in Machiavellian political morality to be fully endorsed by reason-of-state thinkers schooled in the religious imperatives of the

Counter-Reformation. Similarly relevant to the times was the role of the tragic heroine, in whose fate playwrights articulated the debate on the question of misogyny. In dramatizing issues of major concern to society, the stage was more than a mirror of the times, it was also a force that awakened in the consciousness of cinquecento society the need to confront its cultural prejudice, and define or redefine its changing values. Thus, the debate on the nature of kingship, while pointing out the shortcomings of the humanist notion of princeship, argued for the need to anchor Machiavellian theory on religious morality. On the question of misogyny, Renaissance tragedy dramatized its pernicious effect both on its victims and on its perpetrators. It also showed, albeit obliquely, that the overcoming of prejudice does not normally happen overnight, nor is it always readily perceptible; it is an evolving mental and cultural process that is as slow as the issue is complex. Indeed, misogyny is so deeply rooted in man's thinking that the reconceptualization of woman that started then is far from complete today.

There was general consensus that the purpose of theater, just like that of poetry in general, was to teach and to entertain. The first was easily accomplished mainly because playwrights, following the example of the ancients, informed the stage with their own living realities. The second, however, was not so easily achieved because theater, unlike any other poetry, amuses mostly through visual and audible perceptions. This "spectacular" or theatrical dimension of tragedy had to be invented or reinvented, since there was hardly any tradition of stage representations or other similar spectacles, as Muratori lamented. In the main, tragedies had been thought of as literary works written to be read rather than acted out. The dramatist's first task, then, was to get the genre out of the closet and onto the stage. This happened very slowly. In fact, although Italian tragedies had been written since early sixteenth century, *Orbecche* was the first tragedy to be represented on stage (1541). It was this performance that gave Giraldi reason to boast that it was he who restored tragedy to the stage. The first and perhaps most important contribution to the staging of tragedy, and theater in general, was the use of perspective, which opened the way for a new conception of dramatic space. Dramatic space was expanded beyond the physical barriers of the scene to include the buildings, the houses, the streets, and the squares painted on the backdrop. It virtually extended its boundaries anywhere where dramatic events could be sensorially perceived as taking place. All these spaces fostered the theatrical illusion that the development of the action and the roles of the characters were not limited to the visible stage. Dramatists could represent the unrepresentable, such as unusually bloody scenes or gatherings of large crowds, by simply signifying it through loud noises, shrill cries, and other appropriate sounds. In some instances, an eyewitness would describe the unrepresentable event as it was taking place out sight but within earshot of the audience.

In either case, the spectators were made to feel very close to the developing action. The resulting temporal and spatial proximity added a sense of realistic urgency to the happenings on stage, causing the spectators to be easily drawn into the action taking place there and then. No longer did they have to learn of the dramatic action through a messenger, that is, after it took place somewhere away from the stage. The role of the messenger could now be limited to confirming or explaining to anxious spectators the meaning of a loud crash or the sound of a horn already heard in the entire auditorium. The spectators were in the hall not to hear a story being told, but to see it develop before their very eyes or within hearing range. They did not have to rely only on the spoken word for information about the action and the characters. Sounds and movements, tone and gestures, colors and smell, physical appearance and facial expressions were all effective means of communication. They heard and saw a language of signs that was either complementary to the language of words or produced a meaning of its own. Either way, the semiotics text contributed significantly to their understanding of the play and to their theatrical experience overall.

Regretfully, traditional scholarship never appreciated fully this aspect of theater, as it focused its attention mostly on the literary aspect of the written text. Such a limited approach contributed to the persisting characterization of Renaissance tragedy as static and "talky." It also failed to appreciate that the genre, which at the turn of the century represented a mere infatuation with the ancients, eventually became a theater in its own right, grounded in living realities and on aesthetic preferences that reflected and often inspired the taste of the times. It spoke, as theater should, to its audiences about their problems and predilections in a manner that was both intelligible and entertaining.

Both its accomplishments and its failures became an important legacy of the art of theater in Italy and abroad, for all the Italian experiences became a presence in the theaters of all of Europe. On the French and English stage in particular, the Italian Renaissance tragedy, while showing the pitfalls to be avoided, inspired "stately-written tragedies" about which Kyd's Hieronimo tells Balthazar, "The Italian tragedians were so sharp of wit" (*Spanish Tragedy*, 4.1). But the Italians' most important legacy lies in having discovered classical tragedy, restoring it onto the stage, and giving it a modern identity. Appropriately it became known as the Italian Renaissance tragedy because it was the living traditions and the artistic genius of that period that brought to life the ancient genre and guaranteed its survival in Western culture.

Notes

Preface

1. Lienhard Bergel, speaking of the low esteem that for centuries has characterized Italian Renaissance tragedy, writes that in the past critics looked upon these tragedies "mainly as school exercises in practicing the prescriptions contained in Aristotle's *Poetics* and in the interpretations which the text had received in the sixteenth century. The plays were tested in regard to their faithfulness to the famous three unities and other technical details; the texts themselves were discussed only in passing." (Bergel, "The Rise of Cinquecento Tragedy," *Renaissance Drama* 8 [1965]: 199).

2. For Jonas Barish, closet plays are "plays designed to be read rather than played—experienced, that is, in the closet, some enclosed or intimate space like a library, a study, a chapel, or room for meditation." (Barish, "The Problem with Closet Drama in the Italian Renaissance," *Italica* 71, 1 [1994]: 4). For the origin of the term see the footnote to his definition. He also discusses the term within the context of the nineteenth century in his *The Antitheatrical Prejudice* (Berkeley: University of California Press, 1981), 325.

3. Benedetts Croce, dwelling on the question why Italian Renaissance tragedy was not great theater, invokes Cattaneo's view that "ciò dipese dal caso che fece nascere lo Shakespeare sulle sponde dell'Avon e non sulle rive di un fiume italiano" [it depended from chance which made it so that Shakespeare was born on the banks of the Avon and not on the banks of an Italian river] (Croce, *La letteratura italiana*, vol. 1 [Bari: Laterza, 1967], 432).

Chapter 1. The Making of Italian Renaissance Tragedy

1. For the dissemination of Aristotle's *Poetics* and its influence on dramatic theory during the Italian Renaissance, see Marvin Carlson, *Theories of the Theater: A Historical and Critical Survey* (Ithaca: Cornell University Press, 1984), 37–38.

2. Arguments for the unities centered on *The Poetics*, 5.9, where Aristotle merely compares tragedy and epic poetry, observing that, among other differences, they "differ also in the time consumed by the events treated." Without intending to set a rigid unity of time, he concludes that although the two genres were originally alike in this respect, "tragedy [now] tries as far as possible to limit the time of its action to one revolution of the sun or to depart only slightly from that rule, but epic poetry does not so limit itself in time." *The Poetics of Aristotle*, trans. P. H. Epps [Chapel Hill: University of North Carolina Press, 1970], 5.9).

3. This is how Muratori begins "Dissertatio" XXIX: "Qui Ludi publici, quæ magnifica Spectacula & oblectamenta Populo præberentur Italico post declinationem Imperii Romani, atque ante Annum Christi Millesimum, pauca novimus, quia ne Historias quidem illius ævi nisi pauculas habemus. Præterea suspicandi locus est, barbarica illa tempora, ac rudes gentes parum sibi procurasse, quæ tanta pecuniæ effusione a Græcis ac Romanis olim edebantur, ac tanto studio Populus spectatum accurrebat. . . . Præter militares Ludos, qui oblectarent Langobardorum gentem, postquam Italia potita est, alios frustra in Chartis quærimus" [As to what public games, what magnificent spectacles and pastimes were offered to the Italian people after the fall of the Roman empire and before the year one thousand, we know little, since we have but few stories of that period. In addition, there is room to assume that the barbarous times and the primitive people cared little about those things which were once built with great effusion of money by the Greeks and the Romans, and which the people eagerly came to watch. . . . Besides the military games which entertained the Longobards, after Italy was conquered, in vain do we search the documents for information about other forms of entertainment] (Ludovico Muratori, *De Speculis et Ludi*, in *Antiquitates Italicae Medii Aevi* [Mediolani, 1739; rpt. an., Bologna, 1975], 831).

4. Aelius Donatus, comparing tragedy to comedy, observes that whereas comedy deals with men in ordinary situations, small dangers, and actions with happy endings, "in Tragoedia omnia contraria, ingentes personae, magni timores, exitus funesti habentur" [tragedy, to the contrary, features great characters, deep fears, and a sorrowful conclusion] (Aelius Donatus, *De tragoedia et comoedia*, in *Handbook of French Renaissance Dramatic Theory*, ed. H. W. Lawton [Manchester: Manchester University Press, 1949], 11).

5. For a detailed discussion of Isidore's concept of tragedy, see Henry Ansgar Kelly, *Ideas and Forms of Tragedy from Aristotle to the Middle Ages* (Cambridge: Cambridge University Press, 1993), 36–50, especially where he writes that the "upshot of Isidore's central teaching on tragedy" is that it deals with "*facinora sceleratum regum luctuosa*, evil and sorrowful deeds of evil kings" (49). On Lucan's view of the genre, see p. 92.

6. In explaining the title of his poem to Cangrande, Dante points out that contrary to comedy "tragedia in principio est admirabilis et quieta, in fine seu exitu est fetida et horribilis" [tragedy at the beginning is admirable and serene, at the end, its conclusion is foul and horrible] ("Epistola," 13.29). Also, in *De vulgari eloquentia*, having noted that contrary to the ordinary style of comedy, tragedy uses the higher style, Dante observes that "Stilo equidem tragico tunc uti videmur quando cum gravitate sententie tam superbia carminum quam constructionis elatio et excellentia vocabulorum concordat" [the tragic style is clearly to be used whenever both the magnificence of the verses and the lofty excellence of construction and vocabulary accord with the gravity of the subject-matter] (2.4.7). In the *Inferno*, Virgil, in pointing out the alleged diviner Eurypylus, says: "Euripilo ebbe nome, e così 'l canta / l'alta mia tragedìa" [Eurypylus was his name, / as my high tragedy sings] (20.113). And later, when he meets Ulysses and Diomedes, he begs them to speak to him, reminding them that he immortalized them "quando nel mondo gli alti versi scrissi" [when in the world I wrote my high verses] (*Inferno*, 26, 82).

7. Barish, "The Problem with Closet Drama," 6. Also, noting that Medieval notions of theater were based on misreading of authors like Isidore who, in turn, misread authors like Livy, Barish concludes that the "theoretical pronouncements of medieval authors often make it clear that they did not think of tragedy as a theatrical form at all. Rather, the term denoted a certain kind of story, presented in a certain elevated style."

8. Kelly, having suggested that only Pietro Alighieri had any knowledge of the actable dimension of tragedy, which was Isidore's idea of dumb show with voice-over, concludes: "other commentators remained completely in the dark about the form of the tragedies as stage-plays, and the same holds for Albertino Mussato, who took the momentous step of writing an imitation of Senecan tragedy" (Kelly, *Ideas and Forms of Tragedy*, 219).

9. H. B. Charleton, *The Senecan Tradition in Renaissance Tragedy* (Manchester: Manchester University Press, 1946), 67.

10. We have no evidence that the play was actually performed in Rome "par les soins de Léon X, en 1515" [in 1515, under the auspices of Leo X], as suggested by H.-J. Molinier, *Mellin De Saint-Gelays* (Genève: Slatkine Reprints, 1968), 488. Carmelo Musumarra erroneously gives 1556 as the date of the first performance of *Sofonisba* in Vicenza (*La poesia tragica* [Florence: Olsehki, 1972], 55). There was a 1556 performance, but, according to Paulette Leblanc (*Les écrits théoriques et critiques* [Paris: A.-G. Nizet, 1972], 106) and to Raymond Lebègue (*Études sur le Théatre Français* [Paris: A.-G. Nizet, 1977], 164), it was in the French version of Mellin de Saint-Gelais at Blois, before Henry II and Catherine de Medici. However, Molinier (*Mellin De Saint-Gelays*, 489) gives 1554 as the date of that representation. The discrepancy persists in contemporary scholarship, as critics such as Federico Doglio (*Il teatro tragico italiano* [Bologna: Guanda, 1960], lxxi), Marco Ariani (*Il teatro italiano* [Turin: Einaudi, 1977], 1.8; there is no actual page number in Ariani's bio-bibliographical note preceding *Sofonisba*), and Mary Morrison (*The Tragedies of G.-B. Giraldi Cinthio* [Lewiston: Edwin Mellen Press, 1997], 2) accept 1554 as the actual date of the performance. Others, such as Renzo Cremante (*Teatro del Cinquecento* [Milan and Naples: Ricciardi, 1988], 17), prefer the later date of 1556. The inconsistency is accentuated by the confusion as to whose wedding occasioned the performance at Blois. Lebègue writes that the play was staged in occasion of the double weddings of "M. de Sipierre avec Mlle de Piennes et de M. de Saint-Amant Barbazan avec Mlle d'Humières" (*Études sur le Théatre Français*,160). But, both Leblanc (174) and Molinier (489) indicate that the wedding was that of the Marquis d'Elboeuf.

11. Though we know that it was first printed in 1525, the date of composition oscillates between 1515 and 1516. Guido Mazzoni, suggesting that Trissino and Rucellai were writing their respective plays at the same time and were engaged in friendly rivalry, concludes that both *Sofonisba* and *Rosmunda* "furono compiute dentro il 1515" [were finished within the year 1515] (Guido Mazzoni, ed., *Le opere di Giovanni Rucellai* [Bologna: Zanichelli, 1887], xvii).

12. Alessandro Pazzi, "Prefatione" to his *Cyclope*, in *Le tragedie metriche* (Bologna: Commissione per i testi di lingua, 1969), 141, 144. In the 1524 "Prefatione" to his *Dido in Cartagine* and *Iphigenia in Tauris,* Pazzi refers to either of the plays as "poema." This designation was also common among later playwrights such as Dell'Anguillara, who defines tragedy as "Poesia . . . alta di stile" [poetry written in high style] (*Edippo*, in *Teatro italiano antico*, ed. Gaetano Poggiali [Milan: Società Tipografica de' Classici Italiani, 1808–12], 8.6).

13. Trissino points out that the play had to be written in Italian because, "havendosi a rappresentare in Italia, non potrebbe essere intesa da tutto il popolo s'ella fosse in altra lingua che Italiana composta; et appresso i Costumi, le Sentenzie et il Discorso non arrecherebbono universale utilitate e diletto, se non fossero intese da li' ascoltanti. Sì che, per non le tòrre la Rappresentazione, la quale (come dice Aristotele) è la più dilettevole parte de la Tragedia . . . , elessi di scriverla in questo idioma" [since it would be represented in Italy, it would not be understood by the people if it were composed in a language other than Italian. Furthermore, the

customs, the speeches and the discourse, would not bring profit and pleasure if they were not intelligible to the listeners. Thus, in order not to take the Representation away from it, which (as Aristotle says) is the most delightful part of Tragedy . . . , I chose to write it in this idiom] (in Cremante, *Teatro del Cinquecento,* 31). Giraldi defends his tragedies "a lieto fine" [with happy endings], arguing that rather than pleasing the academicians he prefers to please the spectators, that is, those "per piacere dei quali la favola si conduce in scena" [for whom the story is represented on stage] (Giambattista Giraldi Cinthio, "Discorso intorno al comporre delle commedie e delle tragedie," *Scritti critici,* ed. Camillo Crocetti [Milan: Marzorati, 1973], 184).

14. Giovani Giorgio Trissino, *La Quinta divisione della poetic* (Weinberg, *Trattati* 2:7–44), 2.16. Also, in the same treatise, Trissino, having noted repeatedly the presence and the significance of the spectators, writes that the sixth element of tragedy, following plot, character, thought, etc., is the representation which, "per essere quella che primamente s'appresenta agli occhi dei spettatori, pare essere la prima e principale parte della tragedia" [since it is the first thing that appears before the eyes of the spectators, seems to be the first and principal part of tragedy] (2.15).

15. Alessandro Pazzi, in the dedication of his tragedies to Pope Clement VII, noting that of all the great tragedians of the past only Seneca, Aeschylus, Euripides, and Sophocles were known, suspects that "ancora di questi molte et molte Tragedie alle tempi nostri non si truovino" [many of their tragedies are still missing] (*Le tragedie metriche,* 44). Eugenio Garin, speaking of the enthusiasm with which humanists searched for ancient texts, writes that in 1413 the Sicilian scholar Giovanni Aurispa "comprava codici di Sofocle e Euripide a Chio" [was buying Sophoclean and Eurpidean manuscripts in Chios], and in 1421 he was in Greece from which he would return with an entire library of 238 manuscripts (Eugenio Garin, *La cultura del Rinascimento* [Milan: Il Saggiatore, 1995], 32). Agostino Pertusi, citing A. Turyn, states that by the end of the sixteenth century more than one hundred Euripidean manuscripts (out of a total of 368) were owned by Italian, French and English humanists (Agostino Pertusi, "Il ritorno alle fonti," *Venezia e l'Oriente fra tardo Medioevo e Rinascimento,* ed. Pertusi [Florence: Sansoni, 1966], 210).

16. Pertusi, "Il ritorno alle fonti," 217. He also observes that the Latin translations of Euripides were meant to render the Greek tragedies "più accessibili al pubblico degli studiosi—ed anche dei letterati in senso generico" [more accessible to the community of scholars—and also of *litterati* in a general sense] (221).

17. Speaking of Dolce's commitment to revitalize ancient texts, which he thought readers would find useful, Terpening notes that Dolce "fulfilled his debt to these authors by translating their works in a way that brought them to life for a new class of readers" (Ronnie Terpening, *Lodovico Dolce* [Toronto: University of Toronto Press, 1997], 166).

18. Russo argued most convincingly that "l'intervento dei vari Castelvetro nel Cinquecento, fu benefico, in quanto evitò che il nostro teatro popolare si dissipasse e si sciogliesse e prolungasse in una serie infinita di cronache (come approssimativamente i serials dei cinematografi moderni o degli autori televisivi). Le tre unità, di cui discutevano il Castelvetro, il Maggi, lo Scaligero, e altri sulle loro traccie, richiamavano ad una più rigorosa coerenza e strettezza la composizione delle parti di una tragedia" [The intervention by the various Castelvetro in the Cinquecento was beneficial in that it prevented our popular theater from dissipating into an endless series of stories (somewhat like modern movie sequels or television writers). The three unities discussed by Castelvetro, Maggi, Scaligero, and others called for a more rigorous coherence and a closer link between the parts of a tragedy] (Luigi Russo "La tragedia nel Cinque e Seicento," *Belfagor* 1 [1959]: 15).

19. Speaking of the successful reception accorded to his *Marianna*, Dolce, in his dedicatory letter to Antonio Molino, writes that the 1565 performance in the house of the Venetian Sebastiano Erizzo, though without scenography or music, "ella fu comunemente lodata da trecento e più gentiluomini che vi si erano raunati per udirla" [it was applauded by more than three hundred gentlemen spectators who had come to see it] (in Cremante, *Teatro del Cinquecento*, 745). Antonio Cicogna writes that in 1566 Dolce's *Le troiane* was successfully represented with beautiful music and costumes by Antonio Molino and by Gradenigo, and, quoting Dolce "colla onoratissima compagnia di egregi cittadini, parte de' quali con sommissima laude di dottrina e di eloquenza trattano le diverse cause che occorrono dinanzi ai tribunali ed alle corone de' giudici, e parte ancora esercitano diversi uffici civili onoratamente" [with the honorable company of important citizens, some of whom are lauded for the great doctrine and eloquence with which they argue before judges and state tribunals, while others hold civic offices with honor and distinction] (Cicogna, "Memoria intorno la vita," in *Memorie dell' I.R. Intituto venteto di scienze, lettere ed arti* II [Venice: Presso la segretaria dell' I. R. Instituto nel Palazzo Ducale, 1862], 160).

20. Giraldi wrote no fewer than nine tragedies and is second only to Lodovico Dolce who wrote two original tragedies, translated all of Seneca's dramas, and imitated many Greek plays. Neri referred to them as "i due grandi divulgatori della tragedia" [the two great promoters of tragedy] (Ferdinando Neri, *La tragedia Italiana nel Cinquecento* [Firenze: Galletti e Cocci, 1904] 94).

21. Giambattista Giraldi Cinthio, "Lettera sulla tragedia (1543)," in *Trattati di poetica e retorica del Cinquecento*, ed. Bernard (Bari: Laterza, 1970), 1.480.

22. On the enthusiastic reception of *Orbecche*, see Giraldi's dedicatory letter to Ercole II ("Lettera," 1.480), and Cremante, *Teatro del Cinquecento*, 283–85.

23. Dolce, in informing Antonio Molino that in 1565 his *Marianna* was represented twice in the palace of the Duke of Ferrara, proudly points out that "quantunque la prima volta per la gran moltitudine fosse turbato il rappresentarla, la seconda fu confermato il giudizio primiero" [though the first performance was hindered by the unusually large audience, the second was highly acclaimed] (in Cremante, *Teatro del Cinquecento*, 745).

24. Attributing tragedy's lack of popularity, among other things, to its high cost, Ingegneri writes that if we were to represent *Oedipus the King* according to modern royal decorum, expenses would be so high that "ricercano a punto borsa reale" [would rightly require a royal purse] (Angelo Ingegheri, *Della poesia rappresentativa*, in *Storia documentaria del teatro italiano*, ed. Ferruccio Marotti [Milan: Feltrinelli: 1974], 275). Financial support by wealthy sponsors was necessary even when performances were given at private residences, as it was the case in several of Giraldi's plays which were performed at his house. For specifics, see Giulio Bertoni's letter in *Giornale storico*, XCIX (1932): 282–83, n. 2. In this context, Iacopo Castellini, in a letter to Giovan Battista Strozzi, admits his inability to provide stage instructions for the eventual representation of his *Asdrubale* mainly because he did not have the "commodità di farla recitare a mie spese" [financial resources to have it represented at my expenses] (in Ariani, *Il Teatro*, 2.983). And Leone de' Sommi underscores the importance of sumptuous costumes "massimamente a questi tempi che sono le pompe nel lor sommo grado" [especially in our times when pomp has gone to extremes] (*Quattro dialoghi in materia di rappresentazioni sceniche*, ed. Ferruccio Marotti [Milan: Il Polifilo, 1968], 3.48).

25. On conspiracies and jealousies among Renaissance petty nobles, see Burckhardt's chapters on tyranny in his *The Civilization of the Renaissance in Italy* (New York:

Harper & Row, 1975), especially 1.26–81. See, also, Luciano Chiappini's version of the conspiracy against Borso d'Este, and the attempt against Erocle I (*Gli Estensi* [Milan: Dall'Oglio, 1967], 136–38; 151–54).

26. Joseph Kennard suggests that "all the literature of the cinquecento, and especially that of the theater, though it owed much to the perception and taste of the whole people, was composed for the most part by men of the middle rank for the amusement of citizens and nobles" (Kennard, *The Italian Theatre* [New York: Benjamin Bloom, 1964], 136). Ariani too, claims that "per tutto il Cinquecento i tragediografi vengono o dall'aristocrazia o da una burocrazia gentilizia o alto borghese asservita alla corte" [throughout the sixteenth century dramatists come either from the aristocracy or from a noble or bourgeois bureaucracy typically servile to the court] (Ariani, *Il teatro*, 1. XI). However, Ruggiero Romano points out that not every writer was totally subservient to the court, for "molto spesso, il fondo di dignità, la capacità di protesta tacita, che si trovano in questi personaggi è nettamente superiore a tutto quanto una certa tradizione di studi vorrebbe far credere" [very often the sense of dignity and the ability for tacit protest that one finds in this sense, are far more than a certain scholarly tradition would want us to believe] (Romano *Tra due crisi* [Torino: Einaudi, 1971], 126). For a discussion of the notion of "protesta tacita," see my "Blaime-by-praise Irony."

27. For biographical details on Aretino, see Cleugh's *The Divine Aretino* (New York: Stein and Davis, 1966); on Dolce's life, see Terpening, *Lodovico Dolce,* especially 8–9; on Groto, see Bocchi's *Luigi Groto (il Cieco d'Andria)* (Adria, 1886).

28. Harold Bloom, *The Western Canon: The Books and School of the Ages* (New York: Harcourt Brace, 1994), 34; but, see the whole chapter for a stimulating discussion on poetic freedom and creativity.

29. Peter Burke, *The Italian Renaissance: Culture and Society in Italy* (Princeton: Princeton University Press, 1986), 109. For a fuller discussion of the issue, see chapter 4 "Patrons and Clients," especially the section "Patrons v. Artists," 100–110.

30. In his December 1546 letter to Valerio Amano, Farnese's secretary, Aretino hopes that the Duke will prevail upon the Pope to show some generosity, for "senza i suoi doni ho da vivere come son visso. Imperoché solo la fama, solo l'onore, solo la lode è cibo, alimento e vitto de la virtù" [without his gifts I must go on living in much the same way I have lived. Although, only fame, only honor, only praise is virtue's food, aliments and nourishment] (in Cremante, *Teatro del Cinquecento,* 577–78).

31. Marvin Herrick, *Italian Tragedy in the Renaissance* (Urbana: University of Illinois Press, 1965), 287.

32. Ariani, *Il teatro,* 2. 997. Tadeusz Kowzan observes that from the Greeks to the Romans to eighteenth-century Europe there has always been a preference for plots from known sources, such as myths and historical events. With specific reference to Renaissance playwrights, he writes that they "ne tenaient pas à l'originalité absolue de leurs oeuvres; il leur suffisait d'être les premiers dans leur langue" [they were not interested in the absolute originality of their works; they were satisfied to be first in their language] (Kowzan, *Littérature et spectacle* [Warsaw, 1975], 158). And Hamilton suggests that dramatists should visit the old and through their ideas and creative ability make it relevant to the audience. For him, old material is best for new plays (Clayton Hamilton, *The Theory of the Theater* [New York: Henry Holt, 1939], 163–64). Against this prevailing view, Giraldi argued that new plots were equally effective, for the spectator, upon learning of the novelty of the plot, "alza la mente e cerca di non perderne parola" [pays close attention and tries not to miss a word] ("Discorso," 177).

33. Antiphanes. "Fragments of the Comedies," in *The Fragments of Attic Comedy,* ed. John Maxwell (Leiden: E. J. Brill, 1959), fragment 191, 2:257–59.

NOTES 215

34. In the "Argomento" preceding his *Didone,* Dolce defends his departure from the Virgilian source by noting that "questa licentia diedero già ad alcune delle sue Tragedie non meno Sofocle, che Euripide" [Sophocles as well as Euripides took similar liberties with some of their tragedies].

35. Petrarch writes: "Standum denique Senece consilio, quod ante Senecam Flacci erat, ut scribamus scilicet sicut apes mellificant, non servatis floribus sed in favos versis, ut ex multis et variis unum fiat, idque aliud et melius." [Thus according to Seneca's advice, first suggested by Flaccus, we must write as the bees make honey, not by picking flowers but by turning them into honeycombs, so that from the many and the various only one is made that is different and better] (*Rerum familiarum,* 23.19). For a full discussion of Petrarch's view on imitation, see Umberto Bosco, *Francesco Petrarca,* (Bari: Laterza, 1961), 128–30. For a wide perspective on the concept of imitation in the cultural and philosophical context of the Renaissance, see Ferruccio Ulivi, *L'imitazione nella poetica del Rinascimento* (Milan: Marzorati, 1959). On the use of the simile of the bees in the Renaissance, see Giovanni Rucellai's *Api,* pp.4–5; Poliziano's *Stanze,* vv. 200–201; Baldesar Castiglione, *Il libro del Cortegiano,* ed. Guilio Preti (Turin: Einaudi, 1960) 1.26; Dolce's *Apologia,* 2.v^r.

36. Castelvetro, after pointing out that a poet would be considered a "ladro o vile" [thief or a coward] if he were to appropriate "le figure delle parole usate dagli altri, come sono le traslationi, e 'l rimanente dell'altre figure" [the figures of speech used by others, such as metaphors and other figures], distinguishes between natural and poetic imitation, noting that poetry "non solamente non seguita l'essempio altrui proposto, o non fa quella cosa medesima che già è stata fatta . . . , ma fa una cosa del tutto divisa dalle fatte in fino a quel dì, & proponesi altrui, così si può dire, essempio da seguitare" [not only does not copy existing models or duplicate something already made . . . , but makes a thing that stands clearly apart from all the others made before that day, and it becomes, so to speak, a model for others to follow]. Imitation, then, "è, o si dee, o si può appellare gareggiamento del poeta, & della dispositione della fortuna, o del corso delle mondane cose in trovare uno accidente d'attione humana più dilettevole ad ascoltare, & più maraviglioso" [is or should or could be called a contest between the poet and the disposition of fortune or the course of worldly events to find an instance of human actions that is both delightful and marvelous to behold] (Lodovico Castelvetro, *Poetica d'Aristotele Vulgarizzata* [Munich: Wilhelm Fink Verlag, 1968], 2.1.37–38).

37. With reference to the advance knowledge of the plot and to the audience's tendency to appreciate variants and innovations, Manfred Pfister notes that advance knowledge "releases the attention of the audience to appreciate the particular variant and interpretation of the myth enacted in the play. [. . . It also tends to form a] contrasting inter textual background which emphasizes the elements that deviate from the older version, thus enduing those elements with greater informational significance" (Pfister, *The Theory and Analysis of Drama,* trans. John Halliday [Cambridge: Cambridge University Press, 1988], 43). And Marvin Carlson, expanding on Kowzan's view (see note 32 above) that theatrical plots were usually reworkings of well known subjects or characters, writes that "previous acquaintance with a particular dramatic action added further preparation for audience members" (Carlson, "Audiences and the Reading of Performance," in *Interpreting the Theatrical Past,* ed. Thomas Postlewait and Bruce A. McConachie [Iowa City: University of Iowa Press, 1989], 87).

38. This same moral tone is present in Giraldi's *Euphimia,* where Prologue warns the spectators against placing their trust in ungrateful men: "Così vi guardi il Ciel di havere à porre / In ingrat'huomo i benefici vostri" [May Heaven protect you from entrusting / the ungrateful with your good deeds]. Speaking of the moral

didacticism of Giraldi's plays, Philip Horne believes that it "is subordinate to an overriding religious belief in the existence of Divine Providence" He adds that "all his tragedies with happy endings are in a way dramatic *exampla*, illustrating how, despite all the ups and downs of Fortune, human destinies are in the hands of a benevolent Higher Intelligence" (Horne, *The Tragedies of Giambattista Cinthio Giraldi* [Oxford: Oxford University Press, 1962], 38). Dolce, too, believed in the didactic function of theater, as evinced by the character Tragedia (appended to his *Ifigenia*, p. 53) who warns the audience to let the misfortunes of others be of example to them: "il mal d'altrui vi porga esempio" [may the misfortunes of others be of example to you].

39. For a discussion of the role of the merchants and the social value placed on their activities, see Vittore Branca, especially the chapter entitled "L'epopea dei mercanti," where merchants are called pioneers, "veri eroi dell'intrapendenza e della tenacia umana" [true heroes of human enterprise and tenacity] (Branca, *Boccaccio medievale* [Florence: Sansoni, 1970], 134), and "precursori della società moderna . . . paladini di mercatura" [precursors of modern society . . . paladins of commerce] (164).

40. William G. McCollum, *Tragedy* (New York: Macmillan, 1957), 113. Hamilton echoes this same notion as he suggests that the "dramatist's thoughts must fall within the mental range of the multitude he is writing for" (Hamilton, *The Theory of the Theater*, 103).

41. For a comprehensive view of Machiavellism in Renaissance Europe, see, inter alia, Peter Donaldson, *Machiavelli and the Mystery of State* (Cambridge: Cambridge University Press, 1988). For the presence of Machiavelli in the politics of Renaissance England, see Victoria Kahn, *Machiavellian Rhetoric: From the Counter-Reformation to Milton* (Princeton: Princeton University Press, 1994).

42. Russo writes that "quanto alla nascita della tragedia nel secondo Cinquecento e nel Seicento, noi siamo d'avviso che la tragedia nasce tutte le volte che c'è nella civiltà una profonda crisi etico-politica e religiosa. . . . Ripetiamo: non sono gli avvenimenti luttuosi, i sublimi e orripilanti delitti, che determinano il nascere della tragedia in senso poetico o teatrale, ma sono le profonde crisi spirituali, che portano . . . a cotesto genere letterario della tragedia" [concerning the birth of tragedy in the second half of the Cinquecento and in the Seicento, we believe that tragedy is born whenever the culture experiences a profound ethico-political and religious crisis . . . We repeat: it is not the mournful events, the sublime and horrifying crimes that determine the birth of tragedy in the poetic or theatrical sense, but the profound spiritual crises which lead to the literary genre of tragedy] (Russo, "La tragedia,"18).

43. Also, in Giraldi's *Antivalomeni*, Prologue proposes to teach and amuse the spectators

> Col condurre in scena,
> Con sembianza del ver, la miglior forma
> De le migliori, fra le attioni humane.
>
> (p. 10)

[By bringing on the stage, / with as much realism as possible, / the best of human actions.]

On the relationship between the fictional place of the representation and the real place of the spectator, see Cesare Molinari, "Les rapports entre la scène et les spectateurs dans le théatre italien du XVIe Siècle," in *Le lieu théatral a la Renaissance*, ed. Jean Jacquot (Paris: Editions du Centre National de la Recherche Scientifique, 1964), 61–71.

44. Deploring the length of monologues, Ingegneri noted with sarcasm that "se ne trovano (in diversi moderni particolarmente) alcuni di tanta lunghezza, e di così poca verisimilitudine, che chi potesse dormire tutto quel tempo, e risvegliarsi poi a suo buon piacere quando ne vengono l'altre scene in dialogo, credo che ne sentirebbe assai più diletto" [there are (especially among many contemporaries) some scenes of so much length and of so little verisimilitude that the spectators who could sleep through them and leisurely wake up when there is a scene with dialogue would enjoy it more] (Ingegneri, *Della poesia rappresentativa*, 284).

45. Molinari, noting that Cinquecento tragedy was more concerned with certain aspects of its poetic structure, such as the Aristotelian reversal and recognition, rather than with its theatrical aspect, concludes that "solo raramente la struttura drammatica viene messa in relazione al fatto rappresentativo o spettacolare, per il resto quasi totalmente ignorato" [only rarely is the dramatic structure seen in relationship with the representative or spectacular element, for the rest almost totally ignored] (Cesare Molinari, "Scenografia e spettacolo nelle poetiche del '500," *Il Veltro* vi (1964): 894).

46. Giraldi reminded Giulio Ponzio Ponzoni, the actor who played Oronte, that "Guerriera vostra . . . veduta la testa di Oronte . . . subito cadde come morta" [your lady friend Guerriera, upon seeing Oronte's head, immediately fainted and fell as if she were dead] (Giraldi, "Discorso," 198).

47. Responding to his critics, Giraldi argues that actors may speak out their thoughts aloud without fear of being overheard by the spectators, for "gli spettatori non sono in considerazione agli istrioni, ma che ragionano come se fossero nelle proprie case" [because spectators are not taken into account by the actors, who may speak as if they were in the privacy of their own homes] (Giraldi, "Lettera," 1.483). In the "Discorso," he insists that for the sake of verisimilitude actors must recite as if "non vi fossero spettatori, i quali son solo in considerazione alla persone (sic) che fa il prologo" [here were no spectators, whose presence is acknowledged only by the character in the role of Prologue] (221).

48. Leone de' Sommi, *Quattro dialoghi*, 1.19.

49. Giraldi writes: "è meglio che compaia nella scena favola di non molto pregio, che sia ben rappresentata, che averne una lodevolissima che abbia gli istrioni freddi ed inetti nell'azione" [it is better to represent a play of little worth, but well performed, rather than to stage a well known play that features actors that are both cold and inept] (Giraldi, "Discorso," 220). He also recognized the importance of the scene or *apparato* that, "quantunque egli non entri nella favola e non sia parte né del nodo, né della soluzione, è egli però necessario alla rappresentazione" [although it is not an integral part of the plot or of the conflict or the solution, is necessary to the representation] (219). This, however, should not be taken to mean that the spectacle was considered more important than the written text, for Giraldi strongly believed, following Aristotle, in the importance of the literary text. In his own words, "non è lo spettacolo che da sé induca la commiserazione, ma le affettuosissime parole. . . . E questo è quello che dice Aristotile essere officio de' migliori poeti" [it is not the spectacle in itself that brings about the tragic effect, but moving words . . . And this is what Aristotle calls the office of good poets] (188). Trissino shared this view as he noted that "la tragedia ancora ch'ella non fosse rappresentata non starebbe di essere tragedia e di fare la sua dottrina" [even if tragedy were not represented, it would still fulfill its purpose] (Trissino, *La Quinta divisione della poetica*, 1.44).

50. Ingegneri points out that one of the most common mistake playwrights tend to make when composing dramas is that they "non si fingono (sì come essi arrebbono a fare) spettatori di quelle. Ma mettendo giù talora a caso le cose che loro vengono in fantasia, non badano più che tanto se ciò ch'essi fanno s'accommodi o

218   NOTES

non s'accommodi al palco: al cui compartimento non hanno un riguardo al mondo" [do not put themselves, as they should, in the place of the spectators. But putting down haphazardly whatever comes to their minds, they do not consider if what they do is suitable or not for the stage, for which they have no care in the world] (Ingegneri, *Della poesia rappresentativa*, 290).

51. Giorgio Vasari writes that Bastiano San Gallo, better known as Aristotile, surpassed himself in arranging the scene for the 1539 performance of Landi's *Commondo* in occasion of Cosimo's wedding to Leonora of Toledo. Among the numerous representations in perspective, Vasari recalls, Aristotile "ordinò con molto ingegno una lanterna di legname a uso d'arco dietro a tutti i casamenti, con un sole alto un braccio, fatto con una palla di cristallo piena d'acqua stillata, dietro la quale erano due torchi accesi, che la facevano in modo risplendere, che ella rendeva luminoso il cielo della scena e la prospettiva in guisa, che pareva veramente il sole vivo e naturale; e questo sole, dico, avendo intorno un ornamento di razzi d'oro che coprivano la cortina, era di mano in mano per via d'un arganetto tirato con sí fatt'ordine, che a principio della comedia pareva che si levasse il sole, e che salito infino al mezzo dell'arco scendesse in guisa, che al fine della comedia entrasse sotto e tramontasse" [ingeniously placed a wooden lantern in the shape of an arch behind the buildings, and a sun a *braccio* tall about two feet in diameter made of a crystal ball filled with distilled water. Two lighted torches behind it made it so bright that it illuminated the sky of the scenery and the perspective, just like the real sun. And this sun, I say, adorned with golden rays covering the curtain, was slowly hoisted by a windlass so as to give the impression that at the beginning of the play it was rising. Having reached the middle of the arch, the sun began to sink, setting in the west just as the play was nearing the end] (Giorgio Vasari, *Le vite de' più eccellenti pittori scultori ed architettori scritte da Giorgio Vasari pittore aretino*, ed. Gaetano Milanesi [Florence: Sansoni, 1906], 6.442).

52. Serlio, *Il secondo libro di prospettiva*, in *Storia docummtaria del teatro italiano*, ed. Ferruccio Marotti [Milan: Feltrinelli, 1974], 204–5)

53. Jean Jacquot, speaking of scenic decor and dynamism in the Italian stage of the Renaissance, suggests that the major force behind its technical innovations was "l'exigence d'un public de cour avide de divertissement et de sensations neuves" [the demand of a courtly public athirst for amusement and new sensations] (Jean Jacquot, "Les types de lieu théatral et leurs transformations de la fin du Moyen Age au milieu du XVIIe siècle," in *Le lieu théatral a la Renaissance*, ed. Jean Jacquot [Paris: Éditions du Centre National de la Recherche Scientifique, 1964], 479).

54. Among the things that bring "gran diletto" to the spectators, Serlio lists such things as "uno squadrone di gente, chi a piedi e chi a cavallo, le quali con alcune voci o gridi sordi, strepiti di tamburri e suono di trombe, pascono molto gli spettatori" [a troop of people (running), some on foot others on horseback, who, with the sound of voices or muffled screams and the uproar of drums and trumpets, delight the spectators] (ibid., 204).

CHAPTER 2. RENAISSANCE LIVING TRADITIONS AND THE REVIVAL OF ANCIENT TRAGEDY

1. At the end of *Iphigenia* Dolce appended a Prologue in which Tragedy speaks to the spectators and identifies herself this way:

> Io son colei, ch'addimandaro i Greci
> Tragedia; e nacqui alhor, ch'in terra nacque
> La Tirannide iniqua, . . .
> . . . . . . a me non piacque
> D'habitar sopra il Tebro. Hor sopra l'Arno
> Volger mi fece il piede assai pomposa
> Quel, che già pianse il fin di Sofonisba,
> E quello, che d'Antigone e di Hemone
> Rinovò la pietà, la fè, e l'amore,
> E quell'altro da poi, che estinse Orbecche,
> E chi cantò lo sdegno di Rosmunda;
> E chi con nuovo e non più visto esempio
> Lo scelerato amor di Macareo,
> Ne men quell'altro ingegno, che fe degna
> L'Horatia del'orecchio del gran padre . . .
>
> (p. 52)

[I am the one which the Greeks called / Tragedy, and was born at the same time that on earth was born / iniquitous tyranny . . . / . . . I did not like / to live on the Tiber. So towards Arno / directed my feet with great pomp / he who mourned the end of Sofonisba; / and the one who, of Antigone and Haemon, / sang anew the piety, the faith, and the love; / and then that other who killed Orbecche; / and he who sang of Rosmunda's disdain; / and he who with a new and never seen example / [sang] of Macareo's infamous love; / not least, that other genius who made / Horatia worthy of the great father's ears [the Pope] . . .

2. In the prologue to *La strega* (1566), Grazzini, reiterating what he had already pointed out in the prologue to *La gelosia* (1550), spoke against imitating the classics on the grounds that theater should reflect the culture in which it is produced. He argued that "Aristotile e Orazio viddero i tempi loro, ma i nostri sono d'un'altra maniera: abbiamo altri costumi, altra religione e altro modo di vivere . . . in Firenze non si vive come si viveva già in Atene e in Roma" [Aristotle and Horace saw their times, but our times are different from theirs: we have other customs, another religion, and another way of life; . . . in Florence one does not live as one lived in Athens and in Rome] (Antonfrancesco Grazzini, *Commedie di Antonfrancesco Grazzini*, ed. Pietro Fanfani [Firenze: Le monnier, 1859], p. 173).

3. D'Alembert, *Discours Préliminaire de l'Encyclopédie*, ed. F. Picavet [Paris: Librarie Armand Colin, 1929], 78.

4. Speaking of the Renaissance tendency to rival the Ancients, D'Alembert writes that "Enfin on ne se borna plus à copier les Romains et les Grecs, ou même à les imiter; on tâcha de les surpasser, s'il était possible, et de penser d'après soi" [finally they no longer limited themselves to copying or even imitating the Greeks and the Romans; they proposed to surpass them, if possible, and to rely on their own] (ibid., 83).

5. On the importance of theatrical verisimilitude, see Marvin Carlson, *Theories of the Theater*, 39–42. Also, Giraldi insisted that dramatic action be expressed in the context of the costumes, decorum, and manners of the times in which the poet is writing: "E nello eleggersi o formarsi queste azioni illustri, . . . non è se non bene averle tali quali le ricercano verisimilmente i tempi nei quali scrive il poeta, quanto ai ragionamenti, ai costumi, al decoro ed alle altre circostanze della persona" [And in choosing or proposing these illustrious actions, . . . it is but appropriate to represent them realistically according to the times about which the poet is writing. Especially as it regards speech, costumes, decorum, and other aspects of the character] (Giraldi, "Discorso," 182). On Giraldi's independence from the classics, see Weinberg, *A*

History of Literary Criticism in the Italian Renaissance, 2 vols. (Chicago: University of Chicago Press, 1961), 2.914.

6. Of all Seneca's plays only *Hercules on Oeta* exceeds 2,000 lines; the other nine are all between 800 and 1,400 lines. Sophocles's *Oedipus at Colonus* is the only Greek tragedy that reaches 2,000 lines, the others are between 1,000 and 1,600 lines.

7. Charleton, *The Senecan Tradition,* 67.

8. Noting that spectators might be more receptive to the stage representation of tragedies with happy ending than they might be to tragedies of horror, Giraldi writes: "Quelle terribile (se gli animi degli spettatori forse le abboriscono) possono essere delle scritture, queste di fin lieto delle rappresentazioni" [The terrible ones (if the spectators abhor them) might be written texts (to be read), these with happy ending may be represented in stage representations] (Giraldi, "Discorso," 184).

9. Ibid., 219.

10. In his letter to Isabella, dated 9–13 February 1499, Pencaro writes that "refferendo al conspecto d'alcuni huomini da bene della spesa quale faceva questo Illmo Duca, non solo non mi fu creduto, ma quasi fui stimato mendace, allegando montare dicta spesa circa duomillia ducati" [speaking to some honorable men of the sum of money that this Most Illustrious Duke spent (for the performance), not only was I not believed, but was also called a liar for saying that the cost was about two thousand ducats] (in Emilio Faccioli, *Il teatro italiano I: Dalli origini al Quattrocento,* 2 vols. [Torino: Einaudi, 1975], 2.700).

11. The anonymous observer, after providing a long list of the most important nobles in attendance, observes that the rest of the auditorium "era pieno di tutta la nobiltà di Lombardia, né vi era alcuno di Reggio, essendo così piaciuto al S. Duca, per dar luogo a' forestieri in quel giorno che senza numero vi erano concorsi" [was full of the entire nobility of Lombardy, nor was there anyone from Reggio, as it pleased the Duke, in order to make room for the out of town guests who in this particular day had come in droves] ("Il Successo dell'*Alidoro,*" in Ariani, *Il teatro,* 2.985). In this same volume, 1031–38, see also Dolfin's and Pigafetta's accounts of the 1585 representation of *Edippo il tiranno.* I quote both of these letters from Gallo's *La prima rappresentazione,* Ariani's source.

12. Filippo Pigafetta, "Lettera di Filippo Pigafetta," in *La prima rappresentazione al teatro Olimpico,* ed. Alberto Gallo (Milan: Il Polifilo, 1973), 55. Pigafetta also reports that "alle porte stavano compagnie di soldati armati per sicurezza della porta e per ogn'altro buon rispetto" [soldiers were stationed at every door both for reasons of security and for any other good purpose] (56).

13. The Anonymous describes the seating arrangements for the *Alidoro,* noting with great accuracy who was sitting where with relation to the ruling prince's seat (Ariani, *Il teatro,* 2. 985). On the importance of seating arrangements, see also Giovanni Attolini, *Teatro e spettacolo nel Rinascimento* (Bari: Laterza, 1988), 73 and, especially, 67, where he discusses the mise-en-scène of Landi's *Commodo* on the occasion of Cosimo I's wedding with Eleanor of Toledo, in 1539. See, also his discussion of the 1513 performance of Bibbiena's *Calandria* in Urbino (114). On the political significance of the stage, see Alessandro Fontana, "La scena," in *Storia d'Italia* (Turin: Einaudi, 1972), 793–866.

14. Giraldi, "Lettera," 485.

15. "Il Successo dell'*Alidoro,*" in Ariani, *Il teatro,* 2.996–97.

16. "Lettera di Filippo Pigafetta," 55–56.

17. Ibid., 34.

18. After noting that a dramatist should use common sense in determining the length of a play, Giraldi notes that the representation "della commedia non voglia

meno di tre ore, né quella della tragedia meno di quattro"[of a comedy should not last fewer than three hours, nor should that of tragedy last fewer than four hours] (Giraldi, "Discorso," 174). Angelo Ingegneri, too, argues that a dramatic performance should not last "più di tre ore e mezza in quattro" [more than three and a half to four hours] (Ingegneri, *Della poesia rappresentativa*, 284).

19. Paraphrasing Aristotle, Trissino stresses that the story must be presented "con parole belle et accomodate" [in beautiful and appropriate words] (Trissino, *La Quinta divisione della poetica*, 1.31) and concludes that the poet should not concern himself with music or representation, since "la tragedia ancora che ella non fosse rappresentata non starebbe di essere tragedia e di fare la sua dottrina" [tragedy even if it were not performed is still tragedy and its function is not diminished] (44). In other words, the tragic effect can actually be derived from reading alone, provided that the play is written in beautiful verses. Also, Giovanni Andrea Dell'Anguillara, in dedicating his *Edippo* to Heronimo Foccari, hopes that his tragedy is "così alta di stile, come richiede il nome, che ella tiene" [of such high style as is befitting to Tragedy], for only then he would be sure of sending him "Opera degna" [a worthy work] (Giovanni Andrea dell' Anguillara, *Edippo*, in *Teatro italiano antico*, ed. Gaetano Poggiali, 6). On the sociopolitical implications of the Renaissance preference for *bene dicere*, see Ariani's "Introduzione," in his *Il teatro*.

20. The Anonymous says that *Alidoro* was performed with such perfection as to rival the ancients at their best. He specifically praises the actors, who recited with "tanta grazia che gli spettatori, pieni d'insolita meraviglia, fecero giudizio che l'età nostra in questa parte fosse molto più felice delle passate" [so much grace that the spectators, full of unusual *meraviglia*, thought that our age had surpassed the past in this respect] (in Ariani, *Il teatro*, 2.998).

21. Of Alamanni's poetry, Neri believes that it "può meritar qualche lode" [may be worthy of some praise] (Neri, *La tragedia*, 49); and Musumarra suggests that it represents "l'espressione genuina d'un gusto e d'un clima" [the genuine expression of a taste and a climate] (Musumarra, *La poesia tragica*, 74).

22. In *Altile*, Giraldi boasts that he intends to depart from traditional norm in order to reflect the taste of the times and please the spectators. He promises the dramatization of a story never touched before "o da poeta antico o da moderno" [either by ancient or modern poet] (13). And in the prologue to *Giocasta*, Dolce informs the audience that the atrocities they are about to see "mai per carte, o per altrui favelle / Pervenir all'orecchie de' mortali" [neither on paper nor in speech / Did they ever reach human ears] (9).

23. The longest monologue I have seen in any drama is the 349 lines spoken by Latino in *Adriana*, 2.2, followed by Torrismondo's 308 line account of his journey from Norway (*Torrismondo*, 1.3.68–376).

24. Mazzoni writes that Rucellai began working on *Oreste* immediately after the completion of *Rosmunda* (1516) and that the play was still incomplete in 1520 ("Introduzione," in Mazzoni, *Le opere di Giovanni Rucellai*, LI). Since Rucellai died on 3 April 1525, it is conceivable that he worked on it until his death.

25. Consider the scene in which Pylades argues against leaving Orestes behind in Tauris to die. In the original, the protestation is only fourteen lines long (673–87), in the Italian version, the same protestation is about eighty-four lines (3.321–405). And, the scene in which Thoas exhorts his people to give chase to the fugitives is barely fourteen lines long (1422–34), in the Italian version, the same scene counts approximately sixty lines (5.259–319). I use Mazzoni's edition of *Oreste* because it is divided into acts with numbered lines, making for easy reference.

26. The uncommon references to bees reflect Rucellai's familiarity with the insect, which is the topic of his poem *Api*, a reworking of Virgil's *Georgics*, 4.

27. Aristotle notes that of "all forms of recognition the best is that which results from the incidents themselves in which the astonishment too results from what is probable. Such are the recognitions in Sophocles's *Oedipus Tyrannus* and in the *Iphigenia*" (Aristotle, *The Poetics of Aristotle*, 16.33).

28. Leopardi observes that classical dramatists, contrary to modern playwrights, preferred to dwell on the mythological and the supra human aspect of vices and virtues. The moderns, he points out, propose to explore human passions, whereas the ancients focus on the imagination. This is partly due to the fact that ancient tragedians were "molto inferiori a' moderni nella cognizione del cuore umano" [very inferior to the modern regarding the understanding of human emotions] (Giacomo Leopardi, *Zibaldone*, in *Tutte le opere*, ed. Walter Binni, vol. 2 [Florence: Sansoni, 1969], 2.869).

29. Neri (*La tragedia*, 47) endorses the prevailing negative view of the play, including Poggiali's suggestion that its emphasis on gentle and noble emotions reflects the taste of an age "quasi alla mollezza inclinato" [somewhat inclined towards softness] (Poggiali, *Teatro italiano antico*, 2.5)

30. This may serve as a partial answer to Neri's question why the representation of tragedy failed on stage, but succeeded in "novelle mirabili" [great short stories] (Neri, *La tragedia*, 146). The means of representation in narrative is basically verbal, which leaves the reader to imagine the narrated event on the stage of the mind. When this same linguistic means was employed in theater it failed noticeably because the stage communicates mostly through actions not words.

31. Giraldi, "La Tragedia che parla," appended to *Orbecche*, in *Teatro del Cinquecento*, ed. Renzo Cremante, 3272–73.

32. *Inferno*, 33.4–5.

33. *Rime*, 1.11.

34. It was indeed common for cinquecento poets to display erudition by echoing what Bembo called the "modern classics": Dante, Petrarch, and Boccaccio. Here are a few examples from Rucellai's *Oreste*: Ifigenia's wish to die with both Oreste and Pilade so that she can be "terza tra cotanto amore" (2.173) echoes Dante's happiness in being sixth "tra cotanto senno" (*Inferno*, 4.102); and her exclamation upon hearing of Agamemnon's murder: "Ahi cruda terra, come non apristi / Un cieco iato." (2.355), is a conscious reference to Dante's Ugolino "Ahi dura terra perché non t'apristi" (*Inferno*, 33. 66). The chorus's apostrophe "Superstizion, di quanto mal sei madre!" (2.419), is reminiscent of Dante's invective against the Simonist Popes: "Ahi, Costantin, di quanto mal fu matre" (*Inferno*, 19.115). The chorus's conclusion that it is better to die than to witness human sacrifices, "Ch'un bel morir tutta la vita onora" (1.212) is identical to Petrarch's begging Love to put an end to his misery "ch'un bel morir tutta la vita onora" (*Rime*, 207:65). And Oreste's description of Agamemnon's bed "Di bianco avorio, e d'ebano contesto" (4.377) recalls Petrarch's ship "tutta d'avorio e d'ebeno contesta" (*Rime*, 323:15). Tasso's *Torrismondo*, among other tragedies, is another rich source of literary allusions to the "modern classics." Some allusions to Dante: "nessun amato amar perdoni" (1.3.264): cfr. *Inferno*, 5.103: "a nullo amato amar perdona"; "Questo quel punto fu che sol mi vinse" (1.3.331): cfr. *Inferno*, 5.132: "ma solo un punto fu quel che ci vinse"; "Fortuna errò, che volse i lieti giochi / in tristi lutti" (4.7.14–15): cfr. *Inferno*, 13.69: "che' lieti onor tornaro in tristi lutti." A few allusions to Petrarch: "venti contrari a la serena vita" (2.1.42): cfr. *Rime*, 128.105: "vènti contrari a la vita serena"; "per l'estreme giornate di mia vita" (2.4.124): cfr. *Rime*, 16.6: "per l'estreme giornate di

sua vita"; "or mi sovviene / di quel che spesso ho già pensato e letto" (3.1.1–2): cfr. *Rime*, 56.12: "Et or di quel ch'i' ho letto mi sovene"; "Bello e dolce morire era allor quando" (5.6.47): cfr. *Rime*, 331.43: "Bello e dolce morire era allor quando."

35. Arguing that armies, not fortresses, are the best means of defense, Machiavelli invokes the ancients' mistrust of fortresses as reliable means of defense: "ché se i Romani non edificavano fortezze, gli Spartani non solamente si astenevano da quelle, ma non permettevano di avere mura alle loro città" [for, if the Romans did not build fortresses, the Spartans not only abstained from them, they also refused to have walls around their cities] (Niccolò Machiavelli, *Il Principe e Discorsi*, ed. Sergio Bertelli [Milan: Feltrinelli, 1968], 2.24.355).

36. Euripides, *The Phoenician Women*, in *The Complete Greek Tragedies*, eds. Grene and Lattimore (Chicago: University of Chicago Press, 1959), 63–65.

37. For a detailed account of the episode, see Ernst Breisach, *Caterina Sforza: A Renaissance Virago* (Chicago: University of Chicago Press, 1967), 212–18.

38. Mazzoni's edition lists only one character as "Cavaliere o Barone del Re," whereas Maffei's edition lists "Cavalieri, o Baroni."

39. On the function of modern names, see Carlson, *Theater*, 26–38.

40. Giraldi, "Lettera," 482.

41. Pigafetta, "Lettera di Filippo Pigafetta," 56.

42. Werner Gundersheimer, having noted that Ercole d'Este had a bodyguard of twenty-five armed soldiers who guarded him day and night, comments that it was "the first such force of which we have record in Quattrocento Ferrara" (Werner Gundersheimer, *Ferrara: The Style of Renaissance Despotism* [Princeton: Princeton University Press, 1973], 184).

43. Ferruccio Marotti, *Storia documentaria del teatro italicano* (Milan: Feltrinelli, 1974), 303. Inexplicably, Ingegneri gives 1584 as the date of the representation whereas both Pigafetta and Dolfin give 1585.

44. Angelo Ingegneri, "Progetto di Angelo Ingegneri," in *La prima rappresentazione del teatro Olimpico*, ed. Alberto Gallo, 13.

45. For details, see Richmond Lattimore's introduction to Aeschylus, *The Complete Greek Tragedies. Oresteia Aeschylus* I: eds. Grene and Lattimore (Chicago: University of Chicago Press, 1953), 18–19.

46. In his criticism of the performance, Sperone Speroni pointed out that Thebes was afflicted by the plague and both the people and the king were "in stato di supplicare e non di pompeggiare" [were in a state of suffering and worshipping and not in a mood for festivities] (Sperone Speroni, "Proposte di Sperone Speroni," in *La prima rappresentazione del teatro Olimpico*, ed. Alberto Gallo, 31). In the same vein as Speroni, Antonio Riccoboni found it "strano che in un tempo calamitosissimo di peste si adoperassero quelle vesti tanto pompose" [strange that in a time so ravaged by pestilence they would use costumes so sumptuous] (Antonio Riccoboni "Lettera di Antonio Riccoboni," ibid., 47).

47. In Ariani, *Il teatro*, 996. Leone de' Sommi recommends sumptuous stage costumes because they enhance the reputation of tragedy "massimamente a questi tempi che sono le pompe nel lor sommo grado" [especially in these times of ours when pomp has reached its highest expression;] (Sommi, *Quattro dialoghi*, 3.48).

48. Giraldi points out that royal deeds are events of great importance in which many people participate, and their presence underscores "la reale maiestà dell'azione" [the true majesty of the action] (Giraldi, "Lettera" 481). In his *Della poesia rappresentativa*, Angelo Ingegneri argues that "non pare verisimile che all'uscire del Principe in publico . . . la città si ritrovi vuota, né vi sia chi il rimiri e chi il riverisca"

[it is not realistic for a prince to walk through the city without a following and without being greeted by obsequious subjects] (279).

49. Luciano Chiappini quotes Alphonse's letter, and details the bloody incident (Chiappini, *Gli Estensi*, 218–20).

50. Beatrice Corrigan, ed. *Two Renaissance Plays* [Manchester: Manchester University Press, 1975], 11).

51. Niccolò Machiavelli, *Lettere,* ed. Franco Gaeta (Milan: Feltrinelli, 1961), 41.

52. Pietro Aretino, *Tutti le opere. Le Lettere,* ed. Francesco Flora (Milan: Mondadori, 1960), 161, 198.

53. On the presence and activities of pirates in the Mediterranean, see Francesco Cognasso, *L'Italia nel Rinascimento* (Torino: UTET, 1965), 2.251; and Alberto Tenenti, *Piracy and the Decline of Venice* (Berkeley: University of California Press, 1967), 3–55.

54. Judith Hook, *The Sack of Rome: 1527* (London: Macmillan, 1972), 282.

55. Peter Laven, speaking of the danger of land travel, notes that merchants would often form large caravans to "defend themselves against highway banditry" and that land routes "had to contend with armed bands whose raids were often organized by a powerful local feudatory" (Peter Laven, *Renaissance Italy: 1464–1534* (London: Batsford, 1966], 87–88). Jack F. Bernard writes that Renaissance Florence "was greatly hampered by the conditions in the surrounding countryside. Outside her walls, for a radius of fifteen or twenty miles, there were numerous castles, or rather lairs, of "robber barons," whose wealth was founded and multiplied almost entirely on the proceeds or highway robbery" (Jack Bernard, *Up from Caesar* [Garden City, N.Y.: Doubleday, 1970], 191). Relying on Montaigne's account of his journey in Italy (1580–1581), Bernard notes that bandits in the Papal States "succeeded in robbing, burning, pillaging, raping, and murdering with perfect impunity." He offers the example of the notorious highwayman Piccolomini, who confessed "to three hundred and seventy murders" (301).

56. According to P. J. Jones, the woman fled to Verona where she died of grief (P. J. Jones, *The Malatesta of Rimini and the Papal State* [London: Cambridge University Press, 1974], 202–03).

57. Ludovico Ariosto, *The Satires of Ludovico Ariosto,* trans. Peter Desa Wiggins (Athens: Ohio State University Press, 1976), 4.160.

58. Burckhardt, *The Civilization of the Renaissance in Italy*, 2.438–39.

Chapter 3. Their Gods, Our God: Christian Religion in the Tragic World of Myth

1. Humanists went as far as to suggest that humans had the spiritual and intellectual potential to be equal to celestial creatures. Giovanni Pico della Mirandola, for instance, argued that humans should not consider themselves second to the angels, for "erimus illis, cum voluerimus, nihilo inferiores" [if and when we wish it, we shall be inferior to them in nothing] (*De Hominis Dignitate,*14). Humanists also claimed that humans could determine the course of their own lives against adverse Fortune, for, as Alberti writes in the Prologue to his *I libri della famiglia*, "gli uomini le più volte aversi d'ogni suo bene cagione e d'ogni suo male" [individuals most often are the cause of all good and evil that befalls them] (Leon Battista Alberti, *I libri della famiglia*, eds. Ruggero Romano and Alberto Tenenti [Turin: Einaudi, 1969], 4). He further argues that Fortune is "invalida e debolissima a rapirci qualunque nostra minima virtù, e dobbiamo giudicare la virtù sufficiente a conscendere e occupare

ogni sublime ed eccelsa cosa, amplissimi principati, suppreme laude, eterna fama e immortal gloria" [most weak and incapable of robbing us of our smallest *virtù*. We must judge *virtù* sufficient to attain and maintain great things, such as great principalities, high praise, eternal fame and immortal glory] (10). For more on Fortune, see my "Divine Order, Fate, Fortune."

2. Disheartened by the bloodshed, the cruelty, and the destruction of the invasion, Vettori writes: "io voglio attendere a vivere questo resto che mi avanza di tempo e non voglio dibattermi il cervello a investigare le ragioni delle cose, nè volgio pensare a quello ebbi a essere" [I want to concern myself only with living out the rest of my life, and do not want to beat my brains investigating the causes and the origin of things nor do I want to reflect upon how things should be] (Franceso Vettori, "Sacco di Roma: Dialogo," in *Scritti storici e politici*, ed. E. Niccolini [Bari: Laterza, 1972], 296).

3. Regarding the Sack of Rome and the religious restlessness of the period, Grendler writes: "the political and social problems stimulated an awareness of man's fragility and impermanence, and turned attention to God" (Paul F. Grendler *Critics of the Italian World* [Madison: University of Wisconsin Press, 1969], 104). The effect of the crisis was especially felt by Francesco Guicciardini. But, as I noted in my "Narratorial Strategy," reading through the highly stylized self-accusations and argumentation of Guicciardini's personal writings ("Accusatoria," "Defensoria," and "Consolatoria"), we have the impression that his demise was symptomatic of a crisis that went beyond a personal setback and affected instead an entire way of thinking. Vittorio De Caprariis, observing that the impact of the Sack of Rome went beyond Guicciardini's personal crisis, writes that it was "una crisi assai più vasta e grave: lo sbigottimento per il fallimento non tanto del suo successo, quanto del suo sistema" [a crisis much bigger and much deeper: it was the shock of the failure not so much of his success, but of his entire system] (Vittorio De Caprariis, ed., *Francesco Guicciardini: Opere* [Milan: Ricciardi, 1953], xiii). Felix Gilbert, too, suggested that "because Guicciardini had been inspired by the belief in man's power to control events and in his own talent to manage his affairs, the shock caused by the events of 1527 was profound" (Felix Gilbert, *Machiavelli and Guicciardini* [Princeton: Princeton University Press, 1965], 280–81).

4. Trissino, in *La Quinta divisione della poetica*, writes:"le buone soluzioni delle favole denno venire dalla istessa favola e non dallo introdurvi per via della machina della scena qualche iddio che la solva" [a good plot solution must come from the story itself and not from the introduction, by means of the *machina*, of some gods who might solve it]. He goes on to note that "i déi non si denno introdurre se non per chiarire le cose che sono fuori della favola . . . et . . . per predire le cose future quando hanno bisogno di essere predicte" [the gods must be used only to clarify events outside the plot [and . . .] to foretell future events when necessary] (2.27).

5. Herrick, *Italian Tragedy*, 288–891.

6. The following are but a few samples typical of the dozens of invocations that are found throughout the tragedy: Prologue I: "giustizia santa," 86; "figliuol di Dio," 94. Prologue II: Plutone: "de la Vergine il figliuolo," 159. Marianna: "Dio clemente e giusto," 2.1220. Coro: "padre del ciel pietoso e giusto," 4.2815. Beniamino: "bontà di Dio," 2.1375. Herod: "o giustizia di Dio," 2.1333. Alessandro: "Re celeste," 3.1518. Nunzio: "giusto Dio," 5.3107.

7. For Cremante, the"pietosa Madre" in line 350 is "anacrosticamente, la Vergine" [anachronistically, the Virgin] (Cremante, *Teatro del Cinquecento*, 220).

8. Cremante notes that the theme of chastity and honor first expressed in lines 312–15, is "più esplicitamente e cattolicamente ribadito" [re-iterated in terms more explicit and more catholic in lines 337–39] (ibid., 206 n. 312).

9. Consider also the despair of Seneca's Thyestes as he feels abandoned by the uncaring gods "wherever ye have fled," (5.5.1149).

10. Garin points out that "gli déi antichi tornano nella poesia e nell'arte, da cui per altro non erano scomparsi mai. Vi tornano, se mai, nella bellezza autentica dei miti antichi, restaurati e storicizzati: non più demoni orribili, ma giovani divinità del mondo greco e romano" [ancient gods reappear in art and poetry from which they had never disappeared. They return in the authentic beauty of their ancient myths, restored and historicized: no longer horrible demons, but youthful divinities of the Greek and Roman worlds] (Garin, *La cultura*, 97). Musumarra sees the coexistence of Christian and pagan elements as the writers' tendency "di fondere tradizioni diverse per renderle più moderne e accessibili alle nuove esigence culturali dei dotti o, più genericamente, alle mutate esigenze moralistiche e religiose della società" [to fuse diverse traditions in order to render them more modern and more in line with the changing cultural expectations of the learned, or more generally, with society's changing moral and religious realities] (Musumarra, *La poesia tragica*, 28).

11. Dante, *Purgatory*, 6.118.

12. Notice also Altile's reference to the creation of humankind as she refers to God as the Eternal Mover of the stars who "in far noi divise le prime membra, onde viviamo" [in making us, divided the first members, and so we live] (Giraldi, *Altile*, ed. Peggy Osborn [Lewiston, N.Y.: Edwin Mellen Press, 1992], 1.5.531). Speaking of religion in Giraldi's plays, including those in far away lands, Morrison concludes that "religion in Giraldi conforms more or less with the spirit of Christian religion" (Morrison, *The Tragedies of G.-B. Giraldi Cinthio*, 32). On Giraldi's sense of Christian morality, see Horne, *The Tragedies of Giambattista Cinthio Giraldi*, 37–39, and Peggy Osborn, *G. B. Giraldi's Altile* (Lewiston, N.Y.: Edwin Mellen Press, 1992), 59.

13. Dante, *Paradise*, 2.127.

14. Ibid., 33.145. Cfr. Giraldi's "supremo Motor che il tutto regge" [supreme Mover who rules all] (Giraldi, *Altile*, Prologue), "l'eterno Motor che il tutto regge" [the eternal Mover who rules all] (*Antivalomeni*, Prologue), and "il Motor eterno delle stelle" [the stars' eternal Mover] (Dolce, *Didone*, 3. 7. p.82). Commenting on Publio's reference to Jupiter as the maker and mover of the universe in *Orazia* 1.340–43, Cremante recalls similar invocations in other cinquecento playwrights and concludes that the deity is represented "come Dio cristiano, fattore e motore dell'universo" [as a Christian God, maker and mover of the universe] (Cremante, *Teatro del Cinquecento*, 609).

15. Interestingly, in Seneca's *Oedipus* this is not seen as sin, for, as Jocasta puts it, "None sins in living out his destiny." (5.3.1067).

16. This biblical tone is also heard in *Adriana* as well as in Dolce's *Didone*:

> Pensati, o uom, che sei,
> pensati, che esser déi.
> . . . .
> E pensa che sei terra,
> pensa che sarai terra
> . . . .
> la morte ti dissolve,
> e in fumo, in ombra, e in polve
> il corpo infin risolve,
> e in vermi e in serpi il volve.
>
> (*Adriana* 4.4.1–91)

[Reflect, man, on what you are / reflect on what you will be / . . . / Consider that you are dust, / consider that you will be dust / . . . / death will dissolve you, / and in smoke, shadow and dust. / and ultimately will turn the body / in vermin and serpents.]

> Quel dì, ch'el miser huomo
> Veste quà giuso l'alma
> Di questo corporal caduco velo,
> La sù con lettere salde, e adamantine
> E' discritto il suo fine.
> Però ai fati cedete
> Voi, che felici, o sventurati sete:
> Ch'ogni cosa mortal governa il Cielo.
>
> (*Didone*, 5. p. 40)

[That day that wretched humans / put on, here on earth, / the vestige of this corporal veil, / up there with firm and adamantine letters / their end is already written. / Thus, do not fight your fate / whether you are happy or wretched, / For Heaven governs all mortal things.]

17. Cremante notes that all these terms are thomistic designations of the divine (Cremante, *Teatro del Cinquecento*, 300). On these attributes, see, also, the final chorus in Dolce's *Thieste*.

18. Actually, both the ancient and the Italian Thyestes invoke revenge; but, whereas in Seneca the revenge represents the individual's need for gratification, in Dolce it is invoked in the name of God's justice.

19. Aristotle, *Poetics*, 15.30.

20. Recalling Aristotle's criticism of Euripides's use of the *machina* in *Iphigenia in Tauris*, Giraldi states that the resolution of the dramatic action "deve venire dalla natura del soggetto e dall'ingegno del poeta, e quando manca questo e quello a ciò fare, e vi si introduce la macchina che porti lo dio che il fine v'impogna, come si vede nella Ifigenia nella taurica regione, . . . non merita ciò punto lode" [must issue from the nature of the subject and from the poet's ability. Where both genius and ability are lacking, one imposes the resolution by means of the deus ex machina, as is the case in *Iphigenia in Tauris*, . . . this expedient is not at all praiseworthy] (Giraldi, "Lettera" 1. 475).

21. Anguillara's Edippo expresses this same view when he reminds his children that "la religion governa il mondo" [religion rules the world] (18).

22. For a detailed discussion of this question, see Poggiali's "Ragionamento," in *Teatro Italiano*, 3.16–18.

23. Herrick suggests that the voice heard on stage is that of Jove: "The whole action is resolved by the voice of Jove" (Herrick, *Italian Tragedy*, 141). For Marco Ariani, instead, it is the voice of Mars (Marco Ariani, *Tra classicismo e Manierismo* [Florence: Olschki, 1974], 194). More likely, it is the voice of Minerva, since she is the deity most frequently mentioned in the play. Also, the divine whisper is heard coming from the roof of the goddess's temple that dominates the dramatic space.

24. Neri laments that the deus ex machina "non è il miglior modo per risolvere la tragedia: sebbene in fondo sia piú un difetto formale, che reale, poiché non reca decisioni inattese o avvenimenti soprannaturali, ma solo piega al giogo l'ostinazione di Orazio" [it is not the best way to resolve the tragedy, although it is a flaw more formal than real, since it does not bring about unexpected decisions or supernatural events, but only subdues Horace's obstinacy] (Neri, *La tragedia*, 89). Also Herrick, having pointed out that the use of the ex machina must not have pleased Aretino's contemporaries, opines that the intervention "was unnecessary" and that Aretino "probably introduced it for theatrical effect" (Herrick, *Italian Tragedy*, 136).

25. On the titanic nature of Orazio's character, see Croce, *La letteratura italiana*, 1. 440, and Bergel, "The Rise of Cinquecento Tragedy," 215–38. It is difficult to agree with Mercuri's suggestion that Orazio is a modest individual, and that his modesty "conferisce legittimità alla sua azione omicida" [confers legitimacy to his murderous

act] (Roberto Mercuri, "*Orazia* dell'Aretino," in *La letteratura italiana storia e testi*, ed. Carlo Muscetta [Bari: Laterza, 1973], 78).

26. Speaking of the type of tragic reconciliation in which the individual surrenders his/her own point of view, Hegel writes: "In this betrayal by personality of its essential pathos, however, it cannot fail to appear destitute of character.... The individual, therefore, can only submit to a higher Power and its counsel or command, to the effect that while on his own account he adheres to such a pathos, the will is nevertheless broken in its bare obstinacy by a god's authority. In such a case the knot is not loosened, but, as in the case of Philoctetes, it is severed by a *deus ex machina*" (G. W. F. Hegel, *The Philosophy of Fine Art*, trans. F. P. B. Osmaston, 4 vols. [London: G. Bell and Sons, 1920], 325).

27. Neri argues that Aretino "avrebbe certo potuto aggiustare diversamente (v. Ginguenè, loc. cit.) sol anche seguendo Livio" [certainly could have taken a different approach (see Ginguenè, loc. cit.) by simply following Livy] (Neri, *La tragedia*, note p. 87).

28. Mercuri believes that the intervention has actually an exculpatory ("scagionatorio") function in that it serves to clear Orazio of the charges against him (Mercuri, "*Orazia* dell'Aretino," 78).

29. Speaking of the religious impact that the sack of Rome had on the people of the Renaissance, Grendler observes that the event "was seen as a divine retribution for clerical sins, and Italians took up the issues of faith, predestination, and Scripture raised by thoughtful people, orthodox and protestant" (Grendler, *Critics of the Italian World*,16). With reference to the religious restlessness that characterized the first quarter of the century, he notes that "only after the penetration of the new ideas from the north and the disasters of war, climaxed by the shock of the sack of Rome, did latent Italian religious unrest find focus. Then the reform-minded saw the sack of Rome as a warning from God to correct abuses" (105).

CHAPTER 4. THE NATURE OF KINGSHIP: THE DEBATE ON MACHIAVELLISM

1. See Kelly, *Ideas and Forms of Tragedy*, especially 32, 46, 218.

2.
>Io, qual vedete a questi oscuri panni,
>A questo scettro, a questa ignuda spada
>Et a questa corona, son colei
>Che Tragedia nomar gli antichi Greci.
>. . . . .
>Né, come la Comedia, apporto giuochi
>E diletti e piacer, ma doglie e pianti,
>Rappresentando morti atre e funeste
>O di Tiranni, o di Re giusti, oppressi
>Da nimica Fortuna, o di Reine.
>
>(*Marianna*, Prologue 1, 1–12)

[I, as you can see from these dark cloths, / this scepter, this drawn sword / and this crown, am the one / whom the ancient Greeks called Tragedia./ ... / Unlike Comedy, I do not bring you games, / delights and pleasure, but cries and pain / by representing gruesome and sorrowful deaths / of Tyrants, or of just kings oppressed / by adverse Fortune, or of Queens.]

See, also, Tragedia's characterization appended to Dolce's *Ifigenia*.

3. Also, in *Torrismondo*, 5.4, Alvida kills herself, suspecting erroneously that Torrismondo was unfaithful. Torrismondo is so devastated by her death that, unable to endure the sorrow and the guilt, he stabs himself to death.

4. Neri writes that stage violence was a good "arma per iscuotere i nervi degli spettatori" [weapon to shake the nerves of the spectators] (Neri, *La tragedia*, 146). Apollonio, having noted that as a tragedian Giraldi was a "conformista" like all other dilettanti, attributes all the horrors in *Orbecche* to the "moda letteraria dell'anno" [literary fashion of the times] (Mario Apollonio, *Storia del teatro* [Florence: Sansoni, 1951], 2.227). He also believes that Giraldi "accetta da Seneca e da ogni altro tragico, con una specie di indifferenza, quel che gli capita: segno che è scomparso il tipo dell'imitar-critico" [accepts with indifference from Seneca and from any other tragedian whatever he can find: a sign that the type of critical imitation has disappeared] (227).

5. For a discussion of the counselor's role in *Rosmunda* and *Marianna*, see Ronnie H. Terpening, "Between Lord and Lady," *Forum Italicum* 15 (1981).

6. Donaldson, *Machiavelli and the Mystery of State*, xi.

7. Machiavelli, *Discorsi*, 3.30.468. The biblical reference is to *Exodus*, 32:27–29, where the sons of Levi, on the orders of Moses, killed "about three thousand men." Besides the story of Lucius Brutus's execution of his own sons (*Discorsi*, 1.16.174), and Marcus Brutus's murder of Caesar (ibid., 3.6.392), Machiavelli also cites and discusses the examples of Cyrus, Lycurgus, and Romulus (ibid.,1.9.153–55, and *Prince*, 6.26). For more details, see Donaldson's discussion of Louis Mochon's *Apologie* in *Machiavelli and the Mystery of State*,194–96.

8. On the humanist notion of virtù and its Roman background, see Quentin Skinner, *Machaivelli* (New York: Hill and Wang, 1981), especially 34–37.

9. Among the most important works on reason of state literature, one should include Girolamo Frachetta's *L'idea del libro de' governi di stato e di guerra* (1592), Scipione Ammirato's *Discorsi sopra Cornelio Tacito* (1594), and Ludovico Zuccolo's *Della ragion di stato* (1621).

10. Machiavelli, *Discorsi*, 1.9.154.

11. For a detailed account of Federico's political activities for the preservation of his duchy, see Walter Tommasoli's interesting biography of the Duke, *La Vita di Federico da Montfeltro* (Urbino: Argalia, 1978).

12. Perry Anderson, *Lineages of the Absolutist State* (London: N. L. B., 1974), 9.

13. Malecche, defending Orbecche's choice to marry poor Oronte, points out to Sulmone that "i ben de la fortuna, ch'oggi sono / D'uno e diman d'un altro, son caduchi" [fortune's favors, which today are enjoyed / by one and tomorrow by another, are fleeting] (3.2.1355). This notion of Fortune is reminiscent of the argument that Boccaccio's Ghismunda, whose story parallels that of Orbecche, uses in favor of her low-born lover Guiscardo. She reminds her father, Prince Tancredi, that "molti re, molti gran prencipi furon già poveri, e molti di quegli che la terra zappano e guardan le pecore già ricchissimi furono" [many kings and many great princes were once poor, and many of those who now till the land and care for sheep were once very rich] (Giovanni Boccaccio, *Decameron*, ed. Carlo Salinari, 2 vols. [Bari: Laterza, 1966], 4.1.295). The chorus at the end of Dolce's *Giocasta* echoes this same idea of Fortune. Here, the chorus invites all rulers to reflect upon Oedipus's fate and see how in a world ruled by whimsical Fortune today's powerful can become tomorrow's paupers. See also *Rosmunda*, where the chorus warns rulers to pay heed to Rosmunda, who in a very short time was reduced from queen to wife of her enemy (230–32). For other allusions to Fortune, see *Rosmunda*, 142–54, 810, and especially

the end of the play where the chorus reminds rulers to learn from Alboino's fate and to govern justly. Also in *Orazia*, 43, Fame talks of Fortune's whims.

14. Malecche's view that true nobility resides only in virtue "Parmi che sia ne la virtute sola / (Stabil bene de l'uom) nobilità vera" [it seems to me that true nobility resides only in virtue / (man's lasting goodness)] (Giraldi, *Orbecche*, 3.2.1365–66) evokes a similar notion in Boccaccio. In *Decameron*, 4.1, Ghismunda reminds her father that "(L)a vertù primieramente noi, che tutti nascemmo e nasciamo uguali, ne distinse; e quegli che di lei maggior parte avevano ed adoperavano nobili furon detti, ed il rimanente rimase non nobile" [since we were all born and are still born equal, it was virtue that set us apart from one another. Those who possessed and displayed great virtues were called nobles, the rest remained commoners] (295). Also, in Buonaccorso da Montemagno's *De Nobilitate*, Flaminius, who is arguing before the Roman senate against Cornelius's proposition that nobility resides in one's birth, points out that one's nobility is not in the glory of others but "in propria nostra animi virtute" [in the virtue of our soul] (142). He goes on to note that virtue is acquired through "proprio labore" [one's own deeds] (150) and should not be sought in one's ancestry, for "frustra in bonis hereditariis virtus quaeritur" [in vain does one look for virtue in his heredity] (160). There were a series of treatises on *De vera nobilitate* which, in the words of Eugene Rice, "put true nobility in virtue and personal merit rather than in birth and taught that virtue is acquired, not inherited" (Eugene Rice, *The Foundations of Early Modern Europe, 1460–1559* [New York: W. W. Norton, 1970], 56).

15. Burckhardt, having noted that the example of Ludovico Sforza's great accomplishments was contagious, cites Aeneas Sylvius: "In our change-loving Italy, where nothing stands firm, and where no ancient dynasty exists, a servant can easily become a king. One man in particular," continues Burckhardt, "who styled himself 'the man of fortune,' filled the imagination of the whole country: Jacopo Piccinino" (Burkhardt, *The Civilization of the Renaissance in Italy*,1.43). See, also, Wayne A. Rebhorn, *Foxes and Lions: Machiavelli's Confidence Men* (Ithaca: Cornell University Press, 1988), 26–36.

16. John F. D'Amico, *Renaissance Humanism in Papal Rome* (Baltimore: Johns Hopkins University Press, 1983), 17.

17. For a comprehensive discussion of critical reactions to Giraldi's use of violence, see Ariani, *Tra classicismo*, 15–71.

18. Horne, arguing against those who viewed the playwright's descriptions of torture and bloodshed as an indication of "his sadistic or morbid inclinations," suggests that the horrific element in *Orbecche* should be seen "as an æsthetic phenomenon—a dramatic device intended to sharpen the emotional impact made by the tragic spectacle" (Horne, *The Tragedies of Giambattista Cinthio Giraldi*,147–48).

19. Maecenas offers a similar advice to Octavius, who is about to execute Marc Anthony, his enemy and now his prisoner:

> Cosa non è più generosa, e degna
> Più di gran prence, che donar perdono
> A chi disposto si è di fargli offesa.

(*Cleopatra*, 2.5. 1215–25; also 1360–61)

[There is no deed more generous, and more worthy / of a great prince, than to forgive / those who tried to harm him.]

20. Castiglione writes that the courtier among other qualities must be wise enough to show "al suo principe quanto onore ed utile nasca a lui ed alli suoi dalla

giustizia, dalla liberalità, dalla magnanimità, dalla mansuetudine e dall'altre virtù che si convengono a bon principe" [the prince how much honor and utility comes to him and his people from the justice, the liberality, the magnanimity, the docility and other virtues becoming to a prince] (Castiglione, *Il libro del Cortegiano*, 4.5.354).

21. Dante, *Purgatory*, 15.97–104.

22. Musumarra notes that Sulmone and Malecche represent "due opposte mentalità: la tradizione e il rinnovamento" [two opposite mentalities: tradition and renewal], and argues that the counselor "sconvolge la teoria machiavellica dei re cui tutto è concesso" [upsets the Machiavellian theory that kings are allowed everything] (Musumarra, *La poesia tragica*, 108–9). A similar oppostion is present in *Cleopatra*, especially in act 2.5, where Agrippa's Machiavellian advice stand in sharp contrast with Maecenas's humanistic ideals of personal glory.

23. Machiavelli, *Prince*, 18.

24. Speroni's Eolo follows the same logic as he orders the murder of his daughter Canace's illegitimate baby:

> Mora per nostro onore
> L'infamia del mio regno,
> La vergogna del mondo, una *memoria*
> *Del vituperio eterno*
> Della mia casa.
>
> (*Canace*, 1335–39)

[For the sake of our honor must die / the infamy of my kingdom, / the shame of the world, a memory / of the eternal disgrace / of my house.]

25. Machiavelli, *Prince*, 4, 8. Also, using Tarquinius Priscus and Servius Tullus as examples, Machiavelli underscores the need to eliminate surviving enemies, concluding that a prince cannot feel safe in his newly acquired principality "finché vivono coloro che ne sono stati spogliati" [as long as those whom he defeated are still alive] (Machiavelli, *Discorsi*, 3.4.387). On the need to eliminate those who might inspire rebellion, such as members of the family of the defeated ruler, *Cleopatra*'s Agrippa argues that people are eager for change and are always ready to join a rebellion or conspiracy; however, if they see that those who incited them are dead

> il simil temon tutti,
> E non avendo chi lor dia favore,
> Non ardiscono piú di alzar la testa.
>
> (*Cleopatra*, 2.5.1172–76)

[they all fear a similar fate, / and, not finding anyone to aid them, / they do not dare to rebel again.]

Also, Dolce's Herod decides to murder his two children because he fears that one day they might plot against his life:

> S'ambi costoro in sì immatura etade
> Sono vèr me sì audaci e sì crudeli,
> Or che farian col trappassar del tempo?
> Bisogna estinguer l'uno e l'altro serpe,
> Prima ch'accresca in lor veneno e forza.
>
> (*Marianna*, 4.2673–77)

[If both of them in such tender age / are so daring and so cruel towards me / what will they not do as they grow older? / It is necessary to extinguish both of these serpents / before they grow in strength and venom.]

26. Robert M. Adams, ed. and trans. *Niccolò Machiavelli: The Prince* (New York: W. W. Norton, 1977), 267.

27. He tells his servants Alllocche and Tamule that his scheme is worthy of a true king:

> Certo ch'anch'io mi pregio che nel fine
> Quasi de la mia vita abbia mostrato
> Con opra di me degna esser Re vero.
>
> (5.1.2523–25)

[Certainly, I pride myself that toward the end / of my life I was able to show / through a worthy deed that I am a true King.]

Although not quite as proud as Sulmone, King Eolo, too, intends to erase the stain upon his honor by means of a "memorabil vendetta" (1300), namely, the plan to poison Canace and the order to strangle the baby and throw him to the wolves (1397).

28. Like Sulmone, King Lamano wants to punish Norrino "accioch'agli altri essempio / Dia di servar la fede al suo signore" [so that it may serve as a warning to others / to keep their loyalty to their lord] (Giraldi, *Altile*, 1.1.59). He also wants the punishment to discourage all attempts against the crown: "Che non fia alcun, che tal delitto ordisca" [so that there will be no one / who might dare to commit such a crime] (3.5.1615).

29. Machiavelli, *Prince*, 19.

30. Machiavelli believes that it is better for a prince to be feared than to be loved, "perché l'amore è tenuto da un vinculo di obligo il quale per essere li uomini tristi, da ogni occasione di propria utilità è rotto; ma il timore è tenuto da una paura di pena che non ti abbandona mai" [because love is held by a bond of obligation which, men being selfish by nature, is broken whenever is convenient; but fear is held by the fear of punishment which never leaves you] (Machiavelli, *Prince*, 17.70). Botero echoes Machiavelli's reasoning as he, too, concludes that a ruler's reputation should be based on fear "perché l'amore è in podestà del suddito; ma il timore dipende da chi si fà temere" [because love is determined by the subjects, whereas fear depends on those who make themselves feared] (*Aggiunte*, 2.420). With obvious reference to Machiavelli, Alessandro Tassoni points out that " 'l legame dell'amore è molto più agevole da sciorre, che non è quel del timore: perché l'amore riguarda il comodo altrui: ma il timore, tutto si volge al nostro proprio interesse" [it is much easier to loosen a bond of love than it is a bond of fear because love is directed at others, whereas fear turns its effects on us] (Alessandro Tassoni, *Pensieri diversi in Prose politiche e morali*, vol. 1, ed. Piero Puliatti [Bari: Laterza, rpt. 1978], 8.25.216). The idea of fear as the basis of political rule is a common topos in ancient tragedy. Sophocles's Menelaus, for instance, prohibits the burial of Ajax because he wants the body left out in the open as a warning to others. In his words, "laws will never be rightly kept in a city / That knows no fear or reverence, and no army / Without its shield of fear can be well governed (*Ajax*, 1073–75). Also, Seneca's Oedipus tells Creon that "he who fears such hate [from the subjects] too much / Has never learned to rule; fear guards the realm." Ominously, Creon warns him that "the king who holds his throne with cruel sway / Must fear the fearful; on its author's head will fear return"

(Sophocles *Oedipus the King*, in *The Complete Greek Tragedies*, ed. Grene and Lattimore [Chicago: University of Chicago Press, 1969], 753–56).

31. Machiavelli, *Prince*, 7.

32. This attempt to see kings in the *imitatio dei* tradition is also apparent in *Cleopatra*, where Maecenas notes that by killing one man, the king induces as much fear as God does with his thunderbolts (2.5.1344–45). Also, in Aretino's *Orazia*, the Duumviri point out that kings rule by divine disposition and that "chi ottiene lo scettro et il diadema, / Di Dio la volontate have esseguita" [those who obtain the scepter and the crown / do so by the will of God] (4.1951–54).

33. Giovanni Botero, *Della ragion di stato*, ed. Luigi Firpo (Turin: VTET, 1948), 2.15.135–36.

34. In his discussion of Botero's life and works, Gioda finds it interesting that Botero calls for a few, symbolic executions not because of his adversity to violence, but because men were needed in dangerous activities such as war. He cites from Botero's *Aggiunte*, 2: "non essendo oggi maggior carestia di cosa alcuna, che di uomini per la guerra, per le galere e per altri affari, conviene risparmiare le lor vite il più che si possa" [now days there is such a scarcity of able men needed for wars, the operations of galleys, and other activities that is reasonable to spare their lives whenever possible] (Carlo Gioda, *La vita e le opere di Giovanni Botero*, vol. 1 [Milan: Ulrico Hoepli, 1894], 1.320).

35. Machiavelli, *Prince*, 15.65. For a detailed discussion on the compatibility between Machiavellism and reason of state theory, see Kahn, *Machiavellian Rhetoric*, 60–84, and Donaldson, *Machiavelli*, especially 111–140.

36. In Dolce's *Didone*, Prefetto expresses this same thought as he swears to avenge the dead queen with the blood of Eneas and all his Trojans:

> Nessun liquore
> E' a Dio piu' grato, o vittima piu' cara,
> Che quella d'un tiran crudele, et empio.
>
> (5, p. 38)

[no nectar / is more pleasing to the gods, O dearest victim, / than that of a cruel and godless tyrant.]

37. See, also, the chorus's long characterization of Fortune in Alamanni's *Antingone* (p. 196–98) and at the conclusion of Dolce's *Giocasta*.

38.
> ... Forse penserete
> In Ferrara trovarvi, città piena
> D'ogni virtù, città felice
> ....
> Mercé de la giustizia e del valore,
> Del consiglio matur, de la prudenza
> Del suo Signor, al par d'ogni altro saggio.
> E fuor del credere vostro
> ....
> Vi troverete in uno instante in Susa,
> Città nobil di Persia, antica stanza
> Già di felici Re, com'or d'affanno
> E di calamitadi è crudo albergo.
>
> (*Orbecche*, Prologue 54–66)

[... Perhaps you will think / that you are in Ferrara, a city full / of all sort of virtues, a happy city / ... / Thanks to the justice, the valor, / the mature wisdom, and the prudence

/ of its Lord, wise as any other wise prince. / And with your surprise and disbelief / . . . / In an instant you will find yourselves in Susa, / a noble city in Persia, once an ancient kingdom / of happy Kings, and now / a cruel place full of grief and calamity.]

This differentiation between the "here" of the theater and the "there" of the action is also found in Dolce's *Marianna*, where Prologue distinguishes between the grieving Jerusalem of the stage and the happy, blessed, free, and illustrious Venice. In his *Giocasta*, Prologue makes a similar distinction between Venice, the most illustrious city in the whole world, and the miserable Thebes.

39. With reference to the 1513 representation of Bibbiena's *Calandria* at the Ducal palace in Urbino, Attolini writes that "gli unici spettatori coinvolti nella rappresentazione sono in realtà i signori, i principi; coinvolti fino al punto da offrirsi essi stessi come spettacolo. Tanto è vero che solitamente vengono fatti sedere su un palco al centro della sala, del tutto separati dal resto del pubblico" [the only spectators involved in the representation are really the nobles and the princes. They are involved to the point of offering themselves as the spectacle. This is evinced by the fact that usually they are seated on a platform in the middle of the hall, totally separated from the rest of the public] (Attolini, *Teatro e spettacolo*, 114).

40. Having noted that theatrical performances at the Elizabethan court had two audiences and two spectacles and that the primary audience was the monarch, Orgel writes that "at these performances what the rest of the spectators watched was not a play but the queen at a play, and their response would have been not simply to the drama, but to the relationship between the drama and its primary audience, the royal spectator" (Stephen Orgel, *The Illusion of Power* [Berkeley: University of California Press, 1975], 9).

41. Attolini cites Paruta in support of his own observation that the political motive behind public festivities was no longer "soltanto quello di divertire il popolo, ma di associarlo, apparentemente, all'esercizio del potere" [only that of amusing the people, but also to associate them, openly, to the exercise of power] (Attolini, *Teatro e spettacolo*, 35).

Chapter 5. Tragic Heroines: The Debate on the Emerging Question of Women

1. These plays are commonly considered the most representative of Italian Renaissance drama. For a list of Renaissance tragedies in Latin and in Italian, including close imitations and translations of Greek and Latin plays, see the index in Herrick, *Italian Tragedy*, 307–9. With reference to *Orazia*, there is enough textual evidence to support the contention that the title may be taken to refer to Celia's character. On this point, see Barish, "The Problem,"13.

2. Lucien Goldmann points out that "all forms of tragic vision have one feature in common: they all express a deep crisis in the relationship between man and his social and spiritual world" (Lucien Goldmann, *The Hidden God*, trans. Philip Thody [London: Routledge & Kegan Paul, 1970], 41). Luigi Russo, with reference to sixteenth and seventeenth-century drama, argues that "la tragedia nasce tutte le volte che c'è nella civiltà una profonda crisi etico-politica e religiosa" [tragedy normally flourishes when in the culture there is a profound crisis of political and religious nature] (Russo, "La tragedia," 18).

3. McCollum, *Tragedy*, 114. McCollum believes that tragic conflicts should reflect the cultural and historical crisis in which the writer lives (12), and that in

trying to determine the meaning of the play, we actually ask: "How does the action of the play apply to the society which produced it?" (113).

4. Kennard, *The Italian Theatre*, 144. Although Kennard correctly identifies the crisis, his assessment of Giraldi must be taken for what it is worth. "In the quarrels of men and women," he writes, "Giraldi sided with the women and praised matrimony. It was a vital question in the literature of the time, and he brought it also on to the tragic stage. All his women are devoted, sincere, virtuous; all are victims of men's cruelty. Had his talent equaled his sympathies, his women would all have been sweet and interesting figures" (ibid.).

5. Among the many excellent books on the traditional concept of womanhood, see in particular, Patricia Labaime, *Beyond their Sex: Learned Women of the European Past;* Julia O'Faolain and Laura Martinez, eds. *Not in God's Image: Women in History from the Greeks to the Victorians*; and Marina Warner, *Alone of All Her Sex*. For the Renaissance, see Ian Maclean, *Woman Triumphant*, and Romeo De Maio's *Donna e Rinascimento*.

6. Barbaro lists these three qualities as the most praiseworthy virtues in a wife: "caritas in maritum, vitae modestia, domesticae rei cura gravis et diligens" [love for the husband, modesty, and great and diligent care of the household] (Francesco Barbaro, "De re uxoria liber," in *Prosatori latini del Quattrocento*, ed. Eugene Garin [Torino: Einaudi, 1976], 110). This concept, which is also discussed in Alberti's *I libri della famiglia*, 2, finds its way in many future treatises on the subject of women and marriage.

7. Boccaccio, *Decameron*, 6.7.

8. Gene Brucker, *Giovanni and Lusanna: Love and Marriage in Renaissance Florence* (Berkeley: University of California Press, 1986), 121.

9. Margaret King, noting the difficulty in determining whether writers defended the intellectual capacity of woman because they believed in it or simply "because of their relation to female patrons," concludes: "Perhaps they shaped laudatory views to conform to the inclination of the listener who had commissioned them, or perhaps, thinking well of women, they addressed their writings to influential paragons of that sex" (Margaret King *Women of the Renaissance* [Chicago: University of Chicago Press, 1991], 184).

10. De Maio, *Donna e Rinascimento*, 68–69.

11. Firenzuola reiterates the equality of the sexes, stressing that everything points to the conclusion that "così nobili siate voi donne come noi uomini, così savie, così atte alle intelligenzie e morali e speculative, così atte alle meccaniche azioni e cognizioni come noi, e quelle medesime potenzie e virtuali abiti sono nell'animo vostro che nel nostro: perciocché, quando il tutto si parte in due parti uguali ugualmente, di necessità tanto è una parte quanto l'altra, tanto buona quanto l'altra, tanto bella quanto l'altra" [you women are as noble as us men, so wise, so apt to moral and intellectual understanding, so apt to material actions and cognition as us men, and those virtues that are in your souls are also in ours. Therefore, when the whole is divided in two equal parts, it follows that one part be as much as the other, as good as the other, as beautiful as the other] (Agnolo Firenzuola, *Dialogo delle bellezze delle donne*, ed. Adriano Seroni [Florence: Sansoni, 1971], 547).

12. Silvia Ruffo-Fiore, "The Silent Scholars of Italian Humanism: Feminism in the Renaissance," in *Interpreting the Italian Renaissance*, ed. Antonio Toscano (Stony Brook: Filibrary, 1991), 20.

13. Ariosto, *Orlando Furioso*, 13.59. In another instance, Ariosto, lamenting that he cannot possibly write about all the women deserving praise, chooses Vittoria Colonna as the one who has achieved immortality through her writings:

> Sceglieronne una; e sceglierolla tale,
> che superato avrà l'invidia in modo,
> che nessun'altra potrà avere a male,
> se l'altre taccio, e se lei sola lodo.
> *Quest'una ha non pur sé fatta immortale*
> *col dolce stil di che il meglior non odo;*
> ma può qualunque di cui parli o scriva,
> trar del sepolcro, e far ch'eterno viva.
>
> (37.16)

> [One will I choose, and such will choose, that she
> All envy shall so well have overthrown,
> No other woman can offend be,
> If, passing others, her I praise alone:
> *Nor joys this one but immortality,*
> *Though her sweet style (and better know I none);*
> But who is honoured in her speech and page,
> Shall burst the tomb, and live through every age
> (trans. Stewart Rose; italics mine)

On the administrative and political ability of women, such as Isabella d'Este and Barbara of Brandenburg, besides established biographies that make for informative and delightful reading, see Ward E. Swain's excellent essay "My excellent & most singular lord," *Journal of Medieval and Renaissance Studies* 2 (1986). On female poets and their works, see Alma Forlani and Marta Savini, *Scrittrici d'Italia* (Rome: Newton Compton, 1991), 11–88, as well as King, *Women of the Renaissance*, especially, 215–18. On women humanists, see Margaret L. King and Albert Rabil, Jr. eds., *Her Immaculate Hand* (Asheville: University of North Carolina Press, 1997), and its useful bibliography.

14. Burckhardt, *The Civilization of the Renaissance in Italy*, 2.389.

15. For details, see De Maio, *Donna e Rinascimento*, 53–54.

16. The Church of the Counter-Reformation, writes Servadio, "riportò le donne alla posizione che avevano prima del Rinascimento: tornarono ad essere il simbolo del peccato" [brought women back to the status they held before the Renaissance: they became once again the symbol of sin] (Gaia Servadio, *La donna nel Rinascimento*, trans. Giovanni Luciani [Milan: Garzanti, 1986], 23). For a broad view on the notion of women before the Renaissance, see Francis and Joseph Gies, *Women in the Middle Ages* (New York: Harper Perennial, 1978).

17. Kelso tells of two incidents in which local women made the authors of misogynist diatribes to repent for their attacks (Ruth Kelso, *Doctrine for the Lady of the Renaissance* [Urbana: University of Illinois Press, 1956], 9). She also identifies and discusses four different aspects of the Renaissance notion of womankind: 1. women as necessary evil; 2. women inferior, but comparable to men in their own special role; 3. woman the equal to man; 4. [women's] superiority argued by extremists (284–85). As for women in epic poetry, suffice the view Ariosto expressed in the *Furioso*:

> *Le donne son venute in eccellenza*
> *di ciascun'arte ove'hanno posto cura;*
> e qualunque all'istorie abbia avvertenza,
> ne sente ancor la fama non oscura.
> Se 'l mondo n'è gran tempo stato senza,
> non però sempre il mal influsso dura;
> e forse ascosi han lor debiti onori
> l'invidia o il non saper degli scrittori.
>
> (20.2)

[*Women have reached the pinnacle of glory,*
In every art by them professed, well seen;
And whosoever turns the leaf of story,
Finds record of them, neither dim nor mean.
The evil influence will be transitory,
If long deprived of such the world has been;
And envious men, and those that never knew
Their worth, have haply hid their honours due]

(trans. S. Rose; italics mine)

But, see also King, *Women of the Renaissance,* 189. For the treatment of woman in the short story, besides Machiavelli's *Belfagor,* see Bandello's *Novelle,* especially Fiorato's discussion of it ("L'image et la condition," 169–286). Comedy is a typical source of misogyny. Aretino's *Il marescalco,* for example, is based primarily on the clash between vituperators (Ambrogio and Marescalco) and defenders of woman (Balia and Jacopo).

18. In his comments on the portrayal of women in thirty-two paintings by various Renaissance artists, De Maio underscores the growing perception of woman as having an increasingly important role in society (De maio, *Donna e Rinascimento,* 154–55).

19. Alessandro Del Vita reports that the writing was sculptured on a marble stone at the entrance of Villa Imperiale near Pesaro. He also puts in context the association of women with the destructive goats and the stupid ducks and cites local sayings reflecting this form of female vituperation (Alessandro Del Vita, *Lusso, donne, amore nel Rinascimento* [Arezzo: Edizioni Rinascimento, 1961], 58).

20. On this tradition, see Kelly, *Ideas and Forms of Tragedy,* 31, 76–77. Also, consider the conclusion of Rucellai's *Oreste,* where King Toante inveighs against women who, like Medea, Ariadne, and Helen of Troy, brought ruin upon their families and/or their states.

21. In a soliloquy of more than one hundred lines long, Orbecche deplores her status thus:

> . . . io veggio
> Ch'altro esser non mi fa trista e infelice
> Che l'esser donna. O sesso al mondo in ira,
> Sesso pien di miserie e pien d'affanni
> Et a te stesso, non ch'ad altri, in odio!

(2.880–85)

[. . . I realize / that nothing makes me more sad and unhappy / that my being a woman. Oh sex, hated by the whole world, / sex full of toils and miseries, / abhorred both by yourself and by others!]

22. Cfr. Dolce's and Euripides's versions:

> *Medea*: Ma, che bisogna dir? Certo noi Donne
> Siam tutte assai piú misere, e infelici
> Di qualunque animale alberga in terra.
> Che primamente non possiam da noi
> Regger lo stato nostro: indi conviene,
> Che col prezzo de l'oro e de l'argento
> Compriamo il *proprio male*: e questo è il nostro
> Marito: anzi per dirlo veramente
> *Il Signor de la vita e de la morte:*

> Il qual non con dolcezza e con amore,
> Ma *con asprezza e crudeltà ci regge.*
>
> (2, p. 12; italics mine)

[*Medea*: But, what can one say? Certainly, we women / are all more unfortunate and unhappy / than any animal that lives on earth. / For, to begin with, we cannot on our own / govern our affairs. Hence, it is necessary / that with gold and silver / we buy our misfortune, namely, a / husband: the true *master of our life and death.* / He rules us not with sweetness and love / but *with harshness and cruelty*]

Euripedes's version:

> We women are the most unfortunate creatures.
> Firstly, with an excess of wealth it is required
> for us to buy a husband and take for our bodies
> a master; for not to take one is even worse.
> And now the question is serious whether we take
> a good or bad one; for there is no easy escape
> for a woman, nor can she say no to her marriage.
> She arrives among new modes of behavior and manners,
> and needs prophetic power, unless she has learned at home,
> how best to manage him who shares the bed with her.
> And if we work out all this well and carefully,
> and the husband lives with us and lightly bears his yoke,
> then life is enviable. If not, I'd rather die.
>
> (231–43)

23. The notion is found in the ancients as well as in Boccaccio and other writers. For references, see Cremante, *Teatro del Cinquecento,* note to lines 871–73, pp. 339–40.

24. Donna di Selene, in Giraldi's *Arrenopia,* 3.10, voices a similar despair when she complains that women live in perpetual servitude: as young virgins they are subject to their parents and brothers, she complains, as married women to their husbands. The theme is echoed in another of Giraldi's tragedies *Altile,* 3.4. And, in Aretino's *Orazia,* Celia wishes that she had been born a man so that she would not have to suffer and mourn the loss of her loved one: "Perchè, lassa, non nacqui maschio anch'io / . . . / Tal che fuora sarei di tanto affanno" [Why, alas, was I not born a male / . . . / So that I would be free of so much anguish] (1.476–93).

25. Luigi Baldacci, ed. *Lirici del Cinquecento* (Milan: Longanesi, 1975), 483. For additional biographical details, see the bibliographical note on p. lii.

26. Pietro Belmonte, elaborating on the recurrent image of the mirror, offers the following advice: "convien che tu [moglie] rida al suo riso, ti attristi al suo scontento, posi al suo posare, camini al suo andare, taccia al suo tacere, e favelli al suo parlare" [it behooves you (wife) to smile when he smiles, be sad when he is sad, stop when he stops, walk when he walks, be quiet when he is quiet, and speak when he speaks] (Pietro Belmonte, *Istitutione della sposa* [Rome: Heredi di Giovanni Osmarino Gigliotto, 1587], qtd. by Daniela del Frigo, "Dal caos all'ordine," *Nel Cerchio della luna,* ed. Marina Zancan [Venice: Marsilio, 1983], 77). Similar views are expressed in Sperone Speroni, "Della dignità delle donne," where one reads comments such as: woman is born to live "come altri vuole" [according to the wishes of others] (580), it is natural for a wife "servire il marito" [to serve her husband] (581), woman should be a servant because "a servire é creata" [she was born to serve] (583).

27. Venus dissuades Aeneas from killing Helen of Troy by reminding him that there is no glory in killing a woman: "nullum memorabile nomen / feminea in poena est nec habet victoria laudem" [there is nothing memorable or worthy of praise in punishing a woman] (Virgil, *The Aeneid of Virgil*, ed. R. M. Williams [London: Macmillan, 1975], 2.583–84). Also, the Prefect in Seneca's *Octavia*, in his attempt to dissuade Nero from killing Octavia, argues that a woman can hardly be considered a serious enemy, and therefore, he asks, how can "Femina hoc nomen capit?" [such epithet describe a woman?] (5.2.867).

28. Daniela Frigo points out that most authors agreed on the two basic roles that women were supposed to play in society: an internal or domestic role, in which she was to exhibit moral virtues and organizational abilities; and an external one, meant to promote the harmonious relationship between the family and its sociopolitical milieu (Frigo, "Dal caos all'ordine," 69).

29. Alberti, *Libro della famiglia*, 3.495.

30. Reflecting a humanist tendency dating back to Petrarch, many wished that procreation could be attained without marriage so that they did not have to live with women. Pietro Lauro, conceding that "se si potesse tener famiglia, haver figliuoli heredi de le facultà e del nome de la casata, senza pigliar moglie, non è dubbio che sarebbe assai meglio il viverne senza. . . . Ma . . . siamo pur astretti à viver tra tanti incomodi con la moglie" [if one could have a family, have heirs worthy of the family name, without having to take a wife, there is no doubt that it would be much better to live without. . . . But . . . we are forced to live with the inconvenience of having a wife] (Pietro Lauro, *De le lettere*, qtd. by Frigo, "Dal caos all'ordine," 92).

31. With reference to the 1488 conspiracy against Count Girolamo Riario of Forlì, Machiavelli tells how the conspirators having murdered the count and taken prisoner the countess and the children proceeded to take over the fortress. When the loyal castellan refused to turn over the stronghold to the conspirators, the captive countess promised its immediate surrender if she were allowed inside to talk to the castellan. To ensure that she would come out, the conspirators held her children as hostages. Once inside, Caterina refused to come out. When the conspirators threatened to kill the children, Caterina "mostrò loro le membra genitali, dicendo che aveva ancora il modo a rifarne" [showed them her genitalia, telling them that she still had the means to make more] (Machiavelli, *Discorsi*, 3: 6.408).

32. Most heroines admit to the physical weakness of their sex and, of course, to their helplessness in a culture that keeps them totally dependent on men for their sustenance. Alamanni's Ismene, for instance, like her Greek counterpart, reminds her sister Antigone that they are women and thus inadequate against men:

> Ma ne convien pensar che già create
> Femine fummo, e che non siam bastanti
> Debili e 'nferme a contrastar con l'uomo.
>
> (*Antigone*, p. 150)

[But, we may do well to remember that we were created / women, and that we are very / weak and ill suited to fight against men.]

In *Acripanda*, Nodrice tells Acripanda that women are by nature "garrule e loquaci" [garrulous and talkative] (p. 62). Adriana's female chorus, having learned of the impending invasion, wonder "dove fuggiremo / donne imbecilli, e stanche?" [where can we flee, / we feeble and tired women] (5.9.95–96). In Dolce's *Giocasta*, Antigone tells her mother, who wishes to prevent the fatal encounter between her two sons, that there is nothing they can do, since "Voi debol vecchia, et io / Impotente fanciulla" [you are a feeble old woman, and I a helpless young girl] (p. 85).

33. Anthony Gable, contrasting French with Italian heroines of drama, writes that in "Italy the lovelorn heroine was a normal figure, and had been since Trissino's Sofonisba had spoken of 'Amore . . . e le dolcissime parole' "(Anthony Gable "Du Monin's Revenge Tragedy *Orbecc-Oronte,*" *Renaissance Drama* 11[1980]: 9).

34. Robert Payne and Nikita Romanoff, *Ivan The Terrible* (New York: Thomas Y. Crowell, 1975), 264. For a transcript of Elizabeth Dirks's trial, torture and subsequent death by drowning, see Roland H. Bainton, *Women of the Reformation in Germany and Italy* (Minneapolis: Augsburg Publishing House, 1971), 145–50.

35. There are striking similarities between the two heroines: Rosmunda swears never to touch Alboino (758), her father's conqueror, and Andromaque prefers to join her dead husband rather than marry the victorious Pyrrhus (3.6). Both succumb to the logic of their nurses' argument, namely, that they should accept the offer of marriage in order to spare the lives of innocent victims. Though after accepting marriage, Rosmunda kills Alboino and Andromaque kills herself, their status as failed tragic heroines is rather similar. Goldmann, in discussing the tragic notion of "refusal" in Racine's play, argues that Andromaque "is tragic in so far as she refuses the alternatives, and confronts the world with her voluntary refusal of life and her freely accepted choice of death. She ceases to be tragic, however, when she decides to accept marriage with Pyrrhus" (Goldmann, *The Hidden God,* 324). This argument can also be made with reference to Rosmunda's character.

36. Da Horte's Acripanda, fearing that she may be taken prisoner and brought to Arabia by the triumphant Arabian king, wishes to emulate the example of Cleopatra, Sofonisba, Cato, and Lucretia among others (*Acripanda,* 2.1). On the meaning of "generosa" as employed by Renaissance writers, Georg Weise notes that the term *generositas* implies "l'idea d'una nobile origine come presupposto di un pensare e di un agire magnanimi" [the idea of noble origins as the basis for magnanimous thoughts and deeds] (Georg Weise, *L'Ideale eroico del Rinascimento e le sue premesse umanistiche* [Naples: Edizioni Sciéntifiche Italiane, 1961], 195). For other connotations, see 198, 217.

37. Dante, *Purgatory,* 1.71–73.

38. Manetti points out that Socrates, Cleombrotus, and Cato committed suicide not out of desperation but in the hope of gaining immortality. Otherwise, he continues, they would not have been praised by so many future writers, since to flee from danger and misfortunes is not typical of the strong but "mollis et enervati hominis" [of the weak man] (Giannozzo Manetti, "De dignitate et excellentia hominis," in *Prosatori latini del Quattrocento,* ed. Eugene Garin [Torino: Einaudi, 1976], 459).

39. Beaty footnotes that over one hundred editions of the *Ars moriendi* itself "are extant from the fifteenth century alone" (Nancy Lee Beaty *The Craft of Dying: A Study of the Literary Tradition of the Ars Moriendi in England* [New Haven: Yale University Press, 1970], 55).

40. Weise, *L'Ideale eroico del Rinascimento,* 224–25. Speaking of the ethical ideals of the Renaissance, Weise concludes that "l'idea del 'bene compositus animus' e della padronanza della ragione sugli affetti e sulle passioni sono di dominio in tutta la letteratura umanistica" [the idea of a 'well balanced mind' and of reason's control over one's emotions and passions are dominant in humanist literature] (ibid.). For a series of examples, see his chapter "Gli ideali etici," 181–238.

41. Mary Ellen Lamb, "The Countess of Pembroke and the Art of Dying," *Women in the Middle Ages and the Renaissance,* ed. Mary Beth Rose [Syracuse: Syracuse University Press, 1986], 220.

42. Maclean, *The Renaissance Notion of Woman*, 187. Maclean also emphasizes the source of *admiratio* in tragedy and underlines the moral elevation associated with this rhetorical technique. This is particularly true when death occurs on stage. When death is narrated as having taken place, the suspense is minimal, as the narrative is cast with enough clues as to leave no doubt that the heroine ultimately kills herself (186–90).

43. Compare Othello's grief as he stares at Desdemona's lifeless body with Herod's wish to join Marianna after he ordered her execution:

> *Othello*: Man but a rush against Othello's breast,
> And he retires. Where should Othello go?
> Now how dost thou look now? O ill-starr'd wench!
> Pale as thy smock! when we shall meet at compt,
> *This look of thine will hurl my soul from heaven,*
> And fiends will snatch at it.
>
> (5.2.271–76)

> *Herod*: A me non saria cosa acerba e grave
> Con le mie proprie mani aprirmi il petto.
> Ma tu, sì come pura et innocente,
> Sciolta da' lacci uman sei gita in cielo,
> *Et io discenderei da te lontano,*
> *Pieno di sceleraggini a l'Inferno.*
>
> (5.3248–53)

[For me, it would be neither repugnant nor onerous a deed / to tear open my breast with my own hands. / But you, so pure and innocent, / freed from your human bonds, have gone to heaven. / And I, with all my iniquities, would descend / in Hell, far away from you.]

44. Besides the female authors who wrote between 1530–1550 (Tullia d'Aragona, Vittoria Colonna, Lucrezia Gonzaga, Veronica Franco, Gaspara Stampa, Veronica Gambara, Laura Terracina), a second group flourished toward the end of the century. Among the better known were Isabella Andreini, Maddalena Campiglia, Isabella Cervoni, Modesta Pozzo de' Zorzi, and Lucrezia Marinelli. For more details on women poets, see Forlani and Savini, *Scrittrici d'Italia*. See, especially, Adriana Chemello's enlightening discussion of Marinelli's treatise *La Nobiltà et eccellenza delle donne*, "La donna, il modello, l'immaginario," in *Nel Cerchio della luna*, ed. Marina Zancan (Venice: Marsilio, 1983), 150–70.

45. In a marginal note to his "Discorso," Giraldi underscores the teaching effectiveness of theater over philosophical or theoretical writings. He points out that the playwright often treats the same topics as the philosopher, but with entertainment, for "per l'artificio ch'egli usa, giova e diletta e porge utile non pure a coloro che son capaci di conoscere i sentimenti ascosi sotto le finzioni, ma anco agli altri che non sono così atti alla profonda intelligenza" [through the use of his art, he delights and teaches not only those capable of perceiving hidden meaning, but also those less intellectually gifted] (275 n. 48).

46. In Dolce's *Marianna*, Prologue appeals to the sensitivity of the

> ... leggiadre donne,
> D'alta beltade e di virtute esempio,
> E chiaro specchio d'onestate invitta.
>
> (65–69)

[... lovely ladies, / paragon of great beauty and virtue, / and clear mirror of unassailable honesty.]

47. Philip Horne gives for granted Giraldi's "feminist sympathies" (Horne, *The Tragedies of Giambattista Cinthio Giraldi*, 78).

48. Compare, for instance, Ariosto's praise of women in *Orlando Furioso*, 20.2 and 37.16 with the misogynist tone of his fifth satire, which he wrote for the coming marriage of his cousin Annibale Malaguzzi. In the satire, he advises the bridegroom that one should domesticate a wife in much the same way one trains a horse or a dog:

> Poi ch'io t'ho posto assai bene a cavallo,
> ti voglio anco mostrar come lo guidi,
> come spinger lo déi, come fermallo.
> . . . .
> Questi animal, che son molto più umani, [women]
> corregger non si dén sempre con sdegno,
> né, al mio parer, mai con menar de mani.
>
> (247–49, 262–64)

[Now that I have mounted you so tightly on your mare, must show you how to guide her, how to urge her on and how to halt her. . . . Creatures which are much more human than these should not be corrected all the time with anger, nor, in my opinion, ever with a slap of the hand.]

(trans. Desa Wiggins)

49. Boccaccio's *De mulieribus claris*, notes King, "paved the way for a rash of catalogues of illustrious women of the biblical, classical, Christian, and local past" (King, *Women of the Renaissance*, 183). Actually, it was more than just a tradition of catalogues, for, as De Maio points out, the *De mulieribus* "crea la biografia laica femminile" [it inaugurates the biographical genre of secular women] (De Maio, *Donna e Rinascimento*, 147).

Chapter 6. The Evolving Concept of Stage and Dramatic Space

1. Kowzan, distinguishing between written text and dramatization, points out that "une oeuvre dramatique implique l'utilisation d'autres moyens d'expression, elle implique le recours à la perception sensorielle du consommateur, la coexistence et l'interpénétration des éléments expressifs verbaux et extra-verbaux, elle est destinée à être recrée continuellement dans l'espace et dans le temps" [a dramatic work implies the utilization of other means of expression. It implies the recourse to the consumer's sensorial perception, the coexistence and the interpenetration of verbal and extra-verbal elements of expression. It is destined to be continually recreated in time and space] (Kowzan, *Littérature et spectacle,* 159). On the difference between reading and representing a dramatic text, see Roman Ingarden, *The Literary Work of Art*, trans. George G. Grabowiz (Evanston, Ill.: Northwestern University Press, 1973), especially pp. 318–22; also Pfister, *The Theory and Analysis of Drama*, 7.

2. Speaking of the function of these different systems, Donahue points out that "the visual, auditory, and linguistic sign systems act as reinforcement for each other, producing redundant messages that ensure that communication takes place

despite momentary lapses of concentration on the part of the spectator" (Thomas John Donahue, *Structures of Meaning* [London and Toronto: Associated University Presses, 1993], 81).

3. Ariani notes that one of the difficulties in dealing with Italian Renaissance drama is "la scarsità di documentazioni e testimonianze attendibili che, quantomeno, vadano oltre la semplice descrizione esterna dello spettacolo tragico cinquecentesco" [the scarcity of viable evidence and documentation which may go, at least, beyond the simple external description of the tragic spectacle in the cinquecento] (Ariani, *Il teatro*,1.VII). On the subject, besides Barish's "The Problem," see also Attolini, *Teatro e spettacolo*, 67, 73, 165.

4. Most critics endorse the distinction that Marco de Marinis makes between the written text and the performance text. However, there are reservations to such an approach. Jean Alter points out that "since the performance lapses into nonexistence at the very moment it comes into being, there is no opportunity either for a second look at a specific feature or for a reproduction of the entire experience for the purposes of verification." Thus the need to "come back to the written text which alone allows for meaningful communication" (Jean Alter, "Waiting for the Referent," in *On Referring in Literature,* ed. Anna Whiteside and Michael Issacharoff [Bloomington: Indiana University Press, 1987], 42–43). For an overall view of the problem, see Anne Ubersfeld, *Lire le Théâtre* (Paris: Éditions Sociales, 1981), 13–24, and Carlson, *Theater,* xii, 95.

5. Donahue observes that "through the use of language the playwright goads the reader into creating a virtual production of the play. The reader is asked to visualize the place of the action, the gestures of the actors, and all the visual and auditory effects that would be part of most contemporary productions" (Donahue, *Structures of Meaning,* 80).

6. Roland Barthes offers a comprehensive definition of theatricality as he answers his own question "Qu'est-ce que la théâtricalité?" For him, theatricality "c'est le théâtre moins le texte, c'est une épaisseur de signes et de sensations qui s'édifie sure la scène à partir de l'argument écrit, c'est cette sorte de perception oecuménique des artifices sensuels, gestes, tons, distances, substances, lumières, qui submerge le texte sous la plénitude de son langage extérieur. Naturellement, la théâtricalité doit être présente dès le premier germe écrit d'une oeuvre, elle est une donnée de création, non de réalisation" [is the theater minus the text, it is a density of signs and sensations that, issuing from the written text, grow on the scene. It is that sort of ecumenical perception of sensual artifices, gestures, tone, distances, substances, lights, which submerge the text under the plenitude of its exterior language. Naturally, theatricality must be present from the first written germ of the work, for it is a question of creation, not of realization] (Roland Barthes, "Le théatre," in *Essais Critiques* [Paris: Éditions du Seuil, 1964], 41–2).

7. Ubersfeld defines scenic space as "la collection des signes provenus du lieu scénique et qui y trouvent leur place. A l'espace scénique appartiendront non seulement des signes comme les practicables ou les accessoires, mais le nombre des comédiens et leur espacement, les figures qu'ils dessinent, leur rapport à l'éclairage et à l'acoustique. La définition de l'espace scénique sera donc extrêmement large; à la limite, il contient tous les événements qui prennent leur place sur la scène" [the collection of signs which issue from the scenic place and find their place in it. To the scenic space, then, will belong non only signs of practicables and accessories, but the number of actors and their blocking, the shadows they cast, their relationship to the lighting and the acoustics. Thus, the definition of scenic space is extremely wide; at least, it contains all the events which take place on the scene] (Anne Ubersfeld *L'école*

du spectateur [Paris: Éditions Sociales, 1981], 56). The concept of space in theater is a problematic one and has received much attention. For an enlightening discussion informed by previous contributions, see Michael Issacharoff's "Space and Reference in Drama," *Poetics Today* 3 (1981).

    8. Arnott, speaking of the evolution of the Greek tragic *skene*, points out that when its temporary structure became permanent, it "retained the entrance doors—no more than three are needed in any one play—and was decorated with statues of the gods" (Peter D. Arnott, *An Introduction to the Greek Theatre* [London: Macmillan, 1959], 33). He also suggests that most Greek "tragedies are set before a temple or a palace" (38), and that apart from the statues and the gods "the most important feature of many plays is the altar around which characters sit in supplication, or to which they fly for protection" (41). Pickard-Cambridge, having discussed the probable structure of the scene in various Greek tragedies, concludes that the "background most often represented a palace or a temple, or one, or two, or three houses [houses were mostly featured in comedy] and admitted of a good deal of adaptation; it might sometimes represent a cliff with a central cave, and when scene-painting was introduced it could be applied to suggest a grove or wooded country" (A. W. Pickard: Cambridge, *The Theatre of Dionysus in Athens* [Oxford: Clarendon Press, 1956], 68).

    9. Pickard-Cambridge believes that in this tragedy "there is a group of altars (as lines 15 and 16 suggest) in front of the palace, or at least an altar of Apollo Lykeios (lines 918 ff.)," in ibid., 47.

    10. Vince gives a concise sketch of the critical and editorial fortunes enjoyed by the *De Re Architectura* in the Renaissance, noting that it was first printed in 1486 in Rome and published again in 1496 and 1497. In 1511 appeared Fra Giocondo's illustrated edition. The work was also translated into Italian in 1521 by Cesare Cesariano, and again in 1556 by Daniello Barbaro, who also provided the original text with illustrations and commentary. Vince writes that "before the end of the seventeenth century more than thirty editions of Vitruvius had appeared in Europe." He goes on to suggest that Vitruvius's "brief comments on and discussion of theater dominated theatrical theory and practice in Renaissance Italy in much the same way Aristotle and Horace dominated Renaissance poetics" (Ronald W. Vince, *Renaissance Theatre* [Westport, Conn.: Greenwood Press, 1984], 11–12).

    11. For a discussion of Alberti's view and its influence on the development of the physical structure of the Renaissance stage, see Marotti, *Storia documentaria*, 27–30, and Attolini, *Teatro e spettacolo*, 54–56.

    12. With few exceptions, in the tragedies that followed closely the Greek tradition, such as Tasso's *Torrismondo* and Torrelli's *Merope*, the scene consisted of the space in front of the royal palace or temple, where most of the dramatic action took place.

    13. Vince, *Renaissance Theatre*, 12.

    14. Franco Mancini, *Scenografia italiana* (Milan: Fratelli Fabbri, 1966), 17–18, notes that the first historically verifiable scene in perspective was painded by Pellegrino da Udine for the 1508 performance of Ariosto's *Cassaria* in the Sala Grande of the Este Court.

    15. Issacharoff defines diegetic space as a place described or "referred to by the characters" (Issacharoff, "Space and Reference in Drama," 215). Veltrusky calls it "imaginary stage or, to use a more accurate term imaginary action space' " (Jirí Veltrusky, "The Prague School Theory of Theater," *Poetics Today* 3 [1981]: 232). Pfister refers to it as "verbal localisation technique," and acknowledges that is it also known as "word-scenery" or " 'spoken space' " (Pfister, *The Theory and Analysis of*

Drama, 267). Donahue, *Structures of Meaning*, 87, distinguishes between verbal space (that which is alluded to in the characters' discourse) and perceptual space (that which is seen). This notion of perceptual space should be expanded, I believe, to include space perceived through sounds, for noises heard from offstage often signify dramatic space.

16. Styan argues that spatial closeness determines "the emotional range of the play, the intimacy or remoteness of the playing and the immediacy or alienation of the response." He further points out that such closeness puts a special pressure on the spectator, since he "is compelled to pay a closer attention to what is said and done on the stage. In intimate conditions he gives a wider range of attention to the actors, calling upon otherwise untapped sources of sympathy and response" (J. L. Styan, *Shakespeare's Stagecraft* [Cambridge: Cambridge University Press, 1967], 14–15).

17. David Cole, noting that in theater a change of place may be accomplished through images, argues that an "image, in manifesting itself, brings its world along with it, just the way a traveller stepping into a restaurant out of a blizzard, carries the storm into the diners' midst." Conversely, a vanishing image takes "its space with it" (David Cole, *The Theatrical Event* [Middletown, Conn.: Wesleyan University Press, 1975], 89).

18. Veltrusky, speaking of dramatic space, both mimetic and diagetic, concludes that "dramatic space unifies all the meanings the various components evoke simultaneously just as dramatic action unifies all the meanings they evoke successively" (Veltrusky, "The Prague School Theory of Theater," 232).

19. Ginguené calls *Orazia* "le premier exemple des tragédies historiques à grand spectacle et à grands mouvements, dont Shakespeare, qui ne parut que cinquante ans après, passe pour l'inventeur et qu'il méla de grossièretès et de licences de tout genre, qu'on ne trouve point dans cette tragédie" [the first example of historical tragedies with a great spectacle and great movements, of which Shakespeare, who came fifty years later, passes for the inventor. He also introduced profanities and all sort of licentious behavior, none of which is to be found in this tragedy] (Pierre Louis Ginguené, *Histoire littéraire d'Italie* [Paris: Michaud, 1813], 140–41). Canello refers to Aretino's play as "un dramma shakespeariano di larghe proporzioni" [a Shakespearean drama of great proportions] (Angelo Ugo Canello, *Storia della letteratura italiana nel secolo XVI* [Milan: Vallardi, 1880], 225). Mario Apollonio called it "una grande tragedia" (Apollonio, *Storia del teatro*, 2.243). Kennard, comparing Aretino to Speroni, concludes: "*Orazia* is far better than *Canace*; it is indeed the least bad of the Italian cinquecento tragedies" (Kennard, *The Italian Theatre*,149). Herrick writes: "*Marianna* is Dolce's masterpiece, and it is among the best Italian tragedies of the sixteenth century. Aretino's *Orazia* is a better play" (Herrick, *Italian Tragedy*, 176–77). George Bull considers *Orazia* "arguably the best Italian tragedy of the century" (George Bull, ed. and trans., *Pietro Aretino. Selected Letters* [Harmondsworth: Penguin, 1976], 33). Ariani points out that structurally *Orazia* "è certo la tragedia cinquecentesca meglio costruita, la più armoniosa, prima almeno della *Merope* del Torelli" [is certainly the best structured and the most harmonious tragedy of the cinquecento, at least prior to Torelli's *Merope*] (Ariani, *Il teatro*, XLIII). For more details on the critical assessment of *Orazia*, see Morano's compendious discussion in Michael Lettieri and Rocco Mario Morano, eds., *Pietro Aretino. L'Orazia* [Rovito: Marra Editore, 1991], especially XI.

20. On these critical perspectives, see Salvatore Di Maria, "Spazio e tematica nell' *Orazia* de Pietro Aretino," in *Pietro Aretino e la cultura del Rinascimento*, ed. M. Lettieri, S. Bancheri, and R. Buranello (Rome: Salerno Editrice, 1995).

21. Larivaille also points out that Aretino's many praises of the Venetian political institutions "donneraient à penser que la royauté romaine de l'Orazia—élective et assortie du contrôle d'une assemblée—, n'est que un régime républicain à la vénetienne, opportunément dissimulé par l'Arétin sous des apparences monarchiques non seulement par respect du texte de Tite-Live et de la vérité historique, mais pour ne pas s'aliéner les monarques dont les largesses emplissent ses coffres" [lead one to believe that the Roman royalty in *Orazia*—elective and with the control of an assembly—, is nothing but a republican regime, Venetian style, conveniently dissimulated by Aretino under monarchical disguise not only out of deference to Livy's text and to historical truth, but also to avoid alienating the monarchs whose generosity filled his coffers] (Paul Larivaille, "L'*Orazia* de l'Arétin," in *Les ecrivains et la pouvoir en Italie*, ed. A. Rochon [Paris: Université de la Sorbonne Nouvelle, 1973], 355). Rocco Morano questions these assertions, noting that Larivaille "rimane al di qua del testo in quanto non ne disvela né l'interna struttura né le relazioni col genere tragico cui appartiene" [remains on this side of the text in so far as he does not deal with its internal structure or its relationship to the tragic genre to which it belongs] (Morano, *Pietro Aretino. L'Orazia*, LXVI). Commenting on Aretino's ideology and political intent, Ariani considers the dedication of the play to Emperor Charles V as Aretino's "accettazione acritica dell'eroe come elemento di fissità tirannica, imperiale, appunto pseudoromana, in realtà spagnolesca e controriformistica" [acritical acceptance of the hero as an element of tyrannical, imperial, more appropriately pseudo Roman presence. In reality (the presence is) Spaniard-like and Counter-Reformist] (Ariani, *Tra Classicismo e Manierismo*, 192–93).

22. Speaking of the virtual scene in *Orazia*, Ariani suggests that "strutturalmente, nei suoi risvolti iconici più facilmente estrapolabili, il testo aretiniano si pone come la prima, esplicita traduzione in scrittura teatrale della scena tragica di Sebastiano Serlio" [structurally, in its iconic elements more easily extrapolated, the Aretinian text emerges as the first explicit realization in theatrical writing of Serlio's tragic scene] (Ariani, *Il teatro*, xxxix).

23. Corneille's Sabine, Celia's French sister-in-law, underscores the importance implied in this spatial demarcation as she tells her husband Horace: "Prenons part en public aux victoires publiques; / Pleurons dans la maison nos malheurs doméstiques" [Let us take part openly in the public victories, / (but) Let us commiserate at home over our domestic misfortunes] (*Horace*, 4.7).

24. On the role of Publio, see Di Maria, "Spazio e tematica."

25. See Neri, *La tragedia*, 87, and Herrick, *Italian Tragedy*, 136.

Chapter 7. Representing the Unrepresentable: The *Hic et Nunc* of Tragedy

1. Aristotle, though noting that tragic experience consists of "destructive or painful actions such as deaths in plain view, extreme pains, and the like" (11.22), points out that those playwrights who strive to arouse fear in the spectators by producing "only what is monstrous are total strangers to [the nature and purpose of] tragedy" (Aristotle *The Poetics*, 14.26–27). In his *Ars poetica*, Horace advises the dramatist not to "bring upon the stage what ought to pass behind the scenes." For the convenience of the reader, and to avoid repetitive references, I quote the entire section where Horace discusses the theater and especially what is and what is not representable:

> Aut agitur res in scenis, aut acta refertur.
> Segniùs irritant animos demissa per aurem,
> Quàm quæ sunt oculis subjecta fidelibus, & quæ
> Ipse sibi tradit spectator. Non tamen intùs
> Digna geri promes in scenam: multaque tolles
> Ex oculis, quæ mox narret facundia præsens
> Nec pueros coram populo Medea trucidet;
> Aut humana palàm coquat extra nefarius Atreus;
> Aut in avem Progne vertatur, Cadmus in anguem.
> Quodcunque ostendis mihi sic, incredulus odi.
>
> (*Ars poetica*, 179–88)

[In plays some things are acted, others only told. What strikes the ear moves us far less, than what passes before the eyes, and the spectator himself is made a witness of. But you are not, on this account, to bring upon the stage what ought to pass behind the scenes: for many thing [*sic*] are to be removed from the eyes of the spectators, which he will afterwards learn better by faithful and moving relation. Medea must not murder her children before the people; nor Atreus prepare his bloody banquet upon the stage; let not Progne be changed into a swallow, or Cadmus into a serpent. Whatever you thus present that contradicts my sense, I hate and disbelieve.]

Echoing this precept, Prologue I in Dolce's *Marianna* says that neither the Greeks nor the Romans allowed murder to be represented on stage:

> Né peró mi ricorda unqua fra' Greci
> Né fra Latin, ch'alcun de' miei seguaci
> Consentisse ch'innanzi a riguardanti
> Omicidio altrui si commettesse.
>
> (14–17)

[Nor do I remember either among the Greeks / or the Latin, that any of my followers / allowed that before the spectators / a homicide be committed.]

However, Castelvetro believed that, within the limits of decorum, certain horrible acts should be represented on stage, since people are moved more "per lo sentimento della veduta che per lo sentimento dell'udita, cioè che siano piú commossi veggendo le cose con gli occhi che udendole narrare" [by the sense of sight than by the sense of hearing, that is, they are moved more by seeing things with their eyes than by hearing them reported] (Castelvestro, *Poetica d'Aristotele Vulgarizzata*, 3.13.160).

2. Bartoli was convinced that violent scenes would be more effective if entertained in the theater of the mind. He specifically points out that certain acts, such as wounding or killing, "molto più movon maraviglia et compassione con immaginarle per via di narazione d'alcuno, che con la vista loro" [arouse greater marvel and compassion when we imagine them through somebody's narrative than when we see them] (quoted and trans. in Weinberg, *History*, 2.930). Piccolomini shared this notion and insisted that audiences grant that theater is an imitation and accept, therefore, the conventions or suggestions of the stage. He specifically points out that "si come l'imitatione non è lo stesso vero, ma in qualche parte mancante da esso, poscia che se punto da quel non mancasse, non sarebbe l'imitatione, ma la cosa vera ... gli spettatori, come discreti, & che non ricercano l'impossibile; tutto quello, che lontan dal vero reca, & richiede necessariamente l'arte dell'imitare, donano, & concedono agli imitatori, & conseguentemente al poeta nelle commedie, & nelle tragedie: come quelli, che ben conoscono, che se questo non donasser loro, & tal licentia, loro non concedessero; l'imitatione non potrebbe haver luogo; &

per conseguente resterebber' essi privi di quel diletto" [since imitation is not the same as reality, but in some parts lacking reality, for if it did not lack it, it would no longer be imitation but reality.... The spectators, being reasonable, do not demand the impossible. They concede to the imitators, and inherently to authors of comedies and tragedies, all that which, though far from the truth, is required by the art of imitation. For, spectators know that if they did not grant this and did not concede this (poetic) license, imitation could not take place, and they would be deprived of such a pleasure] (Alessandro Piccolomini, *Annotationi nel Libro della Poetica d'Aristotile* [Venice: Giovanni Guarisco e Compagni, 1572], 24). Castelvetro was also against the representation of brutal and excessively bloody deeds on the grounds that they could not be faithfully executed and could easily appear ridiculous. He argued that "l'esperienza ha mostrato che simili crudeltà, & horribilità non si possono verisimilmente far vedere in atto, & che fanno anzi ridere che piangere, & che producono non effetto di tragedia ma di comedia" [experience has shown that similar cruelties and horrible acts cannot be shown on stage in a realistic way. They might rouse laughter rather than tears, and produce an effect that is more comic than tragic] (Castelvetro, *Poetica d'Aristotele Vulgarizzata*, 3.13.161).

3. Let us recall the numerous murders that characterize plays such as Thomas Kyd's *The Spanish Tragedie* (c. 1587), Christopher Marlowe's *The Jew of Malta* (c. 1588–92), and John Webster's *The Duchess of Malfi* (produced before 1614). Even Shakespeare was not immune to excessive use of bloodshed on stage. *King Lear*, for instance, is awash with bloody scenes resulting in death on stage (Servant, Oswald) or off stage (Cornwall, Edmund), or murders that, though they take place off stage, the corpses are brought on stage for effect (Regan, Goneril, and Cordelia). Perhaps most violent of them all is the scene where Cornwall puts out Gloucester's eyes. The cruelty of this episode far surpasses its Greek counterpart in Sophocles's *Oedipus*, where the spectators are spared the gruesome sight, as they learn of Oedipus's misdeed through a messenger and see him with his eyes covered. In the English version, instead, not only the audience behold Cornwall's savagery, they also see the old Earl with his face covered with blood streaming down from his hollow eye sockets (3.7). This preference for showing bloodshed contrasts sharply with Anguillara's *Edippo*, where the spectators never see the king after he puts his eyes out.

4. Trans. by William Arrowsmith. Electra having just risen from bed, speaks the prologue:

> But why should I linger on the horrors of my house?
> Atreus feasted him [Thyestes] on his murdered sons.
> I pass over, in the *interests of decorum*,
> the succeeding years.
>
> (14–17)

Also, Giraldi, espousing the argument that a dramatist ought to write "per servire gli spettatori" [to serve the spectators] suggests that contrary to happy-ending tragedies, horrific tragedies are best suited for reading because the spectators may find them abhorring: "quelle terribile (sic) [se gli animi degli spettatori forse le abborriscono] possono essere delle scritture, queste di fin lieto delle rappresentazioni" [the terrible ones (if the spectators abhor them) may be suited for reading, these of happy ending for representation] (Giraldi, *Discorso*, 184). Although Aristotle defines tragic experience as "destructive or painful actions such as deaths in plain view" (Aristotle, *The Poetics*, 11.22), the Greeks do not seem to have followed this advice very often. Horace recommended keeping gruesome scenes off stage (Horace, *Ars poetica*, 185–88); but Cinthio will dismiss the Horatian precept in "La tragedia a chi legge," appended to his *Orbecche,* 3239–47. Interestingly, he defends it in *Discorso* when he expresses surprise that in *Medea* Seneca did not follow Horace's recommendation against staging bloody episodes: "E molto mi sono sempre meravigliato di Seneca che si partisse dal precetto di Orazio nella sua *Medea*" [And I have always been puzzled by Seneca's decision to deviate from Horace's precept in his *Medea*] (185).

  5. For plot discussions and summaries of many cinquecento tragedies, see Herrick's *Italian Tragedy.*

  6. Like *Canace,* Dolce's *Marianna* has little emotional impact on the spectators who hear of Marianna's tragedy after it happened somewhere away from the stage. By means of the traditional messenger, Dolce reveals to the audience that queen Marianna was executed after she was made to watch the murder of her children and of her own mother, as decreed by King Herod. Tasso, too, uses this traditional means of announcing to the audience the double suicide of Alvida and Torrismondo.

  7. Hamilton, speaking of the importance of the audience, points out that "the dramatist is dependent on his audience," and that "without an appreciative audience a play cannot endure: empty the auditorium and the theatrical work of art ceases to exist" (Hamilton, *The Theory of the Theater,* 103). Grotowski, in his attempt to define theater, points out to his interviewer that "the number of definitions of theater is practically unlimited" and that theater can exist without costumes, music, lighting, and even the text. But, he observes, theater cannot exist without an audience, for "at least one spectator is needed to make it a performance" (Jerzy Grotowski, "Theatre's New Testament" in *Towards a Poor Theater* [New York: Simon and Schuster, 1968], 32).

  8. We learn from Iphigenia herself that she was spared at the last moment by Artemis, who substituted "a deer to bleed for me and stole me through / The azure sky" (Euripides, *Iphigenia in Tauris,* 28–29).

  9. Bartoli, arguing that narration often can be more effective than representation, makes the point that with certain acts, such as wounding and killing, whereas "la narrazione fa considerare ogni circostanza, dove il riguardante sempre non vi si accorge et non vi pensa, et chi narra dimora quanto è necessario in alungare qualunque ragionamento amplificando quello che fa et compassione et spavento et maraviglia" [narration makes us consider every circumstance, the spectator is not always aware of them and does not think about them; and he who narrates lingers as long as is necessary to lengthen any passage, amplifying those things which produce compassion and fright and wonder] (quoted and trans. in Weinberg, *History,* 2.930).

  10. Styan argues that the spatial closeness between actors and players, and by inference the action itself, determines "the emotional range of the play, the intimacy or remoteness of the playing and the immediacy or alienation of the response." He further points out that such closeness puts a special pressure on the spectator, as he "is compelled to pay a closer attention to what is said and done on the stage. In intimate conditions he gives a wider range of attention to the actors, calling upon otherwise untapped sources of sympathy and response" (Styan, *Shakespeare's Stagecraft,* 14–15).

  11. Trissino comments "si temono quei mali che ci possono dar morte o grandissime noie e dolori, e questi non ancora si temono sempre, ma solamente li temiamo quando ci appareno vicini e sono per dover essere" [one fears those evils that can bring about death or great hardship and suffering. These we always fear, but we fear them the most when they appear near us and about to happen] (Trissino, *La Quinta divisione della poetica,* 2.33). He makes the same point about pity, which is best aroused in the spectators when the tragic deed happens near the spectators, for "il male che è fatto o che è per doversi fare, ponendosi con le dette cose avanti agli occhi, viene a parer vicino; e quello che è vicino, cioè allora allora fatto o per doversi

fare, è più misericordioso" [the evils which just happened or are about to happen, placing themselves with the aforementioned things before our eyes, seem very near to us; and that which is near, that is, which just happened or is about to happen, is more worthy of compassion] (37). Here Trissino seems to be echoing Horace's view that what the spectators hear is far less moving than what they see (Horace, *Ars poetica,* 180–82).

12. Such was the case in classical drama that T. S. Eliot, speaking of Seneca's penchant for verbal exposition, notes: "In the plays of Seneca, the drama is all in the word, and the word has no further reality behind it" (T. S. Eliot, *Selected Essays* [New York: Harcourt Brace, 1932], 54). Also, H. B. Charleton characterizes Senecan drama as "largely a succession of long speeches . . . most suitable for reading only as a closet drama." (Charleton, *The Senecan Tradition,* 20). He further notes that "as we gather from *Thyestes,* Seneca knew he could narrate horrors better than stage them" (n. 1). For a discussion of the Renaissance dramatists' reliance on the *bene dicere* see, Ariani's *Il teatro,* especially where he argues that "*bene dicere* fu privilegiato, per ragioni squisitamente sociali, come principale funzione dinamica dell'intera complessione rappresentativa, come congengo ideologico e insieme fulcro agogico dell'azione tragica" [high style was privileged, for purely social reasons, as a principal dynamic function of the entire representation genre, as an ideological device and as the driving force of the tragic action] (viii).

13. Max Bluestone observes that kinetic exposition "describes motion through space and appears in every variety of adaptive exposition—in soliloquies, choral speeches, and in reports of events both real and imagined in the past, present, or future." He goes on to suggest, that it "performs a drama without vesting the action in a local habitation [and that] it strains the bounds of language to bring things removed in space and time into ken just short of perceptual knowledge" (Max Bluestone, *From Story to Stage* [The Hague: Mouton, 1974], 135–37).

14. The unreliability of one's recollection is underscored in Sophocles's *Oedipus the King,* where the messenger reports Jocasta's death, promising chorus "in so far as I remember it / you'll hear the end of our unlucky queen" (1239–40).

15. Serva tells the stage audience that after Almachilde severed Alboino's head, she saw

> . . . un gran fiume di sangue
> Con maggior copia di vino e di schiuma
> Dal singultante tronco giù versare
> . . . .
> Così tagliato quello orribil teschio
> Ci fe' paura, perché ben tre volte
> Le sue sagnuigne luci ne' nostri occhi
> travolse, aprì la bocca e battè e denti.
>
> (1205–17)

[. . . a great river of blood / with a large quantity of wine and foam / spewing out of the heaving trunk / . . . / Thus severed, that horrible skull / frightened us, as three times / its bloody eyes toward our eyes / it rolled, opened its mouth, and chattered its teeth.]

16. Use of this technique is found in several Greek tragedies, including Euripides's *Orestes* and *Heracles,* Sophocles's *Electra,* and Æschylus's *The Libation Bearers.* In all these instances the victim's cries for help are heard from within the palace as he or she is being murdered. In *The Libation Bearers,* however, Aegisthus's actual cry for help is not reported, it is simply signified by chorus as she calls for silence: "Listen,

it goes / but how? What has been done in the house?" The question is answered immediately afterwards by a follower of the king who announces that "Aegisthus lives no longer" (870–76). Though in these plays no character actually witnesses the tragic deed, there is, nonetheless, a dramaturgical intent to provide some sort of description either in the form of prophecy (Cassandra) or by having the perpetrators plan the killing on stage prior to carrying it out inside, as in Sophocles's *Electra*.

17. Ironically, in Æschylus's *The Libation Bearers*, Orestes is shown standing over the bodies of Clytemnestra and Aegisthus, whom he has just murdered.

18. To be sure, the technique was used by other playwrights, such as Martelli and Dolce, in *Tullia* and *Marianna* respectively. However, their use of the eyewitness sequence is as rudimentary as in ancient drama in that there is no eyewitness to the events represented as taking place off stage.

19. Herrick assumes that Orbecche carries her father's "severed head and hands into the palace," thus suggesting that the stabbing and the subsequent hacking of the king's body takes place on stage (Herrick, *Italian Tragedy*, 103). Actually, Orbecche kills her father in the palace, where he invited her to come and receive his forgiveness (5.2.2824–25). In fact, the spectators do not see her dismemberment of the body, which is described by semichorus who rushed onto the scene following the king's screams. It would make little sense for semichorus to describe Orbecche's fury to the spectators, if the spectators were actually witnessing the bloody deed. Also, we must suppose that Orbecche killed her father inside, for only then can the semichorus see her come out of the palace with a bloody knife in one hand and the king's severed head and hands in the other:

> Ma veggio che col capo e con le mani
> Del crudo padre e col coltello in mano
> Se ne viene di fore.
>   (5.2.2886–88)

[But I see that with the head and the hands / of her cruel father and with the knife in her hand / she is coming out.]

In addition, in "La tragedia a chi legge," Giraldi defends Orbecche's own death on stage, noting that this deviation from Horace's recommendation reflects and satisfies the cultural taste of the times. Had the king also been killed on stage, the "Tragedia" would certainly have included it in its defense of representing death on stage.

20. Cfr. Orbecche's horror upon seeing the contents of the vessel, "Oimè, ch'è questo?" [Alas! what is this?] with Thyestes's apprehension "Sed quid hoc?" [But what is this?] as he beholds his dinner platter containing his children's body parts (v. 985). On Seneca's influence on Giraldi, see Charleton, *The Senecan Tradition*, 72–94; Riccardo Scrivano, *La Rassegna della letteratura italiana* 44 (1960): 324–26; and Cremante, *Teatro del Cinquecento*, 279.

21. In his *Discorso*, Giraldi warns against assuming that "le azioni sole bastino" [actions alone suffice] to reveal one's inner thoughts, "perché, quantunque uno uccidesse un altro, atto all'orrore e alla compassione, non verrebbe indi né questa né quello, se non vi fosse chi con acconce parole commovesse gli animi degli spettatori" [for, if a person killed another, an act of horror and compassion, neither emotion could be aroused, if there were not someone who with appropriate words moved the hearts of the spectators] (199). He expresses a similar idea on p. 188.

22. Horne insists, and rightly so, that Giraldi is not a writer of horror-tragedies (Horne, *The Tragedies of Giambattista Cinthio Giraldi*, 2). Giraldi himself concedes that horror tragedies may best be suited for reading (Giraldi, *Discorso*, 184). However,

one must agree with Charleton, who, in the context of Senecan influence, argues that Giraldi "had created a new type [of tragedy] with his *Orbecche*" (Charleton, *The Senecan Tradition*, 74).

23. Giraldi defended his choice in "La tragedia a chi legge," especially where Tragedia declares that she chose to follow nature, rather than "con pompose voci una finta arte" [a fake art with pompous words] (3259–61). And in the prologue to his *Altile*, he insisted that poets should be free from rules restricting their creativity. He also argued that death scenes, provided that they were not unrealistic (i.e., Progne turning into a bird) or too cruel (i.e., parents knowingly killing their children) could be represented on stage in order to arouse pity in the spectators. And to those who argued that there is no example of violent death in Greek tragedies, he responded that "non abbiamo tutte quelle che si leggevano al tempo di Aristotile, che se le avessimo vedremmo che le palesi morti non erano tolte alle scene" [we do not possess all those (tragedies) that were available during Aristotle's time, for if we did, we would see that death scenes were not excluded from the stage] (Giraldi, *Discorso*, 186–87). He further noted that Plutarch suggested that Aristotle allowed deaths on stage (ibid.).

24. On Giraldi's tragic language and particularly on Orbecche's soliloquy, see Ariani, "La trasgressione e l'ordine," 117–80. For another example of equally affected soliloquies, see Alvida's preamble to her death in *Torrismondo*, 5.1.115–20.

25. Arguing against the use of rhyme in tragedy, Trissino in his letter presenting the play to Leo X writes that the Pope will find regular discourse, not rhyme, most effective and necessary in arousing pity in the spectators: "Vostra Beatitudine . . . lo vedrà non solamente ne le narrazioni et orazioni utilissimo, ma nel muovere compassione necessario; perciò che quel sermone il quale suol muovere questa [compassione], nasce dal dolore, et il dolore manda fuori non pensate parole" [Your Beatitude . . . will see that it (language) is not only most useful in narratives and speeches, but also necessary for arousing compassion; for the type of speech which tends to arouse this (compassion) is born from sorrow, and sorrow does not produce studied words] (quoted in Cremante, *Teatro del Cinquecento*, 31–32). Speaking of the verbal expression of pathos, Frye points out that "highly articulate pathos is apt to become a factitious appeal to self-pity, or tear-jerking" (Northrup Frye, *Anatomy of Criticism: Four Essays* [Princeton: Princeton University Press, 1957], 39)

26. For admirers of Giraldi, see Charleton, *The Senecan Tradition*, 73–74.

27. By contrast, in Dolce's *Medea*, 5. pp. 37–38, the audience can hear the children's pleas for help as their mother slaughters them inside the palace.

28. Herrick observes incorrectly that the murder takes place on stage: "His only violation of the strictest rules was allowing Orazio to kill his sister on stage." He also calls the play a "debate instead of a drama" (Herrick, *Italian Tragedy*, 137).

29. Kennard, calling *Orazia* one of the best tragedies in the Italian Renaissance, writes that "most of the action occurs before the eyes of the spectators, and that Aretino banished the chorus and the messengers . . . ; the narratives are few and brief compared with those in other tragedies" (Kennard, *The Italian Theatre*, 149).

30. Frye also points out that pathos, which is typical of low mimetic or domestic tragedy, is a "queer ghoulish emotion, and some failure of expression, real or simulated, seems to be peculiar to it" (Frye, *Anatomy of Criticism*, 39).

31. The comparison between these two tragedies dates back to Ginguené, who argued that Aretino's dramaturgical feats "ne peuvent équivaloir aux beautés de sentiment dont la pièce française est remplie" [cannot equal the beauty of emotions with which the French play is replete] (Ginguene, *Histoire littéraire d'Italie*,137). Salfi challenged this view, judging the Italian play "supérieure, quant à ce qui regarde

l'unité d'action, la suite du plan, le spectacle et le mouvement" [superior, as regards the unity of action, the structural cohesion, the spectacle and the movement] (Francesco Saverio Salfi, *Résumé de l'histoire de la littérature italienne* [Paris: Louis Janet, Libraire, 1826], 230–31). For a detailed discussion of the controversy surrounding these two plays, see Rocco Morano, in Lettieri and Morano, *Pietro Aretino. L'Orazia*, especially clxiv–clxxx.

CHAPTER 8. THE THEATRICAL LANGUAGE OF SOUNDS AND MOVEMENTS

1. Speaking of the tragic scene, Serlio notes that "benché alcuni hanno dipinto alcuni personaggi che rappresentano il vivo, come saria una femina ad un balcone o dentro d'una porta, eziandio qualche animale, queste cose non consiglio che si faccino perché non hanno il moto e pure rappresentano il vivo: ma qualche persona che dorma a buon proposito, overo qualche cane o altro animale che dorma, perché non hanno il moto" [although some artists have painted (on the backdrop) figures representing live characters, such as a woman on a balcony or in a doorway, or an animal (in motion), I advise against painting these things because they do not move and yet they imply motion. However, it is appropriate to paint a person asleep or a sleeping dog or some other animal, because their position does not suggest motion] (Serlio, *Il secondo libro di prospettiva*, 200–201).
2. Aristotle, *The Poetics*, 6.11.
3. Neri, while praising *Torrismondo*'s lyrical moments, complains about its oppressive verbosity and observes that Tasso's mental problems "influirono sul *Torrismondo*, appunto nella debole rappresentazione delle figure, nella lentezza dello sviluppo, nei molti tratti prolissi e vacui" [surfaced in *Torrismondo*, especially in the weak representation of its characters, in the slow development, and in the many empty and tediously long passages] (Neri, *La tragedia*, 148). He finds *Merope* equally lyrical, but complains that its "verseggiatura è fiacca, sovrabbondante" [versification is weak and excessive] (163).
4. Herrick, tracing the beginning of the Grecian tradition at the turn of the sixteenth century, notes that "soon after the publication of Greek texts of Sophocles and Euripides a few learned poets began to imitate the Greeks when they composed Italian tragedies. These Grecians not only turned aside from native religious plays but from Seneca as well and tried to imitate Attic tragedy" (Herrick, *Italian Tragedy*, 44). But, see the whole chapter on the "Grecians," 43–71.
5. Mazzoni writes that Rucellai began working on *Oreste* immediately after the completion of *Rosmunda* (1515) and that the play was still incomplete in 1520 (Mazzoni, *Le opere di Giovanni Rucellai*, LI). Since Rucellai died on 3 April 1525, it is conceivable that he worked on it until his death.
6. Early in the eighteenth century Scipione Maffei observed that *Oreste* features enough changes to be rightly considered Rucellai's own play. While granting that the play follows its ancient model, he pointed out that Rucellai introduced so much "diversità . . . che basti a renderla Tragedia sua; avendola anche ingrandita, e nobilitata con motivi sí aritificiosi, e teatrali, che in tempo sí antico par maraviglia" [diversity . . . as to be enough to render it his own tragedy. He expanded and endowed it with innovations so ingenious and so theatrical that, for the times, it is a wonder] (Scipione Maffei, *Teatro italiano o sia Scelta di tragedie per uso della Scena* [Venice: Orlandini, 1746], 1.78–79).

7. This reading of line 174 ("Non vedi quanta gente si raccoglie?") is found in both the 1746 Oralandini edition and in the 1808 edition of *Teatro italiano antico*. In the 1887 Zanichelli edition, Mazzoni, instead, proposes "Ma che fra tante genti posson due?" I prefer the earlier reading because it places more emphasis on the perceptual "vedi," which suggests that the characters can actually see people gathering in the distance.

8. For the proliferation of terms and definitions dealing with the concept of reference, see Alter, "Waiting for the Referent," 42–56. See also Bruce Morrissette, "Referential Intertextuality: Pre-Code, Code, and Post-Code," in *On Referring in Literature*, ed. Whiteside and Issacharoff (Bloomington: Indiana University Press, 1987), 111–21.

9. Toante's penchant for blood and brutality, which brings to mind *Rosmunda's* Alboino, Rucellai's other bloodthirsty king, may be observed in his wish to get his hands on the dead victims and

> con le mie man segar vo' lor le vene:
> E se mi fosse lecito il ber sangue,
> Non vorrei d'altr'umor saziar mia sete.
>
> (3.15–17)

[with my own hands I want to rip their veins: / And if I were permitted to drink blood, / I would not want to quench my thirst with any other fluid.]

10. Ubersfeld, *L'école*, 325–26.

11. Lucien Febvre and Henry-Jean Martin note that Virgil was the most published classical author before 1500, as attested by "une foule d'éditions imprimées" [a legion of published editions] (Lucien Lebvre and Henry-Jean Martin, *L'apparition du livre* [Paris: Albin Michel, 1958], 386). They point out that in the course of the sixteenth century, Virgil's works counted 263 editions in Latin, 72 in Italian, 27 in French, 11 in English, 5 in German, 5 in Spanish, and 2 in Flemish (411).

12. Having offered several arguments in support of his contention that Giraldi was aware of Pazzi's play, Turner concludes that Dolce had to have a general knowledge of the two existing dramatizations, for it would be difficult to explain "le grand nombre de ressemblances qui existent entre ces tragédies" [the numerous similarities that exist within these tragedies] (Robert Elson Turner, *Didon dans la Tragédie de la Renaissance Italienne et Français* [Paris: Fouillot, 1926], 83). Also, he assumes that Jodelle wrote "sous l'influence italienne" [under the influence of the Italians] and that he probably knew and imitated Dolce's *Didone*] (131).

13. Ibid., 130. In Turner's view, Pazzi's *Dido* is as mediocre or worthless as La Grange's *Didon*. Federico Doglio considers Pazzi's play a reflection of Pazzi himself, a meticulous scholar but "incapace di autentica invenzione" [incapable of authentic innovation] (Doglio, *Il teatro tragico italiano*, xxxix). Herrick, also, sees Pazzi's tragedy as "not a good play, for its plot is ill contrived by comparison with Virgil's original story and most of the dialogue is tedious. Since it was not published in the early sixteenth century, it could hardly have been widely known. Nevertheless, it is representative of the learned Italian tragedy that set the pattern for the neoclassical theater of the Renaissance" (Herrick, *Italian Tragedy*, 64). Terpening shares the traditional criticism of Pazzi's play, noting that it "is noteworthy more as an experiment in meter than for its poetic beauty or dramatic innovations" (Terpening, *Lodovico Dolce*, 111).

14. To my knowledge, no scholar has yet examined these tragedies from the theatrical point of view. Critical attention has focused mostly on their literariness, plot structure, source material, themes, characters, and tragic conflicts.

15. With refererence to queen Dido, Turner notes that "elle n'a que des regrets, qui sont fort beaux en poésie, mais dépourvus d'action et ennuyeux sur la scène" [she has but regrets, which are beautiful in poetry, but deprived of action and boring on the stage] (Turner, *Didon dans la Tragédie de la Renaissance Italienne et Français*, 8).

16. In the *Aeneid*, the action develops rather rapidly: Eneas, reminded of his mission by Mercury, tells his men to get ready to sail and, pulling his flaming sword from its scabbard, cut the ropes. The men incited by so much ardor,

> rapiuntque ruuntque,
> litora deseruere, latet sub classibus aequor,
> adnixi torquent spumas et caerule verrunt.
>
> (4.585–87)

[rushed and ran, and quickly pulled away from the shore. The sea disappeared under the ships, as the men, bending strenuously, beat the foams of the blue sea.]

At daylight, Queen Dido saw "aequitis classem procedere velis" [the ships sailing away].

17. The appearance of daybreak also helps to establish the unity of time, since it marks the twenty-four-hour period in which the action will take place.

18. Female roles were normally played by men, since in the Renaissance it was considered undecorous for women, especially young women, to act on stage.

19. Pazzi's *Dido* is 1,767 lines long, whereas Giraldi's play counts over 3,400 lines. Giraldi's *Didone* features 26 scenes of which 12 are monologues, almost double that of Pazzi's tragedy. Giraldi's cast of 24 is double that of Pazzi. Mary Morrison, calling attention to Dido's long role, points out that Giraldi makes the queen "more introspective and amplifies the inner struggle she experiences, chiefly by giving her one or two invented monologues" (Morrison, *The Tragedies of G.-B. Giraldi Cinthio*, 95). She goes on to say that "*Didone* is unique in Giraldi's theater in that it is a tragedy of inner conflicts. This is rare in the sixteenth century, though in the seventeenth century the inner conflict was to become an almost essential constituent of tragedy" (103).

20. Morrison writes that "the last scene shows Giraldi creating not only a spectacle but a moving finale" (ibid., 95).

21. Both Turner, *Didon dans la Tragédie de la Renaissance Italienne et Français*, 48, and Terpening, *Lodovico Dolce*, 113, find objectionable the excessive repetition of Anna's "oimè."

22. Philip Horne writes that Marlowe's dramatic treatment of Dido's story "affords an interesting comparison with Giraldi's more pedestrian imitation." He goes on to say that Giraldi follows Virgil faithfully, adding "nothing of his own invention to the events narrated in the *Aeneid*" (Horne, *The Tragedies of Giambattista Cinthio Giraldi*, 75–76).

23. Herrick, though recognizing *Orbecche* as a trendsetter, concedes that many other previous examples of tragedies of blood "had already been dramatized before the 1540s" (Herrick, *Italian Tragedy*, 178). One must add, however, that, unlike *Orbecche*, some of the earlier tragedies tended to report rather than show blood and violence.

24. Interestingly, Jodelle's *Didon*, which Turner considers the best of four dramatizations, has no theatrical dimension. The death scene is entirely reported by Barce at the end of the play.

25. Morrison, commenting on the dramatic impact of the last scene, writes:

"with true dramatic flair Giraldi now brings Dido on the stage to die" (Morrison, *The Tragedies of G.-B. Giraldi Cinthio*, 100).

26. This is undoubtedly one of the reasons for the play's lukewarm critical assessment. In Neri's view, the play is not "un'altissima tragedia, e neppur terra terra" [a great tragedy, nor is it really bad] (Neri, *La tragedia,* 90).

27. Turner concluded his comparative study by noting that "la meilleure des tragédies italiennes est celle du Giraldi, bien que la *Didon* du Dolce soit moins ennuyeuse: cepandant, la *Didon* de Jodelle les surpasse toutes" [the best of the Italian tragedies is that of Giraldi, although Dolce's *Dido* is less boring; however, Jodelle's *Dido* surpasses them all] (Turner, *Didon dans la Tragédie de la Renaissance Italienne et Français,* 130).

28. Trissino observes that the dramatist in thinking of the scene and the characters must place "avanti agli occhi i gesti e le figure che fanno quelli che sono nelle passioni [. . . poichè] i segni, cioè vesti, camise, et altre cose simili, di quelli che hanno patito . . . muoveno grandemente" [before his eyes the gestures and the appearance of the characters (. . . for) the signs, that is, the clothes, the shirts and other similar things of those who have suffered . . . move greatly] (Trissino, *La Quinta divisione della poetica,* 231, 37–38).

Bibliography

Adams, Robert M., ed. and trans. *Niccolò Machiavelli: The Prince*. New York: W.W. Norton, 1977.

Æschylus, *Agamemnon*. In *The Complete Greek Tragedies. Oresteia: Aeschylus*, I. Edited by David Grene and Richard Lattimore, 35–90. Chicago: University of Chicago Press, 1953.

Alamanni. Luigi. *L'Antigone*. In *Teatro italiano antico*. Edited by Gaetano Poggiali, 2: 145–206. Milan: Società Tipografica de' Classici Italiani, 1808–12.

Alberti, Leon Battista. *I libri della famiglia*. Edited by Ruggero Romano and Alberto Tenenti. Turin: Einaudi, 1969.

Alter, Jean. "Waiting for the Referent, Waiting for Godot: On Referring in Theater," *On Referring in Literature*. Edited by Anna Whiteside and Michael Issacharoff, 42–56. Bloomington: Indiana University Press, 1987.

Anderson, Perry. *Lineages of the Absolutist State*. London: New Left Books, 1974.

Anguillara, Giovanni Andrea dell'. *Edippo*. In *Teatro italiano antico*. Edited by Gaetano Poggiali, 8:3–132. Milan: Società Tipografica de' Classici Italiani, 1808–12.

Anonymous. "Il Successo dell'*Alidoro* tragedia rappresentata in Reggio alla Sereniss. Regina Barbara d'Austria, Duchessa di Ferrara." In *Il teatro italiano: La tragedia del Cinquecento*. Edited by Marco Ariani, 2: 984–1008. Turin: Einaudi, 1977.

Antiphanes. "Fragments of the Comedies." In *The Fragments of Attic Comedy*. Edited by John Maxwell Edmonds, 2:165–310. Leiden: E. J. Brill, 1959.

Apollonio, Mario. *Storia del teatro italiano*. Vol. 2. Florence: Sansoni, 1951.

Aretino, Pietro. *L'Orazia*, Edited by Michael Lettieri and Rocco Mario Morano. Rovito: Marra Editore, 1991.

———. *Orazia*. In *Teatro del Cinquecento: La tragedia*. Edited by Renzo Cremante, 577–727. Milan and Naples: Ricciardi, 1988.

———. *Tutte le opere. Le lettere: Il primo e il secondo libro*. Edited by Francesco Flora. Milan: Mondadori, 1960.

Ariani, Marco. "La trasgressione e l'ordine: *Orbecche* di G. B. Giraldi Cinthio." *Rassegna della letteratura italiana* LXXXIII (1979): 117–80.

———, ed. *Il teatro italiano: La tragedia del Cinquecento*. 2 vols. Turin: Einaudi, 1977.

———. *Tra Classicismo e Manierismo: Il teatro tragico del Cinquecento*. Florence: Olschki, 1974.

Ariosto, Ludovico. *Ludovico Ariosto: Orlando Furioso*. Translated by William Stewart Rose. Edited by Stewart A. Baker and A. Bartlett Giamatti. Indianapolis: Bobbs-Merrill, 1968.

———. *Orlando Furioso*. Edited by Marcello Turchi and Edoardo Sanguineti. 3rd ed. 2 vols. Milan: Garzanti, 1978.

———. *The Satires of Ludovico Ariosto.* Translated by Peter Desa Wiggins. Athens: Ohio State University Press, 1976.

Aristotle. *The Poetics of Aristotle.* Translated by P. H. Epps. Chapel Hill: University of North Carolina Press, 1970.

Arnott, Peter D. *An Introduction to the Greek Theatre.* London: Macmillan, 1959.

Attolini, Giovanni. *Teatro e spettacolo nel Rinascimento.* Bari: Laterza, 1988.

Bainton, Roland H. *Women of the Reformation in Germany and Italy.* Minneapolis: Augsburg Publishing House, 1971.

Baldacci, Luigi, ed. *Lirici del Cinquecento.* Milan: Longanesi, 1975.

Barbaro, Francesco. "De re uxoria liber." In *Prosatori latini del Quattrocento.* Edited by Eugenio Garin, 1: 104–37. Torino: Einuadi, 1976.

Barish, Jonas. *The Antitheatrical Prejudice.* Berkeley: University of California Press, 1981.

———. "The Problem with Closet Drama in the Italian Renaissance." *Italica* 71, 1 (1994): 4–30.

Barthes, Roland. *Essais Critiques.* Paris: Éditions Du Seuil, 1964.

Beaty, Nancy Lee. *The Craft of Dying: A Study of the Literary Tradition of the Ars Moriendi in England.* New Haven: Yale University Press, 1970.

Belmonte, Pietro. *Istitutione della sposa . . . , fatta principalmente per Madonna Laudonia sua figliuola nelle sue nuove nozze.* Rome: Heredi di Giovanni Osmarino Gigliotto, 1587.

Bergel, Lienhard. "The Horatians and the Curiatians in the Dramatic and Political-Moralist Literature Before Corneille." *Renaissance Drama,* New Series 3 (1970): 215–38.

———. "The Rise of Cinquecento Tragedy." *Renaissance Drama* 8 (1965): 197–217.

Bernard, Jack F. *Up from Caesar.* Garden City, N.Y.: Doubleday, 1970.

Bertoni, Giulio. *Giornale storico della letteratura italiana* XCIX (1932): 282–83.

Bloom, Harold. *The Western Canon: The Books and School of the Ages.* New York: Harcourt Brace, 1994.

Bluestone, Max. *From Story to Stage.* The Hague: Mouton, 1974.

Boccaccio, Giovanni. *Decameron.* Edited by Carlo Salinari. 2 vols. Bari: Laterza, 1966.

Bocchi. F. *Luigi Groto (il Cieco d'Andria).* Adria: Eredi Guarnieri, 1886.

Bosco, Umberto. *Francesco Petrarca.* Bari: Laterza, 1961.

Botero, Giovanni. *Della ragion di stato, con tre libri delle cause della grandezza della città, due Aggiunte e un discorso sulla popolazione di Roma.* Edited by Luigi Firpo. Turin: Unione Tipografico-Editrice Torinese, 1948.

Branca, Vittore. *Boccaccio medievale.* Florence: Sansoni, 1970.

Breisach, Ernst. *Caterina Sforza: A Renaissance Virago.* Chicago: Chicago University Press, 1967.

Brucker, Gene. *Giovanni and Lusanna: Love and Marriage in Renaissance Florence.* Berkeley: University of California Press, 1986.

Bull, George, ed. and trans. *Pietro Aretino. Selected Letters.* Harmondsworth: Penguin Books, 1976.

Burckhardt, Jacob. *The Civilization of the Renaissance in Italy.* 2 vols. New York: Harper & Row, 1975.

Burke, Peter. *The Italian Renaissance: Culture and Society in Italy.* Princeton: Princeton University Press, 1986.

Canello, Angelo Ugo. *Storia della letteratura italiana nel secolo XVI.* Milan: Vallardi, 1880.

Carlson, Marvin. "Audiences and the Reading of Performance." In *Interpreting the Theatrical Past.* Edited by Thomas Postlewait and Bruce A. McConachie, 82–98. Iowa City: University of Iowa Press, 1989.

———. *Theater Semiotics: Signs of Life.* Bloomington: Indiana University Press, 1990.

———. *Theories of the Theater. A Historical and Critical Survey, from the Greeks to the Present.* Ithaca: Cornell University Press, 1984.

Castelvetro, Lodovico. *Poetica d'Aristotele Vulgarizzata, et Sposta Per Lodovico Castelvetro.* Vienna, 1570. Munich: Wilhelm Fink Verlag, 1968.

Castiglione, Baldesar. *Il libro del Cortegiano.* Edited by Giulio Preti. Turin: Einaudi, 1960.

Charleton, H. B. *The Senecan Tradition in Renaissance Tragedy.* Manchester: Manchester University Press, 1946.

Chemello, Adriana. "La donna, il modello, l'immaginario: Moderata Fonte e Lucrezia Marinella." In *Nel Cerchio della luna: figure di donna in alcuni testi del XVI secolo.* Edited by Marina Zancan, 95–170. Venice: Marsilio, 1983.

Chiappini, Luciano. *Gli Estensi.* Milan: Dall'Oglio, 1967.

Cicogna, Emmanuel Antonio. "Memoria intorno la vita e gli scritti di Messer Lodovico Dolce letterato veneziano del secolo XVI." In *Memorie dell' I.R. Istituto veneto di scienze, lettere ed arti.* Venice: Presso la segreteria dell'I.R. Istituto nel Palazzo Ducale, 1862.

Cleugh, James. *The Divine Aretino.* New York: Stein and Davis, 1966.

Cognasso, Francesco. *L'Italia nel Rinascimento.* Vol. 2. Torino: UTET, 1965.

Cole, David. *The Theatrical Event: A Mythos, a Vocabulary, a Perspective.* Middletown, Conn.: Wesleyan University Press, 1975.

Corneille, Pierre. *Horace. Théatre complet.* Edited by Pierre Lièvre. Vol. 1. Paris: Gallimard, 1950.

Corrigan, Beatrice, ed. *Two Renaissance Plays: Ludovico Ariosto, Il Negromante; Giangiorgio Tirssino, Sofonisba.* Manchester: Manchester University Press, 1975.

Cremante, Renzo, ed. *Teatro del Cinquecento: La tragedia.* Milan and Naples: Ricciardi, 1988.

Croce, Benedetto. *La letteratura italiana.* Vol. 1. Bari: Laterza, 1967.

D'Alembert, Jean-Baptiste Le Ronde. *Discours Préliminaire de l'Encyclopédie.* 1763. Edited by F. Picavet. 5th ed. Paris: Librairie Armand Colin, 1929.

D'Amico, John F. *Renaissance Humanism in Papal Rome.* Baltimore: Johns Hopkins University Press, 1983.

Da Horte, Antonio Decio. *Acripanda.* In *Teatro italiano antico.* Edited by Gaetano Poggiali, 9: 35–194. Milan: Società Tipografica de' Classici Italiani, 1808–12.

Da Montemagno, Buonaccorso. *De nobilitate.* In *Prosatori latini del Quattrocento.* Edited by Eugenio Garin, 2:142–165. Torino: Einuadi, 1976.

Dante, Alighieri. "Epistola" in *Dante Alighieri: Opere Minori.* Vol. 2. Milano: Ricciardi, 1979.

———. *La divina commedia.* Edited by Natalino Sapegno. Florence: La Nuova Italia, 1885.

———. *De vulgari eloquentia.* Edited and translated by Steven Botterill. Cambridge: Cambridge University Press, 1996.

De Caprariis, Vittorio, ed. *Francesco Guicciardini: Opere.* Milan: Ricciardi, 1953.

De Maio, Romeo. *Donna e Rinascimento.* Milan: Mondadori, 1987.

De Marinis, Marco. "Lo spettacolo come testo." *Versus* 21 (1978): 3–31.

Del Vita, Alessandro. *Lusso, donne, amore nel Rinascimento.* Arezzo: Edizioni Rinascimento, 1961.

Di Maria, Salvatore. "Blame-by-praise Irony in the *Ecatommiti* of Giraldi Cinzio." *Quaderni d'italianistica* 6 (autunno 1985): 178–92.

———. "Divine Order, Fate, Fortune, and Human Action in Guicciardini's *Storia d'Italia.*" *Forum Italicum* 28 (spring 1994): 22–40.

———. "The Dramatic *hic et nunc* in the Tragedy of Renaissance Italy." *Italica* 72 (1995): 275–97.

———. "Narratorial Strategy in Guicciardini's *Storia d'Italia.*" *Stanford Italian Review* IX, 1–2 (1990): 115–32.

———. "Spazio e tematica nell' *Orazia* di Pietro Aretino." In *Pietro Aretino e la cultura del Rinascimento.* Edited by M. Lettieri, S. Bancheri, and R. Buranello. Vol. 2, 803–28. Rome: Salerno Editrice, 1995.

———. "Towards an Italian Theater: Rucellai's *Oreste.*" *M L N* 111 (1996): 123–48.

Doglio, Federico, ed. *Il teatro tragico italiano. Storia e testi del teatro tragico in Italia.* Bologna: Guanda, 1960.

Dolce, Lodovico. *Apologia contra i detrattori dell'Autore.* In *Orlando furioso di Messer Ludovico Ariosto nobile ferrarese con la giunta, novissimamente stampato e corretto. Con una apologia di M. Lodovico Dolcio contra i detrattori dell'Autore.* Turin: Martino Cravoto & Francesco Robi de Savilliano, 1536.

———. *Didone. Tragedia di M. Lodovico Dolce. Nuovamente dal medesimo riveduta e ricorretta.* Venice: Gabriel Giolito De' Ferrari, 1560.

———. *Giocasta.* In *Teatro italiano antico.* Edited by Gaetano Poggiali, 6: 5–118. Milan: Società Tipografica de' Classici Italiani, 1808–12.

———. *Hecuba. Tragedia di M. Lodovico Dolce. Di nuovo ricorretta e ristampata.* Venice: Gabriel Giolito De' Ferrari, 1560.

———. *Ifigenia. Tragedia di M. Lodovico Dolce. Di nuovo ricorretta e ristampata.* Venice: Gabriel Giolito De' Ferrari, 1560.

———. *Marianna.* In *Teatro del Cinquecento: La tragedia,* edited by Renzo Cremante, 741–877. Milan and Naples: Ricciardi, 1988.

———. *La Medea. Tragedia di M. Lodovico Dolce. Di nuovo ricorretta e ristampata.* Venice: Gabriel Giolito De' Ferrari, 1560.

———. *Thieste. Tragedia di M. Lodovico Dolce. Di nuovo ricorretta e ristampata.* Venice: Gabriel Giolito De' Ferrari, 1560.

Dolfin, Giacomo. "Lettera di Giacomo Dolfin." In *La prima rappresentazione al teatro Olimpico.* Edited by Alberto Gallo, 33–37. Milan: Il Polifilo, 1973.

Donahue, Thomas John. *Structures of Meaning: A Semiotic Approach to the Play Text.* London and Toronto: Associated University Presses, 1993.

Donaldson, Peter S. *Machiavelli and the Mystery of State.* Cambridge: Cambridge University Press, 1988.

Donatus, Aelius. *De tragoedia et comoedia.* In *Handbook of French Renaissance Dramatic Theory.* Edited by H. W. Lawton, 2–21. Manchester: Manchester University Press, 1949.

Eliot, T. S. *Selected Essays: 1917–1932.* New York: Harcourt, Brace, 1932.

Euripides. *Iphigenia in Tauris.* In *The Complete Greek Tragedies. Euripides II.* Edited by David Grene and Richard Lattimore, 118–87. Chicago: Univesity of Chicago Press, 1969.

———. *The Medea.* In *The Complete Greek Tragedies. Euripides I.* Edited by David Grene and Richard Lattimore. Translated by Rex Warner, 55–108. Chicago: Univesity of Chicago Press, 1955.

———. *Orestes.* In *The Complete Greek Tragedies. Euripides IV.* Edited by David Grene and Richard Lattimore. Translated by William Arrowsmith, 104–204. New York: Washington Square Press, 1968.

———. *The Phoenician Women.* In *The Complete Greek Tragedies. Euripides V.* Edited by David Grene and Richard Lattimore. Translated by Elizabeth Wyckoff, 71–140. Chicago: Univesity of Chicago Press, 1959.

Faccioli, Emilio, ed. *Il teatro italiano I: Dalle origini al Quattrocento.* 2 vols. Torino: Einaudi, 1975.

Febvre, Lucien, and Henri-Jean Martin. *L'apparition du livre.* Paris: Albin Michel, 1958

Ferguson, John. *A Companion to Greek Tragedy.* Austin: University of Texas Press, 1972.

Fiorato, Adelin-Charles. "L'image et la condition de la femme dans les *Nouvelles de Bandello.*" In *Images de la femme dans la littérature italienne de la Renaissance: Préjugés misogynes et aspirations nouvelles.* Edited by André Rochon, 169–286. Paris: Université de la Sorbonne Nouvelle, 1980.

Firenzuola, Agnolo. *Dialogo delle bellezze delle donne. Discorso primo. Opere.* Edited by Adriano Seroni. Florence: Sansoni, 1971.

Fontana, Alessandro. "La scena." In *Storia d'Italia. I caratteri originali,* 1:793–866. Turin: Einaudi, 1972.

Forlani, Alma, and Savini, Marta, eds. *Scrittrici d'Italia.* Rome: Newton Compton, 1991.

Frigo, Daniela del. "Dal caos all'ordine: sulla questione di 'prender moglie' nella trattatistica del sedicesimo secolo." In *Nel Cerchio della luna: figure di donna in alcuni testi del XVI secolo.* Edited by Marina Zancan, 57–93. Venice: Marsilio, 1983.

Frye, Northrop. *Anatomy of Criticism: Four Essays.* Princeton: Princeton University Press, 1957.

Gable, Anthony. "Du Monin's Revenge Tragedy *Orbecc-Oronte* (1585): Its Debt to Garnier and Giraldi." *Renaissance Drama* 11 (1980): 3–25.

Gallo, Alberto, ed. *La prima rappresentazione al teatro Olimpico.* Milan: Il Polifilo, 1973.

Garin, Eugenio. *La cultura del Rinascimento.* 1964. Milan: Il Saggiatore, 1995.

———, ed. *Prosatori latini del Quattrocento.* 8 vols. Torino: Einuadi, 1976.

Gies, Francis, and Joseph Gies. *Women in the Middle Ages.* New York: Harper Perennial, 1978.

Gilbert, Felix. *Machiavelli and Guicciardini: Politics and History in Sixteenth-Century Florence.* Princeton: Princeton University Press, 1965.

Ginguené, Pierre Louis. *Histoire littéraire d'Italie.* Tome Sixième. Paris: Michaud, 1813.

Gioda, Carlo. *La vita e le opere di Giovanni Botero.* Vol. 1. Milan: Ulrico Hoepli, 1894.

Giraldi, Giambattista Cinthio. *Arrenopia*. In *Teatro italiano antico*. Edited by Gaetano Poggiali 5:51–191. Milan: Società Tipografica de' Classici Italiani, 1808–12.

———. *Altile*. Edited by Peggy Osborn. Lewiston, N.Y.: Edwin Mellen Press, 1992.

———. *Cleopatra Tragedia*. Edited by Mary Morrison and Peggy Osborn. Exeter: Short Run Press, 1985.

———. "Discorso intorno al comporre delle commedie e delle tragedie," *Scritti critici*. Edited by Camillo Guerrieri Crocetti. Milan: Marzorati, 1973.

———. "Lettera sulla tragedia (1543)." In *Trattati di poetica e retorica del Cinquecento*. Edited by Bernard Weinberg, 1: 471–86. Bari: Laterza, 1970.

———. *Orbecche*. In *Teatro del Cinquecento: La tragedia*. Edited by Renzo Cremante, 281–448. Milan and Naples: Ricciardi, 1988.

———. *Selene*. Edited by Philp Horne. Lewiston, N.Y.: Edwin Mellen Press, 1996.

Goldmann, Lucien. *The Hidden God*. Translated by Philip Thody. London: Routledge & Kegan Paul, 1970.

Grazzini, Antonfrancesco. *Commedie di Antonfrancesco Grazzini, detto il Lasca*. Edited by Pietro Fanfani. Firenze: Le monnier, 1859.

Grendler. Paul F. *Critics of the Italian World [1530–1560]: Anton Francesco Doni, Nicolò Franco, and Ortensio Lando*. Madison: University of Wisconsin Press, 1969.

Grene, David, and Richmond Lattimore, eds. *The Complete Greek Tragedies*. 5 vols. New York: Washington Square Press, 1955–69.

Groto, Luigi. *Adriana*. In *Il teatro italiano: La tragedia del Cinquecento*. Edited by Marco Ariani, 1: 287–424. Turin: Einaudi, 1977.

Grotowski, Jerzy. "Theatre's New Testament: An Interview with Eugenio Barba." In *Towards a Poor Theater*. Preface by Peter Brook. New York: Simon and Schuster, 1968.

Gundersheimer, Werner L. *Ferrara: The Style of Renaissance Despotism*. Princeton: Princeton University Press, 1973.

Hamilton, Clayton. *The Theory of the Theater*. New York: Henry Holt, 1939.

Hegel, G. W. F. *The Philosophy of Fine Art*. Translated by F. P. B. Osmaston. 4 vols. London: G. Bell and Sons, 1920.

Herrick, Marvin. *Italian Tragedy in the Renaissance*. Urbana: University of Illinois Press, 1965.

Hook, Judith. *The Sack of Rome: 1527*. London: Macmillan, 1972.

Horace. *Satires, Epistles, and Ars Poetica*. 1929. Translated by H. Rushton Fairclough. London: William Heinemann, 1942.

Horne, Philip R. *Selene: An Italian Renaissance Tragedy by G. B. Giraldi*. Queenston, Ontario: Edwin Mellen Press, 1996.

———. ed. *The Tragedies of Giambattista Cinthio Giraldi*. Oxford: Oxford University Press, 1962.

Hubner, Zygmunt. *Theater and Politics*. Edited and translated by Jadwiga Kosicka. Evanston, Ill.: Northwestern University Press, 1988.

Ingarden, Roman. *The Literary Work of Art*. Translated with an introduction by George G. Grabowiz. Evanston, Ill.: Northwestern University Press, 1973.

Ingegneri, Angelo. *Della poesia rappresentativa e del modo di rappresentare le favole sceniche. Discorso di Angelo Ingegneri*. In *Storia documentaria del teatro italiano: Lo spettacolo dall'Umanesimo al Manierismo*. Edited by Ferruccio Marotti, 271–308. Milan: Feltrinelli, 1974.

———. "Progetto di Angelo Ingegneri." In *La prima rappresentazione al teatro Olimpico.* Edited by Alberto Gallo, 3–25. Milan: Il Polifilo, 1973.

Issacharoff, Michael. "Space and Reference in Drama." *Poetics Today* 3 (1981): 211–24.

Jacquot, Jean. "Les types de lieu théatral et leurs transformations de la fin du Moyen Age au milieu du XVIIe siècle." In *Le lieu théatral a la Renaissance.* Edited by Jean Jacquot, 474–83. Paris: Éditions du Centre National de la Recherche Scientifique, 1964.

Jones, P. J. *The Malatesta of Rimini and the Papal State.* London: Cambridge University Press, 1974.

Kahn, Victoria. *Machiavellian Rhetoric: From the Counter-Reformation to Milton.* Princeton: Princeton University Press, 1994.

Kelly, Henry Ansgar. *Ideas and Forms of Tragedy from Aristotle to the Middle Ages.* Cambridge: Cambridge University Press, 1993.

Kelso, Ruth. *Doctrine for the Lady of the Renaissance.* Urbana: University of Illinois Press, 1956.

Kennard, Joseph S. *The Italian Theatre.* New York: Benjamin Bloom, 1964.

King, Margaret L. *Women of the Renaissance.* Chicago: University of Chicago Press, 1991.

———, and Albert Rabil, Jr., eds. *Her Immaculate Hand.* 2nd ed. Reprint, Asheville, N.C.: Pegasus Press, 1997.

Kowzan, Tadeusz. *Littérature et spectacle.* Hague: Mouton, 1975.

Labaime, Patricia A., ed. *Beyond their Sex: Learned Women of the European Past.* New York: New York University Press, 1980.

Lamb, Mary Ellen. "The Countess of Pembroke and the Art of Dying." *Women in the Middle Ages and the Renaissance: Literary and Historical Perspectives.* Edited by Mary Beth Rose, 207–26. Syracuse: Syracuse University Press, 1986.

Larivaille, Paul. "L'*Orazia* de l'Arétin, tragédie des ambitions déçues." In AA.VV., *Les écrivains et le pouvoir en Italie à l'époque de la Renaissance.* Edited by A. Rochon, 2.279–360. Paris, Université de la Sorbonne Nouvelle, 1973.

Lauro, Pietro. *De le lettere. . . . Il primo libro.* Venice, [M. Tramezzino], 1552 (1553).

———. *De le lettere. . . . Libro secondo.* Venice, 1560.

Laven, Peter. *Renaissance Italy: 1464–1534.* London: Batsford, 1966.

Lebègue, Raymond. *Études sur le Théatre Français. I. Moyen Age, Renaissance, Baroque.* Paris: A.-G. Nizet, 1977.

Leblanc, Paulette. *Les écrits théoriques et critiques français des années 1540–1561 sur la tragedie.* Paris: A.-G. Nizet, 1972.

Leopardi, Giacomo. *Zibaldone.* In *Tutte le opere.* Edited by Walter Binni. Vol. 2. Florence: Sansoni, 1969.

Lettieri, Michael, and Rocco Mario Morano, eds. *Pietro Aretino. L'Orazia.* Rovito: Marra Editore, 1991.

Lotharii Cardinalis (Innocentii III), *De Misera Humane Conditionis.* Edited by Michele Maccarrone. Verona: Thesauri Mundi, 1955.

Lucas, D. W. *The Greek Tragic Poets.* London: Cohen & West, 1959.

Machiavelli, Niccolò. *Lettere.* Edited by Franco Gaeta. Milan: Feltrinelli, 1961.

———. *Il Principe e Discorsi*. Introduction by Giuliano Procacci. Edited by Sergio Bertelli. 2nd ed. Milan: Feltrinelli, 1968.

Maclean, Ian. *The Renaissance Notion of Woman*. Cambridge: Cambridge University Press, 1980.

———. *Woman Triumphant: Feminism in French Literature 1610–1652*. Oxford: Clarendon Press, 1977.

Maffei, Scipione, ed. *Teatro italiano o sia Scelta di tragedie per uso della scena*. Vol 1. Venice: Orlandini, 1746.

Mancini, Franco. *Scenografia italiana: Dal Rinascimento all'età romantica*. Milan: Fratelli Fabbri, 1966.

Manetti, Giannozzo. "De dignitate et excellentia hominis. Liber Quartus: De laudatione et bono mortis et de miseria humanae vitae." In *Prosatori latini del Quattrocento*. Edited by Eugenio Garin, 4: 422–87. Torino: Einuadi, 1976.

Marotti, Ferruccio. *Storia documentaria del teatro italiano: Lo spettacolo dall'Umanesimo al Manierismo*. Milan: Feltrinelli, 1974.

Martelli, Ludovico. *La Tullia*. In *Teatro italiano antico*. Edited by Gaetano Poggiali, 3: 31–112. Milan: Società Tipografica de' Classici Italiani, 1808–12.

Mazzoni. Guido, ed. *Le opere di Giovanni Rucellai*. Bologna: Zanichelli, 1887.

McCollum, William G. *Tragedy*. New York: Macmillan, 1957.

Mercuri, Roberto. "*Orazia* dell'Aretino." In *La letteratura italiana storia e testi: Il Cinquecento*. Edited by Carlo Muscetta, 4.2.77–82. Bari: Laterza, 1973.

Molinari, Cesare. "Les rapports entre la scène et les spectateurs dans le théatre italien du XVIe siècle." In *Le lieu théatral a la Renaissance*. Edited by Jean Jacquot, 61–71. Paris: Éditions du Centre National de la Recherche Scientifique, 1964.

———. "Scenografia e spettacolo nelle poetiche dei '500." *Il Veltro* VI (1964): 885–902.

Molinier, H.-J. *Mellin De Saint-Gelays (1490?–1558). Étude sur sa vie et sur ses oeuvres*. Genève: Slatkine Reprints, 1968.

Morrison. Mary. *The Tragedies of G.-B. Giraldi Cinthio. The Transformation of Narrative Source into Stage Play*. Lewiston, N.Y.: Edwin Mellen Press, 1997.

Morrison, Mary, and Peggy Osborn, eds. *Giovan Battista Giraldi Cintio: Cleopatra Tragedia*. Exeter: University of Exeter Press, 1985.

Morrissette, Bruce. "Referential Intertextuality: Pre-Code, Code, and Post-Code." *On Referring in Literature*. Edited by Anna Whiteside and Michael Issacharoff, 111–21. Bloomington: Indiana University Press, 1987.

Muratori, Ludovico Antonio. *De Speculis et Ludi Publicis Medii Aevi*, "Dissertatio" XXIX. In *Antiquitates Italicae Medii Aevi*, Mediolani, 1739. Reprint Bologna: A. Forni, 1975.

Musumarra, Carmelo. *La poesia tragica italiana nel Rinascimento*. Florence: Olschki, 1972.

Neri, Ferdinando. *La tragedia italiana nel Cinquecento*. Florence: Galletti e Cocci, 1904.

O'Faolain, Julia and Laura Martinez, eds. *Not in God's Image: Women in History from the Greeks to the Victorians*. New York: Harper, 1975.

Orgel, Stephen. *The Illusion of Power*. Berkeley: University of California Press, 1975.

Osborn, Peggy, ed. *G. B. Giraldi's Altile*. Lewiston, N.Y.: Edwin Mellen Press, 1992.

Patrizi, Francesco. *Della Poetica: Il Cornaro ovvero della rettorica perfetta*. Libro 2. Ferrara, 1586.

———. *Della Poetica: La Deca disputata.* Vol 1. Edited by Danilo Aguzzi Barbagli. Florence: Istituto Nazionale di studi sul Rinascimento, 1969.

Payne, Robert, and Nikita Romanoff. *Ivan The Terrible.* New York: Thomas Y. Crowell, 1975.

Pazzi (Paccio) de' Medici, Alessandro. *Le tragedie metriche di Alessandro Pazzi de' Medici.* Collezione di Opere inedite o rare. Dispensa CCXXIV. Edited by Angelo Solerti. 1887. Reprint, Bologna: Commissione per i testi di lingua, 1969.

Pencaro, Jano. "Lettere a Isabella Gonzaga." *Il teatro italiano: Dalle origini al Quattrocento.* Edited by Emilio Faccioli, 2: 700–706. Torino: Einaudi, 1975.

Pertusi, Agostino. "Il ritorno alle fonti del teatro greco classico: Euripide nell'Umanesimo e nel Rinascimento." *Venezia e l'Oriente fra tardo Medioevo e Rinascimento.* Edited by Agostino Pertusi, 205–24. Florence: Sansoni, 1966.

Petrarca, Francesco. *Canzoniere.* Edited by Raffaele Manica. Rome: Newton, 1997.

———. *Rerum Familiarum Libri.* In *Prose.* Edited by Guido Martellotti et al. Milan and Naples, 1955.

Pfister, Manfred. *The Theory and Analysis of Drama.* Translated by John Halliday. Cambridge: Cambridge University Press, 1988.

Piccolomini, Alessandro. *Annotationi nel Libro della Poetica d'Aristotile, con la traduttione del medesimo libro in lingua volgare.* Venice: Giovanni Guarisco e Compagni, 1572.

Pickard-Cambridge, A. W. *The Theatre of Dionysus in Athens.* Oxford: Clarendon Press, 1956.

Pico della Mirandola, Giovanni. *De Hominis Dignitate.* Edited and translated by Bruno Cicognani. Florence: Le Monnier, 1941.

Pigafetta, Filippo. "Lettera di Filippo Pigafetta." In *La prima rappresentazione al teatro Olimpico.* Edited by Alberto Gallo, 53–58. Milan: Il Polifilo, 1973.

Poggiali, Gaetano. "Ragionamento." In *Teatro italiano antico.* Edited by Gaetano Poggiali, 3:3–27. Milan: Società Tipografica de' Classici Italiani, 1808–12.

———, ed. *Teatro italiano antico.* 10 vols. Milan: Società Tipografica de' Classici Italiani, 1808–12.

Poliziano, Angelo. *Stanze per la giostra.* In *Le stanze, l'Orfeo e le rime de messer Angelo Ambrogini Poliziano.* Edited by Giosuè Carducci. Florence: Barbara, 1863.

Rebhorn, Wayne A. *Foxes and Lions: Machiavelli's Confidence Men.* Ithaca: Cornell University Press, 1988.

Rice, Eugene F., Jr. *The Foundations of Early Modern Europe, 1460–1559.* New York: W.W. Norton, 1970.

Riccoboni, Antonio. "Lettera di Antonio Riccoboni." In *La prima rappresentazione al teatro Olimpico.* Edited by Alberto Gallo, 39–51. Milan: Il Polifilo, 1973.

Romano, Ruggiero. *Tra due crisi: L'Italia del Rinascimento.* Torino: Einaudi, 1971.

Rucellai, Giovanni. *Oreste.* In *Le opere di Giovanni Rucellai.* Edited by Guido Mazzoni, 107–229. Bologna: Zanichelli, 1887.

———. *Le Api.* In *Le opere de Giovanni Rucellai.* Edited by Guido Mazzoni, 1–40. Bologna, Zanichelli, 1887.

———. *Rosmunda.* In *Teatro del Cinquecento: La tragedia.* Edited by Renzo Cremante, 83–257, Milan and Naples: Ricciardi, 1988.

Ruffo-Fiore, Silvia. "The Silent Scholars of Italian Humanism: Feminism in the Renaissance." In *Interpreting the Italian Renaissance: Literary Perspectives.* Edited by Antonio Toscano, 5–27. Stony Brook: Filibrary, 1991.

Russo, Luigi. "Il Petrarca e il Petrarchismo." *Belfagor* 5 (1954): 497–509.

———. "La tragedia nel Cinque e Seicento." *Belfagor* 1 (1959): 14–22.

Salfi, Francesco Saverio. *Résumé de l'histoire de la littérature italienne, par F. Salfi.* 2nd ed. Tome Premier. Paris: Louis Janet, Libraire, 1826.

Savonarola, Girolamo. *Prediche sopra Ezechiele* (Sermon XXII, 1497). In Romeo De Maio, *Donna e Rinascimento*. Milan: Mondadori, 1987.

Scrivano, Riccardo. *La Rassegna della letteratura italiana* 44 (1960): 324–26.

Seneca. *Seneca's Tragedies*. Translated by Frank Justus Miller. Vol. 2. 1917. Cambridge: Harvard University Press, 1953.

Serlio, Sebastiano. *Il secondo libro di prospettiva*. In *Storia documentaria del teatro italiano: Lo spettacolo dall'Umanesimo al Manierismo*. Edited by Ferruccio Marotti, 190–205. Milan: Feltrinelli, 1974.

Servadio, Gaia. *La donna nel Rinascimento*. Translated by Giovanni Luciani. Milan: Garzanti, 1986.

Skinner, Quentin. *Machiavelli*. New York: Hill and Wang, 1981.

Sommi, Leone de'. *Quattro dialoghi in materia di rappresentazioni sceniche*. Edited by Ferruccio Marotti. Milan: Il Polifilo, 1968.

Sophocles. *Ajax*. In *The Complete Greek Tragedies. Sophocles II*. Edited by Grene and Lattimore, 7–62. 1957. Reprint, Chicago: University of Chicago Press, 1969.

———. *Electra*. In *The Complete Greek Tragedies. Sophocles II*. Edited by David Grene and Richard Lattimore, 127–87. 1957. Reprint, Chicago: University of Chicago Press, 1969.

———. *Oedipus the King*. In *The Complete Greek Tragedies. Sophocles I*. Edited by David Grene and Richard Lattimore, 9–76. Chicago: University of Chicago Press, 1954.

Speroni, Sperone. *Canace*. In *Teatro del Cinquecento: La tragedia*. Edited by Renzo Cremante, 463–561. Milan and Naples: Ricciardi, 1988.

———. "Della dignità delle donne." In *Trattatisti del Cinquecento*. Edited by Mario Pozzi, 1:565–84. Milan: Ricciardi, 1978.

———. "Proposte di Sperone Speroni." In *La prima rappresentazione al teatro Olimpico*. Edited by Alberto Gallo, 31. Milan: Il Polifilo, 1973.

Styan, J. L. *Shakespeare's Stagecraft*. Cambridge: Cambridge University Press, 1967.

Swain, Ward E. "My excellent & most singular lord." *Journal of Medieval and Renaissance Studies* 2 (1986): 171–95.

Tasso, Torquato. *King Torrismondo*. Translated by Maria Pastore Passaro. New York: Fordham University Press, 1997.

———. *Torrismondo*. In *Il teatro italiano: La tragedia del Cinquecento*. Edited by Marco Ariani, 2: 433–552. Turin: Einaudi, 1977.

Tassoni, Alessandro. *Pensieri diversi in Prose politiche e morali*. Vol. 1. Edited by Piero Puliatti. Bari: Laterza, 1978.

Tenenti, Alberto. *Piracy and the Decline of Venice: 1580–1615*. Berkeley: University of California Press, 1967.

Terpening, Ronnie H. "Between Lord and Lady: The Tyrant's Captain in Rucellai's *Rosmunda* and in Dolce's *Marianna*." *Forum Italicum* 15 (1981): 153–70.

———. *Lodovico Dolce: Renaissance Man of Letters*. Toronto: University of Toronto Press, 1997.

Tommasoli, Walter. *La vita di Federico da Montefeltro*. Urbino: Argalìa, 1978.

Torelli, Pomponio. *Merope*. In *Il teatro italiano: La tragedia del Cinquecento*. Edited by Marco Ariani, 2: 561–637. Turin: Einaudi, 1977.

Trissino, Giovan Giorgio. *La Quinta divisione della poetica*. In *Trattati di poetica e retorica del Cinquecento*. Edited by Bernard Weinberg, 2: 7–44. Bari: Laterza, 1970.

———. *Sofonisba*. In *Teatro del Cinquecento: La tragedia*. Edited by Renzo Cremante, 35–162. Milan and Naples: Ricciardi, 1988.

Turner, Robert Elson. *Didon dans la Tragédie de la Renaissance Italienne et Française*. Paris: Fouillot, 1926.

Ubersfeld, Anne. *L'école du spectateur*. Paris: Éditions Sociales, 1981.

———. *Lire le Théâtre*. Paris: Éditions Sociales, 1978.

Ulivi, Ferruccio. *L'imitazione nella poetica del Rinascimento*. Milan: Marzorati, 1959.

Varchi, Benedetto. *L'Ercolano. Opere di Benedetto Varchi*. Edited by A. Racheli e Gio. Battista Busini. Trieste: Lloyd Austriaco, 1859.

Vasari, Giorgio. *Le vite de' più eccellenti pittori scultori ed architettori scritte da Giorgio Vasari pittore aretino*. Edited by Gaetano Milanesi. Vol. 6. Florence: Sansoni, 1906.

Veltrusky, Jirí. "The Prague School Theory of Theater." *Poetics Today* 3 (1981): 225–35.

Vettori, Francesco. "Sacco di Roma: Dialogo." *Scritti storici e politici*. Edited by E. Niccolini. Bari: Laterza, 1972.

Vince, W. Ronald. *Renaissance Theatre. A Historiographical Handbook*. Westport Conn.: Greenwood Press, 1984.

Virgil. *The Aeneid of Virgil*. Edited by R. M. Williams. 1972. Reprint, London: Macmillan Education Limited, 1975.

Warner, Marina. *Alone of All Her Sex*. New York: Vintage Books. A Division of Random House, 1985.

Weinberg, Bernard. *A History of Literary Criticsm in the Italian Renaissance*. 2 vols. Chicago: University of Chicago Press, 1961.

———, ed. *Trattati di poetica e retorica del Cinquecento*. 2 vols. Bari: Laterza, 1970.

Weise, Georg. *L'Ideale eroico del Rinascimento e le sue premesse umanistiche*. Naples: Edizioni Scientifiche Italiane, 1961.

Zancan, Marina, ed. *Nel Cerchio della luna: figure di donna in alcuni testi del XVI secolo*. Venice: Marsilio, 1983.

Index

Numbers in boldface indicate illustration pages

absconditus, 71
Ab urbo condita (Livy), 171
Acripanda (Da Horte), 101
adaptations, 25–26, 30
Adriana (Groto), 31, 33, 37, 64, 79, 101, 116, 122, 138
Aeneid (Virgil), 18, 180, 193, 195, 196, 199
Æschylus, 19, 24, 165; *Agamemnon,* 133–34, 164; *The Eumenides,* 51; *Oresteia,* 88
Agamemnon (AEschylus), 133–34, 164
agere et intelligere, 39, 87
agnitione, 43
Aicardo, Battista, 56
Alamanni, Luigi, 35, 40
Alberti, Leon Battista, 110, 111, 136
Alidoro (Bombace), 24, 38, 52
Altile (Giraldi), 20
Attolini, Giovanni, 99
ambiance, 46–54
Anderson, Perry, 85–86
angels, 60
Anguillara, Giovanni Andrea dell': *Edippo,* 37, 39, 46, 47, 53, 64, 67, 69, 84
antefactum, 31
Antigone (Alamanni), 40
Antigone (Sophocles), 40
Antiphanes, 24–25
Antivalomeni (Giraldi), 29
Arc, Joan of, 104, 114
Architectura (Serlio), 136
Aretino, Pietro, 22, 31, 35, 53, 56, 116; *Orazia,* 23, 28, 30, 31, 32, 41, 60, 72–78, 101, 138, 139, 144–54, 171–76, 178–79, 180
Ariani, Marco, 9

Ariosto, Ludovico, 30, 42, 48, 104, 105, 113, 123
Aristotle, 17, 33, 35, 40 43; on bloodshed, 156; on characterization, 158; defines tragedy, 178; dramatic theories of, 135; *Poetics,* 20, 160; precepts of, 60, 72; unities of, 17, 20
ars moriendi literature, 118
Ars poetica (Horace), 20, 162
auctoritas, 63, 204
auditory effects, 140

Bandello, Matteo, 118
Barbaro, Francesco, 103
Barish, Jonas, 18
Bembo, Pietro, 66
Barthes, Roland, 131
Bartoli, 156
Beaty, Nancy Lee, 118
bene dicere, 40, 46
Bloom, Harold, 23
Boccaccio, Giovanni, 45, 27; *Corbaccio,* 103, 124; *Decameron,* 103, 123, 145; *De mulieribus claris,* 123
Boiardo, Matteo, 48
Bombace, Gabriele: *Alidoro,* 24, 38, 52
Borgia, Ceasre, 92
Botero Giovanni, 91, 94, 96; *Della Ragion di stato,* 82, 93
Branderburg, Barbara of, 104
brigands and pirates, 54–57
Brucker, Eugene, 103
Burckhardt, Jacob, 104
Burke, Peter, 23

Campano, Antonio, 87
Canace (Speroni), 53, 101, 110, 142, 158
Canterbury Tales (Chaucer), 145

Canzone: Petrarchan, 41
Castellesi, Adriano, 87
Castelvetro, Lodovico, 25, 156
Castiglione, Baldesar, 89, 110, 123
Castracani, Castruccio, 87
casts, 38
Cato of Utica, 116
Charles V, 56, 71, 144
Charles VIII, 81
Charleton, Henry Buckley, 18, 37
Chaucer, Geoffrey: *Canterbury Tales,* 145
Cicero, 81
Clement VII, 144
Colonna, Vittoria, 104
comedy: popularity of, 21
contrappasso, 90
Corbaccio (Boccaccio), 103, 124
Corneille: *Horace,* 173–75, 176
Correggio, Niccolò da: *Fabula di Cefalo,* 37
Corrigan, Beatrice, 55
Counter-Reformation, 7, 73, 93, 94, 96, 104, 105, 144, 145, 153, 205
Cyclope (Pazzi de' Medici), 19
Cyclops, The (Euripides), 19

Da Horte: *Acripanda,* 101
D'Alembert, 35
Dante, 30, 45, 58, 67, 89, 116, 203; *De vulgari eloquentia,* 18; *Divine Comedy,* 18, 66, 67; *Inferno,* 27
Decameron (Boccaccio), 103, 123, 145
Della Casa, Giovanni and Susanna, 103
Della perfettione della vita politica (Paruta), 99
Della ragion di stato (Botero), 82, 93
De mulieribus claris (Boccaccio), 123
De Re Architectura (Vitruvius), 135
(deus) ex machina, 60, 71–78, 149
deus in terris, 60
devils, 58, 60
De vulgari eloquentia (Dante), 18
Dido in Cartagine (Pazzi de' Medici), 193–202
Didon se sacrifiant, La (Jodelle), 193–202
Didone (Dolce), 25, 193–202
Didone (Giraldi), 39, 52, 72, 193–202
Dirks, Elisabeth, 114
Dispute over the Trinity (del Sarto), **109**
Divine Comedy (Dante), 18, 66, 67
Docere et diligere, 26

Dolce, Lodovico, 19, 22, 25, 29, 106, 107, 114, 116, 117, 180; *Didone,* 25, 193–202; *Giocasta.* 29, 36, 41, 66, 83; *Ifigenia,* 9, 30, 35, 84; *Marianna,* 21, 36, 61, 79, 83, 101, 119, 132, 133, 139, 141; *Medea,* 21, 30, 37, 48, 84, 122; *Thieste,* 70–71
Dolfin, Giacomo, 39
Donaldson, Peter, 81
Donatus, 17
dramatic space, 129–54
Draperio, Francisco, 56

Ecerinus (Mussato), 18, 37
Edippo (Anguillara), 37, 39, 46, 47, 53, 64, 67, 69, 84
Edippo (Giustiniano), 48, 52
Edippo tiranno, l' (Maganza), **50**
Este, Ercole d', 39
Este, Isabella d', 104
Este family, 54
Eumenides, The (AEschylus), 51
Eunuch, The (Terence), 38
Euripides, 24, 25, 46: *The Cyclops,* 19; *Iphigenia in Aulis,* 159; *Iphigenia in Tauris,* 42, 134, 142, 180, 181, 191, 192; *Medea,* 156, 163; *Orestes,* 156; *The Phoenician Women,* 51, 68, 139
Evdokia, Princess, 114
eyewitness: role of, 162–64

fabula di Cefalo (Correggio), 37
Farfa, abbot of, 56
Farnese, Luigi, 23
Ferrara, duke of, 38
Filippa, Madonna, 103
Firenzuola, Agnolo, 104
florilegia, 103, 110
Fonte, Moderata, 121
forma mentis, 77
fortitudo, 101; of women, 114, 121, 123
Francis I, 144
Franco, Veronica, 104
Fregoso, Paolo, 56

Galen, 103
Gambara, Veronica, 104
Garin, Eugenio, 66
Gesta, 42
Giocasta (Dolce), 29, 36, 41, 66, 83
Giraldi, Giambattista Cinthio, 21, 30, 33, 35, 38, 40, 41, 45, 49, 102, 110,

113, 115, 122, 157; *Altile,* 20–21, 35;
Antivalomeni, 29; *Didone,* 39, 52, 72,
193–202; *Orbecche,* 31, 36, 38, 41, 53,
62–71, 85–97, 101, 110, 113, 119, 157,
158, 180, 205; *Selene,* 26
Giustiniano, Orsato: *Edippo il tiranno,*
39, 49, **50,** 52
gods/goddesses: in Renaissance drama,
58–78
Gonzaga, Isabella, 38
Grazzini, Anton Francesco, 30, 35
Grimaldi, Giovanni, 56
Groto, Luigi, 2, 31, 111, 157; *Adriana,*
31, 33, 37, 64, 79, 101, 116, 122, 138
Ginguené, Pierre Louis, 144

Herrick, Marvin, 24, 60
hic et nunc technique, 140, 155–76, 177,
195
Homer, 66
Hook, Judith, 56
Horace, 25, 35, 160; *Ars poetica,* 20, 162;
on bloodshed, 156; precepts of, 155
Horace (Corneille), 173–75, 176
humanism, 59
humilitas, 105

Ifigenia (Dolce), 9, 30, 35, 84
illud tempus, 48, 52
imbecillitas, 105
imitatio dei, 92
Inferno (Dante), 27
infirmitas, 105
Ingegneri, Angelo, 21, 30–31, 33, 40, 52
intelligere, 104
Iphigenia in Aulis (Euripides), 159
Iphigenia in Tauris (Euripides), 42, 134,
142, 180, 181, **182,** 191, 192
Iphigenia in Tauris (Pompeii), **182**
Isidore of Seville, 17
Ivan the Terrible, 114

Jans, Anneken, 114
Jodelle, Etienne: *La Didon se sacrifiant,*
193–202

Kennard, Joseph, 102
kingship, 27; nature, of, 79–100
Kyd, Thomas, 206

Lauro, Pietro, 111

Larivaille, Paul, 145
legibus soluti, 80, 96
Leo X (Pope), 19
Leopardi, Giacomo, 45
Livy, 75; *Ab urbe condita,* 171
Lucan, 17

Machiavelli, Niccolò, 46, 53, 59, 92, 93,
94, 96, 204, 205; *Mandragola,* 55–56;
The Prince, 84, 91
Machiavellism, 79–100
Maclean, Ian, 119
Maganza, Giovan Battista: *l'Edippo
tiranno,* **50**
Malatesta, Sigismondo, 56
Mandragola (Machiavelli), 55–56
Manetti, Giannozzo, 116
Marianna (Dolce), 21, 36, 61, 79, 83,
101, 119, 132, 133, 139, 141
Marinella, Lucrezia, 121
Marlowe, Christopher, 156
Martelli, Ludovico: *Tullia,* 41, 60, 72–78,
101, 112, 133, 141, 142
McCollum, William, 27
Medea (Dolce), 21, 30, 37, 48, 84, 122
Medea (Euripides), 156, 163
Medea (Seneca), 37, 156, 170–71
Medici family, 81
Merope (Torelli), 83, 97, 101, 180
messengers: role of, 155, 158–62
Michelangelo, 105; *The Original Sin,*
107; *The Sacrifice of Noah,* **106**
misogyny, 205
Molinari, Cesare, 31
Montefeltro, Federico da, 83
Morra, Isabella, 109
mulier taceat in ecclesia, 104
Muratori, Lodovico, 17, 205
Mussato, Albertino: *Ecerinis,* 18, 37
Martelli, Ludovico: *Tullia,* 41

Naldi, Dionigi, 47
narration: limits of, 158–62

Oedipus (Seneca), 51, 64, 66
Oedipus the King (Sophocles), 37, 39, 61,
64, 134
Orazia (Aretino), 23, 28, 30, 31, 32,
41, 60, 72–78, 101, 138, 139, 144–54,
171–76, 178–79, 180

Orebecche (Giraldi), 21, 31, 36, 38, 41, 53, 69, 85–97, 101, 110, 113, 114, 119, 157, 158, 162–71, 180, 205
Original Sin (Raphael), **108**
Original Sin, The (Michelangelo), **107**
Orco, Remirro de, 92, 94
Oreste (Rucellai), 42–43, 46, 48, 64, 65, 68, 69, 142; dramaturgical elements in, 180–93
Oresteia (AEschylus), 88
Orestes (Euripides), 157
Orgel, Stephen, 99
Ovid, 24

pageantry/stage entertainment, 22, 38, 39–40, 98–99
Palladio, Andrea: *Teatro Olimpico*, **51**
Paruta, Paolo: *Della perfettione della vita politica*, 99
patrons/patronage, 23–24
Paul III, (Pope), 23
Pazzi de Medici, Alessandro, 18–19, 180; *Cyclope*, 19; *Dido in Cartagine*, 193–202
Pelegati, Don Niccolò de', 56
Pencaro, Jano, 38
performances: cost of, 38
Pertusi, Agostino, 19
Peruzzi, Baldassare, 131, 136; *Prospettiva per Scena Comica*, **135**
Petrarch, 25, 30, 43, 45, 66, 203; *Rime*, 118; *Triumph of Death*, 118
Pfister, Manfred, 25
Phoenician Women, The (Euripides), 51, 68, 139
Piccolomini, 156
Pigafetta, Filippo, 39, 48
Pisan, Christine de, 104
plot material, 24
Poetica (Trissino), 19, 60
Poetics (Aristotle), 20, 160
Pole, Reginald, 82
Poliziano, Angelo, 66
Prince, The (Machiavelli), 84, 91
Priene, theater at, **134**
Prisciano, Pellegrino, 136
Prospettiva per Scena Comica (Peruzzi), **135**

querelle des femmes, 28, 105
Quiñones, Alvarode, 56

Racine, Jean-Jacques, 115, 158

Raphael: *Original Sin*, **108**
realism: and the stage, 29–32
religion: in Christian and mythological settings, 61–71
Rime (Petrarch), 118
Romano, Ezzelino da II, 18
Rosmunda (Rucellai), 18, 20, 31, 62, 96, 101, 113, 160–62, 175
Rucellai, Giovanni, 20, 35, 54, 102, 110; *Oreste*, 42–43, 46, 48, 64, 65, 68, 69, 142, 180–93; *Rosmunda*, 18, 20, 31, 62, 96, 101, 113, 160–62, 175
Ruffo-Fiore, Silvia, 104
Russo, Luigi, 20, 29
Ruzzante, Angelo Beolco, 30

sacre rappresentazioni, 71, 98
Sacrifice of Noah, The (Michelangelo), **106**
Salutati, Coluccio, 118
Sandoval De Vcastro, Diego, 109
Sangallo, Aristotile da, 131
San Gallo, Bastiano da: *Urban Scene for Theatre*, **136**
Sarto, Andrea del, 105; *Dispute over the Trinity*, **109**
Savonarola, Fra Girolamo, 59, 104
Scala, Bartolomeo della, 87
Scala, Cangrande della, 18
Scena tragica (Serlio), **137**
scenic space, 136–44
Selene (Giraldi), 26
Seneca, 18, 24, 25, 40, 41, 80, 81, 84, 88, 169; *Antigone*, 40; on bloodshed, 158; *Medea*, 37, 156, 170–71; *Oedipus*, 51, 64, 66; *Thyestes*, 156, 166, 196
Serlio, Sebastiano, 34; *Architectura*, 136; on backdrops, 178; defines tragedy, 178; *Scena tragica*, **137;** on stage setting, 177–78
Servadio, Gaia, 105
Sforza, Caterina, 47, 104, 112
Sforza family, 87
Shakespeare, William, 120, 144
Siena, Catherine of, 104
Socrates, 116
Sofonisba (Trissino), 18, 19, 20, 41, 45, 55, 101
Sommi, Leone de', 32
Sophoclean conflict, 144, 145

Sophocles, 19, 24, 25, 28, 49, 82; *Oedipus the King*, 37, 39, 64, 66, 134
sounds and dramatic space, 32–34
spatial setting, 46–54
special effects, 131, 205–6
spectators, 38–39
Speroni, Sperone, 35, 52; *Canace*, 53, 101, 110, 142, 158
stage, the: and dramatic space, 129–54
stage productions: costs of, 21–22; and pageantry, 22
stage setting/architecture, 129–54
Stampa, Gaspara, 104
studia litterarum, 46
Styan, J. L., 139

Tasso, Torquato, 113; *Torrismondo*, 43–44, 55, 101, 142, 180
Tassoni, Alessandro, 91
Teatro Olimpico (Palladio), **51**
Terence: *The Eunuch*, 38
texts, written: length of, 37–46
theater: didactic function of, 26–27, 205–6; revitalization of, 20–29; as rhetoric of power, 97–100; as spectacle, 205–6
theatrical innovation: in sound and movement, 177–202
Thieste (Dolce), 70–71
Thyestes (Seneca), 156, 166, 196
Torelli, Pomponio: *Merope*, 83, 97, 101, 180

Torrismondo (Tasso), 43–44, 55, 101, 142, 180
tragedy: aim of, 155–56; revival of, 35–57; victims in, 101
Trissino, Gian Giorgio, 20, 35, 102, 157, 160, 170; *Poetica*, 19, 60; *Sofonisba*, 18, 19, 20, 41, 45, 55, 101
Triumph of Death (Petrarch), 118
Tullia (Martelli), 41, 60, 72–78, 101, 112, 133, 141, 142
Turner, Robert, 193–94

Ugolino, Gherardesca della, 45
Urban Scene for Theatre (San Gallo), **136**
utile, 82, 83, 84, 88
utramque partem, 93

Vasari, Giorgio, 131
Vettori, Francesco, 59
violence: representation of, 156
Virgil, 24, 66; *Aeneid*, 18, 180, 193, 195, 196, 199
virtù, 81–82, 87, 96
Vitruvius, 136; *De Re Architectura*, 135
Vladimir of Starista, Prince, 114

Webster, John, 156
womanhood: traditional notions of, 103–5; endorsed by theater, 121–25; as tragic heroine, 101–25; view of, 27–28